3DS MAX 5 FUNDAMENTALS

By Ted Boardman

New Riders

201 West 103rd Street, Indianapolis, Indiana 46290

3ds max 5 Fundamentals

Copyright © 2003 by New Riders Publishing

International Standard Book Number: 0-7357-1318-9

Library of Congress Catalog Card Number: 2002107814

Printed in the United States of America

First Printing: November 2002

06 05 04 03   7 6 5 4 3

Interpretation of the printing code: The rightmost double-digit number is the year of the book's printing; the rightmost single-digit number is the number of the book's printing. For example, the printing code 02-1 shows that the first printing of the book occurred in 2002.

Publisher
David Dwyer

Associate Publisher
Stephanie Wall

Production Manager
Gina Kanouse

Managing Editor
Kristy Knoop

Acquisitions Editor
Jody Kennen

Development Editor
Lisa M. Lord

Project Editor
Suzanne Pettypiece

Senior Marketing Manager
Tammy Detrich

Publicity Manager
Susan Nixon

Manufacturing Coordinator
Jim Conway

Cover Designer
Aren Howell

Interior Designer
Louisa Adair

Compositor
Scan Communications Group, Inc.

Indexer
Joy Dean Lee

Media Developer
Jay Payne

Trademarks

All terms mentioned in this book that are known to be trademarks or service marks have been appropriately capitalized. New Riders Publishing cannot attest to the accuracy of this information. Use of a term in this book should not be regarded as affecting the validity of any trademark or service mark. 3ds max 5 is a registered trademark of Discreet, a division of Autodesk, Inc.; Autodesk VIZ is a registered trademark of Autodesk, Inc.; Reactor is a registered trademark of Havok, Inc.; Windows is a registered trademark of Microsoft, Inc.; Segway is a registered trademark of Segway LLC.

Warning and Disclaimer

Every effort has been made to make this book as complete and as accurate as possible, but no warranty of fitness is implied. The information provided is on an "as is" basis. The authors and the publisher shall have neither liability nor responsibility to any person or entity with respect to any loss or damages arising from the information contained in this book or from the use of the CD or programs accompanying it.

Contents at a Glance

Table of Contents

About the Author

Currently, **Ted Boardman**'s primary job description is that of a traveling Discreet 3ds max and Autodesk 3D Studio VIZ training consultant. Ted is one of a handful of Authorized Discreet Training Specialists. Training sessions are custom classes designed to increase 3D modeling and animation productivity for a wide range of clients, from architecture, to aerospace, to television and computer gaming.

An integral part of Ted's training process is authoring and co-authoring books for New Riders Publishing on the production issues encountered in using 3ds max and 3D Studio VIZ, including *3ds max 4 Fundamentals* and several books from the Inside 3D Studio Max and Inside 3D Studio VIZ 3 series. Ted has contributed to several other books on the subject as well as Discreet Advanced Modules and currently has a monthly column covering topics related to max and VIZ at the `http://www.cgarchitect.com` Web site. Ted also had a column in *Cadence* magazine.

Ted is an award-winning speaker at the annual Autodesk University symposium covering CAD and visualization topics and is founder of the Boston Area 3D Studio User Group.

Outside the 3D world, Ted has traveled, lived, and worked in Europe for many years and, for nearly 18 years, ran a small architectural design/build firm that specialized in hand-cut post-and-beam structures. Long-distance bicycle travel and 28,000 miles of blue water yacht deliveries served as a diversion from work for many years. Photography, painting, and opera are other interests.

Ted lives in Portsmouth, New Hampshire.

About the Tech Editors

David Marks is a member of the Quality Engineering team at Discreet and a veteran user of AutoCAD, 3D Studio, and 3ds max. He lives in the San Francisco Bay area with his wife and two daughters. In his spare time, he enjoys gourmet cooking, listening to progressive rock music, and attempting to play piano. Other hobbies include restoration of vintage arcade games, competitive bowling, and Japanese taiko drumming.

Eric Schuck, a graduate of Purdue University's technical graphics program, has been working in the 3D industry for seven years. During that time, he has taught 3D computer graphics at ITT Technical Institute and Indiana University/Purdue University at Indianapolis. Eric also has designed several computer graphics course curricula for all campuses of ITT Technical Institute across the country. In addition to his work in the educational setting, Eric currently serves as the Secretary of the Indianapolis User Group and is employed as the 3D Visualization Director at Outside Source Design Studio, Inc. in Indianapolis, Indiana.

Dedication

I'd like to dedicate this book to Sally Turner, my long-time companion and friend who helps me stay on track.

Acknowledgments

A good book is possible only with a great team of editors to keep an author on track stylistically and technically, and a production crew to assemble the variety of data. A special thanks go to Lisa Lord, Jody Kennen, and Jay Payne at New Riders for their publishing and production expertise.

David Marks and Eric Schuck, my technical editors, offered invaluable contributions to the accuracy and workflow of the exercises and technical content.

Thanks all, for a job well done.

A Message from New Riders

As the reader of this book, you are our most important critic and commentator. We value your opinion and want to know what we're doing right, what we could do better, in what areas you'd like to see us publish, and any other words of wisdom you're willing to pass our way.

As Associate Publisher at New Riders, I welcome your comments. You can fax, email, or write me directly to let me know what you did or didn't like about this book—as well as what we can do to make our books better. When you write, please be sure to include this book's title, ISBN, and author, as well as your name and phone or fax number. I will carefully review your comments and share them with the authors and editors who worked on the book.

Please note that I cannot help you with technical problems related to the topic of this book, and that due to the high volume of email I receive, I might not be able to reply to every message. Thanks.

Fax: 317-581-4663

Email: stephanie.wall@newriders.com

Mail: Stephanie Wall
          Associate Publisher
          New Riders Publishing
          201 West 103rd Street
          Indianapolis, IN 46290 USA

Visit Our Web Site: *www.newriders.com*

On our Web site, you'll find information about our other books, the authors we partner with, book updates and file downloads, promotions, discussion boards for online interaction with other users and with technology experts, and a calendar of trade shows and other professional events with which we'll be involved. We hope to see you around.

Email Us from Our Web Site

Go to www.newriders.com and click on the Contact Us link if you

- Have comments or questions about this book.
- Want to report errors that you have found in this book.
- Have a book proposal or are interested in writing for New Riders.
- Would like us to send you one of our author kits.
- Are an expert in a computer topic or technology and are interested in being a reviewer or technical editor.
- Want to find a distributor for our titles in your area.
- Are an educator/instructor who wants to preview New Riders books for classroom use. In the body/comments area, include your name, school, department, address, phone number, office days/hours, text currently in use, and enrollment in your department, along with your request for either desk/examination copies or additional information.

Introduction

Would you like to create a medieval fantasy world and fire objects from a catapult or skim along on a personal transporter? Even if gaming or fantasy films is not your chosen profession, why not have a little fun while you learn 3ds max 5? With examples and exercises that are enjoyable to do and create a good basis for your own creative talents, you will get more from the learning process.

Who Should Read This Book?

3ds max 5 has some powerful new features that will increase your production by making creation and editing faster and more powerful. As the book title implies, you will learn some fundamentals of 3ds max 5—not necessarily topics only for first-time users, but for anyone who wants to learn work methods and techniques that are fundamental to creating scenes in a timely manner.

Every level of user, from raw beginner to advanced intermediate, can find information in this book that helps speed day-to-day workflow. The book is intended to show by example methods of working through some typical scenarios you might encounter during production—from layout to final rendering. Along the way, you will learn techniques that are applicable to all types of 3D scene creation. Although it is possible to produce good work without a grounding in the fundamentals in any profession, you will be working much harder than necessary and restrict the time available for creativity.

The Fundamentals

The discussions and exercises in this book walk you through the concepts and work methods that, although fundamental, are essential to understanding how 3ds max 5 functions and how to apply the basic knowledge into a workflow that will make you productive.

You will learn important fundamentals, such as the following:

- The concepts of working in 2D to set up complex 3D objects that can be edited quickly and easily.
- Reducing scene overhead to get the most out of the hardware you have available.
- Using efficient materials to simulate complex geometry so that you can increase rendering speed.
- Applying lighting to scenes with the new radiosity and global illumination features, which are both cost effective and convincing to the viewer.
- Using new animation controls, such as the Function Curve Editor and Character Assemblies.

As new users or users anxious to dive into the new features introduced in 3ds max 5, you will want to get stunning results as soon as possible from your new purchase. Take the time to get a good grounding in these fundamentals, and the fancy work will come much more naturally as you dig deeper into the software.

The Exercises

The many exercises walk you step by step through a process similar to what you might encounter in a real-life project. The processes and methods are designed to help you form work habits that will be relevant whether you are a gamer, a background artist, a stage or set designer, or an engineer.

Use the lessons learned from each exercise to come up with scenes of your own, incorporating the techniques and methods until you understand the process. Start with simple scenes that enable you to focus on understanding the concepts, and the fundamentals will quickly become part of your daily routine.

While you are working through the exercises, try to project how you might apply the methods and techniques in your line of work. When you learn to create a building in an exercise, you might be planning to use the same process to create the rough form of an automobile.

When you work on your own projects, I hope you will not think "I learned this or that from Ted Boardman." Instead, the lessons you learn in this book will become instinctive reactions to challenges.

The CD Files and Content

The CD-ROM that accompanies this book includes the files you'll need for the exercises as well as other files and images that you can use as inspiration for creating new scenes of your own. Look for demo content from third-party vendors that will expand the functionality of 3ds max 5, too.

As you're working through the exercises in this book, you'll notice filenames next to a CD icon, as shown here, at the beginning of most exercises:

On the CD

exercises\CH02\
House04.max

If you like, you can load these files when starting an exercise instead of opening the last file you saved. The scene files on the CD can come in handy if you make a mistake partway through a chapter's exercises, or if you're a more advanced user who doesn't need to start at the beginning.

Try opening all the files in the book and analyzing how the objects were modeled, how the lights were placed, and how the materials and animation were created. Play with those scenes to come up with other approaches to improving them. Try to learn something new every day you work with 3ds max 5, and let these lessons become the foundation for your artistry.

The New Features

I've taken some different approaches to developing scenes for the exercises that use as many of the new 3ds max 5 features, both basic and advanced, as practical and still stay true to the fundamentals of 3ds max.

New Editable Poly editing features are introduced and used extensively in building the objects in the scenes.

Lighting has some new features in 3ds max 5, with global illumination and radiosity renderers. I have divided the exercises into three parts: an exterior medieval hamlet, the interior of a small building, and a freestanding personal transporter. The intent is to introduce you to the fundamentals of three specific types of rendering lighting scenarios—daylight, light fixtures, and global illumination.

Animation also has been improved significantly in 3ds max 5, and the animation exercises walk you through these improvements and explain the fundamental aspects of new animation features.

Overview

This book is organized into the following components:

Part I, "Concepts and Scene Development," includes the following chapter:

- Chapter 1, "Graphics and 3ds max 5 Concepts: Laying the Groundwork," introduces traditional art concepts and computer graphics concepts for you to build on.

Part II, "A Street Scene" encompasses the following chapters:

- Chapter 2, "Modeling: A Medieval Street Scene," leads you through new box modeling techniques and lofting for quick and flexible 3D object creation.
- Chapter 3, "Applying Materials and Maps for a Convincing Outdoor Scene," explains mapping and material techniques that will transform a computer world into a fantasy world.
- Chapter 4, "Exterior Lighting: Standard and Advanced Methods," adds depth to your scene with new lighting techniques.
- Chapter 5, "New Animation Concepts," introduces the new Set Key animation method for better control and new Character Assemblies—containers for animation.

Part III, "An Interior Scene," steps you through the following processes:

- Chapter 6, "Modeling for Radiosity and Efficiency," covers modeling techniques that enhance radiosity rendering efficiency.
- Chapter 7, "Materials and Mapping: Deeper into the Details," introduces mapping techniques and reflections for more realism.
- Chapter 8, "Interior Lighting with New Photometric Lights," explains a new lighting paradigm and shadow creation methods.
- Chapter 9, "Taking Control with Animation Controllers," introduces the concept of specialized controllers for animation.

In Part IV, "A Personal Transporter," you learn to model, light, and animate a vehicle based on the Segway Scooter in the following chapters:

- Chapter 10, "Introduction to Freeform Modeling," covers modeling techniques ideal for flowing surfaces.
- Chapter 11, "Materials and Lighting: The Magic Combination," explores lighting methods and material attributes that make your scenes sparkle.
- Chapter 12, "Animation: Animating in World Space," explains space warping and more, with tools to move the earth.
- Chapter 13, "Effects: Reacting to Reactor," introduces rigid and soft body dynamics.
- Chapter 14, "Video Post: Tying It All Together," explains techniques for producing a cohesive presentation.

Conventions

This book follows a few typographical conventions:

- A new term is set in *italics* the first time it is introduced.
- Text the user types in and other "computer language" terms, such as script and variables, are set in a fixed-pitch font—for example, "enter -4" in the Extrusion Height field."
- Keyboard shortcuts and hotkeys, such as **Alt+w**, are set in **boldface**.

You also will find several boxed elements used in these chapters:

Key Terms

Defines important terminology you need to know when performing exercises.

Hot Keys and Keyboard Shortcuts

Efficient production requires speed in accessing commands, so common shortcuts are highlighted.

tip   Tips offer useful information to extend your knowledge or clarify concepts and techniques.

note   Notes introduce you to optional work methods and ideas or my opinions on a topic.

caution   Cautions point out factors that could slow your workflow or reduce your flexibility.

warning   Warnings alert you to trouble areas or processes that could result in file damage or loss of work.

The Source

The exercises and work methods are derived from situations that develop in my max classes and during consulting. I try to incorporate methods that have been proved in the field to increase productivity and make your job easier and more enjoyable.

Wherever 3ds max 5 may take you, good luck and have fun.

note   Ted Boardman can be reached by visiting his Web site at http://www.tbmax.com or by emailing him at tedb@tbmax.com or tbdesign1@earthlink.net if you have questions about the book or about training.

PART I

Concepts and Scene Development

CHAPTER 1

Graphics and 3ds max 5 Concepts: Laying the Groundwork

In This Chapter

Computer graphics is just that—*graphics*. It is a 2D representation of a 3D scene created to evoke an intended emotional response from the viewer.

Over the centuries, countless resources have been poured into determining what makes effective graphics in many disciplines, from primitive cave drawings to painting and drawing, photography and film, and now, 3D computer graphics.

The 3D part of 3D graphics is evident only during the development phase. The result, except in very few 3D viewing methods, is ultimately presented as a 2D static or moving image. You must still be aware of the principles of what has been accepted, or at least promoted, as good design over the years and apply those same principles to your development of 3D scenes.

Good art is often about bending the established rules to come up with something that makes the viewer sit up and take notice at first glance. That is the emotional response you should be striving for. However, you cannot bend the rules until you know what the rules are. Some of the principles and concepts you will learn to look for include

- Storyboarding
- Color and lighting—traditional and 3ds max 5
- Animation and movement

- Object naming standards
- Understanding compound shapes
- Cloning objects
- Applying and adjusting modifiers
- Materials and maps
- Keyframe animation concepts
- Mathematical accuracy

If you have a chance to take a class in painting, film, or video, the time spent in class is well worth the effort. The more time you can dedicate for hands-on art classes or art appreciation sessions, the more comfortable you will be with incorporating the fundamental principles learned in those classes into your own work.

In working with 3ds max 5, especially for new users, getting absorbed in the technology of creating 3D scenes is very easy. You must remember that no matter how technical the presentation will be, the end result is still art. You are trying to extract an emotional response from the viewer.

Key Terms

Cloning   Making copies of objects in 3ds max 5.

Compound shapes   2D shapes composed of more than one spline sub-object.

Keyframe animation   An animation style in which the user sets poses over time and 3ds max 5 interpolates the in-between steps.

Maps   Patterns to alter the appearance of materials.

Materials   Surface attributes assigned to objects.

Modifier stack   A history of applied modifiers.

Modifiers   Discrete processes applied to edit objects.

Shapes   2D construction objects that do not render.

Basic Graphics Concepts

This chapter is not intended to teach you the principles of good design, but to bring your attention to some topics you'll need to learn more about to become a better 3D artist. Read the descriptions in the chapter, play with the examples, and check out the bibliography for books on related subjects. Then try to condition yourself to look with a critical eye at magazine images, television and movies, and other animators' work to see what strikes you as relevant and how you might apply the concepts to your work.

Some of the discussion refers to theory in painting, and other parts refer to those theories as they are translated into a more modern media, such as TV or film. However, the principles remain the same, with slight variations in actual values.

The specific 3ds max 5 fundamental topics also are included to give you a "heads up" on important subjects that you can investigate more deeply on your own, not necessarily topics that will be addressed directly in the following chapters.

You do not want to directly copy techniques and methods, but you do want to use the fundamental principles to develop a style of your own. Your work will then become art, not just a lucky guess—or worse, a yucky mess.

Storyboarding

A *storyboard* is nothing more than an outline, usually in graphical form, of what the project will contain and how the scenes will be laid out. It can be as simple as a few quick sketches on a pad of paper to a complex airbrushed comic book–style description of the story. The purpose of the storyboard is to organize your thoughts and portray them in a manner that your client and co-workers will know what the plan is and how it will be executed.

Often the individual panels of a storyboard cover the action at an animation's keyframe. Other times, it includes information about the scene's composition and color information.

Although animations can probably benefit more from a good storyboard, still images should also be planned and sketched to show color information, lighting and camera angles, highlight locations, or cropping information. See Figure 1.1 for a quick and dirty storyboard sketch of four panels to show the build up of a scene for an architectural presentation.

No matter how simple the project is, do not take the storyboard for granted. Get into the habit early of creating a storyboard for every project, no matter how small.

In tight production schedules, working out a comprehensive storyboard and getting all parties to sign off before any 3D work starts is a process that will save you countless hours of wasted time and talent down the road.

FIGURE 1.1   *Four fine examples of panels from a storyboard by Andrew Pacquette, © 2001.*

Color and Lighting

Color and lighting are two powerful tools that help you enhance a scene's mood that has already been established by composition, camera angles, and characters. Again, this discussion is about color and lighting as they have traditionally been used in art.

Light is what images are all about in the first place. Everything you view is the result of light being bounced off a surface to your eyes. Color is a quality of the light returned from a surface, based on what range of light wave frequencies can escape from the surface.

Lighting Effects

Lighting refers to not only the light that comes from a light source, such as the sun or a light bulb, but also the relationships between light and dark areas in a scene.

Artists have spent many hours studying the relationships of light and dark. Monet did studies of haystacks and the Rouen Cathedral in France to portray the "transformation of a subject" caused by the effect of light itself. Georges Seurat used pointillism—painting dots of color to represent light in outdoor scenes. The illusion of light was created by using color, not by actually lighting the scene.

Light areas in a scene come forward and dark areas recede. The Old Masters—Rembrandt being one of the more famous—used this concept to develop a painting technique that focuses the viewer's eye on important areas of the image. This technique can be applied to computer-generated images just as effectively.

In the Luminist school of painting, very bright light is often the center of attention and noticeably influences everything in the scene. Search the Internet for examples from some notable Luminist painters, such as Fitz Hugh Lane, J.M.W Turner, and George Curtis to see how they created the illusion of bright light and how it affected the overall mood (see Figure 1.2).

FIGURE 1.2   The Fighting Temeraire *by J.M.W. Turner, an example of the Luminist painting style.*

Color Principles Based on Traditional Theories

As you can see from the lack of color in this book's black-and-white figures, color can be an important element in any image. Although some important artists—Ansel Adams and Alfred Hitchcock, for example—have produced spectacular works in

note

Full color versions of all the figures in this book are available on the accompanying CD-ROM.

grayscale images, they relied on composition, form, camera angles, and lighting to enhance the story they were trying to tell. Even subtle color changes can produce dramatic changes in the mood and 3D depth illusion of scenes.

An important factor in color theory is that of complementary colors, "complementary" being derived from *complete*. Complementary colors are derived from primary colors; in computer renderings, the primary colors are red, green, and blue.

note

Painters' primary pigment colors are red, blue, and yellow, but some of the practical information, such as the effect one color has on another, can be transferred from paint pigments to computer or electric light.

When primary light colors are mixed in equal amounts, these are the results:

red + green = yellow

red + blue = magenta

blue + green = cyan

The complementary colors are those diametrically opposed from each other in the color wheel. In the color wheel in Figure 1.3, the arrow shows that the complementary color of blue is yellow. To see the color version, open the file noted next to the CD icon.

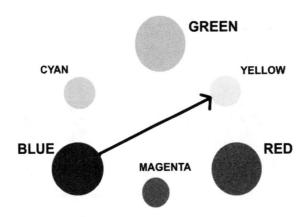

FIGURE 1.3   *The complementary color of blue is yellow, as seen in the color wheel.*

Figure 1.4 shows two dark rectangles with two lighter rectangles in the center of each. The dark patch on the left is a slightly purple shade of blue, and the dark patch on the right is pure blue. Both the small rectangles are the same shade of yellow. In this grayscale image, you might be able to see a difference in the small rectangles' shading, but if you open the

On the CD

images\01MSF04.png

01MSF04.png file from the CD-ROM, you'll see a noticeable difference in the two yellow rectangles. The oneon the right, paired with its complementary color, looks much brighter andmore vibrant.

FIGURE 1.4   *Complementary colors in action. The yellow paired with its complement color, blue, looks more vibrant and clean.*

Figure 1.5 shows a more practical example of using yellow with pure blue. Three lemons are depicted on a velvety blue drape. Open the 01MSF05.png file from the CD-ROM to see the color version.

On the CD

images/01MSF05.png

FIGURE 1.5   *A scene applying the complementary color theory in a more practical setting.*

Lighting Variables

Lighting as an art form in this section refers more to photography and film than to painting. The light's mood and color as well as the physical considerations of when to put which light values on which objects can have a profound effect on the audience.

You should look into two broad areas of lighting concepts from television and film to help improve your overall lighting skills:

- The temperature of light, a purely technical aspect that can affect the mood of your scenes.
- The placement of light values, which has been used to generate an overall mood in scenes since the early days of photography and film.

Temperature of Light

Essentially, the temperature of light is a physical aspect of the light source that affects the light's color. It is not the same as the color of objects, however, nor the same as using colored filters over lights to generate color. Light temperature is given in degrees Kelvin.

What you should be looking at in light temperature is whether it lends a warm or cool feeling to the scene. In photography, warm lighting is lighting with temperatures below 4000K. The colors tend to run to the yellow and red ranges. Warm colors lend a balance and peacefulness to a scene. Here are examples of warm lighting and the corresponding temperatures:

- **Candlelight**   Very warm, with a temperature of around 1900K and a red-orange hue. The mood generated by candlelight is legendary.

- **Incandescent**   Regular household light bulbs are incandescent and cast a yellowish-red light at a temperature of around 2800K. This light conveys a close, warm feeling.

- **Floodlights**   Running a bit cooler at around 3200K and up, floodlight effects work well for exterior night scenes, where you want to open the scene up or make the viewer slightly uncomfortable by giving the scene a contrasting light effect.

> **note**
>
> "Warm" and "cool" are terms that have been coined to define light quality; they have nothing to do with the actual scientific light temperature. So light that generates a "warm" color has lower temperatures than light that produces a "cool" color—the terms are seemingly at odds with each other.

On the cool side of the equation, as you get into higher light temperatures, the scene becomes more harsh or dramatic. The viewer is not lulled into such a sense of well-being and comfort. These are examples of cool light:

- **Daylight** At around 5200K, direct daylight is still somewhat yellow. The mood generated is not uncomfortable, but is more open and expansive.

- **Strobe light** Strobe lighting is definitely moving into the realm of cold and somewhat threatening light temperatures. Most strobes are in the range of 6000K and can be used to heighten the tension in a scene.

- **Skylight** Skylight is the light bounced back from water and particles in the northern sky, where it picks up a decidedly cold effect, with a temperature of around 11000K. It can be bright and very harsh.

Look into incorporating the effects of changing light temperature to set viewers on edge or to calm them, as needed. It has traditionally been a very effective tool in both films and television. Study these mediums to see where lighting temperature changes create changes in mood.

Placement of Light Values

One of the most noticeable detractions in a film or computer-generated image is flat lighting, a scene with no differentiation between foreground and background lighting. Having a range of lighting throughout the scene heightens the feeling of three dimensions.

Overall, light placement and quality can play a large role in how the audience reacts to an image or a scene. Again, it is not only the actual positioning of lights in a setting, but the juxtaposition of light and dark values created by those lights that define the scene's space and mood.

- **Foreground lighting** Lighting the foreground brighter than the background tends to compress the scene somewhat—not in the same way that flat lighting does, but in a way that puts the viewer into the scene. The change in value from light to dark does not have to be dramatic to be effective.

- **Background lighting** When the background is lit brighter than the foreground, the viewer feels more detached from the action and the tension is increased. The greater the difference in the light intensity, the more anonymity the viewer feels.

- **Soft or hard light**   This softness or hardness of light and shadows is projected into the viewer's perception, making the viewer either more at ease or at odds with the scene. For example, a night street scene with soft shadows of a character on the buildings is not as dramatic as hard-edged shadows. The contrast between the dimmest and brightest lights in that scene can also enhance or diminish the effect.

- **Backlighting**   Backlighting, used almost constantly and very prominently in film and television, often seems to be ignored in 3D graphics. Strong backlighting on characters and objects in a scene, which outlines them with a very thin bright edge, separates them from the background and helps focus the viewer's attention on them.

Watch film and television with the preceding topics in mind. We have grown accustomed to seeing these effects on a day-to-day basis and do not even notice them. After you begin looking for foreground lighting or backlighting, for example, you will be amazed that you took it for granted all these years. You cannot incorporate these effects into your work until you become aware of how they might be used, and experience is often the best teacher.

Motion and Movement

You can and should refer to current or past techniques used in more established art forms for cues to making your moving presentations and animations elicit an emotional response from the viewer to support and reinforce the color and composition elements.

Learning more about the following aspects of motion and movement will help increase the impact of the message you are trying to convey with your scenes:

- Object movement
- Camera movement
- Content editing

Review the fundamental concepts in the following sections, and then investigate them further on the Internet or try taking courses that are not necessarily aimed at computer animation, but at the more traditional fields of film, video, and photography.

Object Movement

Objects moving in your scenes should be kept to a minimum. Objects should not move just because they can, but as an integral part of the story you are trying to tell. Unnecessary movement by minor characters or objects, especially at the edges of the main action, can distract the viewer from the point being stressed in the story.

Your main actors, whether human or animal characters or animated objects, should appear to have weight and a specific center of gravity that influences their movement. It is much better to have limited movement reinforced by gestures that show the character's weight, such as shifting the hips or moving the arms to maintain balance. The viewer will read a lot more into these gestures than in the character moving all over the frame.

Taking cues from theater and movies, exaggerating movement to make sure the viewer has gotten the point is an effective tool. Exaggerated movement is not unnecessary movement because it enhances the story. This technique, one you can learn from traditional cartoon artists, works with inanimate objects as well. For example, if a rubber ball rolls in front of the viewer and stops, a slight skewing of the objects in the direction of travel (an effect traditionally known as follow-through) and a spring backward will reinforce the ball's weight and movement.

Camera Movement

Camera movement is a delicate balancing act in film and video. You want to let viewers know that movement has taken place, but you do not want to tamper with their equilibrium, except in rare dramatic cases, such as car chases or cliff climbing.

These four basic camera moves are used in the film and video industry for most scenes:

- **Zoom**   Zooming is accomplished by changing the focal length of the lens—say, from a wide-angle far shot to a telephoto closeup shot. The effect is a very steady movement with changes in perspective that can accentuate your distance from the subject.

- **Dolly**   Dollying physically moves the camera while leaving the perspective intact. It is best used for indicating a first-person character's movement in the scene. A variation of this camera method, called Vertigo, was introduced to Hollywood in Alfred Hitchcock's film of the same name. The camera is dollied out and zoomed in at the same time—tricky to accomplish, but very dramatic, as it seems to leave the viewer in the same position while it distorts the background.

- **Pan**   With this method, the camera is physically moved sideways in the scene. It must be done very slowly to avoid disorienting the viewer.

- **Handheld**   A relatively new camera move, this technique replicates a light handheld camera being walked or run through the scene. Overdone, this method is disconcerting to most viewers, but in moderation, it can add impact to the action.

Turning a camera on a point—for example, standing in one spot and turning around while pointing the camera straight ahead—is rarely done. Without peripheral vision, the turning motion is extremely uncomfortable even for a few degrees. Try to avoid turning the camera at all costs.

Editing as a Tool to Manage Motion

Traditionally, movies are made or ruined in the editing room. Editors stitch short scenes together into a coherent stream, with smooth transitions that give the illusion of a seamless story. Only the most relevant action in the scene is used, and the motion that doesn't directly enhance the story is discarded.

tip

An effective method of getting quick results from computer still images is to borrow from the Ken Burns's television series on the Civil War or from traditional cartoon methods. Use a large image, and pan the camera across the image to create the illusion of movement. It is quick, easy, and effective.

You should incorporate some of the following basic techniques into your work to make the viewer comfortable with the presentation, whether you are working on an entertainment feature or trying to sell a client on a new idea for a machine:

- **Cut** In a cut—the most common technique in film and television—the scene changes abruptly from one frame to the next. Timing the cut is of utmost importance to make it seamless to the viewer.

- **Fade or Dissolve** The transition from one scene to the next is blended, with the first scene fading out as the next fades in. It must be done quickly to avoid the distraction of half of one scene bleeding through the next. Fades, which tend to be shorter, and dissolves usually indicate a shift of time or distance between two scenes—from an exterior shot to an interior shot, for example.

- **Wipe** A wipe transition is similar to a fade, but there is a clear line of demarcation between one scene and the other. It could be a widening circle or a page turn, for example, and is used to indicate a greater time or distance span than the fade or dissolve.

- **Cutaway** In a cutaway transition, the viewer is shown something else in the scene during the transition. For example, in a conversation between two characters, the camera could leave one character, pan to the horizon, and then back to the second character. It indicates a break in the story flow.

3ds max 5 Specific Concepts

Earlier in this chapter, you learned about the concepts helpful in presenting graphics in any form—traditional media or computer generated—for the maximum impact on your intended audience. In this section, you will learn concepts specific to

3ds max 5 that will help make sense of the designers and programmers' intentions and help you make full use of the software's features. Just learning the correct buttons to push is not going to make you a productive artist. You must develop a feel for the toolset and an understanding of the underlying concepts to be able to combine tools and work methods efficiently and effectively.

Read through the description of each concept and absorb what you can from it. Place a bookmark in sections covering concepts that are unfamiliar to you, and refer back to them when you encounter applications of the concepts later in the book's exercises.

After you know *what* to look for, referring back to this chapter or using the 3ds max 5 online User Reference from the menu will be much easier. Making you aware that a concept exists is the main objective of this section.

Object-Naming Standards

Naming objects in 3ds max 5 might not seem important, but proper and logical naming schemes can increase productivity, especially in offices with many modelers and animators or offices that collaborate with other teams.

As you create each 2D or 3D object, 3ds max 5 automatically assigns a name to that object. The name is usually derived from the type of object with a sequential number added to the end: Box01, Line05, Torus433, and so forth.

After applying only a few modifications to the object, you'll quickly realize that it bears no resemblance to its original name, and there is no clue as to what Box01 might refer to when searching a list of named objects. For example, you might open a file containing a landscape with a pond and trees, looking for a listing of all the objects, and see Plane01 through Plane236 and Cylinder01 through Cylinder1021. The result is a long search and select process to pick a specific object in the scene. Renaming objects with logical names in the beginning speeds the selection process when you're editing the file.

Figure 1.6 shows an extremely simple scene with objects that have their original automatically assigned names. It might be difficult to determine which of the objects was an ellipse.

Figure 1.7 shows the same scene with the object names edited to be more descriptive of what the object is actually representing. The properly named objects are easier to choose in the Named Selection Sets dialog box.

Objects can be renamed in the Create panel at the time you create them, or you can change them later by selecting the object, highlighting the name in the Modify panel, and overwriting the text with a new name.

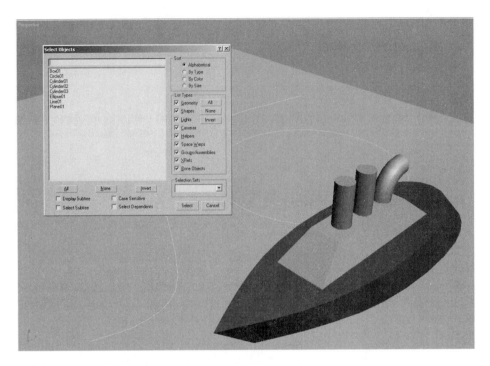

FIGURE 1.6   *A simple ship with original object names in the Select Objects dialog box.*

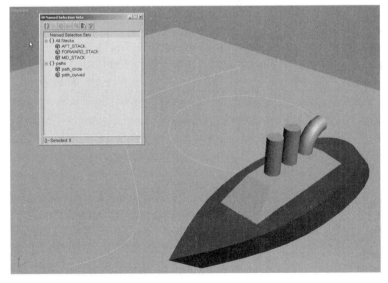

FIGURE 1.7   *A simple ship with logical object names in the Named Selection Sets dialog box.*

Set Up a Naming Standard

For any company using 3ds max 5, developing a set of naming standards for everyone to use would be helpful. If enforced, this standard enables everyone to recognize and find objects in a scene much more quickly and use sorting techniques in the Select by Name dialog boxes. A simple example to start with is shown in the following list:

- **MAJOR ACTORS**   Use all caps to name major objects or characters in your scene. The caps make the objects easier to identify and cause the name to be sorted at the top of the Select by Name list when the Case Sensitive check box is selected (see Figure 1.8).

- **Minor Actors**   Objects with less importance in the scene or background objects can have the first letter capped and the rest of the letters lowercase. This method separates them from the more frequently selected main objects, but indicates a 3D background object.

- **2D objects and shapes**   2D objects and shapes used in the scene as motion paths can be named with all lowercase letters. Lowercase names migrate toward the bottom of the Select by Name list when the Case Sensitive check box is selected.

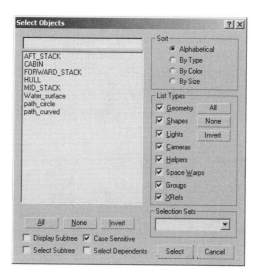

FIGURE 1.8   *Selecting the Case Sensitive option for sorting.*

Another possibility would be to start all object names with 2D- or 3D- to distinguish them in the Select by Name list.

In short, object naming is not something you can leave to 3ds max 5 and still expect to work productively. The time you spend upfront on developing a naming scheme and typing the name when you create objects will be rewarded many times over.

Other Naming and Notation Options

Not only 2D and 3D objects have names. Other areas benefit from logical naming or, in some cases, adding notations to clarify a feature's function or purpose. The following list indicates a few places where logical names can be helpful:

When you have many objects in your scene and you find yourself scrolling through the Select by Name list even with a logical naming scheme, you can edit the names of objects by starting their names with the number 1. This forces those objects to the top of the list for the current editing session when Case Sensitive is selected. Delete the 1 when you are finished with that group of objects.

- **Graph Editors** Track Views, Dope Sheets, Function Curve Editors, and Schematic Views can be named for later recall (see Figure 1.9).

- **Modifiers** You can add to or change names of modifiers by right-clicking the name in the Modifier Stack and choosing Rename in the menu (see Figure 1.10).

- **Named Selection Sets** Multiple selected objects or sub-object sets can be given a common name to make it easier to select them later. This feature was available in 3ds max 4 but has been considerably enhanced in 3ds max 5 to make it more accessible and useful (see Figure 1.11).

- **Groups** The Group command combines multiple objects into a single logical entity for editing (see Figure 1.12). Group names appear in brackets in Select by Name lists—[SHIP], for example.

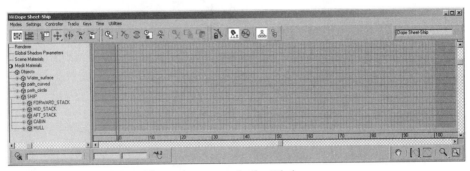

FIGURE 1.9   *The Dope Sheet with a unique name in the title bar.*

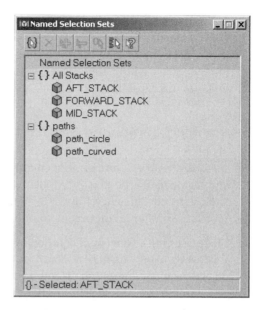

FIGURE 1.10
Adding a notation to the Bend modifier in the Modifier Stack.

FIGURE 1.11
The Named Selection Sets dialog box.

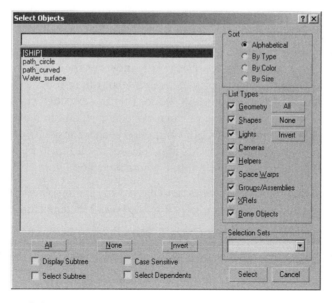

FIGURE 1.12   *Groups are shown in brackets in a Select By Name list.*

Get in the habit early of using short, concise names throughout 3ds max 5 and set a naming standard for your office to increase productivity and ease of use. While working in a Select By Name list, for example, you can select all objects that begin with "TRE" just by typing those three letters. Without logical names, you would lose much of this capability.

Understanding Compound Shapes

2D objects in 3ds max 5 are known collectively as *shapes*. Shapes are composed of sub-object entities, vertices, segments, and splines. You will learn more about vertices and segments in Chapters 2, "Modeling: A Medieval Street Scene," 6, "Modeling for Radiosity and Efficiency," and 10, "An Introduction to Freeform Modeling," but splines are an important part of compound shapes.

There is a simple concept of compound shapes that you should be aware of from the start when using 3ds max 5. Much of the power of converting 2D shapes into 3D objects requires you to understand how using compound shapes affects the model's end result. It is a simple yet important concept.

In 3ds max 5, shapes have names and, when created, are assigned a color in the viewports. Each shape is made up of at least one spline by definition. For example, a Circle 2D primitive is a shape containing one spline, as is a complex curving Line primitive. A Donut primitive is a single shape composed of two concentric round splines. A Donut has a single name, and both round splines are the same color in the viewport.

If two circles, one inside the other, are converted to 3D objects with the Extrude modifier, for example, the result is two cylinders of the same height, one inside the other. If a Donut compound shape is extruded, the result is a cylinder with a hole through the center. In Figure 1.13, notice that the extruded circles on the left share surfaces on the top (and bottom) when extruded, which can make editing and applying materials difficult. The Donut compound shape, consisting of two splines, results in a radically different object. 3ds max 5 builds a solid from the outside spline until it encounters a closed "island" spline where it creates a void.

Understanding compound shapes can help you in creating objects as varied as building elevations with window openings or a splined collar for a machine (see Figure 1.14).

Compound shapes can be created with two common methods:

- Using the Start New Shape button at creation time
- Attaching at the Editable Spline level during editing

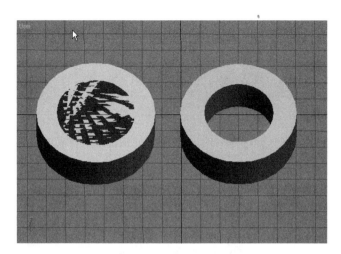

FIGURE 1.13 *3D objects created from extruding two Circle shapes on the left and a Donut compound shape on the right.*

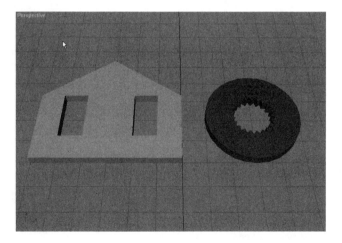

FIGURE 1.14 *Two examples of more practical extruded compound shapes.*

If, after creating a primitive 2D shape, you deselect the Start New Shape check box in the Create panel, any subsequent shapes are added as new splines to the original (see Figure 1.15). If you convert any shape to an editable spline (as discussed in Chapters 2, 6, and 10), use the Attach option so that you can add any valid shape as a new spline (see Figure 1.16).

Again, the concept of compound shapes might seem confusing until you have a chance to use them during a project. However, reading through this part of the chapter will introduce you to the concept, and you will more readily recognize the importance of compound shapes and how to deal with them when you get into chapters that make use of them in the exercises.

Cloning Objects

The process of copying objects to create new objects in 3ds max 5 is known as *cloning*. Making a copy is just one option of cloning, as you will see. You can use cloning to give your objects flexible editing capabilities that can increase productivity enormously.

Primarily, cloning objects is accomplished by *transforming* an object while holding the Shift key down.

Transforming an object with the Shift key held down opens the Clone Options dialog box (see Figure 1.17) with three primary options available:

- **Copy**   A Copy clone looks exactly the same as the original object, but there is no connection between the two. Editing one has no effect on the other.

- **Instance**   An Instance clone has a two-way connection between any modifications to either object. Edit the original, and the Instance clone is also edited; edit the Instance clone, and the original changes.

- **Reference**   A Reference clone has a one-way connection, from the original object to the reference object established, but not from the reference to the original. Edit the original object, and the Reference object also changes. Edit the Reference object, and no changes are passed back to the original.

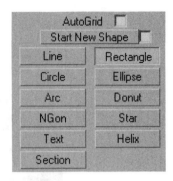

FIGURE 1.15
Clear the Start New Shape check box after creating the first shape to create new splines added to the shape.

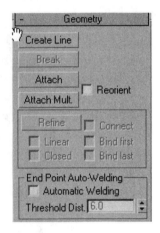

FIGURE 1.16
Click the Attach button in the Modify panel to add splines to a compound shape.

tip

Conversely, single or multiple splines that are part of compound shapes can be selected and detached to create new simple or compound shapes.

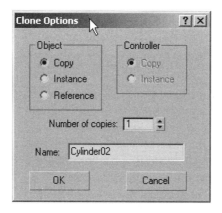

FIGURE 1.17   *The Clone Options dialog box.*

Some 3ds max 5 tools offer Instance as one of the creation methods. The Loft command, a tool for extruding one or more 2D shapes along a 2D path, defaults to Instance when you choose a 2D shape as the Loft cross-section (see Figure 1.18). This allows you to modify the original 2D cross-section to affect the complex 3D lofted object.

As you can easily see, the concept of cloning is a far-reaching, integral part of 3ds max 5 for reducing memory overhead (because instances and references take up less space) and for adding editing flexibility by enabling you to change many clones by editing only one. Learning the concept is simple, but applying the concept efficiently in production work requires a little practice and planning. As with all aspects of 3ds max 5, start with simple examples and work your way into more complex situations to develop a feel for how the tool or concept works.

Transform is a collective term in 3ds max 5 for any of three actions: Move, Rotate, and Scale.

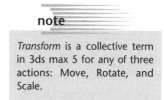

An additional benefit of using Instance or Reference clones is that their memory footprint is considerably smaller than the original object or Copy clones. This increases the efficiency of your scene for better system performance and faster rendering.

Applying Modifiers

Building models in 3ds max 5 is essentially a two-step process: *create and modify*. First, you create a basic 2D or 3D object, and then you modify it into the final form.

One of the primary forms of modifying objects in 3ds max 5 is the core of its power and flexibility: the ability to add discrete modifiers to objects. Modifiers are generally independent of each other and of the base object, which allows you to change, add, or remove them at any point in the construction history without affecting any modifications made before or after that point.

The order in which modifiers are applied to objects often has a profound effect on the end result. For example, if you apply a Bend modifier, followed by a Taper modifier to a cylinder, and then make adjustments, the result is very different from applying the Taper modifier and then the Bend modifier with the same settings. See Figure 1.19 for a comparison of applying modifiers in different orders.

Learning to use modifiers with their wide variety of adjustments should be a high priority in your quest to master 3ds max 5. When you are comfortable with individual modifiers, experiment with combinations to achieve your modeling goals. Use your imagination to apply even the most unlikely sounding combinations of modifiers, and you will soon develop a feeling for what works for your particular situation.

FIGURE 1.18
Selecting the Instance option as the default on a Loft cross-section.

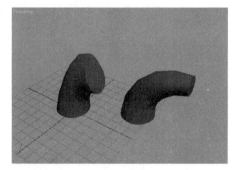

FIGURE 1.19 *On the left, applying a Bend modifier and then a Taper modifier to a cylinder. On the right, applying the Taper modifier before the Bend modifier.*

The Modifier Stack

As you apply modifiers to objects, 3ds max 5 keeps track of their order in the Modifier Stack. Think of the Modifier Stack, shown in Figure 1.20, as the history of editing your object.

Generally, you can select a modifier in the stack and make changes to it without affecting the settings of modifiers above or below that point in the stack. This gives you the freedom to design and experiment with your models that's not found in most other software packages. Dropping to the Cylinder level, for example, gives you access to its base parameters, such as radius, height, and number of segments, again without affecting the settings of the modifiers higher in the stack yet changing the end result.

FIGURE 1.20
The Modifier Stack for a cylinder with four modifiers applied.

You can reposition modifiers in the stack by dragging and dropping them up or down, and you can also completely remove them from the stack. New right-click menus in 3ds max 5 (see Figure 1.21) allow you to perform various operations, such as Cut and Paste, to modifiers to move them to new locations in the stack or to apply them other objects in the scene.

With the right-click menu, you can also rename modifiers to add notations, as mentioned earlier, and you can *collapse* the stack to "bake" the modifications into the model and clear the stack. You can also disable modifiers in the viewports or the renderer or both. Disabling modifiers is a great tool for analyzing models that you obtain from other sources, if you need to edit the object or just want to see how it was built.

You can also expand the modifiers in the stack to access sub-object editing options. Figure 1.22 shows an example of an expanded modifier with access to its Control Points, Lattice, and Set Volume controls.

In Chapters 2, 6, and 10, you will learn to apply modifiers to 2D and 3D objects to build complex models of real-world objects and learn to navigate and edit the Modifier Stack to make changes to your models.

FIGURE 1.21
New right-click menu for the Modifier Stack.

Becoming comfortable with all aspects of the Modifier Stack is an essential part of working with 3ds max 5. The full depth of its possibilities is beyond the scope of this fundamental book. But if you use the information you learn here as a basis to work from, and you experiment with new combinations and permutations, you will quickly learn your way around and develop your own style of modeling.

FIGURE 1.22
Expanding a modifier to access sub-object controls.

Sub-Object Editing

Up to this point, you have heard about working with objects, both 2D and 3D, in a 3ds max 5 scene. Primitive objects are created and then modified at the object level by applying and adjusting modifiers. Another whole world of control exists in 3ds max 5 at what is known as the sub-object level. Usually, you do sub-object editing on 2D or 3D objects to gain access to the fundamental building blocks that make up the objects.

To access the sub-object levels of a 3D surface, you must either convert the primitive—a Box or Cylinder, for example—to an editable mesh, or apply a modifier, such as Edit Mesh, that has options at the sub-object level. These are the sub-object levels associated with a 3D mesh:

- **Face**   Faces are the triangular flat planes that define the surface of a model and can be selected as faces, the triangles themselves, or polygons, which are groups of faces defined by solid edges. Another form of face selection is by element, which is a group of faces defined as an entity.

- **Edge**   Edges are the boundaries of each triangular face and can be visible or invisible to affect how modifiers such as Lattice function or how materials set to Wire show in the rendering. Visible edges can be selected and edited in many ways.

- **Vertex**   Vertices are the non-dimensional points at the apex of each triangular face. Like faces and edges, vertices can be selected and edited.

You can use the selection tools built into 3ds max 5 to select a set of faces, for example, and then edit that selection set with the options available in the Modifier Stack, as shown in Figure 1.23.

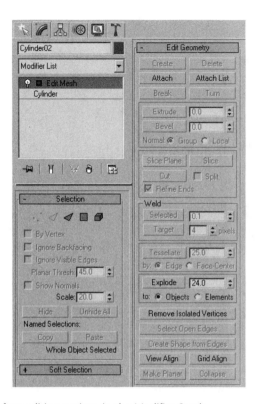

Figure 1.23 *Sub-object face editing options in the Modifier Stack.*

As an alternative, almost any modifier can be applied directly to the selection set of faces and will affect only those faces. For example, you could select only faces on the top half of a cylinder, applying a Bend modifier to those faces and adjusting the modifier controls. The result is a cylinder bent only on the top half rather than the whole cylinder, as shown in Figure 1.24.

Just as 3D surface objects have sub-object editing capabilities, so do 2D shapes. These are the sub-object levels associated with 2D shapes:

- **Spline**   Splines are sub-object level entities that are formed by clearing the Start New Shape check box at creation or by attaching two or more shapes together, as discussed earlier in this chapter.
- **Segment**   Segments are the visible 2D connectors between vertices.
- **Vertex**   Vertices are the non-dimensional points at each end of a segment.

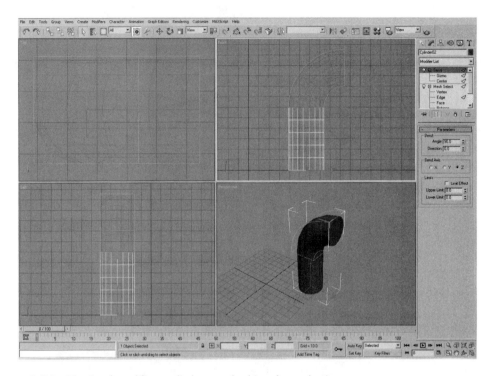

FIGURE 1.24   *The Bend modifier applied to a sub-object face selection.*

Like a surface object, the sub-object levels of 2D shapes can be accessed by converting to an editable spline or by applying a modifier that allows access to the sub-object level. As an example, Figure 1.25 shows the spline sub-object editing options of an editable spline.

There are even special modifiers that their primary function is to create sub-object level selection sets. Other modifiers are then applied above those selections in the Modifier Stack to create highly editable entities. Those modifiers include the following:

- MeshSelect
- SplineSelect
- PolySelect
- PatchSelect
- Vol.Select (volume select)

caution

After you have applied modifiers at the sub-object level that change the mesh's topology—deleting or adding faces, for example—usually you cannot drop below that point in the Modifier Stack without causing problems with the object. 3ds max 5 issues a warning that there could be potential problems.

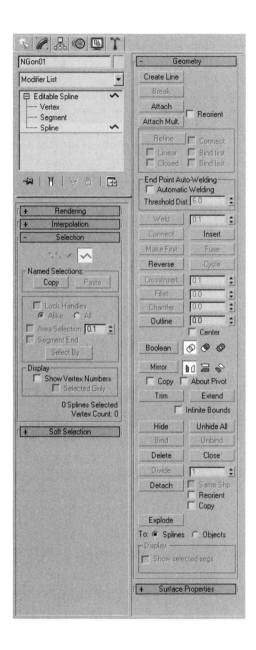

FIGURE 1.25   *The spline sub-object editing options include Outline and Boolean, for example.*

Materials and Maps

Understanding the concept of materials and maps in 3ds max 5 is fundamental to working with the software. The two terms are used throughout the printed and online documentation, and it is assumed that both terms make sense to the new user. Not always so! The efficient use of materials is probably more important than the ability to model well in 3ds max 5; for example, it would be entirely possible to have a perfectly modeled scene but make it look terrible with bad materials. Conversely, it would be possible to take a mediocre model and make it look great with good materials. Understanding the basic concepts and differences between materials and maps will help you create good materials more quickly.

Materials

Materials make up the surface information assigned to 3D mesh objects in the scene. This surface information cues the viewer to what an object is supposed to represent in the scene. Certainly an object's form or shape is a hint as to what it's supposed to be, but the key is to apply a material that convinces the viewer that an object is steel, wood, cloth, or jelly.

The surface information for even the simplest Max 5 materials is generally made up of several components that, when combined, define simulated real-world materials. The components include, but are not limited to the following:

- Surface color
- Texture
- Shininess
- Highlights
- Transparency
- Reflectivity

Study your surroundings to develop a feel for how different materials look to your eye, and you will be on the path to re-creating those materials in 3ds max 5.

Materials are stored on the hard disk in files called *material libraries*. It is a good habit to develop your material libraries early and systemize the process, much as you do with naming conventions. This will save a lot of "reinventing the wheel" and speed production. You will learn more about materials and material libraries in Chapters 3, "Applying Materials and Maps for a Convincing Outdoor Scene," 7, "Materials and Mapping: Deeper into the Details," and 11, "Materials and Lighting: The Magic Combination."

Maps

Materials are surface attributes assigned to objects in a scene, but *maps* are the patterns that make up the material's components. Maps are not assigned directly to objects in the scene, but are used in the material definition of color, bumpiness, transparency, and so on. Maps, however, can also be loaded directly as projected images in 3ds max 5 lights or as background images in the viewports or the rendered image. Figure 1.26 shows two Material Editor sample windows, one with an image loaded as a background or projector map, and the other with the same image as the material's Diffuse Color pattern.

FIGURE 1.26 *On the left, the sample window is a map only. On the right, the sample window is the same map applied as a material's Diffuse Color attribute.*

New users are often confused by the two and try to apply a map created for backgrounds or projectors directly to objects in the scene with no results.

As mentioned, maps are used as patterns for the components of a material, such as color and reflectivity. In many of the component channels, however, it is not the color information that the material uses, but the whiteness of each pixel; you can see this best in Bump maps. You can use a material to give the illusion that a surface is bumpy without the need to generate any extra geometry. This is a time- and resource-saving method of creating convincing objects. The white pixels in the map image appear to cause a surface to bump up, but the black pixels do nothing. Gray pixels appear to bump based on their whiteness value. Figure 1.27 shows an example of a Bump map called Cellular used in a material and applied to a flat plane. Although color maps can be used as Bump, Opacity, or Glossiness maps, for example, often converting them to grayscale images makes it easier to visualize their effectiveness in a material.

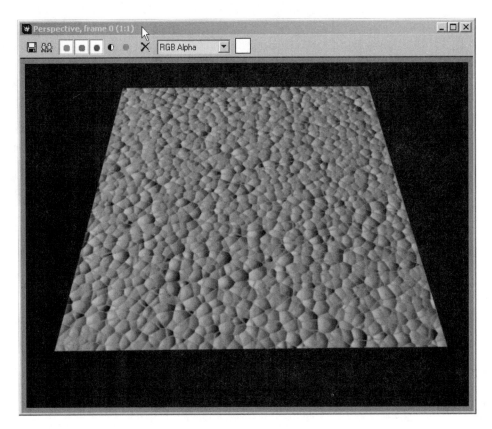

FIGURE 1.27 *A map used for a material's Bump map and applied to a flat plane. The surface texture is an illusion caused by the whiteness values of the pixels in the map.*

Mapping Coordinates

Any discussion of materials and maps is not complete without mentioning mapping coordinates. When a map is used in most material components, the user must indicate the placement, orientation, and scale of the pattern within the material. Reflection, refraction, and 3D procedural maps are exceptions.

Objects require that mapping coordinates be applied to describe how the pattern is to be repeated over the surface. Adjusting this pattern repetition is important to give the patterns a more convincing look. Several methods of generating mapping coordinates are available, including

- **General mapping coordinates** An option for specific mapping coordinates for primitive objects. They are not adjustable and are only for general use.

- **Apply UVW Map modifier**   This modifier has a plethora of adjustments for very accurate map placement and scaling.
- **Special mapping coordinates**   Lofted objects—that is, objects created with cross-sections extruded along a path—generate mapping coordinates that follow the path's curvature. Adjustments for scaling along the length and around the perimeter of the object are available.

Start creating materials with simple map assignments, and work your way up to more complexity after you understand the fundamentals. Study the materials that ship with 3ds max 5 to see how they were created, and assign them to primitive objects for mapping coordinates. The fundamental concepts of materials and maps can be applied over and over to create complex, deep materials that will make you an artist.

Lighting Concepts

Lighting a scene in 3ds max 5 is one of the most important aspects of achieving the desired end result, but often new users give this part of the process the least attention.

Many of us have limited or no training or experience in lighting as a art. Traditional forms of lighting in media such as film or painting were discussed earlier, but this section is more directly related to 3ds max 5, without getting into the details. Understanding the process of lighting scenes in 3ds max 5 will make it easier to learn the specific tools as you encounter them in your work. Chapters 4, "Exterior Lighting: Standard and Advanced Methods," 8, "Interior Lighting with New Photometric Lights," and 11, "Materials and Lighting: The Magic Combination" introduce you to lighting concepts in detail.

Radiosity

3ds max 5 has two new rendering engines and new photometric lights designed to make lighting a scene more realistic for the user:

- **Photometric lights**   Lights based on real-world physical data.
- **Light Tracer**   A multiple-bounce classic Path Tracing renderer intended for outdoor scenes or scenes with large areas lit by direct light. It can be faster than radiosity rendering.
- **Radiosity**   Uses photometric lights with real-world physical attributes to calculate the direct and bounced light in a scene.

The new radiosity lighting concepts are covered in Chapters 4, 8, and 12, "Animation: Animating in World Space," in more depth.

Keyframe Animation Concepts

The term *keyframe* comes from traditional animation, in which a master artist drew keyframes of characters to indicate various poses during motion. Junior artists then traced the in-between steps over the keyframe drawings on acetate or film to get the character from one pose to the next. When the acetates were photographed and played back in sequence, the character came to life in an animation.

3ds max 5 is considered a keyframe animation program because the creation process is similar. You, the master artist, pose objects and characters at points in time to generate a key, recording that position or setting. 3ds max 5 fills in the in-between frames to generate an animation that plays back smoothly. This section of the chapter is not intended to teach you how the Track View works, but to familiarize you with the concepts of keyframe animation in the hope that the Track View will make more sense when you encounter it in the exercises to come in later chapters.

Much of the control the user has over animation is controlled in four places: the standard Track Bar, the new extended Track Bar, the Dope Sheet, and the Function Curve Editor.

Track View and Track Bar

Figure 1.28 is a typical Function Curve Editor dialog box, showing a hierarchical list of the scene elements on the left and a graphical representation of the keyframes on the right. Each curve on the graph represents a position value change or rotation value change over time.

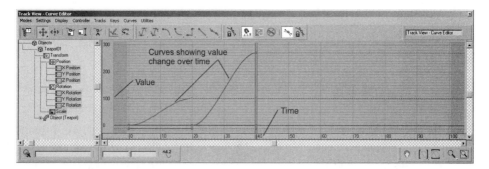

FIGURE 1.28 *The Track View for the animated Teapot01. You see a hierarchical list of scenes on the left and individual keys in time on the right.*

Individual curves or groups of curves can be selected and moved in time to change the speed of events. The steeper the curve in the Track View, the faster the event happens because it takes place in less time.

The new expanded Track bar (see Figure 1.29) is an abbreviated view of the Position, Rotation, and Scale curves accessed with the button to the left of the time ruler in the display.

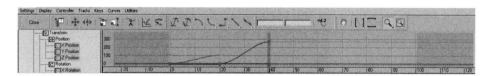

FIGURE 1.29 *The Track bar for the same animated box represented in the Track View of Figure 1.28.*

Mathematical Accuracy

The mathematical accuracy of 3ds max 5 is not necessarily a concept, but causes enough confusion among new users that it is worth discussing in a chapter on concepts.

First, a little background. CAD software and other programs designed primarily for modeling are considered *double precision* math programs. That is, the internal calculations are all evaluated at an accuracy of 64 decimal places. This enables the software to provide accurate detail in scenes ranging from extremely large, like the planet Earth, to very small, like microscopic machine parts, with the resources available on today's common PC computers and workstations.

In a typical 3ds max 5 scene, a large portion of the computer's resources must go into calculations such as high-resolution bitmaps, shadow and lighting effects, bump mapping, and reflections. To free enough resources to accomplish these tasks quickly enough to be cost-effective, the software designers have used *single precision* math, 32-decimal-place internal calculations.

Although 32 decimal places might seem like more than you would ever need, very large and very small objects use a majority of the available decimal places, and rounding errors start to manifest themselves rather quickly. Typical scenes in which you might experience effects from having only 32 decimal places available include the following:

- **Large scenes** Cityscapes or landscapes that cover more than, perhaps, two miles by two miles.

- **Scene with large and small objects** A large building with areas of detail smaller than, say, two inches.

- **Scenes with objects far from the workspace origin** Objects with pivot point absolute coordinates in the hundreds of thousands of units.

Solutions for each scenario would vary, but increasing or decreasing the object's scale by a factor of 10 or 100, breaking a single scene up into low-detail scenes and high-detail scenes, and moving the entire scene close to the workspace origin are possible solutions for the preceding list of problems.

note

Cameras or other objects that jitter when animated far from the workspace origin are symptoms of accuracy problems.

Summary

The intent of this chapter is not so much to teach you specific concepts, but to make you aware of the many aspects of art and 3D graphics that have been historically proved to enhance a viewing experience. These are some topics for you to investigate further:

- **Storyboarding**   You have learned the importance of storyboarding to firm up the scene development cycle. A good storyboard clarifies the thought process and sets the stage for good workflow.

- **Color and lighting**   There are both physical and psychological sides to color. Traditional art forms have long recognized the effect of color and of light and dark contrasts on human emotions. You have been introduced to some of the fundamentals of color as it pertains to a scene and its lighting.

- **Animation and movement**   You have learned to look for the basic techniques used in film and video, both with object and camera movement in a scene and some of the issues in editing story segments into a coherent story.

- **Object-naming standards**   A logical naming scheme will make you much more productive, especially when collaborating with others.

- **Understanding compound shapes**   Compound shapes (shapes containing multiple splines) are an important concept in modeling in 3ds max 5.

- **Cloning objects**   Cloning objects as Copies, Instances, or References allows different levels of linking between modifications for editing control. Instance and Reference clones also have a smaller memory footprint for more efficiency.

- **Applying modifiers**   A fundamental concept in 3ds max 5 is that of applying discrete modifiers to give you flexible editing control.

- **Using the Modifier Stack**   After applying modifiers in 3ds max 5, the Modifier Stack enables you to move up and down in the modification history for unprecedented freedom to experiment with or change your models.

- **Sub-object editing**   In addition to editing objects, whether they are splines, meshes, or modifiers, you also have access to sub-levels of editing on the components that make up the object.

- **Materials and maps**   Materials make up the surface appearance of objects in your scene, and maps are the patterns in material components. You learned the concept of mapping coordinates to describe the position and scale of those patterns.

- **Lighting concepts**   You learned that there are two lighting features in 3ds max 5, Radiosity and Light Tracer, that calculate bounced light based on physical properties of photometric lights and materials. You also have learned about methods of "painting" the scene with standard lights.

- **Keyframe animation concepts**   3ds max 5 uses keys placed in time to record changes in the scene, and then interpolates the changes between keyframes to create smooth animation.

- **Mathematical accuracy**   The internal mathematics that are essential to describing scenes in 3ds max 5 are limited to 32 decimal places to make it one of the fastest rendering programs available. With a working knowledge of mathematical accuracy, you can spot and work around potential problems caused by accuracy levels.

Bibliography

This short compilation of books on this chapter's topics is a starting place for further study. As your time and interests permit, the Internet will be your best resource for more investigation.

Drawing Figures

Blair, Preston. *Cartoon Animation*. Walter Foster Pub., 1995. ISBN: 1560100842.

Culhane, Shamus. *Animation from Script to Screen*. St. Martins Press, 1990. ISBN: 0312050526.

Faigin, Gary. *The Artist's Complete Guide to Facial Expression*. Watson–Guptill Publishing, 1990. ISBN: 0823016285.

Hogarth, Burne. *Dynamic Figure Drawing*. Watson–Guptill Publishing, 1996. ISBN: 0823015777.

Katz, Steven D. *Film Directing Shot by Shot*. Focal Press, 1991. ISBN: 0941188108.

Staake, Bob. *The Complete Book of Caricature*. North Light Books, 1991. ISBN: 0891343679.

Art History

Berger, John. *Ways of Seeing*. Viking Press, 1995. ISBN: 0140135154.

Fleming, William. *Arts and Ideas*. HBJ College and School Division, 1997. ISBN: 0155011049.

Anatomy

Feher, Gyorgy, and Andras Szunyoghy (illus.). *Cyclopedia Anatomicae*. Black Dog and Leventhal Press, 1996. ISBN: 1884822878.

Gray, Henry. *Gray's Anatomy*. Running Press, 1978. ISBN: 0914294083.

Animation

Lutz, Edwin George. *Animated Cartoons: How They Are Made, Their Origin and Development*. Applewood Books, 1998. ISBN: 1557094748.

Thomas, Frank, and Ollie Johnston. *The Illusion of Life: Disney Animation*. Hyperion, 1995. ISBN: 0786860707.

White, Tony. *The Animators Workbook*. Watson-Guptill Publishing, 1988. ISBN: 0823002292.

Color Theory

Lamb, Trevor, and Janine Bourriau (eds.). *Colour Art and Science*. Cambridge University Press, 1995. ISBN: 0521499631.

Walch, Margaret, and Augustine Hope. *Living Colors: The Definitive Guide to Color Palettes Through the Ages*. Chronicle Books, 1995. ISBN: 0811805581.

Lighting and Rendering

Birn, Jeremy. *Digital Lighting & Rendering*. New Riders Publishing, 2000. ISBN: 1562059548.

Cameron, Steven G., and Stuart Simms. *Advanced Courseware: Lighting Module*. Autodesk Inc., 2001. ISBN: 1564440036.

PART II

A Street Scene

CHAPTER 2

Modeling: A Medieval Street Scene

In This Chapter

Let's dive headfirst into 3ds max 5 and create a medieval street scene in a small hamlet somewhere this side of the dark ages.

There is no better place to start the creation process than modeling because you cannot do much with materials, lights, and animation without some models to render. You could generate a complex scene with many objects; however, the exercises in this chapter introduce you to important techniques more slowly. You can use the work methods outlined here to form good work habits for your career in 3D modeling. You also get an opportunity to put into practice some of the 3ds max 5 concepts mentioned in Chapter 1, "Graphics and 3ds max 5 Concepts: Laying the Groundwork."

Although the exercises use the technique on relatively simple buildings, the process is one that you can apply to much more complex models—from automobiles to alien characters—after a little practice. Learn the fundamentals of how the tools work, and then let your imagination take you to worlds unknown when the process becomes familiar. A good traditional artist does not have to look at the brushes and the palette; the act of painting becomes as natural as breathing. The same will happen for you with 3ds max 5: You'll know instinctively which tools will work for you in different situations. In addition, you will learn the following techniques and concepts:

- **Editable Poly** You will learn about the fantastic new Editable Poly editing capabilities that allow you to take a simple box and work it into a building in no time flat.

- **Efficient workflow**   You will learn about working with 2D shapes to create a basis for your 3D objects that can be easily modified to make changes in the 3D objects. This process will give you more freedom in the design stages.

- **Flexible editing**   Applying modifiers to 2D or 3D objects is a method of modeling that allows you to traverse up and down the history of your changes via the Modifier Stack. With this workflow method, you can often make changes to modeling stages without adversely affecting modifications above or below that point in the creation history.

- **Lofting**   You will learn about a unique and powerful modeling tool called lofting, which allows you to create complex meshes by extruding 2D shapes along other 2D shapes. With this tool, you can easily optimize models for rendering efficiency and assign and adjust materials applied to the lofted objects.

Key Terms

Editable Poly   A type of mesh object with powerful editing capabilities.

Face normals   A vector perpendicular to a face or polygon that determines whether the face is visible to the viewer. If the vector points toward the viewer, the face is visible. If the vector points away, the face is invisible in the viewports and the rendered image.

Lofting   The process of extruding one or more 2D shapes along another 2D shape to create a 3D mesh.

Material IDs   Numbers assigned to each face of an object so that corresponding materials can be applied more easily.

Modifier   A discrete operation added to an object to edit or change it. Modifiers can be moved within or removed from the stack.

Quad Patch   A type of deformable surface that can be edited into gentle curves.

Sub-objects   Component parts of 3D objects, 2D shapes, or modifiers, used for editing.

Hotkeys and Keyboard Shortcuts

Alt+w   Toggle from multiple-viewport display mode to full screen mode for the active viewport

Ctrl+b   Exit sub-object mode

Ctrl+s   Save the file with its current name

g   Toggle grid off or on

h   Open Select Objects or Pick Object dialog box

Setting Up the Scene

This section introduces you to the basic 3ds max 5 interface and has you set up a default scene and display settings. You will learn about viewports, scene units, grids, and the basic coordinate system. You have probably been through some of the tutorials that ship with 3ds max 5 and are not completely new to the interface. If you are, just follow along and try to concentrate more on the process rather than the individual steps.

Try not to be intimidated by the seemingly complex 3ds max 5 interface; with a little practice, you will learn your way around and, more important, learn to use the keyboard shortcut keys that are critical to being productive.

Exercise 2.1: Investigating the Interface

In this exercise, you open 3ds max 5 and change the display units to feet and inches, a standard unit of measurement in U.S. architecture. Internally, 3ds max 5 uses inches as the default measurement; the display units are only the format for entering units into numeric fields throughout the interface.

tip

You can set 3ds max 5 to use the standard U.S. or metric system by choosing Customize, Units Setup from the menu and clicking the System Unit Setup button.

You can override the default display unit simply by typing a measurement unit after the number. For example, if your display is set to feet and inches and you type 100mm in a numeric field, it is automatically entered as 0'3 7/8".

1. Start 3ds max 5. You'll see the default screen shown in Figure 2.1. There are four active viewports (three orthographic—Left, Front, and Top—and one perspective), menus and a toolbar along the top, the Command panel along the right side, and the Frame Slider, Track bar, and some settings buttons along the bottom. A group of eight viewport navigation buttons are in the lower-right corner of the display.

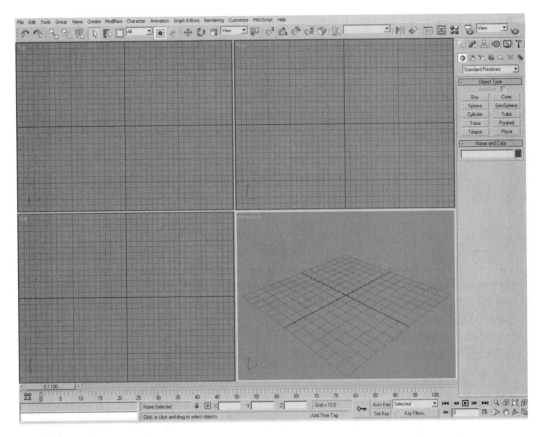

FIGURE 2.1   *The default startup display for 3ds max 5.*

2. The Perspective viewport has a yellow border to indicate that it is the active viewport. Right-click in the other viewports, one at a time, to activate them.

3. Choose File, Save As from the menu and in the Save File As dialog box, name the file maxstart. Click the Save button. The filename has .max appended automatically and is saved in the default \3dsmax5\scenes subdirectory unless you specify otherwise. The maxstart file has no objects, but will save the settings changes. Maxstart.max will be read each time you open or reset 3ds max 5, and the settings will be automatically entered in the new scene.

caution

Although it is possible to activate viewports by left-clicking, it is not a good habit. Often, you're in Select and Move, Rotate, or Scale mode and could inadvertently transform an object without realizing it. Always right-click to activate viewports.

4. Right-click in the Perspective viewport to activate it. You will notice a gray grid with black lines running through the center. The gray grid defines the default Home Grid construction plane in World XY coordinates. The Home Grid is seen in the Top and Perspective viewports. In the Left and Front viewports, the Home Grid is represented by the horizontal black line. The construction plane for the Left and Front viewports is represented by the black lines, as seen in the Top viewport, representing the World YZ and World XZ coordinates, respectively.

5. In the Create panel, click the Geometry category button. In the Object Type rollout, click the Box button (see Figure 2.2).

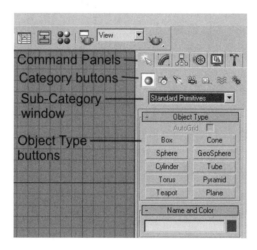

FIGURE 2.2   *Navigate in the Command panel, Geometry category, Standard Primitives sub-category to click the Box button in the Object Type rollout.*

6. In the Perspective viewport, click near the center of the grid. Hold down the left mouse button, and drag to define the opposite corner of the box's base. Any size will do. Release the mouse button, and move the mouse up to indicate a height for the box; any height will do. Click to set the height.

note   Creating primitive objects in 3ds max 5 is essentially as simple as step 6. If you have not had a chance to do so, leave this exercise and practice creating a few of each type of primitive. From this point, the exercises do not walk you through each step; rather, the instructions just say to create a box, cylinder, and so forth.

7. In the Create panel, Parameters rollout, randomly change the Box01 parameters by clicking on the black spinners (see Figure 2.3) to the right of the Length, Width, or Height numeric fields, holding down the mouse button on the spinners, and then moving the mouse. You can also type specific amounts in the numeric fields. Both are valid data entry methods.

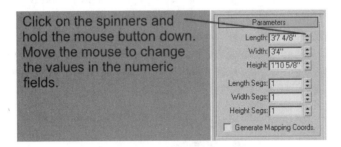

Click on the spinners and hold the mouse button down. Move the mouse to change the values in the numeric fields.

FIGURE 2.3   *You can adjust numeric field values by clicking on the spinners and holding the mouse button down. Move the mouse to change the values.*

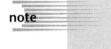

note   If you change the numbers and the box in the viewports does not respond to the changes, you have probably deselected and then reselected the box. After you leave the creation process, the numeric fields no longer affect the box. You must click the Modify panel button and select Box01 in the viewport to make any changes.

8. Click the Modify panel button and make sure the Box01 object is selected. Change the numeric fields to see how the box responds to changes. The numbers are displayed in the fields as decimal inches.

9. Choose Customize, Units Setup from the menu. In the Units Setup dialog box, select the US Standard radio button and choose Feet w/Fractional Inches from the list. Setting display accuracy at the nearest 1/8" is fine (see Figure 2.4). Click the OK button, and you will see that the numeric fields in the Modify panel are now displayed in that format. The box size does not change, of course, as these are just unit display settings.

note   There are radio buttons in the Units Setup dialog box for setting Default Units to feet or inches. Setting them to Feet means that if you enter a number in a numeric field without any designating marks, it is understood as feet. If you want inches, you must specify inches with the inch mark (").

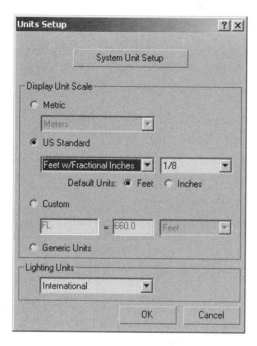

FIGURE 2.4   *You will be working with units displayed in Feet w/Fractional Inches rounded to the nearest 1/8 inch.*

10. Choose Customize, Grid and Snap Settings from the menu, and in the Grid and Snap Settings dialog box, click the Home Grid tab (see Figure 2.5).

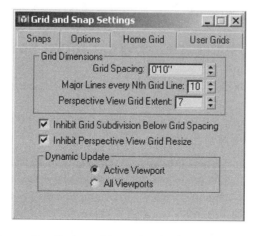

FIGURE 2.5   *You can change the display grid spacing in the Home Grid tab of the Grid and Snap Settings dialog box.*

11. In the Grid and Snap Settings dialog box, enter 1" in the Grid Spacing field (to specify the minimum grid spacing allowed), 12 in Major Lines Every Nth Grid Line (to adjust the spacing of heavier gray reference lines in the grid), and 240 in Perspective View Grid Extent (to set the size, in inches, of the grid seen in the Perspective viewport). You can leave the other settings at the defaults. Close the dialog box. These settings can help with accuracy during object creation by snapping to grid intersections and give you a better perception of where you are in 3D space. However, the grids are optional and can be toggled on and off with the **g** hotkey.

12. Exit 3ds max by choosing File, Exit from the menu. Click No when prompted to save your changes. You will not save this file.

note   At the lower middle right of the display, you will see a window that reads Grid = 1'0" even though you set a grid spacing of 1". The grid is dynamic and adjusts as you zoom in or out of a viewport. Each change is based on the Major Lines Every Nth Grid Line setting. In this case, the grid setting of 1" × 12 = 1 foot. If you zoom out, the display grid becomes 12', and if you zoom in, it switches to 1".

The settings you changed will be remembered in the maxstart.max file. When you start a new file or reset 3ds max 5, the maxstart.max file is automatically read and the current settings are changed to reflect your prototype file settings so that you do not have to re-enter the setting changes each time you start a new file.

note   The grids in the orthographic viewports are work planes that pass through the 0,0,0 world coordinate point represented by the heavy black lines in the grid. Any primitive objects you create will be on the corresponding grid. Try creating a few boxes or cylinders in the viewports and see how they relate to each other and the grid lines in other viewports.

Building a House with the New Editable Poly Object

In the exercises in this section, you shape a Box object into the basic shape of a house. You will learn about converting primitive objects into an enhanced object type called *Editable Poly*. This conversion gives you access to what is known as *sub-object editing*, or editing the building blocks of Editable Poly objects: vertices, edges, borders, polygons, and elements.

Although there are other techniques you could use to build a house in 3ds max 5, you can use Editable Poly's power and flexibility for building all sorts of other objects, such as airplanes, character heads, or furniture. Learn the fundamental technique, and then apply the methods to forge your own ideas into 3D forms.

Roughing the Building from an Editable Poly Object

You will convert a box similar to the one from Exercise 2.1 into an Editable Poly by using Quad menus, which are accessed by right-clicking with the mouse. The Quad menu appears under the cursor.

tip

Depending on the state of the program and the object or space under the cursor when you right-click, you open different Quad menus. It is good practice when you are new to 3ds max 5 to spend some time right-clicking to see what options are displayed.

Right-clicking with the Shift, Ctrl, or Alt keys often displays different Quad menus with more options.

tip

Get into the habit of modeling only what the viewer will see, with only as much detail as needed to make the scene convincing. Any extra vertices and faces in a model slow the workflow and rendering times, causing low productivity and wasting computer resources. Each situation is different, and you must be the judge of how much is enough, but it should always be the minimum that meets your requirements. For example, a building scene from a distance could be a box with very little detail. If you added small details, it would slow production, and the details might be smaller than one pixel in the rendered image and not show at all. However, if you will be viewing the building at a closer viewpoint, you would need the extra detail.

This next exercise teaches you to access sub-objects of an Editable Poly and *transform* (move, rotate, or scale) them. The result will actually be only half a house—the portion that the viewer can see from the camera position in the scene.

Exercise 2.2: Editable Poly Mode and Sub-Object Editing

1. Open the House01.max file noted next to the CD icon. It is a simple Box primitive. Click the Select button on the main toolbar at the top of the display, and pick the box in the Perspective viewport.

On the CD

\exercises\CH02\
House01.max

2. Choose File, Save As from the menu, and click the + button to the left of the Save button in the Save File As dialog box (see Figure 2.6). This increments the filename from House01.max to House02.max and saves the new file in the current subdirectory. The current active file becomes House02.max. Using incremental saves gives you a history of your work so that you can revert back to a previous file if you have a bad file or a design change.

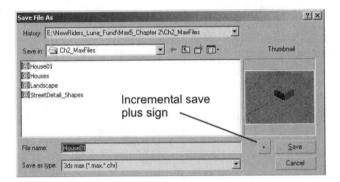

FIGURE 2.6   *In the Save File As dialog box, use the + button to automatically increment your filename.*

3. In the Modify panel, change the box name from Box01 to House01 (see Figure 2.7). To edit the box size, enter 12 in the Length field, 24 in Width, and 16 in Height.

4. Click the Zoom Extents All button in the lower-right corner of the display. It is at the upper right of the group of eight navigation buttons. This fills all viewports with all objects in the scene. Right-click on the Perspective label at the upper left of the Perspective viewport, and choose Edged Faces in the pop-up menu. This allows you to view both the shaded and wireframe versions of the object to make editing easier.

5. With the House01 object selected, move the cursor over the object in the Perspective viewport and right-click. Choose Convert To at the bottom of the Quad menu, and then Convert to Editable Poly in the submenu (see Figure 2.8). Notice that the Modify panel now shows options for editing an Editable Poly rather than the Box primitive parameters.

FIGURE 2.7
In the Modify panel, change the object name, and then change the box size in the Parameters rollout.

tip

The default numeric display has been set to feet, so entering an integer in a numeric field without any unit specified is understood as feet. If you want inches, you must type the number as 6", for example. For feet and inches, the format must be 5'6".

tip

Review Chapter 1 for ideas on logical naming schemes for your scenes. Using names that are easy for you and your coworkers to recognize is critical.

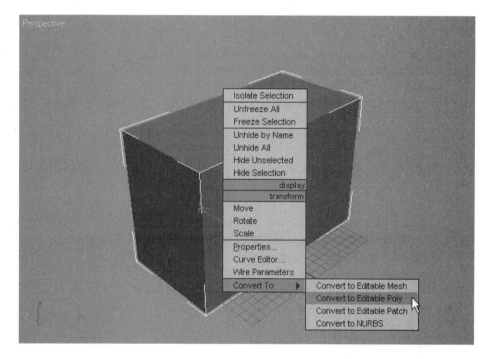

FIGURE 2.8   *The Quad menu showing conversion options for your House01 object.*

6. In the Modify panel, Stack display (the large field below the Modifier List), click the + sign to the left of Editable Poly to expand the sub-object choices, and select Edge. In the Selection rollout, select the Ignore Backfacing check box to help prevent picking edges you can't see (see Figure 2.9).

7. With the Select button highlighted in the main toolbar, pick the vertical front edge of House01 closest to you in the Perspective viewport. It will turn red in the viewport. Hold down the Ctrl key and pick the right edge to add it to the selection set. Both vertical edges on the front should now be red.

8. In the Modify panel, Edit Edges rollout, click the Connect button once. This cuts a new edge from the middle of one selected edge to the middle of the other, effectively dividing the front polygon of House01 into two new polygons (see Figure 2.10). The new polygon on the top will be the overhanging second floor for your house.

9. In Stack display, choose Polygon mode, and pick the upper new polygon you created in step 8. It will turn transparent red. In the Modify panel, Edit Polygons rollout, click the Settings icon to the right of the Extrude button. In the Extrude Polygons dialog box, enter 2 in the Extrusion Height field (see Figure 2.11), and press Enter. When you press Enter, the polygon is moved 2 feet in its own positive-Z axis and four new polygons form sides. Click the OK button.

10. Next, you will use the Connect button again to split the new polygon for use as the roof overhang. In the Stack display, click Edge. On the main toolbar, click the Select button and select a vertical edge of the new polygon. Hold down Ctrl while selecting the other vertical edge of the new polygon to add it to the selection set. In the Modify panel, Edit Edges rollout, click Connect to create the new horizontal edge.

11. Right-click in the Front viewport and select the new horizontal edge only. On the main toolbar, click the Select and Move transform button. You will see the Transform Gizmo appear.

12. Pick the shaft of the vertical Y-axis Transform Gizmo arrow, and move the edge to within about 1 foot of the top edge of the box, as shown in Figure 2.12 (use the grid as a visual aid).

FIGURE 2.9
The Modify panel with Edge selected in the Stack display.

note

The new settings icons in 3ds max 5 can improve workflow by allowing you to preview the effect of changes before committing them and to repeat the action with the Apply button.

tip

The Transform Gizmo is an aid to moving only along the restricted axis in 3ds max 5. You can pick the shafts of the axis arrows to restrict movement in that axis or pick the shaded box to restrict movement in a plane defined by two axis.

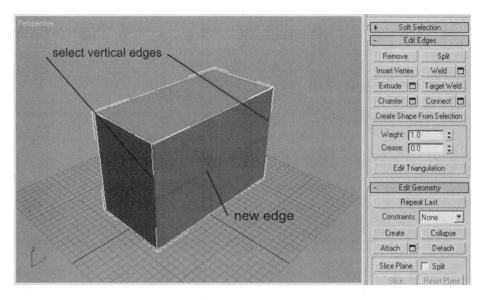

FIGURE 2.10 *Defining a new edge in the Edit Edges rollout to create two polygons from one with Connect.*

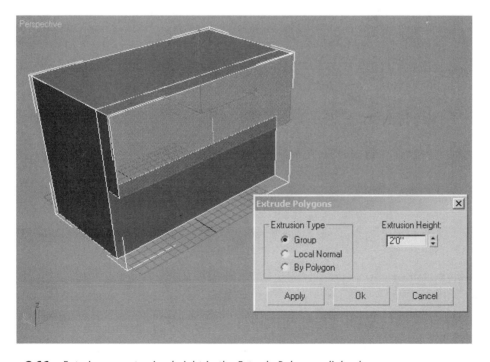

FIGURE 2.11 *Entering an extrusion height in the Extrude Polygons dialog box.*

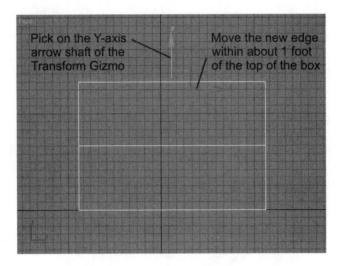

FIGURE 2.12 *Move the selected horizontal line in the Front viewport by picking the Y-axis arrow shaft, thus restricting movement to that axis in the viewport.*

13. In the Stack display, choose Polygon mode, click the Select button, and in the Perspective viewport, pick the new polygon at the top front of the building. Click the Settings icon for Extrude in the Edit Polygons rollout. Enter 1 in the Extrusion Height field and click OK to form the roof overhang (see Figure 2.13).

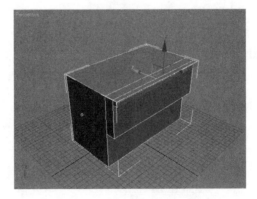

FIGURE 2.13 *Extrude the new top polygon 1 foot to form the roof overhang.*

14. Now you will make the roof slope at a 45-degree angle. Choose Edge sub-object mode in the Stack display, and pick the back top horizontal edge. You need to move this edge an exact amount, so you'll use the Transform Type-In fields at the bottom center of the interface. Right now, they display the Absolute coordinates of the cursor position in world coordinates. Click the Absolute Mode button in the Status Bar to the left of the three numeric fields, and toggle to Offset Mode (see Figure 2.14).

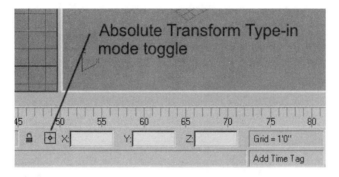

FIGURE 2.14   *Toggle from Absolute to Offset Mode in the Status Bar.*

15. The fields are now blank. Click the Select and Move transform button on the main toolbar, and the fields show that 0'0" of the edge is still selected. When you enter 15 in the Z axis field and press Enter, the edge moves 15 feet in the positive-Z direction. The numeric field reverts to 0'0" because the edge has a new current position and there is no offset from that current position (see Figure 2.15).

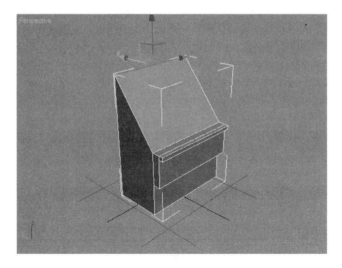

FIGURE 2.15   *In Offset Mode, move the top back edge 15 feet in the positive-Z axis.*

16. Select the next edge forward and move it 3 feet in the Z axis, and then select the next edge and move it up 1 foot. This makes a flat sloping roof at a 45-degree angle to the ground (see Figure 2.16). Exit Edge sub-object mode by picking Editable Poly at the top of the Stack display or by pressing **Ctrl+b**.

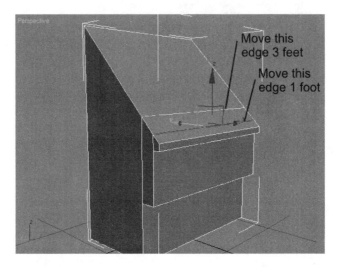

FIGURE 2.16 *Move the next two edges to create a 45-degree sloped roof.*

17. Save the file; it should already be named House02.max.

    With the conversion of a Box primitive object to an Editable Poly object, you have opened new editing possibilities by manipulating sub-object selections. You have connected edges with a new edge and extruded polygons to edit and create new geometry in the form of half a house.

tip

Exiting sub-object mode is an important habit to get into because it helps avoid inadvertent edits and is the only way you can select other objects in the scene.

Creating a Half-Timbered Look

Medieval houses were often constructed by first building a heavy timber frame, and then filling in between the timbers with mud and sticks to form the walls. This characteristic half-timbered look leaves the timbers partially exposed on the outside.

In this section, you learn several new Editable Poly tools and prepare to apply materials to the house elements, such as timbers and walls, in Chapter 3, "Applying Materials and Maps for a Convincing Outdoor Scene." This is accomplished by assigning Material ID numbers to polygons. Each assigned number corresponds to a number in a Multi/Sub-Object material. The Material ID numbers can be changed at any time, but if you know what they are used for now, you can more easily factor them into your modeling process.

The following list shows the Material ID numbers and the building parts they relate to:

1—Roof

2—Trim

3—Side and back walls

4—Timbers

5—Infill walls

6—Window sash

7—Window glass

8—Door

note

3ds max 5 primitive objects automatically get Material IDs assigned to polygons. Your Box object, for example, had an ID number assigned to each side. For a Cylinder primitive, the top cap, bottom cap, and sides all get IDs assigned.

A stand-in material has been applied to the house (see Figure 2.17). A *stand-in material* has only a basic color to help visualize the material assignments when you change Material ID numbers in later exercises.

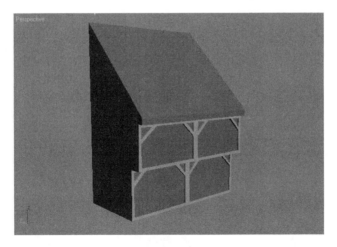

FIGURE 2.17   *By editing polygons and changing Material ID numbers, you'll create a half-timbered house with stand-in material assignments.*

Exercise 2.3: More Sub-Object Editing and Material Assignment by Material ID Numbers

You can open files that you have created in the previous exercise and saved to your hard drive, or you can open the files noted next to the CD icon from the book's CD-ROM for each exercise.

1. Open House02.max, if it is not the current active file. Choose File, Save As from the menu, and click the + button to save the file as House03.max.

On the CD

exercises\CH02\
House02.max

Until you become much more familiar with 3ds max 5, always click the Select button before selecting anything in the scene. Remember that the transform tools are called Select and Move, Select and Rotate, and Select and Scale. It is possible to select and move an object or sub-object in a single motion. This feature is great when you intend to do it, but can cause much confusion when you think you are only selecting.

2. Click the Select button on the main toolbar, and select the house in the Perspective viewport. In the Stack display, choose Polygon mode and pick the two front wall polygons, using the Ctrl key to add to the selection set. In the Modify panel, scroll down to the Polygon Properties rollout, and you will see that the selected polygons have Material ID 5 assigned to them. Change the number to 4 (see Figure 2.18).

3. Arc-rotate the view by clicking the Arc Rotate button (the lower-right button in the group of eight navigation buttons) or by holding the mouse wheel down while pressing the Alt key to position the view for better selections. See Figure 2.19 for the view angle.

FIGURE 2.18
The Material ID number has been changed to 4 for the timber material.

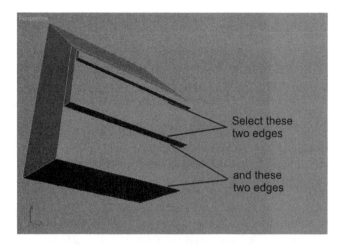

Select these
two edges

and these
two edges

FIGURE 2.19 *Use Arc Rotate to view the front of the building from below, and select the four horizontal edges at the top and bottom of each front wall.*

4. Next you will split these polygons with the Connect tool. Choose Edge in the Stack display, and select the four horizontal edges that form the top and bottom of the two front walls (see Figure 2.19). Click the Connect button in the Modify panel, Edit Edges rollout to create a new vertical edge in the middle of each wall.

5. You will use the new Inset tool in Polygon mode to create wall surfaces between exposed timbers. In the Stack display, choose Polygon; the four front polygons should still be selected. In the Edit Faces rollout, click the Settings icon for the Inset button to open the Inset Selected Faces dialog box. Leave Group selected in the Inset Type section, enter 6" in the Inset Amount field, and press Enter (see Figure 2.20).

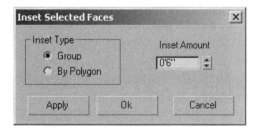

FIGURE 2.20 *Using Inset to create edges that define wall surfaces between exposed timbers.*

6. Notice in the Perspective viewport that the inset takes place only around each group of two polygons. That is not exactly what you want because you need a vertical post in the middle of each wall. Select the By Polygon radio button in the Inset Selected Faces dialog box. Each individual polygon is now inset by 6" (see Figure 2.21). Click the OK button.

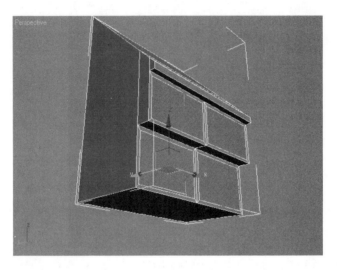

FIGURE 2.21   *Using the By Polygon option to apply the 6" inset to each individual polygon. The Group option would apply the inset to all polygons as a contiguous selection. The Local Normal option could be used to control the direction of the action.*

7. Next, you'll use another tool in the Front viewport at the Edge sub-object level to cut diagonal braces for each new wall panel. Right-click in the Front viewport to make it active. Press **Alt+w** to maximize the Front viewport. Choose Edge in the Stack display, and click the Cut button in the Edit Geometry rollout.

warning

Do not click the Apply button in any Settings dialog boxes unless you want to repeat the current settings again.

8. Click on a vertical edge and then a horizontal edge to cut a new diagonal edge, and then right-click to finish the cut before starting the next one. Repeat this process until you have eight diagonal braces, similar to Figure 2.22.

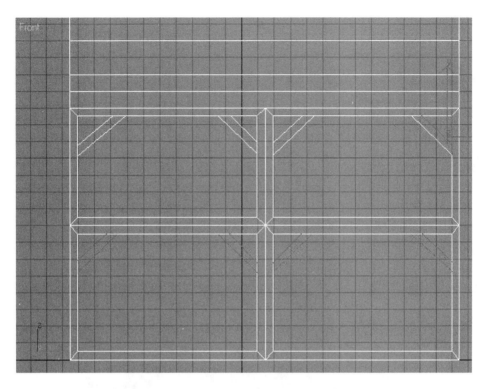

FIGURE 2.22   *Create eight diagonal braces by using the Edge Cut tool.*

9. Do not worry about being exact or about the actual sizes of the braces; after all, this is medieval
   times. Press **Alt+w** to return to four viewports. To
   edit the layout of the braces, choose Vertex in the
   Stack display. In the Front viewport, select a vertex
   at the end of a brace edge. Click Select and Move
   on the main toolbar and move the vertex to adjust
   the brace (see Figure 2.23).

10. Right-click in the Perspective viewport to activate
    it. Go to Polygon sub-object mode and select the
    infill wall areas of the front walls, including the
    new triangular areas inside the diagonal braces
    (see Figure 2.24).

note

With a little practice, cutting
new edges is a powerful tool. If
you have problems with steps
8 and 9, you can open the
House02_Braces.max file noted
next to the CD icon, which has
the braces already created.

On the CD

\exercises\CH02\
House02_Braces.max

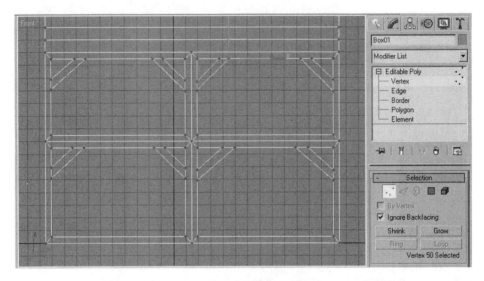

FIGURE 2.23   *You can easily edit the braces in Vertex sub-object mode with the Select and Move command. Use the Transform Gizmo to restrict movement to the horizontal and vertical axes.*

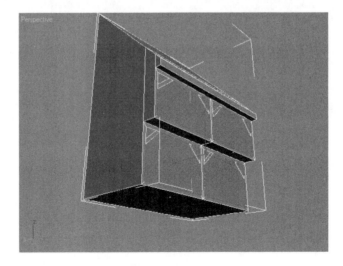

FIGURE 2.24   *Selecting all the wall areas for extrusion.*

11. In the Edit Polygons rollout, click the Settings icon for Extrude. In the Extrude Polygons dialog box, enter –4" in the Extrusion Height field and select the By Polygon radio button (see Figure 2.25). Click OK. In the Modify panel, Polygon Properties rollout, change the Material ID number to 5.

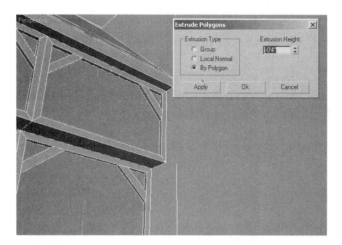

FIGURE 2.25 *Selecting extrusion settings for the wall areas. A negative Extrusion Height value moves the walls areas inward from the timbers.*

12. Exit sub-object mode by choosing Editable Poly at the top of the Stack display. Save the file; it should already be called House03.max.

You now have a house that is developing some character. It has a steep sloping roof and heavy half-timber construction with diagonal bracing. You also have assigned Material ID numbers to various polygons while you were modifying the Editable Poly to save time later.

Adding Windows to the House

It certainly would be handy to see out of your house, so you'll add windows to the upper and lower front wall areas. In this section, you will learn more controls in Editable Poly and manipulate multiple polygons simultaneously so that you can create many similar details at once. You also get more practice with sub-object selections.

Exercise 2.4: Creating Multiple Details at Once

1. Open the House03.max file you saved in the previous exercise, or open it from the CD-ROM. Choose File, Save As to save an incremental copy called House04.max. When you are working on a project, this is a good way to make copies of the file as backup in case you have problems or decide a previous version was better.

On the CD

exercises\CH02\
House03.max

2. Right-click in the Perspective viewport to activate it, click the Select button on the main toolbar, and pick the house in the Perspective viewport. Right-click on the Perspective label, and choose Wireframe in the pop-up menu. In the Modify panel, Stack display, choose the Edge sub-object. Click the Select button, and select the top edge between each brace and the bottom edge of each wall infill area, using the Ctrl key to add to the selection set (see Figure 2.26).

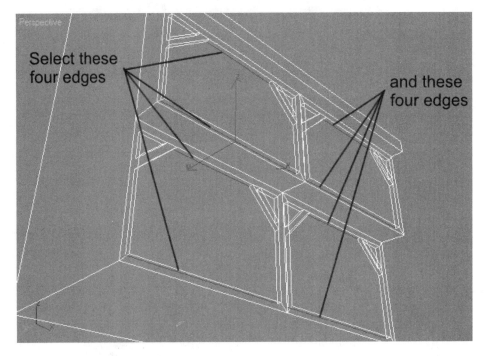

FIGURE 2.26 *Selecting edges for applying detail.*

3. In the Modify panel, Edit Edges rollout, click the Settings icon for Connect. In the Connect Edges dialog box, change the Connect Edge Segments setting to 2 (see Figure 2.27), and click OK. The edges are not vertical because the new edges are based on the midpoints of each segment, and the top is shorter than the bottom in each pair.

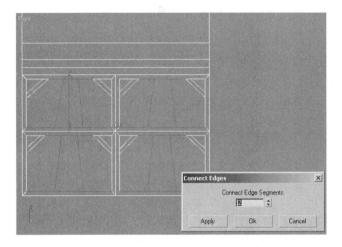

FIGURE 2.27   *Changing the number of segments for connecting edges in the Connect Edges dialog box.*

4. In the Stack display, choose Vertex. Pick the top vertex of a new vertical edge, and using Select and Move, move it left or right until the edge is nearly vertical (see Figure 2.28). Use the Transform Gizmo's X-axis arrow shaft to restrict movement to that axis only. The edges that define the sides of windows do not need to be perfectly vertical.

5. In the Perspective viewport, choose Edge sub-object level in the Stack display, and select the eight new vertical edges. Click the Connect button in the Edit Edges rollout. Connect Edge Segments is still set to 2. This creates two horizontal edges between each pair of vertical edges to define the window openings.

6. In Edge sub-object level, select the four new horizontal edges that define the tops of windows, and using Select and Move, move them closer to the top of the wall area (see Figure 2.29).

FIGURE 2.28   *Refining the sides of the windows to make them more vertical.*

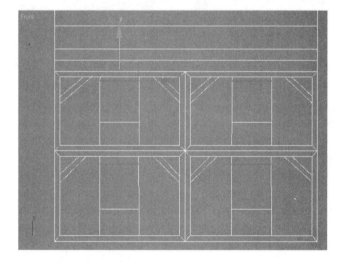

FIGURE 2.29   *Move the top four edges of the new window openings closer to the top of the walls.*

tip

Another good work habit to acquire is using the **Ctrl+s** keyboard shortcut often to save the file to disk with its current name—just in case.

7. In Polygon sub-object mode, select the four new polygons that will become windows. Change the Material ID number in the Modify panel, Polygon Properties rollout, to 2, the Material ID number for trim surfaces. In the Edit Faces rollout, click the Settings icon for Inset. It should still be set to 6" and By Polygon should still be selected. Click the OK button in the Inset Selected Faces dialog box. Change the Material ID number of the new polygons to 6 to assign the ID for the window sash material.

8. Go to Edge sub-object level, click the Select button, and select the horizontal inside edges of each window. Click Connect in the Modify panel, Edit Edges rollout to create two new vertical edges in each window (see Figure 2.30).

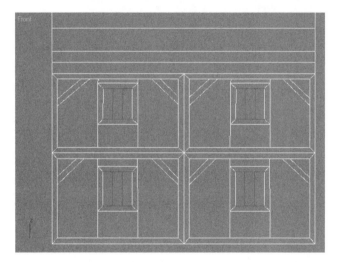

FIGURE 2.30 *Connecting the inside horizontal edges of each window. Connect is still set to create two new edges.*

9. Next, you'll select the four inside vertical edges of each window, but instead of picking them individually, you will use Crossing selection mode to select them in groups of four. Crossing mode selects all objects inside or touching a selection shape that you drag in the viewport. Click the Select button on the main toolbar, and toggle the Window/Crossing button to the right of Select. It will change from a black sphere inside a dotted box to a black sphere half out of the dotted box to indicate Crossing mode.

10. Click just left of an inside vertical window edge, and drag a selection box across the other three edges (see Figure 2.31). Release the mouse button, and select the remaining edges. Hold the Ctrl key down to add to the selection set, and repeat the Crossing selection for each window. Click the Settings icon for Connect in the Edit Edges rollout, and change Connect Edge Segments to 1. Click OK. This creates a new horizontal edge across the middle of each window.

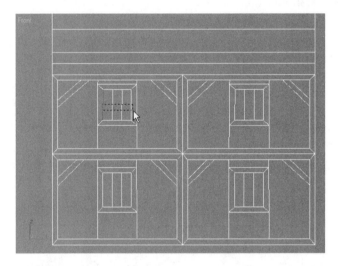

FIGURE 2.31 *Dragging a selection box across the vertical inside edges of a window.*

11. In the Stack display, choose Polygon sub-object level. The window polygons should be automatically selected. If they are not, you can use Crossing mode to select them as you did for the edges in steps 9 and 10. Click the Settings icon for Inset. In the Inset Polygons dialog box, change the Inset Amount to 0.25", and make sure By Polygon is selected. Click OK. This forms the front surfaces of the window sashes, as seen in Figure 2.32.

12. In the Modify panel, Edit Polygons rollout, click the Settings icon for Bevel. This tool is like Extrude, but with an extra level to create beveled sash sides for the window panes. In the Bevel Selection dialog box, enter -1" in the Height field and -1" in Outline Amount, and select the By Polygon radio button. Click OK. The windows now have beveled sashes, as seen in Figure 2.33. Change the Material ID number of the selected polygons to 7 in the Polygon Properties rollout to correspond with the glass material.

FIGURE 2.32   *Inset the window polygons to form the front surface of the window sashes.*

FIGURE 2.33   *Use Bevel settings to create sloped sides for the window sashes.*

13. Click the Select button. In the Front viewport, select the four polygons around each window that define the 6-inch-wide window frames. In the Modify panel, Edit Polygons rollout, click the Settings icon for Extrude. Enter 2″ in the Extrusion Height field, and in the Extrusion Type section, select the Group radio button. Click OK. This extrudes the window frames as a group, rather than individual sections, for each window.

14. Exit sub-object mode by choosing Editable Poly at the top of the Stack display. Save the file; it should already be called House04.max.

You should now have a pretty well-defined house, created with the few simple editing steps on the Editable Poly that started its existence as a lowly box. Again, focus on the process and methods used in these exercises, and practice them on your own. As you learn each tool and its adjustments, you will be able to apply it logically to modeling challenges you encounter in a typical work setting.

Modifying a Window into a Door

Often, if you analyze what you already have in a scene, you can modify existing 2D or 3D geometry to reuse all or parts of what you have. With 2D objects, you might have a rectangle that defines the outer edges of a window frame, and you need a shape that fits three sides of that frame for some window molding. Rather than re-create the line to fit, you could use sub-object segments, select the segments, and use Detach as Copy to extract the data for the new spline. This method cuts down on potential errors and is quick and easy. For 3D objects, you might be able to edit 3D geometry into something else, rather than start the whole process over.

In this section, you take one of the existing windows in the medieval house and rework it into a door with glazing and raised panels.

Exercise 2.5: Reworking Existing Geometry

In the previous exercise, you built four windows into the front with various Editable Poly tools. The client has called and said that the left front window must be a door. You have some artistic license, so the style is up to you, and you would rather not redo the entire model.

1. Open the House04.max file, and save it as House05.max.

2. Right-click in the Front viewport to activate it and select House01. Zoom in on the lower-left area of the front wall. In the Modify panel, Stack display, expand Editable Poly, and choose Vertex sub-object level. Click the Select button, and in the Front viewport, drag a selection box around the vertices that make up the horizontal mullion (the horizontal piece between the upper and lower panes that holds the glass) of the window (see Figure 2.34).

On the CD

exercises\CH02\
House04.max

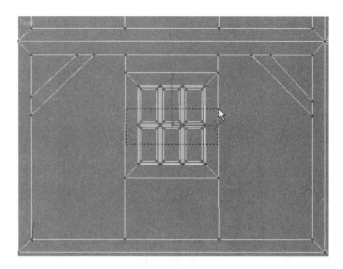

FIGURE 2.34 *In Vertex sub-object level, drag a selection box around the horizontal mullions of the lower-left window.*

3. Click the Select and Move button and move the vertices up in the Y axis until the top window panes are nearly square (see Figure 2.35).

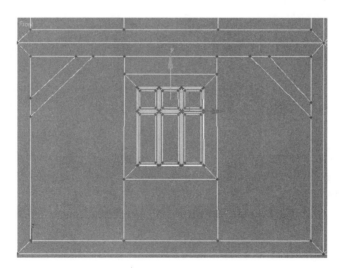

FIGURE 2.35 *You have moved the center window mullions up to create smaller top panes for your door.*

4. Drag a selection box around the bottom two trim vertices and move them down in the Y axis nearly to the house trim line, and then drag a selection box around the bottom mullion vertices and move them down to the trim. The result should look similar to Figure 2.36.

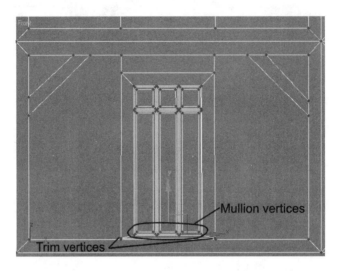

FIGURE 2.36 *You can create a door with long lower panes by moving the trim and bottom mullions near the house trim edge.*

5. Next, you'll move the new long "panes" outward to become the door's raised panels. In the Stack display, choose Polygon. In the Front viewport, select the three long vertical panels of the door, using Ctrl to add to the selection set. In the Transform Type-In area of the Status Bar, toggle the Absolute Mode button to Offset Mode. Enter 2" in the Z field and press Enter. The panels move 2" toward you in the Front viewport to become raised panels in the door.

6. Ensure that the three long panels in the door are still selected, and in the Modify panel, Polygon Properties rollout, change the Material ID number from 7 to 6 to switch from glass to sash material.

7. In the Stack display, exit Polygon sub-object mode. Save the file; it should already be called House05.max.

In this exercise, it was easier to modify existing geometry to create a new detail from an old one than it would be to start again and re-create the whole building. Although this might not always be the case, use your imagination to look for possibilities to increase production.

Creating External Braces

The building needs diagonal bracing to help support the overhanging second story. No geometry on the house lends itself to creating these braces, so you make separate objects and align them into place. You also learn to use the Align tool and the Bevel modifier, which can be applied only to 2D shapes for extruding up to three levels. Its primary use is to create 3D objects—often text—with chamfered edges at the top and bottom.

Exercise 2.6: Creating a Brace with Chamfered Edges

1. Open House05.max, and save the file as House06.max. Click the Zoom Extents All viewport navigation button to fill all viewports with the whole house. Activate the Left viewport, and zoom in to the 2-foot second-story overhang (see Figure 2.37).

On the CD

exercises\CH02\
House05.max

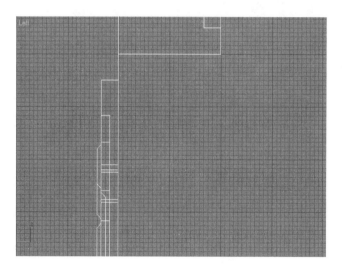

FIGURE 2.37   *In the Left viewport, zoom in to the second-story overhang.*

2. On the main toolbar, toggle the Snap button on. It should be set to Grid Point snap mode by default. You can check by right-clicking the Snap Toggle button and making sure the Grid Points check box is selected in the Snaps tab of the Grid and Snap Settings dialog box.

caution

Simply setting the Snap mode does not activate the Snap tool. You must make sure the Snap Toggle button is pressed down. When it's active, you see a cyan cursor indicator when you move the mouse in the active viewport over a valid object for the current snap settings.

3. In the Create panel, Shapes category, click Line. In the Creation Method rollout, under the Initial Type section, select the Corner radio button, and under Drag Type, select the Corner radio button to ensure that you don't create any curved sections for this line. In the Left viewport, create a closed polyline by snapping to grid points to form a diagonal brace shape at about a 45-degree angle, from under the overhang to the face of the timbers (see Figure 2.38). Click Yes when prompted to close the spline. Rename the shape Brace01 in the Modify panel, and toggle the Snap button off.

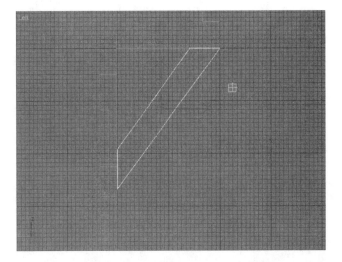

Figure 2.38 *Use Grid Point snap mode to draw a 2D brace holding up the second story.*

caution

If you do not click Yes in the Spline dialog box when prompted, the polygon will be open and the Bevel modifier will not create a contiguous 3D object. Closing the spline welds the last vertex created to the first.

4. In the Modify panel, Modifier List, choose the Bevel modifier. The chamfer you apply will be 0.5", so in the Bevel Values rollout, enter -0.5" in the Start Outline field. This reduces the shape's overall size by 1/2 all around to compensate for the amount of the chamfer.

5. Enter the following amounts in the Bevel Values rollout:

- Under Level 1

  Height: 0.5"

  Outline: 0.5"

- Under Level 2

  Height: 5"

  Outline: 0"

- Under Level 3

  Height: 0.5"

  Outline: -0.5"

The result is a chamfered brace, as shown in Figure 2.39.

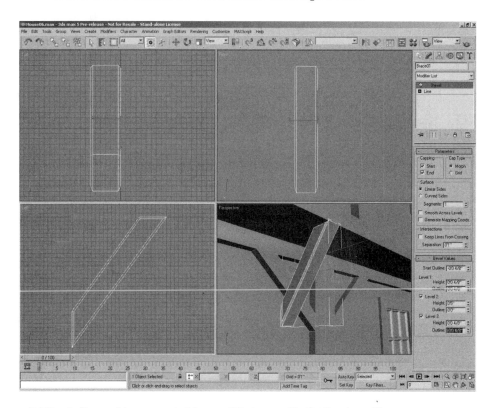

FIGURE 2.39 *A diagonal brace created from a 2D shape with the Bevel modifier.*

6. In the Front viewport, with Brace01 selected, click the Select and Move button, hold down the Shift key, and move Brace01 a little to the right by picking the Transform Gizmo's yellow X restrict arrow. In the Clone Options dialog box that opens when you release the mouse button, select the Instance radio button and enter 2 in the Number of Copies field (see Figure 2.40). Click OK to make two new copies of the brace.

7. Click the Zoom Extents All button to fill all viewports with all objects in the scene. Activate the Front viewport and make sure Brace03 is still selected. On the main toolbar, click the Align button and click anywhere on House01. In the Align Selection (House01) dialog box, select the X Position check box and the Maximum radio button in both the Current Object and Target Object sections (see Figure 2.41). Click OK. These settings align the maximum side of Brace03's bounding box in the positive-X axis to House01's maximum side in the positive-X axis.

note

You must select the check boxes for Level 2 and Level 3 before you can enter numbers in the fields.

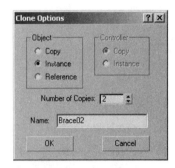

FIGURE 2.40
Cloning two new copies of Brace01.

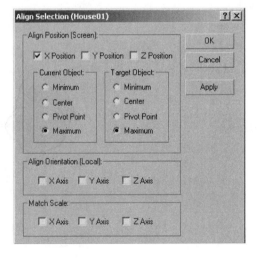

FIGURE 2.41   *Selecting the X Position and the Maximum options for both objects aligns the far right side of Brace01 with the far right side of House01.*

8. In the Front viewport, click the Select button and select Brace02. Click the Align button, and select House01. In the Align Selection dialog box, select X Position and select Center for both objects to align the center of Brace02 with the center of House01. Click OK.

9. In the Front viewport, select Brace01. Click the Align button and select House01. Select X Position and select Minimum for both objects to align the left side of Brace01 with the left side of House01. Figure 2.42 shows the aligned braces in the Perspective viewport.

FIGURE 2.42   *The braces have been aligned in the X axis of the Front viewport.*

10. Next, you will make the braces part of the House01 mesh. Select House01. In the Edit Geometry rollout, click the Attach button and select each brace in the Front viewport. Click the Attach button again to turn it off. Notice that each brace acquires House01's color as it is attached. The braces are now elements of House01 and no longer individual objects. In the Modify panel, Stack display, choose Element and select each brace with the Ctrl key held down. The braces all turn transparent red. In the Polygon Properties rollout, change the Material ID number to 4, the Timber material. Exit sub-object mode.

11. In the Perspective viewport, right-click on the Perspective label and choose Smooth + Highlights. The shaded viewport shows the stand-in material and new Material ID assignments. Save the file. It should already be named House06.max.

Attaching the braces to the house makes it easier to keep track of them, yet you can still edit and transform them individually at the Element sub-object level. House01 is again a single object in the scene.

Creating a Landscape Environment for the Medieval Street Scene

Now that you have a building created, you need an environment for it. In this section, you open a file with a simple landscape made from an object called a *Quad Patch*. It is a flat plane object with mathematical properties that cause weighting from one vertex to the next when vertices are moved. In contrast, when you move a vertex of a mesh plane, the surface just spikes to the vertex location with no regard for neighboring vertices.

Quad Patch surfaces can be helpful in making objects such as hilly landscapes, character faces, automobiles, and curved furniture, for example. Mesh and polygon objects can be converted to Editable Patches, and 2D spline cage structures can be skinned with Patch surfaces and a Surface modifier, too. You will not be working directly with Patch objects in this book, but you might want to investigate them on your own.

The landscape file also has two 2D shapes. One defines a road centerline on the landscape and the other describes a street cross-section.

You also learn a modeling process called *lofting*, the art of extruding a 2D shape along a 2D path shape to define a 3D mesh object—in this section, a road surface. An important aspect of lofting in 3ds max 5 is the ability to easily adjust the resulting 3D mesh's density for a balance of visual quality and a low face and vertex count for efficiency. You then edit the 2D shapes to change the simple road into one with sidewalks and gutters. You also learn to use Loft Deformations to scale the road so that it seems to recede in the distant hills.

You also create a skydome object that serves as a sky in the scene's background. Because it wraps around the scene, it can be viewed from most positions and viewpoints, making it especially useful in animations.

Creating a Roadway in an Environment

In the next exercise, you learn the fundamentals of lofting while creating a road on the surface of landscape. The road's centerline was created with a NURBS curve snapped to the faces of the landscape object. A NURBS curve was used because of its inherent smoothness, although a Line object also could have been used. You also use the loft object's Scale Deformation controls to taper the road as it disappears over the hills, adding the illusion of distance to the scene.

Exercise 2.7: Using Lofting to Create a Roadway

1. Open the Landscape01.max file, and save it as
   Landscape02.max. Click the Select button on the
   main toolbar, and press **h** to open the Select
   Objects dialog box. The dialog box shows that the
   scene contains a camera and target, a landscape
   Quad Patch, a 2D road centerline, and a 2D road
   cross-section (see Figure 2.43). Double-click
   road_centerline in the list to select it.

On the CD

exercises\CH02\
Landscape01.max

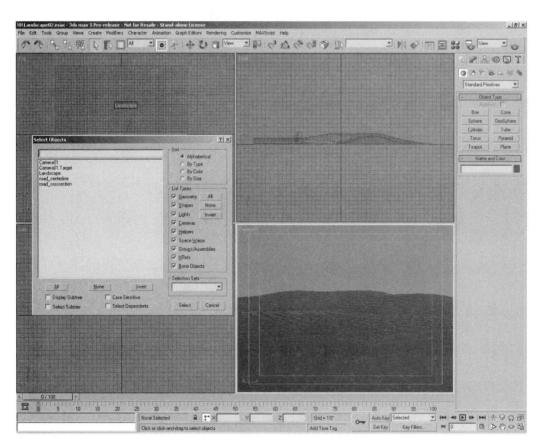

FIGURE 2.43 *The Select Objects dialog box lists the objects in the landscape scene.*

2. In the Create panel, Geometry category, click Standard Primitives and choose Compound Objects in the list (see Figure 2.44). In the Object Type rollout, click the Loft button.

3. The loft path is the road's selected centerline, so you will use Get Shape to choose a 2D shape as the loft shape. Click the Get Shape button and press **h** to open the Pick Object dialog box (see Figure 2.45). It looks like the Select Objects dialog box, but allows you to select a loft shape by name rather than just select an object. Double-click on road_crossection in the list to extrude the shape along the path. Name the object Roadway.

FIGURE 2.44
Selecting Com-pound Objects to find the Loft button.

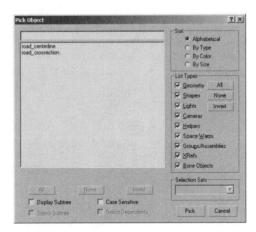

FIGURE 2.45   *Select road_crossection for the loft shape in the Pick Object dialog box instead of selecting the object in the scene.*

tip

In the Loft, Creation Method rollout, the Instance option is selected under Get Shape. That means there is a connection between the original 2D shape and the shape on the path. If you change the original, the shape on the path automatically updates and changes the 3D mesh. Automatic updating of the 3D object when you edit the 2D shapes is one of the most useful features of lofting in 3ds max 5. It allows you to create very complex objects with simple 2D shapes.

4. The hills are only about 400 feet in the distance, and the camera is only a slight wide angle lens at 35mm, so there is a lack of *convergence*, or visual narrowing, of the road to give the illusion of distance. You will use some artistic license to taper the road at the far end to enhance the convergence effect. With Roadway selected, go to the Modify panel, and expand the Deformations rollout (see Figure 2.46). Click the Scale button to open the Scale Deformation dialog box.

5. The Scale Deformation (X) dialog box shows a red line representing the scale factor of the road_crossection shape along the loft path. It is 100% by default. Click the black control point at the right end of the red scale line to turn it white (see Figure 2.47). Enter 35 in the rightmost numeric field at the bottom of the dialog box, and press Enter. This scales the far end of Roadway to 35% of its original size.

6. You have just performed a symmetrical scale, so the roadway has gotten smaller in two axes. In the Scale Deformation (X) dialog box, click the yellow Make Symmetrical button at the upper left to toggle it off. Now click the Display Y Axis button, the third button from the left, with a single green line. This shows that the Y axis scaling is the same as X axis. Click the Reset Curve button at the far right to reset the Y axis scaling to 100% over the entire loft (see Figure 2.48). The horizon now appears farther away in the camera viewport.

7. Close the Scale Deformation dialog box. Save the file; it should already be named Landscape02.max and should look similar to Figure 2.49.

FIGURE 2.46
In the Modify panel, expand the Deform-ations rollout for the selected Roadway object.

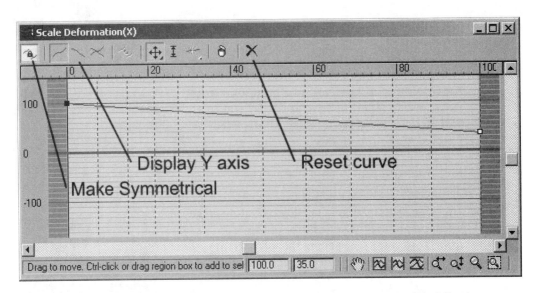

FIGURE 2.47 *Scaling Roadway to 35% of its original size in the Scale Deformation dialog box.*

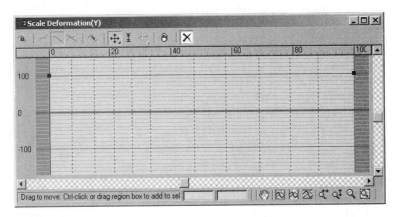

FIGURE 2.48 *Resetting the curve in the Y axis to 100% makes the horizon seem further away.*

You can easily edit the lofted roadway at any time, and the patterns in the materials you assign later will follow the road's curvature for a more convincing look. Lofting's power and ease of editing makes it a modeling technique worth using, even when other methods would create similar mesh objects.

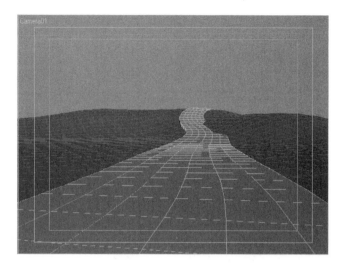

FIGURE 2.49   *A lofted road with Scale Deformation used to enhance the illusion of distance in your scene.*

Major Roadway Changes with Simple Shape Editing

The roadway you have created is a simple flat surface. Even though this is a medieval hamlet, the highway department is fairly sophisticated and wants you to add sidewalks and gutters. Because you have lofted the roadway, you can take advantage of the shapes on the loft being instance clones of the originals, meaning there's a link between the original and the shape on the loft. Changing the original 2D elements will affect the 3D mesh. The edits you make in the next exercise are vastly easier than they would be with other creation methods.

Exercise 2.8: Editing a Loft Object by Changing the 2D Shapes

1. Open Landscape02.max, and save it as
   Landscape03.max. The roadway looks like a simple
   flat surface that you want to turn into a more
   detailed road surface with sidewalks and gutters.
   In the Top viewport, select Roadway, if is not
   already selected. In the Modify panel, Skin
   Parameters rollout, clear the Transform Degrade
   check box in the Options area to keep the loft
   object from disappearing when you edit its shapes later.

On the CD

exercises\CH02\
Landscape02.max

2. Right-click in the Top viewport to activate it. Click the Select button, press **h** to open the Select Objects dialog box, and double-click road_crossection. Click the Zoom Extents Selected button by clicking and holding on the Zoom Extents button and choosing the button with the white box in the flyout buttons. This fills the Top viewport with only the currently selected object.

note

Transform Degrade is a holdover from the days of slow graphics cards, when editing the shape of a complex loft object would bring the graphics subsystem to its knees, halting production.

3. To add gutters and sidewalks, you need extra vertices along the top of the road_crossection shape. This can be done at the Segment sub-object level with the Divide option. In the Modify panel, Stack display, choose the Segment sub-object level. Pick the top horizontal segment of the rectangle in the Top viewport to turn it red. In the Geometry rollout, enter 9 in the numeric field to the right of the Divide button, and then click the Divide button. This adds nine equally spaced vertices to the segment, as shown in Figure 2.50.

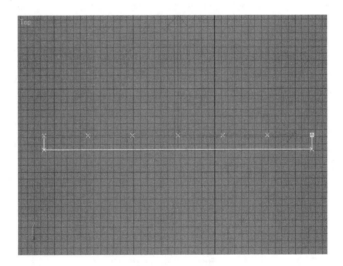

FIGURE 2.50 *The result of using Divide to add nine new vertices to the segment.*

4. In the Modify panel, Stack display, choose Vertex. In the Top viewport, drag a selection box around all vertices to turn them red. Position the cursor over any red vertex, right-click, and choose the Corner tangency option from the Tools 1 Quad menu. This removes all curvature from the new vertices of the shape.

caution

If you position the cursor on a green tangency handle instead of a red selected vertex, you will not get the correct Quad menus.

5. Choose Vertex in the Stack display, and in the Top viewport, Select and Move vertices to transform the shape into something similar to Figure 2.51. This is the road_crossection shape with gutters and sidewalks. The Roadway object in the scene changes accordingly.

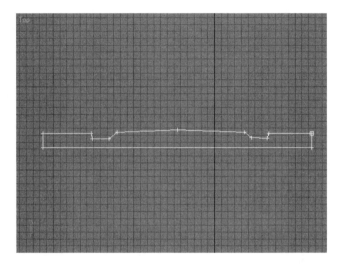

FIGURE 2.51   *By moving vertices of road_crossection, you can create a shape with sidewalks and gutters.*

You do not have to be overly concerned with exactly what the roadway looks like right now. At any time, you can edit the shape to change the road without affecting anything else in the scene. Allow yourself to "sketch" the objects to enhance your creativity.

6. In the Stack display, exit sub-object mode. Save the file; it should already be named Landscape03.max.

Through this simple exercise, you have learned some of the power of lofting objects over other methods of modeling. The ease of editing is unparalleled. In later exercises, you will learn more tools for optimizing lofted objects and assigning materials to different areas easily.

Optimizing Lofted Models

If there is anything you should be learning from the exercises in this book, it is the importance of creating models with the absolute minimum number of faces and vertices that will get you the look you want. Each extra face and vertex adds overhead to the display and rendering process by using RAM that would be better applied elsewhere. Designing for a computer game is usually known as a "low poly" job, but everyone creating scenes in 3ds max 5 should strive for a low polygon count.

A major benefit of modeling with 3ds max 5 lofting is that controlling the mesh's density is easy on several fronts. You can do the following:

- Adjust the loft object's Path Steps and Shape Steps settings.
- Add or delete vertices on the original shapes.
- Adjust the Interpolation settings of the original shapes.

In the next exercise, you will optimize the road from Exercise 2.8 by adjusting the Path and Shape Steps of the lofted Roadway object.

Path and Shape Steps settings are found in the Skin Parameters rollout of the loft object's Modify panel. These settings are defined as intermediate steps between vertices that define curvature. In Exercise 2.9, you reduce the Path and Shape Steps until the object has a minimum number of faces and still looks acceptable. This, of course, is somewhat subjective. Objects can often be optimized more when busy materials or background disguise the faceted look of highly optimized objects. The same optimized object against a plain background or with a solid color might be unacceptable.

Exercise 2.9: Using Path and Shape Steps to Optimize the Lofted Roadway

1. Open Landscape03.max, and save the file as Landscape04.max. You can see plainly in the Camera01 viewport that the mesh of Roadway is quite complex because Edged Faces is activated, revealing the wireframe and shaded view simultaneously. Click the Zoom Extents All button to fill all viewports with all objects.

On the CD

exercises\CH02\
Landscape03.max

2. Click the Select button, press **h**, and double-click Roadway in the Select Objects dialog box to select it. In the Camera01 viewport, place the cursor over Roadway, right-click, and choose Properties in the Quad menu (see Figure 2.52). In the Object Properties dialog box, you will see that the object has 5,226 vertices and 10,448 faces (see Figure 2.53). Close the Object Properties dialog box.

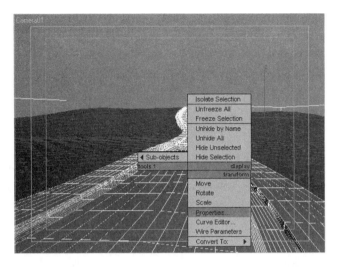

FIGURE 2.52   *Using the Quad menu to see the properties for a selected object.*

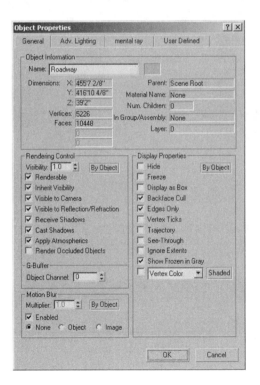

FIGURE 2.53   *Viewing the number of vertices and faces for Roadway in the Object Properties dialog box.*

3. In the Modify panel, Skin Parameters rollout, Options area, you will see that Shape Steps and Path Steps both default to 5. Again, the steps define curvature between vertices. Remember that you selected all the vertices of the road_crossection shape in the previous exercise and converted the vertices to Corner type. That took all the tangency curvature out of the shape. Therefore, Roadway has no curvature from side to side, so the Shape Steps are adding extra geometry that does nothing for the look of the road. Decrement the Shape Steps from 5 to 0 and watch the Roadway change with each lower step count. The Roadway does not look much different with 0 Shape Steps (see Figure 2.54). The face count has dropped from 10,448 to 1,738, a significant savings.

tip

If you press **7**, the Polygon Counter for the selected object is displayed in the upper left of the currently active viewport.

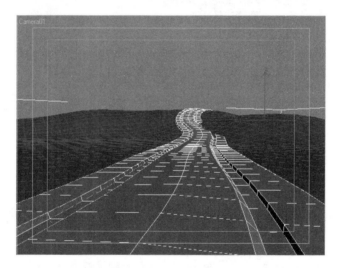

FIGURE 2.54 *Because the Roadway has no curvature across the object, reducing the Shape Steps to 0 has no adverse affect on the appearance but reduces the number of faces significantly.*

tip

For this example, selecting the Optimize Shapes check box would have produced the same results as setting Shape Steps to 0. Optimize Shapes analyzes the cross-section shape and reduces Shape Steps where there is no curvature, but leaves the detail where curvature exists.

4. In the Modify panel, Skin Parameters rollout, decrement the Path Steps from 5 to 0. At this setting, Roadway becomes very faceted and does not have enough curvature as it curves over the hills (see Figure 2.55). Although it reduces the face count to 708, the object does not have enough curvature to meet minimum visual standards. Increase Path Steps to 2, and you have a good compromise with an acceptable look and only 880 faces.

FIGURE 2.55 *Reducing the Path Steps to 0 for Roadway is too severe to keep the road on the surface of the landscape.*

5. Next, you will learn to merge models from other scenes into the current scene by merging an array of houses to run along the street, plus a small chapel for the hilltop beyond. Choose File, Merge from the menu.

6. In the Merge File dialog box, load the Houses.max file noted next to the CD icon, and click Open. In the Merge - Houses.max dialog box, click the All button to select all houses (see Figure 2.56), and click OK. Two rows of houses and a chapel will appear in the scene (see Figure 2.57). All the houses are similar to the house you built in previous exercises.

On the CD

exercises\CH02\
Houses.max

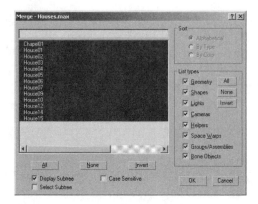

FIGURE 2.56   *Selecting all houses in the file to merge into the scene.*

FIGURE 2.57   *The landscape file with merged houses and a chapel.*

note   The houses have been assigned a Multi/Sub-Object stand-in material that corresponds to the Material ID numbers assigned to the various parts, so they look multi-colored in the viewport.

caution   When merging files, the merged objects are selected. It is a good idea to pick somewhere in space after clicking OK in the Merge dialog box to deselect them. This avoids moving them inadvertently.

7. Save the file; it should already be named Landscape04.max.

You have learned about optimizing lofted objects in this exercise to increase your efficiency while retaining the look your project requires. You also have used File, Merge to import several houses into your scene to line the street.

Creating a Sky for the Street Scene

In this section, you learn about a couple of new modifiers and the concept of face normals in 3ds max to create a hemisphere dome over the landscape that eventually becomes the sky for your scene.

The modifiers you'll use are Xform and Normal modifiers. *Xform* stands for "transform" and can be used as sort of a container to move objects while retaining the ability to remove the modifier and return the object to its original location. You will learn another use for it, however: to enable you to scale objects safely. You have not learned about using the Scale transform yet for good reason. It can be a dangerous transform until you know how it actually works.

3ds max 5 is constantly evaluating the history of objects in this order: Objects are created, modifiers can be applied, SpaceWarps (affect space and objects bound to that space) can be used, and objects can be transformed (moved, rotated, and scaled). Because transforms are evaluated last, problems can arise with the Scale transform because it can change the topology of objects—that is, the relationship between faces and vertices. When that happens at the top of the evaluation stack, modifiers below that evaluation might have already changed topology and strange things could happen. You might get away with it in certain cases, especially when scaling uniformly in all axes, but I recommend against it. However, you can safely scale sub-object selections at any time, as they are always evaluated at the point you perform them in the evaluation stack.

> **warning**
>
> *Do not scale objects in 3ds max 5!* Always apply an Xform modifier and scale its Gizmo. That way, the scaling is evaluated at the proper point in the stack. An alternative fix is to go to the Utilities panel and choose Reset Xform. This applies the Xform after the fact to correct scaling problems.

Face normals are vectors that project perpendicular from each face. The rule is that if a face normal points toward the viewer, the face is visible. If the face normal points away, the face is invisible. You will take advantage of that fact to make the sky surface visible from inside the dome.

Exercise 2.10: Creating a Skydome and Making It Visible from Within

1. Open Landscape04.max, and save it as
   `Landscape05.max`. Right-click in the Top viewport
   to activate it. In the Create panel, Geometry
   panel, click the GeoSphere button, and click and
   drag from near the center of the landscape to near
   an outer edge of the landscape (see Figure 2.58).
   Name the object `Skydome`.

On the CD

exercises\CH02\
Landscape04.max

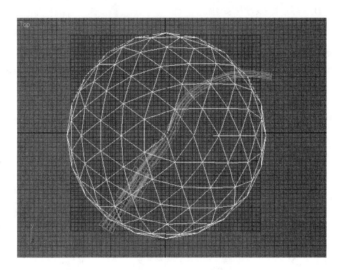

FIGURE 2.58   *Creating a GeoSphere in the Top viewport for the sky surface.*

2. In the Modify panel, Parameters rollout, select the Hemisphere check box. Right-click in the Front viewport, click the Select and Move button, and using the Y-axis restrict arrow, move Skydome down about 1 grid spacing below the landscape (see Figure 2.59). This prevents the faces at the base of Skydome from being coincident—that is, occupying the same space—with the faces of the landscape.

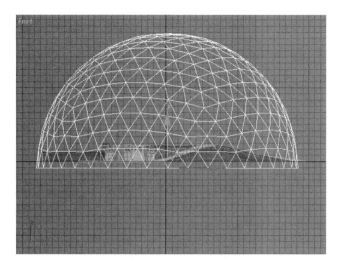

FIGURE 2.59   *Moving Skydome down in the Front viewport.*

3. In the Modify panel, Modifier List, choose the Normal modifier. Skydome then becomes visible in the Camera01 viewport.

4. The high hemisphere creates a near vertical wall over the horizon of your scene. You will apply an Xform modifier and scale it to flatten Skydome somewhat, enhancing the feeling of convergence on the horizon when materials are applied. In the Modify panel, Modifier List, choose Xform modifier. It automatically opens at the Gizmo sub-object.

5. Click and hold on the Select and Scale button and choose the Non-uniform Scale button (the middle button in the flyout, as seen in Figure 2.60). In the Front viewport, click on the Y-axis restrict arrow and scale the Gizmo down to roughly 80%. You can read the scaling percent in the Y Coordinate field at the bottom of the display as you are scaling. Skydome should look similar to Figure 2.61 in the Front viewport. Exit sub-object mode for the Xform modifier.

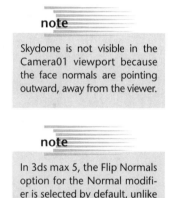

note

Skydome is not visible in the Camera01 viewport because the face normals are pointing outward, away from the viewer.

note

In 3ds max 5, the Flip Normals option for the Normal modifier is selected by default, unlike previous versions.

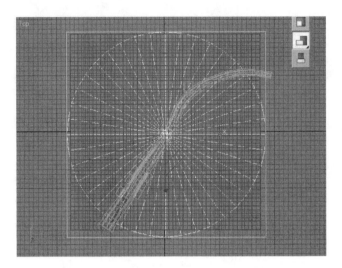

FIGURE 2.60   *Selecting the Non-uniform Scale button.*

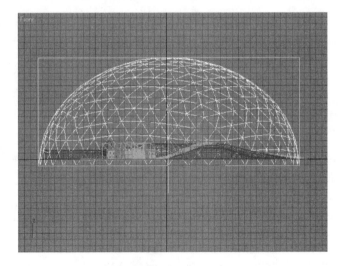

FIGURE 2.61   *Flattening Skydome with the Xform Gizmo to about 80% in the Y axis.*

6. Save the file; it should already be called Landscape05.max. You now have a surface that will act as a sky in your scene.

In this exercise, you have learned that scaling is not recommended without first applying an Xform modifier to the object. You also have learned that objects' faces can be flipped to make them visible from one direction or the other.

Summary

You have learned some important modeling concepts in this chapter, including

- **Maxstart file**   You set new display units and new grid spacing settings and saved them in a file called maxstart.max that loads each time you reset or start a new file.

- **Editable Poly**   Although Editable Poly is not new to 3ds max 5, you have learned some of the new techniques in this vastly improved feature.

- **Sub-object editing**   You learned to access sub-object components of objects—vertices, segments, edges, faces, polygons, and elements—to make changes to the 2D and 3D objects.

- **Applying modifiers**   You have learned to add modifiers to 2D shapes to create 3D objects; in this chapter's exercises, you applied a Bevel modifier to create chamfered braces.

- **Material ID numbers**   You learned to change Material ID numbers to selected polygons in Editable Poly to facilitate applying multiple materials to single objects.

- **Lofting**   You learned the fundamentals of lofting and optimizing lofted objects. This makes use of efficient and easily edited 2D shapes to create complex 3D objects.

- **File Merge**   You learned to merge objects from other 3ds max scenes into your current scene.

- **Xform modifier**   You learned that scaling objects in 3ds max 5 can cause problems, but that applying a Xform modifier and scaling it is an easy solution to the problem.

CHAPTER 3

Applying Materials and Maps for a Convincing Outdoor Scene

In This Chapter

In Chapter 2, "Modeling: A Medieval Street Scene," you created a moderately detailed, efficient scene. When you render an image to show your friends, they are impressed but might ask why everything has funny colors. The colors are either the default object color as it was created or, for the houses, a stand-in material that was added just as a placeholder to save you a few steps in the following exercises.

Materials, along with lighting, can make the scene. By applying good materials to your objects, you can evoke a mood, such as somber or cheery; you can add the illusion of depth to the scene by following the principle that dark objects recede and bright objects appear close and you can create the illusion of extra geometry with bump or opacity mapping.

In this chapter, you learn how to construct and apply basic materials to make your scene much more convincing to the viewer. Although an entire book could be dedicated to materials alone, for this book you will focus on a few important aspects:

- **Color and patterns in materials**   You'll focus on color aspects of materials and the use of 3ds max 5 procedural maps, maps that are generated mathematically within the program.

- **Multiple materials on single objects**   You also will learn about Multi/Sub-Object materials, which are made of any number of sub-materials assigned to faces of an object, based on the Material ID numbers of those faces. In Chapter 2 you assigned certain Material ID numbers to specific faces during the construction of the sample building.

- **Lofting and materials**   You will learn the unique advantages of lofted objects in terms of material assignment and mapping and how to create a convincing sky that can be easily adjusted for mood changes.

While going through these exercises, use your imagination to think of ways you might improve on the fundamentals. There is no end to the possibilities of combining materials and maps to give your scenes a distinct look that others will come to recognize as your signature style.

Key Terms

Bump mapping   Using Luminance values of maps to give the illusion of extra geometry; for example, raised tiles can be simulated with bump maps.

Luminance values   The brightness values of pixels in a map that affect bumpiness, opacity, and masking, among other attributes in a material.

Maps   Patterns, such as bumpiness, color, and displacement, used within attributes of a material or as projected or background images.

Mapping coordinates   A description of the way a map repeats over a surfaces. Accessed through the map itself or by applying a UVW Map modifier.

Materials   Surface information that gets assigned to objects in the scene. Materials can be composed of many attributes, such as color, opacity, and shininess.

Multi/Sub-Object material   A material type comprising any number of other materials that are assigned to faces of an object, based on Material ID numbers.

Procedural maps   Maps that are mathematically generated by the program, usually in random patterns.

Hotkeys and Keyboard Shortcuts

Alt+w   Toggle minimizing/maximizing the viewport

h   Select by Name

m   Open the Material Editor

The Material Editor

The Material Editor, which can be accessed by clicking the Material Editor button on the main toolbar or by pressing **m**, is where all materials are created in 3ds max 5. You should already have been through at least some of the tutorials that ship with 3ds max 5, but a refresher never hurts.

Figure 3.1 shows the Material Editor in Landcape05.max that you will open in Exercise 3.1. It already has one material in the upper-left sample window; the rest of the sample windows are default materials.

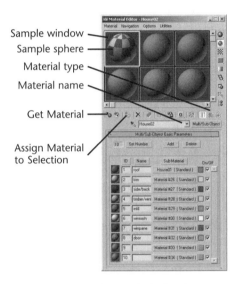

Sample window
Sample sphere
Material type
Material name
Get Material
Assign Material to Selection

Figure 3.1   *The Material Editor with a Multi/Sub-Object material in the upper-left sample window.*

Having only six sample windows certainly does not restrict you to six materials. If you right-click on a sample window, you can choose a 6 × 4 display for 24 sample windows. That is not the limit of materials, only the limit of what you can view at one time.

To retrieve materials from the scene to a sample window, use the eyedropper to the left of the material name in the Material Editor.

You save materials in special files called *material libraries*. If you click the Get Material button on the left, below the sample windows, the Material/Map Browser opens. In this dialog box, you can view a listing of materials in the scene, in material libraries, on selected objects, or in the Material Editor, or create new materials from a list of available map types. Select the Mtl Library radio button in the Browse From section, and you will see a listing of materials (blue sphere icons) and maps (green or red parallelograms), similar to Figure 3.2.

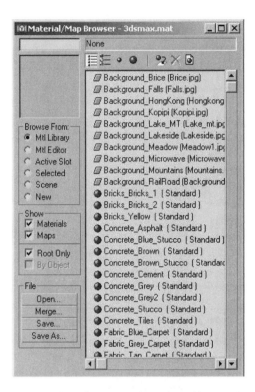

FIGURE 3.2   *View available materials and maps in the Material/Map Browser.*

The best method of working with material libraries is to create a new one for each project, and as you create new materials, drag and drop them from the sample window to the library. The materials are then listed in the material library file, which has a .mat file extension, and you can open the material library from any other file to reuse the materials.

You will be working with several material types in the following exercises, including Standard and Multi/Sub-Object. Figure 3.3 lists the material types you can access by clicking the Standard button at the right in the Material Editor.

tip

You also can create separate material library files that contain all your wood, plastic, or sky materials, for example. You can drag them from the library into a sample window for use in your current scene and library.

FIGURE 3.3   *The Material/Map Browser, listing the available material types for the Standard material.*

Materials and Maps

New users are sometimes confused as to the difference between materials and maps, but it is quite simple, actually:

- **Materials**   Materials are the surface attributes that get applied to objects or faces in a scene. They include color, shininess, reflections, bumpiness, and opacity, among others.

- **Maps**   Maps are used to define patterns within the material—color patterns or bump patterns, for example. Maps cannot be assigned directly to objects in the scene, but they can be used as background images or as projector images for lights.

The maps you will be using in this chapter are mostly *procedural maps*—patterns generated mathematically by the program, as opposed to a picture file or other bitmap.

Creating Materials for the Houses in Your Scene

What better way to learn about materials than to dive right in to the creation process? In this chapter's exercises, you create the materials applied to the houses as individual materials first, and then combine them with the House02 Multi/Sub-Object material in the Material Editor. This Multi/Sub-Object material then gets assigned to the houses in the scene, and your scene will transform itself into a more convincing hamlet.

Budget your project time to spend 50% or less of the total time on modeling. For a much more cost-effective workflow, use the time you save during modeling to work on lighting and materials.

Paint Material for Window Sashes

The first material you will create seems simple enough, but never underestimate the difficulty of getting the materials looking "just right." After you have a material looking good in the sample window, be prepared for a shock when you apply it to your scene and render a test image. The final appearance of materials in your scene depends heavily on the surface shape and the lighting, and you will undoubtedly have to return to the Material Editor several times to tweak the materials.

Exercise 3.1: Glossy Paint

1. Open the Landscape05.max file, noted next to the CD icon. It is the last file saved from Chapter 2. Save it as `StreetMatl01.max`. Click the Material Editor button on the main toolbar. The Material Editor will look like Figure 3.1 at the beginning of this chapter.

On the CD

exercises\CH03\
Landscape05.max

2. Click on the top-middle sample window in the group of six to activate it. A white border appears around a sample window when it is active. Rename the material PAINT_RED.

3. The basics of any material are usually adjusted first. You will focus on two attributes to start: color and specular highlights. In the Material Editor, Blinn Basic Parameters rollout, click on the color swatch to the right of Diffuse to open the Color Selector. In the numeric fields, enter 175 for Red, 50 for Green, and 25 for Blue to get a burnt-orange color (see Figure 3.4).

Using the name PAINT_RED, rather than RED_PAINT, helps keep materials in a list sorted by the type of material. The caps and the underscore are added for clarity and are optional.

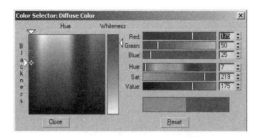

FIGURE 3.4   *Selecting a burnt-orange color in the Color Selector.*

4. In the Specular Highlights area of the Blinn Basic Parameters rollout, set Specular Level to 60 and Glossiness to 50. This makes the material much shinier, as shown in Figure 3.5, as though it were a glossy paint. Using Blinn as the Shader Type creates a round highlight with a moderately soft edge, such as what you might find in many man-made materials.

note

The Ambient color swatch is locked to the Diffuse color swatch to keep them in sync with each other. Unlocking them would allow a different color to be set in each slot, generally for special effects. The Diffuse Color setting is the color of a material in direct light, and Ambient Color> is the color in shaded areas.

tip

Good specular highlights are critical for making materials convincing. In the physical world, a specular highlight is the light scattered from the surface, based on the material's molecular makeup and surface condition. In the 3D world, it is the single biggest clue to the viewer what the material is supposed to represent. Specular highlights in 3ds max 5 have four important attributes that you can set: Specular Color is the color of the scattered light (generally white); Specular Level is the brightness of the highlight; Glossiness is the size of the highlight; and the Shader Type (Blinn, in this example) determines the shape of the highlight.

Study the specular highlights on materials in the world around you and try to reproduce them by using these four settings.

5. Click the Get Material button in the Material Editor. Select Mtl Library in the Browse From section of Material/Map Browser. Click the Clear Material Library button at the top right of the Material/Map Browser (see Figure 3.6). Click Yes in the warning dialog box. This clears the Material/Map Browser, but does not delete materials from the scene or any material library files on disk.

note

Clearing material libraries is completely non-destructive to your materials. 3ds max 5 even prevents you from accidentally saving an empty library over an existing one. You must first assign a new name or choose a specific file to overwrite.

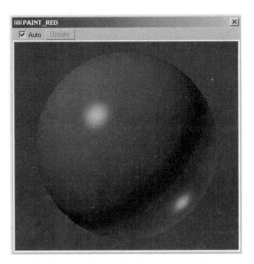

FIGURE 3.5   *The glossy paint look achieved after changing settings for specular highlights.*

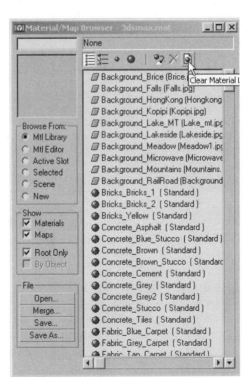

FIGURE 3.6   *Clicking the Clear Material Library button simply clears the Material/Map Browser. No scene materials or material library files are deleted.*

6. Drag the sample window with PAINT_RED into the Material/Map Browser's list of materials. In the Material/Map Browser, click the Save As button in the File section, and choose a subdirectory for your new library. Name the new file StreetScene.mat.

7. Close all windows and dialog boxes. Save the file; it should already be called StreetMatl01.max.

This exercise has introduced you to two simple concepts: color and the much more important specular highlights. Do not create a material without considering the specular highlights for maximum convinciblity. Traditional artists have worked to perfect specular highlights in painting for centuries, and you must give them the same weight.

tip

If you have Microsoft Access on your machine, the file type .mat might be set for Access files. If so, change the file association in Windows to associate .mat files with 3ds max 5. You will not change the functionality of Microsoft Access in any way.

Materials for the Back and Sides of the Houses

In a medieval hamlet with the houses packed close together and open street gutters, there is apt to be some dampness. The sides and backs of your houses will be stucco that has seen better days, so you'll learn to create color that is not homogenous and solid, but blotchy and discolored. To do this, you will learn how to apply maps to materials to give them repeatable patterns. You also will learn about *bump mapping*, using maps to create the illusion of extra geometry without actually adding faces and vertices. Bump mapping works on the Luminance values (brightness) of pixels in the map. White causes the illusion of a raised area, and black does nothing. Levels of gray are somewhere in between, depending on their brightness.

tip

Although color maps can be used for bump mapping, this method is not advised because judging the brightness of colors is difficult for most of us. Bright green and bright red look very different as colors, but have no differentiation in a bump map.

Procedural maps, such as Noise or Smoke, have special coding that actually generates the bumps, but the Luminance values are useful as a guide.

The Cellular procedural map is an exception to this rule.

Exercise 3.2: Dull and Damp Bumpy Stucco

1. Open StreetMatl01.max, and save it as StreetMatl02.max. Open the Material Editor (keyboard shortcut: **m**) and activate the top-right sample window. Name this material STUCCO_MOSSY.

On the CD

exercises\CH03\
StreetMatl01.max

2. You will now go down in the material hierarchy to a mapping level to apply the bump map. Expand the Maps rollout in the Material Editor (see Figure 3.7). It contains a column of attribute names, a column of Amount settings, and a column of map slots, all of which have None as the current map. Click the None button to the right of Bump to display the list of maps in the Material/ Map Browser (see Figure 3.8), and double-click Smoke.

note

There is a specific procedural map called Stucco, but it is more useful for new stucco materials. The Smoke map used in this exercise will create the illusion of years of stucco layers.

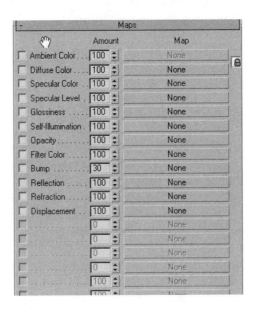

Figure 3.7   *Expand the Maps rollout for a list of material attributes that will accept maps.*

3. The Smoke map is a randomly generated grayscale pattern that looks like Figure 3.9. The white pixels cause the sample sphere's surface to look raised, based on the brightness of the pixels in the map (see Figure 3.10). In the Smoke Parameters rollout, set Size to 30, # Iterations to 3, and Exponent to 3. These settings adjust the relative size of the pattern, the roughness of the transition from black to white, and the ratio of white to black pixels.

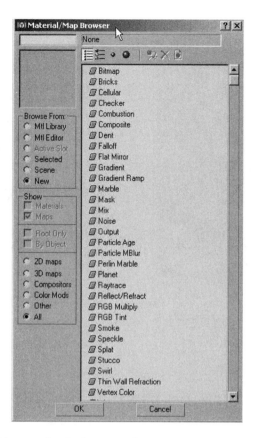

FIGURE 3.8   *The available maps for the Bump attribute.*

4. In the Material Editor, click the Material/Map Navigator button (looks like two vertical blue spheres) at the lower right of the sample windows. It shows a hierarchical list of the current material's attributes and is the best method for navigating the levels of a material (see Figure 3.11). Click the top level, STUCCO_MOSSY, to go to that level.

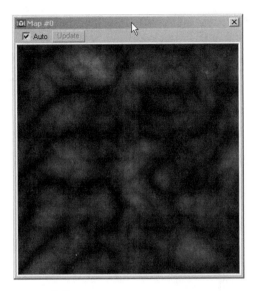

FIGURE 3.9
The Smoke map is a random pattern of black and white pixels.

FIGURE 3.10
Applying a Smoke map to the Bump attribute causes the STUCCO_MOSSY material to look rough without creating any new geometry.

FIGURE 3.11   *Use the Material/Map Navigator to easily traverse a material's hierarchy. This feature is especially useful with complex materials.*

5. In the Maps rollout in the Material Editor, drag the Smoke map from the Bump slot to the None button next to Diffuse Color. Click the Copy radio button in the Copy (Instance) Map dialog box (see Figure 3.12), and click OK. This makes a copy of the map with no connection to the map in Bump, so the colors can be changed without affecting the Bump map. In contrast, the Instance option would make both occurrences of Smoke map share the same settings.

6. Use the Material/Map Navigator to go to the Diffuse Map level. The pattern matches the Bump map just fine, but the black and white colors are not appropriate. In the Smoke Parameters rollout (see Figure 3.13), click on the Color #1 swatch and change the values for Red to 170, Green to 145, and Blue to 105 for a tan stucco color. Click on the Color #2 swatch to change Red to 85, Green to 115, and Blue to 70 for a mossy green that corresponds to the material's bump pattern. Close the Color Selector and use the Material/Map Navigator to return to the top of the material to see the results of the material changes.

FIGURE 3.12
Selecting the Copy option so that colors can be changed without affecting the Bump map.

tip

When you are dragging and dropping maps, the cursor shows an arrow to indicate that you are over a valid slot. The arrow must be on the button, not the black box outline attached to the cursor. Dragging and dropping ensures that the map settings are the same, cutting down on setup time for the maps.

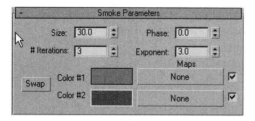

FIGURE 3.13   *Change the color values of the Smoke map in the Diffuse Color slot for a color that has the same pattern as the Bump map.*

tip

The default specular highlights settings are fine for this material. With the Specular Level at 0 and Glossiness at 10, the material has a soft porous quality.

7. Close all windows and dialog boxes, and save the file. It should already be named StreetMatl02.max. The sample sphere appears as a soft dull surface with two distinct patterns: a bump pattern to give the illusion of a rough surface, and a color pattern to look like mossy green patches where the bumps are on the surface.

note

At this point, you should open your material library and drag this material into it. This is a good habit to get into during production to keep your materials organized.

In this exercise, you have delved a little deeper into the hierarchy of materials and learned that with a little adjustment, maps can be reused as different attributes. You also have learned that bump maps create the illusion of bumps without the need for a more complex surface.

Mapping Coordinates Introduction

You might not have noticed, but the materials you have been creating so far are set in the map's Coordinates rollout; you have been using the XYZ coordinates of an object to determine how the materials fit onto the surface when you apply them. This method can be an advantage of procedural maps, such as Smoke. However, at times you need to apply specific mapping coordinates to a map to get it to fit and repeat exactly as you want on the surface. The next exercise starts you toward that goal by making a wood-grain material for the doors of your houses. Using specific mapping coordinates gives you better control so that you can make materials more convincing to viewers.

You also learn about the Color Clipboard, which acts as a palette of colors for your scene. You will open a bitmap image of wood, extract color information, and store it in the Color Clipboard for use in your wood map.

Exercise 3.3: Wood Grain Material and Mapping Coordinates

1. Open StreetMatl02.max, and save it as StreetMatl03.max. Open the Material Editor and click the bottom-left sample window to activate it. Rename the material WOOD_DOOR. The wood should have a slight shine to it, so set Specular Level to 15 to increase the brightness of the specular highlights. The default Blinn Shader Type is fine.

On the CD

exercises\CH03\
StreetMatl02.max

2. Expand the Maps rollout and click the None button for Diffuse Color to go to the map level. Double-click Wood in the Material/Map Browser. In the Coordinates rollout, click the Source drop-down arrow, and select Explicit Map Channel (see Figure 3.14). By default, the Explicit Map Channel is set to 1 in the Map Channel field, which corresponds to a map channel setting in a UVW Map modifier that you will apply later to adjust the pattern's size in the scene.

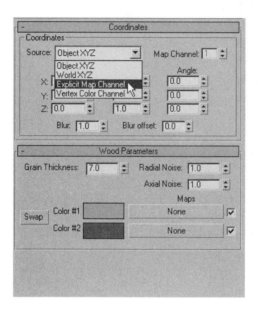

FIGURE 3.14 *In the map's Coordinates rollout, change the Source setting from Object XYZ to Explicit Map Channel.*

3. In the Wood Parameters rollout, set Grain Thickness to 0.02 and Radial and Axial Noise to 0. These settings make the grain pattern much smaller and straighter, as you can see on the sample sphere. In the Coordinates rollout, enter 90 in the Angle column for the W row to rotate the wood grain map 90 degrees in the Z direction.

tip

In 3ds max 5, a good formula to remember is RGB=XYZ=UVW. Red, green, and blue are the colors that often represent the XYZ axes; *UVW* are just the next three letters in the alphabet and refer to the coordinates of maps. They all represent the same directions in space for different purposes.

4. Next, to change the color, you will use the Color Clipboard feature. First, choose File, View Image File from the menu, and load the OLDWOOD.JPG file noted next to the CD icon. It should appear in a window, as shown in Figure 3.15.

On the CD

exercises\CH03\
OLDWOOD.JPG

FIGURE 3.15   *The OLDWOOD.JPG material to be used for a color reference.*

5. In the Create panel, Utilities tab, click the Color Clipboard button in the Utilities rollout (see Figure 3.16). You might have to move the View Image File window to see the panel.

6. Right-click on the wood-grain image in the View Image File window, and hold the mouse button down. Move the eyedropper cursor over the image, and you will see that the color under the cursor is being recorded in the small swatch at the top center of the window (see Figure 3.17). Choose a light-brown pixel. Drag and drop the small color swatch from the View Image File window to a swatch on the Color Clipboard, and select Copy in the Copy or Swap Colors dialog box. Repeat the steps to copy a dark pixel color to another swatch in the Color Clipboard. Close the View Image File window.

tip

Try Ctrl-clicking in the View Image File window, if you need to zoom in on one particular section.

7. Now drag, drop, and copy the lighter of the color swatches in the Color Clipboard to the Color #1 swatch in the Wood Parameters rollout, and drag, drop, copy the darker color swatch to Color #2. Your wood grain now has realistic wood colors of your choosing.

8. Close all windows and dialog boxes and save the file. It should already be called StreetMatl03.max.

You have learned to change the type of mapping coordinates for a map and how to use the Color Clipboard to obtain and reuse colors from images or photos.

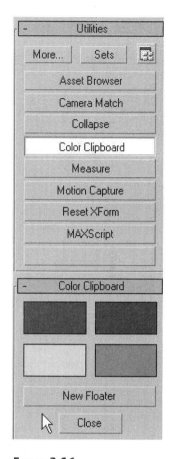

FIGURE 3.16
The Color Clipboard serves as a palette for storing color swatches.

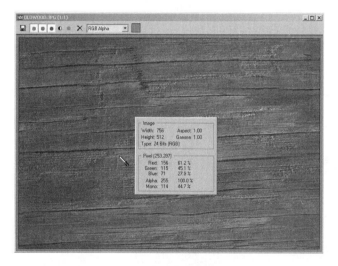

FIGURE 3.17
Right-click and drag the cursor over the View Image File window to record the color under the eyedropper in a color swatch at the top of the window.

Using Maps in Unusual Places

Often you want solid colors in a material, but you don't want the surface to have a boring homogeneous look. Even the best man-made objects have some variations that cause the light to scatter in irregular patterns across the surface.

A technique that can be a good compromise between a smooth surface and a boring surface is applying a map to the Glossiness slot of a material. In the next exercise, you create some trim paint for the buildings. You want a good paint job, but not perfect, so you will add a Noise map to the Glossiness slot to randomly modify the specular highlights on the surface, making it more convincing.

Exercise 3.4: Slight Imperfections with Glossiness Maps

1. Open StreetMatl03.max, and save it as StreetMatl04.max. Open the Material Editor and click the bottom-center sample window to activate it. Name the material PAINT_GLOSSY.

2. Click the Diffuse Color swatch, and set the color for Red to 115, Green to 55, Blue to 0, which gives you a reddish brown. Set the Specular Level to 30.

3. In the Maps rollout, click the None button next to Glossiness and double-click Noise in the Material/Map Browser. This is a random pattern much like the Smoke map, but with generally smoother edges. You will see the specular highlights become quite irregular on the sample sphere, as shown in Figure 3.18.

On the CD

exercises\CH03\
StreetMatl03.max

note

This would be a good time to add this material to your material library, if you want access to the material from other files.

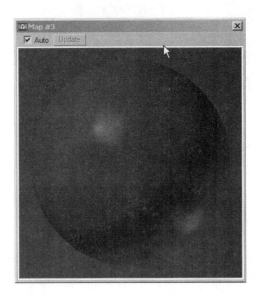

FIGURE 3.18 *Placing a Noise map in the Glossiness slot randomly varies the material's specular highlights, thus making it more convincing.*

4. In the Noise Parameters rollout, set Size to 2.0. Close all windows and dialog boxes and save the file. It should already be named StreetMatl04.max.

Adding the Noise map to the Glossiness slot can enhance a material's look by eliminating the "too-perfect" quality. Subtle adjustments like this one go a long way toward making your materials more believable.

Blend Material: A New World of Possibilities

You will now get deeper into the hierarchy of materials and learn to create a Blend material from two materials in an existing library. You will then use a Mask map to reveal each material in a random pattern to simulate stucco walls that have crumbled and left the underlying brick showing through.

Masking is a technique you will be able to use in many materials. It uses the Luminance values of a map to hide one material and reveal another.

Exercise 3.5: The Blend Material Type

1. Open StreetMatl04.max, and save it as StreetMatl05.max. Open the Material Editor and activate the lower-right sample window. Name it STUCCO_BRICK. Click the Standard button to the right of the name field and double-click Blend in the list of materials in the Material/Map Browser. Select the Discard Old Material radio button in the Replace Material dialog box (see Figure 3.19), and click OK.

On the CD

exercises\CH03\
StreetMatl04.max

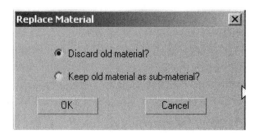

FIGURE 3.19 *Discarding the old material in the Replace Material dialog box.*

2. The Blend material is composed of two other materials with the options of a Mix Amount value or a Mask setting (see Figure 3.20). Click the Get Material button in the Material Editor, and select Mtl Library in the Browse From section. In the File section, click the Open button. Open the InfillBasics.mat file noted next to the CD icon. It contains two materials: BRICK and STUCCO.

On the CD

exercises\CH03\
InfillBasics.mat

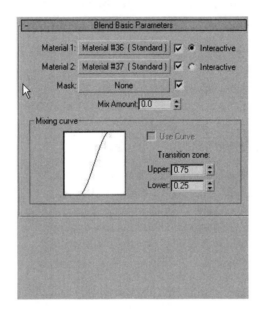

Figure 3.20 *A Blend material is composed of two materials, with options of mixing or masking the materials.*

3. Drag and drop the STUCCO material from the Material/Map Browser onto the Material 1: Standard button in the Material Editor's Blend Basic Parameters roll-out. Drag and drop the BRICK material from the Material/Map Browser onto Material 2: Standard (see Figure 3.21). Close the Material/Map Browser.

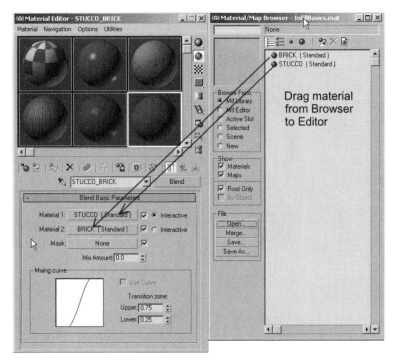

Figure 3.21 *Drag and drop STUCCO and BRICK material from the Material/Map Browser to the Material 1: and Material 2: slots respectively.*

4. The sample window shows the STUCCO material on the sample sphere because it is Material 1. The Mix Amount is 0.0 and there is no mask. In the Blend Basic Parameters rollout, click the None button for the Mask slot and double-click Splat in the Material/Map Browser. The sample window will now show BRICK because of the Mask setting.

5. In the Splat Parameters rollout, set Size to 150 and # Iterations to 2. Make the Color #1 swatch pure black and the Color #2 swatch pure white (see Figure 3.22). The Sample sphere should now show small patches of brick color through the stucco. Save the material to the material library.

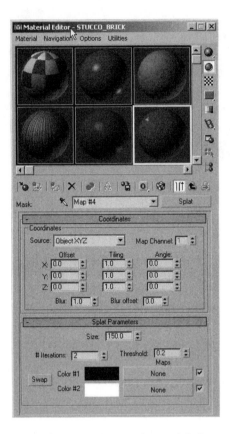

FIGURE 3.22   *The Splat map for the mask in the Blend material shows patches of brick through stucco.*

6. Close any open windows and dialog boxes, and save the file. It should already be called StreetMatl05.max.

You have learned to create a complex material from two other materials and to reveal one through the other with a Mask map—in this case, the Splat map. Blend materials with masks are a great method for creating "grunge" or other compositing effects.

Transparency in Materials

Transparency, or the absence of opacity, is an important element of many materials. You can create it by adjusting the Opacity setting for overall transparency effects or by applying a map to the Opacity slot, where white in the map becomes opaque and black becomes transparent.

In this next section, you are introduced to the Raytrace material type and reflections so that you can create window glass for the street scene.

caution

The Raytrace material type deals with transparency differently than other materials types do. With Raytrace material, you adjust transparency, but for the other material types, you use opacity. The confusion comes with maps, in which the effects of the Brightness values produce opposite results in Raytrace material than in other material types.

Exercise 3.6: Transparency and Reflections for Your Windows

1. Open StreetMatl05.max, and save it as `StreetMatl06.max`. Open the Material Editor and use the slider just below the sample windows to scroll left, revealing more sample windows of the 24 available. Activate the next sample window, and rename the material `WINDOW_GLASS`.

On the CD

exercises\CH03\
StreetMatl05.max

2. Click the Standard button and double-click on Raytrace in the Material/Map Browser. The Raytrace material has many more controls and options than other materials do, but you will make only a few adjustments (see Figure 3.23).

3. In the Raytrace Basic Parameters rollout, select the 2-Sided check box. This tells the material to ignore the object's face normals and show this material on both sides of the object's faces. This is important when a material is transparent; otherwise, the inside surface of closed objects would not be visible through the front.

note

Face normals are vectors projecting from each face that determine visibility.

4. Set the Diffuse Color as follows to produce a dark gray: Red to 50, Green to 50, and Blue to 50. At the upper right of the Material Editor, click the checkered Background button to turn on a multicolored background in the sample window to better see the

transparency. Open the Maps rollout, click the None button next to Transparency, and double-click the Falloff map in the Material/Map Browser. By default, the Falloff map applies color based on the face normal's angles to the viewing direction. That means if an object's face normals are perpendicular to the viewer's line of sight, one color is applied. If the face normal is parallel to the viewer, the other color is applied. The effect is obvious on the sample sphere. The center is opaque (black) and the edges are transparent (white), as shown in Figure 3.24.

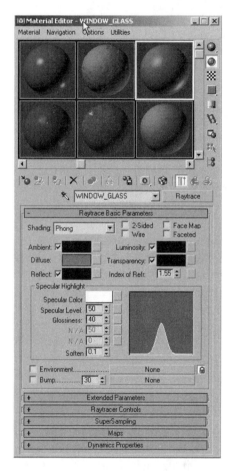

FIGURE 3.23   *The options in the Raytrace Basic Parameters rollout.*

5. In the Falloff Parameters rollout, you can reverse the effect by dragging and dropping one color swatch onto the other and choosing Swap in the dialog box. The center becomes transparent and the edges opaque. On flat windows,

this setting creates a transparent effect when the viewer looks straight on, but opaque when viewed at a sharp angle. Use the Material/Map Navigator to return to the material's top level.

6. In the Maps rollout, drag and drop the Falloff map from the Transparency slot to the Reflect slot, and then select Copy and click OK in the Copy (Instance) Map dialog box. Click on Falloff in the Reflect slot to drop to the map level or use the Material/Map Navigator. Swap black and white back. The windows will now reflect more at a steep viewing angle than when looking straight at them (see Figure 3.25). Add this material to your material library.

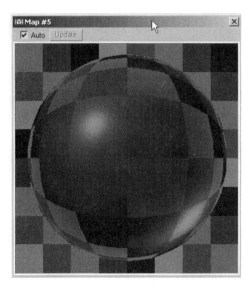

FIGURE 3.24
A Falloff map in the Transparency slot of a Raytrace material causes the center of the sample sphere to be opaque and the edges transparent.

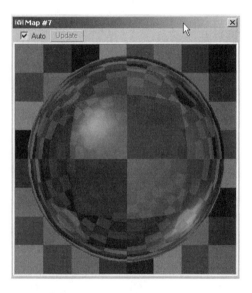

FIGURE 3.25
A Falloff map in the Reflect slot with black in the Front color and white in the Side color will be more reflective at a steep viewing angle.

7. Close the Material Editor and save the file; it should already be called StreetMatl06.max.

You have learned the fundamentals of the Raytrace material type and how to use Falloff maps to affect material attributes based on face normals and viewing angles. The combination is powerful for many transparent or shiny materials, such as glass and paint.

Building a Multi/Sub-Object Material from Existing Materials

In the next exercise, you edit the existing Multi/Sub-Object material applied to the houses to use the materials you have created in previous exercises. The House02 material is just a stand-in material that was created with bright colors to test the Material ID assignments. Many times, it is easier to test as you build, and you'll see that updating the stand-in material for the finished materials is easy.

Exercise 3.7: Taking Advantage of Existing Materials to Build New Multi/Sub-Object Materials

1. Open StreetMatl06.max, and save it as `StreetMatl07.max`. Open the Material Editor, right-click on any sample window, and choose 5 × 3 Sample Windows in the shortcut menu (see Figure 3.26). This allows you to see all materials, including the glass. Activate the House02 Multi/Sub-Object material in the upper left.

On the CD

exercises\CH03\
StreetMatl06.max

2. Drag and drop from the sample windows onto the appropriate Sub-Material buttons in the House02 material, and select Instance so that the materials stay synchronized with each other. These are the assignments (also see Figure 3.27):

   - PAINT_RED to ID 6
   - STUCCO_MOSSY to ID 3
   - WINDOW_GLASS to ID 7
   - WOOD_DOOR to ID 8
   - PAINT_GLOSSY to ID 2
   - STUCCO_BRICK to ID 5

3. This leaves ID 1 and ID 4 with the stand-in material. You have not created the roof and timber materials, but you will get the materials from the library and drop them into the appropriate slot. Click the Get Material button, and select Mtl Library in the Browse From section. Click the Open button in the File section, and open the TimberSlate.mat file noted next to the CD icon. It contains two materials: HEWN_TIMBER and SHINGLE_SLATE.

On the CD

exercises\CH03\
TimberSlate.mat

4. Drag HEWN_TIMBER from the Material/Map Browser to ID 4 and SHINGLE_SLATE to ID 1.

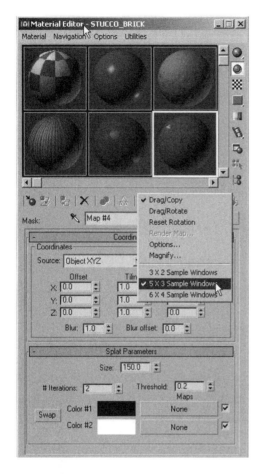

FIGURE 3.27
Creating Instance clones of individual materials within a Multi/Sub-Object material enables you to apply the materials to a single object in the scene.

FIGURE 3.26
The 5 × 3 Sample Windows option enables you to see all the materials.

5. Close all windows and dialog boxes, and save the file. It should be called StreetMatl07.max.

You have learned two methods of using existing materials to construct new materials. First you dragged and dropped directly from the sample windows into the new material, and then you used the Material/Map Browser to open a new Material Library file and drag and drop from there. It is important to manage your materials to avoid reinventing the wheel with each project.

Assigning Materials and Mapping Coordinates

The material you just constructed is not assigned to any objects in the scene yet. In this exercise, you select all the buildings and assign the House02 material to them.

Some of the maps you used in the materials were set to use Object XYZ mapping coordinates. This means the patterns are generated from the center of the object outward to the surface, and the size is adjusted within the map type—for example, the Size setting for the Smoke map.

For other maps, you switched to Explicit Map Channel, but there are no corresponding Explicit Map Channels on the objects. You will apply a UVW Map modifier to the buildings and adjust it to set mapping repeat sizes for maps such as the bricks and the roof shingles.

Exercise 3.8: Object Material Assignments and Mapping Coordinates

Application

1. Open StreetMatl07.max, and save it as StreetMatl08.max. Click the Select button, press **h**, and highlight all the houses and the chapel in the Select Objects dialog box (see Figure 3.28). Click the Select button in the dialog box to select them. On the main toolbar, enter buildings in the Named Selections field and press Enter (see Figure 3.29). This makes it easier to select the buildings as a group again later if you need to.

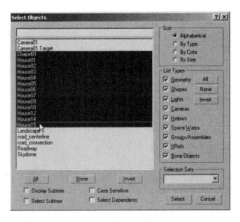

FIGURE 3.28 *Select all buildings by name in the Select Objects dialog box.*

FIGURE 3.29   *Name your selection set to make it easier to select this group of buildings in the future.*

2. Open the Material Editor and make sure House02 is the active sample window. Click the Assign Material to Selection button. In the Assigning Material dialog box, make sure the Replace It radio button is selected (see Figure 3.30), and click OK. This choice replaces the stand-in material with the new material of the same name. Close the Material Editor.

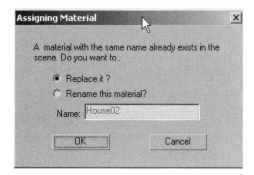

FIGURE 3.30   *The Assigning Material dialog box prevents you from accidentally overwriting same-named materials in your scene. In this case, you're choosing to replace it.*

3. The buildings in your Camera01 viewport will turn mostly gray. Activate the Camera01 viewport and click the Quick Render button, the last teapot button on the main toolbar. You will see a dialog box warning that the buildings all have missing mapping coordinates (see Figure 3.31). Click the Cancel button.

4. Activate the Top viewport, press **Alt+w** to maximize the viewport, and use Zoom Extents All Selected to fill the viewport with the selected buildings. Press **h** and double-click House01 in the list to select it.

5. In the Modify panel, Modifier List, click the UVW Map modifier to apply it to House01. Think of this modifier as a projector for your maps. It is set to Planar Mapping by default, which mean the map is projected in a plane, but in two directions. If you zoom in on House01 in the Top viewport, you will see an orange mapping gizmo that fits the extents of House01.

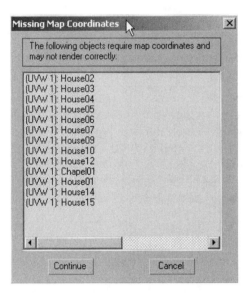

The Missing Map Coordinates dialog box opens when you try to render a scene using materials without the proper UVW mapping coordinates in place.

6. The maps that need coordinates are applied to the sides, front, back, and top of the object, so the Planar setting would make the maps streak on the sides if projected from the top. In the Modify panel, Parameters rollout, select the Box radio button in the Mapping section. Enter 2'0" in the Length, Width, and Height fields (see Figure 3.32).

7. You need to apply the UVW Map to the other buildings, but you can use a shortcut tool to acquire the settings from another UVW Map modifier. Press **h** and double-click House02 in the Select Objects dialog box. In the Modify panel, Modifier List, double-click UVW Map. In the Parameters rollout, click the Acquire button at the lower right. Press **h** and double-click House01 in the Pick Objects dialog box. In the Acquire UVW Mapping dialog box (see Figure 3.33), make sure the Acquire Relative radio button is selected, and click OK. This acquires the setting from House01 to House02 and sets it in a relative position— that is, centered.

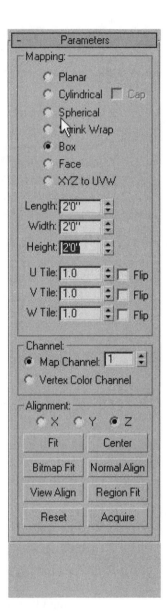

FIGURE 3.32
The Box mapping option projects the map in six directions: up, down, left, right, front, and back.

8. Repeat step 7 for all other buildings, including Chapel01. Render the Camera01 viewport. The buildings should all have appropriate materials on the appropriate surfaces with correct sizing (see Figure 3.34).

9. Close all windows and dialog boxes, and save the file. It should already be called StreetMatl08.max.

For materials with maps to render properly, the object and maps must have mapping coordinates assigned. For many of the procedural maps, such as Smoke and Noise, you used Object XYZ mapping and resized them to fit.

For the Bricks map, you applied a specific UVW Map modifier associated with Map Channel 1 to size one repetition of the map according to real-world sizes. If you analyze the roof shingle material, you will see that it is simply the Bricks map with a different number of bricks in one repetition than the bricks on the walls.

tip

If you analyze a map and determine how much coverage one repetition of the map would cover, you can use that information to accurately size your map. For example, the Bricks map is made of three bricks horizontally by eight bricks vertically. If a standard brick is 8" wide by 3" thick, you use the formula 8×3=24 and 3×8=24, or 2 feet by 2 feet. Because Box mapping has a third dimension, you enter 2 feet in that field as well.

note

Note in the Parameters rollout that the UVW Map modifier is set to work on Map Channel 1. This corresponds to the settings in the Material Editor. You can have as many as 99 different map channels.

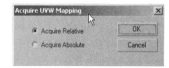

FIGURE 3.33
Using the Acquire button as a shortcut method for applying the UVW map.

FIGURE 3.34 *Notice that the building at the left side closest to you has brick showing through the stucco—the result of the Blend material with the Noise mask.*

Roadway Material and Loft Objects

In Chapter 2, you learned while lofting the Roadway object that one of the benefits of lofting over other modeling techniques is that it gives you some options for control of materials and maps that are not found in other types of modeling.

In the next exercise, you assign a Multi/Sub-Object material to the Roadway object, assign the materials at the Segment sub-object level of the road_crossection 2D shape, and then adjust the loft object to control the size of the maps. This method offers a simple solution to mapping materials on complex lofted objects. For example, it would be difficult to select just the faces of the gutter in the Roadway object because of the compound curves as it winds up over the hill.

Exercise 3.9: Lofted Objects, Mapping, and Material Assignments

1. Open StreetMatl08.max, and save it as
   StreetMatl09.max. Open the Material Editor. You will merge materials from a library on the CD-ROM to the current library. Click the Get Material button, and select Matl Library in the Browse From section. Click the Open button in the File section, and open the StreetScene.mat noted next to the CD icon. It contains PAINT_RED and House02.

On the CD

exercises\CH03\
StreetMatl08.max

2. From the Material Editor, drag the House02 sample window into the Material/Map Browser. It contains all the other materials in your scene to this point. In the Material/Map Browser, click the Merge button in the File section, and double-click

On the CD

exercises\CH03\
StreetScene.mat

   RoadSky.mat in the list. In the Merge - StreetScene.mat dialog box, click the All button to highlight Roadway and Sky (see Figure 3.34), and click OK. The materials are merged into the current library.

3. Drag Roadway and Sky from the Material/Map Browser list to unused sample windows in the Material Editor to make them available for assignment or editing.

4. In the Material Editor, select and activate the Roadway sample window and drag and drop it onto the Roadway object in the Camera01 viewport. The roadway will turn bright blue.

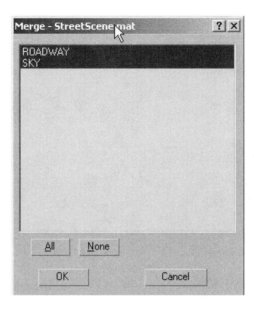

FIGURE 3.35   *Merging the Roadway and Sky materials into the current library.*

5. Select Roadway in the scene, and in the Modifier panel, expand the Surface Parameters rollout. Select Apply Mapping in the Mapping section and Use Shape IDs in the Materials section. These settings tell the loft object to assign materials based on the Material IDs assigned to the road's 2D shape. Obviously, the shape's segments all have Material ID 1 corresponding to the red diffuse color.

6. Right-click in the Top viewport to activate it, click the Select button, and press **h**. Double-click road_crossection in the list. Click the Zoom Extents Selected button to fill the Top viewport with the shape.

7. In the Modify panel, choose the Segment sub-object level, and in the Top viewport, select the six segments that make up the gutter sides and bottom (see Figure 3.36). In the Modify panel, Surface Properties rollout, change the Material IDs of the selected segments to 2. The gutters will become blue in the Camera01 viewport.

8. In the Top viewport, select the two horizontal segments of the sidewalk's top surface and change the Material ID to 3 in the Modify panel, Surface Properties rollout. Exit sub-object mode in the Modify panel and quick render the Camera01 viewport. The road, gutters, and sidewalks now have materials, but the map size is much too large, as can be seen on the road surface (see Figure 3.37).

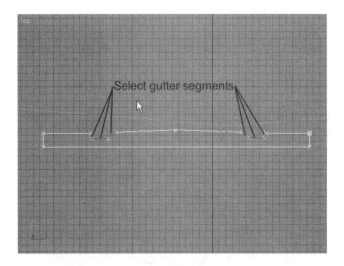

FIGURE 3.36 *Selecting the gutter segments in road_crossection.*

FIGURE 3.37 *Materials are assigned correctly, but the map size is much too large, especially on the road surface.*

9. Select Roadway in the scene. In the Modify panel, expand the Surface Parameters rollout. In the Mapping section, enter 50 in Length Repeat and 12 in Width Repeat (see Figure 3.38). This tells the map how often to repeat along and across the loft object. Render the scene, and you will see that the bricks are sized better.

10. Close all windows and dialog boxes, and save the file. It should already be called StreetMatl09.max.

   You have learned how to take advantage of material assignments at the Segment sub-object level of lofted objects and to use the built-in mapping coordinates to adjust the map's size and retain its ability to follow the curvature of the lofted object.

Sky Materials and Mapping

In the next exercise, you apply a material made from a Gradient Ramp map in the Diffuse Color slot. By default, the Gradient Ramp colors would map over the entire dome, but you will make some adjustments at the map level that limit the area covered to just the visible portion of the sky hemisphere at the end of your street. This compresses the map into a small area to give the illusion of clouds converging toward the horizon.

Exercise 3.10: A Sky Map and Map Tiling

1. Open StreetMatl09.max, and save it as StreetMatl10.max. Open the Material Editor and drag and drop the SKY material sample window onto the Skydome object in the scene.

2. Select Skydome in the scene, and in the Modify panel, Modifier List, choose the UVW Map modifier. In the Parameters rollout, select the Spherical check box. This maps the Gradient Ramp map in SKY from the center of the spherical gizmo outward to the surface.

> **tip**
>
> The other major advantage of lofted objects is that, in this case, the bricks bend with the road. Mapping to a complex object is difficult with other modeling techniques.

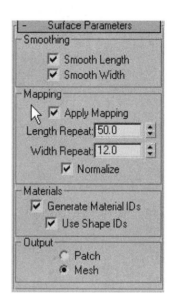

FIGURE 3.38
Changing the repeat for Roadway's material mapping.

On the CD

exercises\CH03\
StreetMatl09.max

3. In the Modify panel, Stack view, expand UVW Mapping and choose the Gizmo sub-object level. Click the Select and Move button, and in the Front viewport, move the spherical gizmo down so that the center is at the bottom of the hemisphere (see Figure 3.39). Exit Gizmo sub-object mode. You should be able to see a dark-to-light transition line to the right of the chapel at the top of the hill. The Gradient Ramp map needs to be adjusted to fit the view better.

tip

In the Material Editor, Gradient Ramp map level, the Show Map in Viewport option is active, so the map is visible on the Skydome object in Camera01 viewport. None of the other maps has this feature turned on.

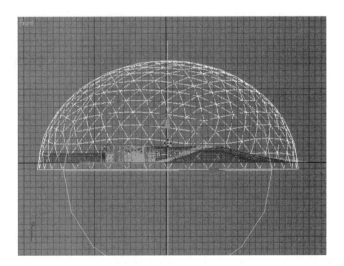

FIGURE 3.39   *Move the gizmo center to the bottom of the Skydome object in the Front viewport.*

4. In the Material Editor, Gradient Ramp map level, Coordinates rollout, you will see that the Tiling check boxes are cleared to keep the map from repeating on the Skydome object. The Tiling setting for U is 3.0 to make the pattern smaller vertically. The Offset setting for U is at 0.25 to move the map up into the viewport (see Figure 3.40). Change this setting to 0.23 and watch the map

tip

In this example, you are adjusting the Offset setting for U to move the map up or down in the scene. The map itself has been rotated 90 degrees, so the horizontal adjustment is actually affecting the vertical position.

move downward in the Camera01 viewport, eliminating the dark-to-light transition line near the horizon. You can now adjust this map easily to fit your view. The exact number will be different, depending on how far you moved the gizmo below the horizon.

5. Quick render the Camera01 viewport, and you will see a sky that ramps from dark blue at the top to a gray haze at the horizon. This convergence heightens the feeling of distance in the scene (see Figure 3.41).

6. Close all windows, and dialog boxes and save the file. It should already be called StreetMatl10.max.

FIGURE 3.40

Changing the Offset setting for U moves the map downward on the hemisphere to hide the dark-to-light line below the horizon.

In this exercise, you have learned to apply and adjust spherical mapping coordinates, and then adjust the Tiling settings of the map to fine-tune its position in the scene.

FIGURE 3.41   *Render the Camera01 viewport to see the Gradient Ramp sky at the end of the road.*

Summary

Maps and mapping coordinates are an essential part of creating a 3ds max 5 scene—in many respects, more important than modeling in creating an illusion that will convince and entertain the viewer. Some of the concepts you learned include the following:

- **Simulated geometry**   You learned that Bump maps create the illusion of bumps without the need for a more complex surface. This chapter introduced you to two simple concepts: object color and, much more important, specular highlights.

- **Adding realism**   You learned that just adding a Noise map to the Glossiness slot can enhance the look of a material by reducing the "too-perfect" quality. Subtle adjustments like that go a long way toward making your materials more believable.

- **Transparency and reflections**   You have learned the fundamentals of the Raytrace material type and how to use Falloff maps to affect material attributes based on face normals and viewing angles. The combination is powerful for many transparent or shiny materials, such as glass and paint.

- **Masking principles**   You have learned to create a complex material from two other materials and to reveal one through the other with a Mask map (in this chapter, the Splat map).

- **Reusing what you have created**   You have learned two methods of using existing materials to construct new materials: dragging and dropping directly from the sample windows into the new material, and using the Material/Map Browser to open a new material library file and drag and drop from there. Managing your materials efficiently keeps you from reinventing the wheel with each project.

- **Mapping coordinates**   You learned to apply and adjust Spherical mapping coordinates, and then adjust the Tiling settings of the map itself to fine-tune its position in the scene. You have learned how to take advantage of material assignments at the Segment sub-object level of lofted objects and to use the built-in mapping coordinates to adjust the size and retain the ability of the map to follow the curvature of the lofted object.

First learn to visualize the world around you, and then start to reproduce it in 3ds max 5. Start slowly with simple materials and setting combinations, and then build your materials, layer upon layer, as you learn how the material attributes react to each other and to the light in the scene.

CHAPTER 4

Exterior Lighting: Standard and Advanced Methods

In This Chapter

Lighting a scene in 3ds max 5 can be approached from two different directions—standard lighting, with no bounced light calculations, or radiosity solutions, which calculate the light bounced from surface to surface. This chapter's exercises lead you through the fundamentals of both lighting methods so that you can compare the techniques to help decide which method will work best for you in different situations. There are no clear rules to help you decide; each case must be evaluated on its own merits, factoring in quality and budget concerns.

Starting with the fundamentals and working in small scenes enables you to build on your knowledge and discover the nuances of both approaches to lighting. Above all, have patience with the process. Good results can take time whichever method you choose—standard or radiosity. Among the topics that will be covered are the following:

- **Standard Sunlight system** A system of direct illumination and a special animation controller that calculates the position of the sun in the sky. No bounced light is calculated.

- **Faking bounced light** Learn to add lights that simulate the effect of bounced light from surface to surface.

- **Daylight system** A new process in 3ds max 5 that uses direct illumination and calculates bounced light, both from surfaces in the model and from a skylight component that simulates light bounced in the atmosphere.

- **Modeling concerns**   The bounced light, or radiosity solution, is stored in mesh objects in the scene. You will learn to adjust the size of that mesh to balance quality and speed.

- **Fine-tuning the process**   Learn some refinement and exposure controls that enable you to fine-tune the basic radiosity calculations.

Key Terms

Angle of incidence   The angle of light to a surface. The steeper the light angle to the surface, the more light on the surface. For example, 90 degrees is full light, and 0 degrees is no light.

Attenuation   The natural diminishing of light intensity away from the light source.

Exposure Control   A light setting that acts like a camera's aperture controls to reduce the amount of bright sunlight reaching the film.

Photometric lights   Lights based on physics principles to mimic real lights more accurately. They have brightness settings in real units and respect the laws of physics for attenuation.

Radiosity   The calculation of bounced light between surfaces to include illumination and transfer of color from one surface to another (color bleeding). The extra light from the surface interaction adds "body" to your lighting.

Radiosity meshing   The process of adding vertices and faces to mesh objects. Radiosity effects are stored in the mesh. The denser the mesh, the more accurate the radiosity solution, but the slower the calculation.

Hotkeys and Keyboard Shortcuts

9   Open the Advanced Lighting dialog box

m   Open the Material Editor

Basic Lighting Concepts

Lighting a 3ds max scene is a process that has always been perhaps 30% technical and 70% art. Essentially, the approach was painting the scene with light rather than lighting the scene as a lighting engineer would. 3ds max 5 changes that approach somewhat with the introduction of photometric lights and new radiosity rendering engines. There are now three approaches to take when lighting your scenes:

caution

Although standard lights and Sunlight can be used with Light Tracer rendering, the bounced light is not calculated, but render times will be much longer.

- **Standard lights with Scanline rendering**   This is the old "painting with light" method, in which the placement of lights bears little resemblance to the real world. The primary advantage of standard lighting techniques is that render times are very fast compared to Radiosity and Light Tracer, although setup time can be longer. Exterior lighting with the Scanline renderer is accomplished with the Sunlight system.

- **Photometric lights with Radiosity renderer**   In this new approach, lighting is based on real-world physics of attenuation and bounced light. Lighting is positioned in the scene as it would be in a real setting, and the software calculates the interaction of light with surfaces. Exterior scenes with the Radiosity renderer use the Daylight system.

- **Skylight with Light Tracer rendering**   Skylight is not so much a source of direct light as a flooding of the scene with light and calculating rays emitted from pixels and bouncing from nearby surfaces. It tends to be faster than the Radiosity renderer, but slower than the Scanline renderer, and is intended for animation and outdoor scenes. Exterior scenes with the Light Tracer renderer can use the Standard Skylight or Daylight system.

In this chapter, you will learn two methods of lighting an exterior scene—one with a standard lighting system called Sunlight and another using the new Daylight system. The Sunlight system uses a standard Direct light that casts light in a cylinder from the light source and is rendered by using the Scanline renderer. The default Daylight system uses a combined IES Sun direct illumination source and an IES Sky light type that fills the scene with parallel rays of direct illumination and a flood of sky light that simulates light bounced in the atmosphere. Daylight is rendered with the Radiosity renderer.

note

IES Sun and IES Sky are based on actual physics parameters.

Each system has its advantages, and you should learn the fundamentals of both so that you can make an intelligent choice when the time comes in a production environment. Here is a quick comparison of the two systems:

- **Sunlight system**   Offers fast render times. It can project image maps to simulate cloud shadows. The Sunlight system requires few parameter settings.

- **Daylight system**   Can stand alone and does not require fill lights to simulate light bounced from surfaces. The lighting is more convincing to viewers, and it has more shadow options. Skylight can also be set to use the color information from images to light scenes.

- **Skylight**   Comes in a variety of forms. Standard Skylight is used with the Light Tracer renderer. Photometric IES Sky is used with the Radiosity renderer as a standalone source or as a component of the Daylight system.

Sunlight System with Exterior Scenes

The Sunlight system is the tried-and-true method of lighting an exterior scene with a Direct light source and a special animation controller that positions the sun according to actual time/date/location data that you enter. This information enables accurate shadow studies over time.

note   Both the Sunlight and Daylight systems use the same animation controller to position the sun in the sky.

In the Sunlight system, the Direct light type casts light in a cylindrical form from the light source to the light target to create parallel rays for more accurate shadow generation. Because the Direct light does not bounce off surfaces to light other surfaces, you need to add lights to the scene to simulate reflected light. You will use non-shadow-casting Omni lights to simulate the light that would typically be scattered through the atmosphere and bounce off adjacent surfaces in the real world.

warning   Omni lights are standard point lights that are actually composed of six standard spotlights facing top, bottom, left, right, front, and back. A special algorithm blends the edges of the spotlight cone intersections. The result is that shadow-casting Omni lights have six times the memory overhead of a single spot. Use them judiciously. A good use might be for open flame sources or bare bulb fixtures.

Although it takes more time to set up a scene with the Sunlight system and Omni lights, the advantages in render speed are usually significant.

Adding a Sunlight System

In this exercise, you add a Sunlight system to the street scene from Chapter 3, "Applying Materials and Maps for a Convincing Outdoor Scene," for the main light source. You then adjust it for time, date, and location and change shadow parameters for rendering efficiency.

Exercise 4.1: Sunlight System for an Exterior Scene

1. Open the Sunlight01.max file noted next to the CD icon. Choose File, Save As from the menu, and select a subdirectory. Click the + button to the left of the Save button to increment the filename to Sunlight02.max and save it to your hard drive.

2. Right-click in the Camera01 viewport to make sure it is active, and click the Quick Render button at the far right of the main toolbar. The Virtual Frame Buffer (VFB) opens, showing a very flat-looking street scene. Close the VFB.

3. Choose Rendering, RAM Player from the menu. Click the Open Last Rendered Image in Channel A button in the RAM Player. Click OK in the RAM Player Configuration dialog box to accept the default settings. This stores the image in RAM and shows it in the RAM Player (see Figure 4.1) so that you can compare changes you make later in the exercise. Minimize the RAM Player; do not close it.

FIGURE 4.1   *The RAM Player showing the rendered street scene with default lighting.*

4. Right-click in the Top viewport to activate it. In the Create panel, Systems category, click the Sunlight button in the Object Type rollout (see Figure 4.2). This enables you to create a Sunlight system with a light source and a positional animation controller based on time and date for a given location.

5. Click and drag slightly in the center of the Landscape object in the Top viewport until you see a gray compass rose. Release the left mouse button, and move your mouse up until the Sun01 object is beyond the Landscape object. Click to set the Sun01 position (see Figure 4.3).

note

The actual size of the compass rose is not important; its center is the important factor in determining where the sun points. Note that the gray compass rose might be difficult to see in the viewports.

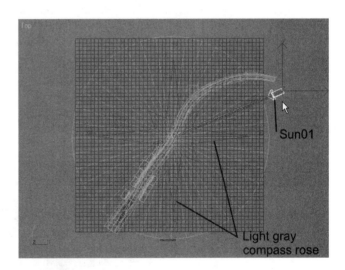

FIGURE 4.2
Creating a Sunlight system with parameters for setting the date, time, and world location for the sun's position.

FIGURE 4.3
The light-gray compass rose in the center of the landscape and the Sun01 object just outside the landscape. The up direction in the viewport represents north.

6. Click the Motion panel button (looks like a wheel). In the Motion panel (see Figure 4.4), the parameters are set to the date and time of your computer clock. Set the time as follows: 11 for Hours, 0 for Mins., 0 for Secs., 6 for Month, 21 for Day, 2002 for Year, and –8 for Time Zone. This sets the sun for the first day of summer at 11 a.m. in the year 2002 for San Francisco. Make sure the Daylight Saving Time check box is selected in the Control Parameters rollout.

7. Right-click in the Camera01 viewport and click the Quick Render button. Close the VFB. Maximize the RAM Player and click the Open Last Rendered Image in Channel B button. You can now pick the images and scrub back and forth to compare Channels A and B (see Figure 4.5). Minimize the RAM Player.

note

The position of your Sun01 will be different from the illustration, depending on the time and date set on your computer when you do the exercise.

tip

Keep Sun01 near the outer edge of objects in the scene. If the light is too far from the objects, shadow casting can become a problem caused by mathematical inaccuracies of large or small numbers in 3ds max 5.

FIGURE 4.4
Use the Motion panel, Control Parameters rollout, to change date, time, and location settings for your Sun01 object.

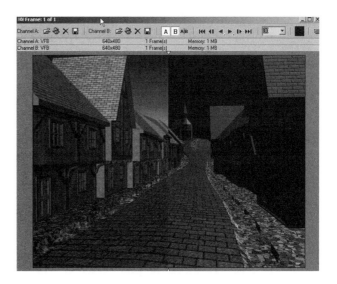

FIGURE 4.5
Comparing renderings in the RAM Player.

note Note that you are in the Motion panel, not the Modify panel. This is where animation parameters can be adjusted and the position of the Sun01 object is set by an animation controller.

tip The distance of standard lights from a surface does not affect the brightness on the surface. The important factor is the *angle of incidence* to the surface. The light is brightest on the roofs to the left that are nearly perpendicular to the sun. There is no light on the right vertical walls or on the skydome, causing them to render black. No bounced light is calculated with standard lights and the Scanline renderer.

warning The buildings are not casting shadows, even though shadow casting is turned on for the Sunlight system by default. This is because of bogus settings in the default Sunlight system that you must change before it will work correctly. This is a source of much frustration for new users who quickly abandon the Sunlight system.

tip The skydome not casting shadows is caused by something else entirely. In Chapter 2, "Modeling: A Medieval Street Scene," you applied a Normal modifier to flip the face normals to the inside of the hemisphere. The backside of the faces is invisible to the viewer and to any lights hitting the backsides.

8. You might notice that when Sun01's blue cylinders (which represent the limit of light) are selected in the viewport, they are very narrow. To fix this problem, first make sure Sun01 is selected. In the Modify panel, Directional Parameters rollout, the Overshoot check box is selected and the Falloff/Field setting is 3'9". Clear the Overshoot check box. Enter 350 in the Hotspot/Beam field and press Enter to cover the entire scene with Sun01's light cylinder. The Falloff/Field radius will automatically remain 2 degrees larger in diameter. Render the Camera01 viewport and open the last rendered image in Channel A of the RAM Player. The amount of light on the surfaces hasn't changed, but the buildings are now casting shadows (see Figure 4.6).

tip Shadows are cast only within the areas described by the Falloff/Field radius of a standard Direct light. The Overshoot option causes the Direct light to act as a Direct *and* a non-shadow-casting Omni light, lighting the scene but casting shadows only on a spot within the Falloff/Field radius.

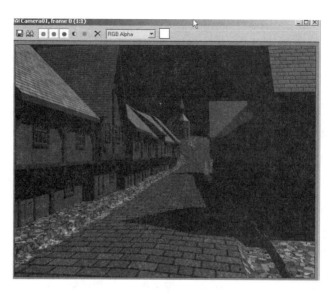

FIGURE 4.6   *After adjusting settings in the Modify panel, Directional Parameters rollout, the buildings cast shadows, as shown in this rendered view.*

The Overshoot option can be used effectively in very large scenes, such as a cityscape, where you need light outside the center of the viewer's focus, but you need to speed rendering by disabling shadow-casting outside the core area.

9. In the Modify panel, Ray Traced Shadow Params rollout, change the Max Quadtree Depth field from 7 to 10. In typical scenes, this setting often produces significant increases in raytraced shadow calculation speed. On a dual PIII 650MHz machine, the times were 23 seconds versus 45 seconds after the change.

10. Close the RAM Player. Click OK in the Exit RAM Player dialog box. Save the file; it should already be called Sunlight02.max.

You have added a Sunlight system to the street scene to replace the default lighting. Upon rendering, no shadows were cast by Sun01, but you learned to disable the Overshoot option and adjust the Falloff/Field radius to cover the entire scene. Shadows are calculated only within the cylinder described by the Falloff/Field radius.

You also have learned that when a light uses ray-traced shadows, increasing the Max Quadtree Depth field to 10 (its highest setting) can speed the rendering. In this case, renderings went from 45 seconds to 23 seconds with no change in quality.

Simulating Bounced Light in a Scene with Standard Lights

Whole areas of your scene are completely dark, either because the light does not hit the surfaces or hits at an angle of incidence too steep to light the surface sufficiently. To fix this problem, you will learn a process called *Fakosity* (fake radiosity), a term coined by Fermi Bertran of Barcelona in the VIZ support forum to describe the technique.

In this exercise, you add and adjust several Omni lights to fill the dark areas; this simulates light bounced from nearby surfaces or scattered in the atmosphere. You also learn the important steps of excluding or including certain objects from the influence of lights.

Exercise 4.2: Adding Lights to Fake Bounced Lighting

1. Open the Sunlight02.max file noted next to the CD icon, and save it as `Sunlight03.max`. Render the Camera01 viewport. The sky is black, as are the buildings on the right. To fix this problem, you will add an Omni light to the left to fill in the lighting around the buildings. This light will simulate the sunlight bouncing from the road and buildings.

On the CD

exercises\CH04\
Sunlight02.max

2. Right-click in the Top viewport to activate it. In the Create panel, Lights category, click the Omni button (see Figure 4.7) in the Object Type rollout. Click in the Top viewport to the left of the Landscape object, so that the light is perpendicular to the street and buildings (see Figure 4.8).

3. The Omni light adds too much light to the buildings on the right side of the street because the angle of incidence is nearly 90 degrees and the light is the same value as the sun. In the Modify panel, Intensity/Color/Attenuation rollout, enter 0.3 in the Multiplier field and press Enter. Quick render the Camera01 viewport, close the VFB, and open the image in Channel A of RAM Player. After checking the rendering, minimize the RAM Player.

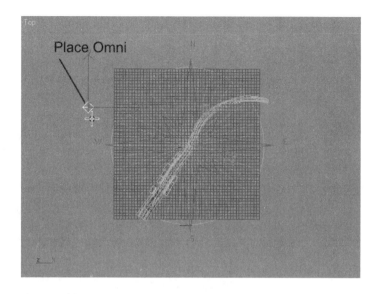

Place Omni

FIGURE 4.8
In the Top viewport, place the Omni light left of Landscape and per-pendicular to the street and buildings as fill lighting.

FIGURE 4.7
Adding an Omni light from the Object Type rollout.

4. The sky is still too dark, however. In the Create panel, Lights category, click the Omni button. In the Top viewport, place this new Omni light (Omni02) in the center of the Skydome object. In the Modify panel, Intensity/Color/Attenuation rollout, set the Multiplier field back to 1.0. This setting lightens the inside of the Skydome object, but adds some unwanted light to the scene. (see Figure 4.9).

5. In the Modify panel, General Parameters rollout, click the Exclude button. In the Exclude/Include dialog box, select Skydome in the left column and click the >> button to send it to the right column. Select the Include radio button at the upper right of the dialog box (see Figure 4.10), and click OK. This tells Omni02 to light only the Skydome and ignore everything else in the scene.

tip

Although you could have excluded all objects *but* Skydome from Omni02 for the same effect, you would have to remember to exclude every new object you create in the scene. The Modify panel button now reads Include to indicate the mode the light is using. This method makes management a little easier.

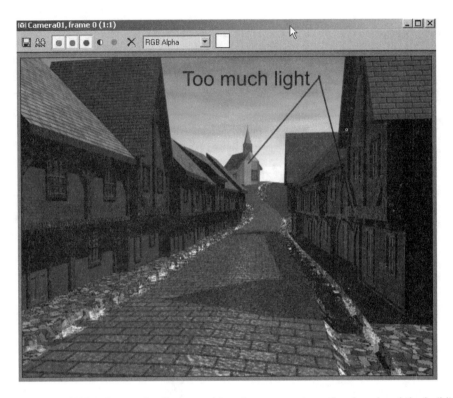

FIGURE 4.9   *The light is fine on the Skydome object, but too much on the chapel and the buildings on the right.*

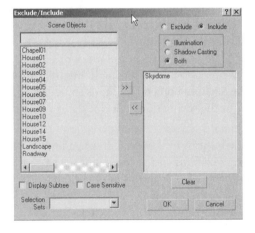

FIGURE 4.10   *Use the Exclude/Include dialog box to specify which objects the Omni02 light should include.*

6. Select Sun01 in the scene, and in the Modify panel, Intensity/Color/Attenuation rollout, set the Multiplier field to 1.75. Render the Camera01 viewport and open the last rendered image in Channel B of the RAM Player you minimized earlier. The sun is now bright, as it should be for late morning, and the balance of direct light to "bounced" light is pleasing when compared to the sunlight alone in Channel A.

7. In the Modify panel, General Parameters rollout, click the Exclude button for Sun01 and exclude Skydome from its effects by moving Skydome from the left column to the right column and leaving the Exclude radio button selected. You would never want the Sun01 light to actually light the sky, especially when the sun is at low angles.

8. Close the VFB and the RAM Player and save the file. It should already be called Sunlight03.max.

You have learned the fundamental steps of placing a Sunlight system in a scene and adjusting for a particular time, date, and location. You then added an Omni light to simulate bounced light from the buildings on the left and the street onto the buildings on the right. You also added an Omni light that lit only the Skydome object with evenly distributed bright light.

> **tip**
>
> For an early morning or late afternoon sun position, you would need another Omni light with a low Multiplier setting high above the landscape to compensate for the sun's low angle of incidence to the landscape.

You could experiment with this scene, perhaps adding small amounts of color to the lights to more accurately simulate real conditions. The sun could have a slight yellow color, and the Omni fill light for the buildings might have a slight orange cast to simulate color bounced from the road and buildings.

You might even try some radical color changes to create otherworldly effects. Remember, you are painting the scene with light, much as a traditional artist might with color wash techniques and transparent colors that apply a base color, perhaps yellow for a sunlit scene, and then build on the base to add darker areas to the picture.

Daylight System with Exterior Scenes

The Daylight system, an entirely new concept in 3ds max 5, is composed of a Sun and a Skylight. The Sun simulates the direct rays of the sun and the Skylight simulates the light scattered by moisture and particles in the atmosphere. This one lighting system is often enough to achieve good results in exterior lighting.

Daylight systems require the use of a new rendering engine called the Radiosity renderer to calculate the light bouncing from surface to surface. As the light bounces, it picks up color from the materials and transmits the color to neighboring surfaces.

However, because Daylight simulates the sun physically, it is very bright. It might be easiest to think of a rendered image as a photograph. If you used a cheap manual camera with no adjustments, many of your daylight pictures would be overexposed. With a quality camera, you could adjust the aperture of the camera lens to reduce the amount of light hitting the film, thereby getting the optimum amount of exposure in the photograph. With the 3ds max 5 Daylight system, you will learn to use the Exposure Control feature to strike that same balance. You can adjust overall brightness as well as contrast and midtone values.

The major downside of Radiosity rendering is the time it takes to calculate the light bouncing between surfaces and the amount of reflectivity of surfaces that determine color bleed in that bounced light. Rendering times can be long, and although there are adjustments to optimize the process, the learning curve can be steep. However, you will learn the fundamentals of the process as applied to an exterior scene and make some adjustments to strike a balance between image quality and render times.

Radiosity rendering information gets calculated and stored in the vertices and faces of a new mesh in your scene. This mesh can be generated automatically or manually. Two forms of light information are generated: direct light (the light from the sun that strikes a surface), and indirect light (the light bounced from surface to surface). This new mesh that contains the solution to the radiosity calculations can significantly increase your scene's file size and affect the performance of viewports and rendering alike.

warning   If you have a slow processor and/or limited RAM in your computer, the test renders to see the effects of adjustments could be very long.

You will learn more about advanced lighting in Chapter 11, "Materials and Lighting: The Magic Combination."

Adding a Daylight System

The following exercises use a different exterior scene that renders a bit more quickly than the street scene. It has an old building on a pond in a hilly landscape. There is a skydome that already has an Omni light, which has been configured to include only the skydome, like the one you created in the Sunlight exercise.

In this exercise, you add a Daylight system and set it to June 21, 2002, at 11 a.m. for San Francisco, as in the last exercise. You then learn to use the Advanced Lighting adjustments and Exposure Control settings to balance quality and speed. The exercise walks you through the process the typical user follows to set up lighting, especially those users with max experience in standard lighting before 3ds max 5. Stay with the steps of the exercise and pay attention to the process. The solution will reveal itself in the end.

Exercise 4.3: Daylight System for an Exterior Scene

1. Open the Daylight01.max file noted next to the CD icon, and save it to your hard drive as Daylight02.max. The Camera01 viewport looks almost totally dark because there is only one standard Omni light that includes just the Skydome object.

On the CD

exercises\CH04\
Daylight01.max

caution

All reflections have been disabled at the material level and in the Render dialog box to speed rendering.

2. In the Create panel, Systems category, click the Daylight button in the Object Type rollout (see Figure 4.11). In the Top viewport, click near the center of the landscape and drag slightly to create a compass rose. Release the left mouse button and move the mouse up to move the Daylight01 object outside the skydome, as seen in the Front viewport. Click to set the position (see Figure 4.12).

3. Switch to the Motion panel by clicking the button that looks like a wheel. In the Motion panel, the parameters are set to the date and time of your computer clock. Set the time as follows: 11 for Hours, 0 for Mins., 0 for Secs., 6 for Month, 21 for Day, 2002 for Year, and –8 for Time Zone. This sets the sun for the first day of summer at 11 a.m. in the year 2002 for San Francisco. Make sure the Daylight Saving Time check box is selected in the Control Parameters rollout.

FIGURE 4.11

In the Create panel, Systems category, click the Daylight button.

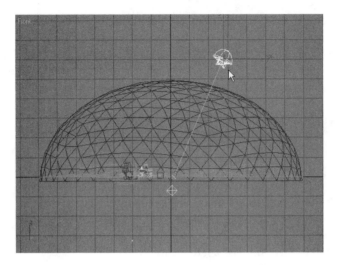

FIGURE 4.12 *Setting the sun's position just outside the skydome.*

note   Unlike the standard Sunlight system, the distance of the light source from the objects is irrelevant because the light is physically based and interacts with scene units.

4. The Scanline renderer does not know how to accurately handle the Daylight system, but a rendering of the scene would show very bright Direct light and soft Sky light. Choose Rendering, Advanced Lighting from the menu or use the **9** keyboard shortcut. In the Advanced Lighting dialog box, click the drop-down arrow next to No Lighting plug-in and select Radiosity in the list (see Figure 4.13). This option calculates the direct and indirect light from the Daylight system's Sun and Sky lights.

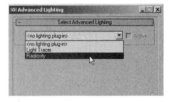

FIGURE 4.13
Selecting the Radiosity option for rendering.

note   A single PIII 1.13GHz with 512MB of RAM takes 3 minutes, 4 seconds to process the solution for this scene. This information can be found in the Statistics rollout of the Advanced Lighting dialog box.

5. In the Radiosity Processing Parameters rollout, click the Start button to begin generating a new mesh with direct and indirect illumination stored in its faces and vertices. The Initial Quality is set to 85%, which is generally the highest setting you need for most scenes. Because the Display Radiosity in Viewport check box is selected, the Camera01 viewport will be very dark with only a few light spots.

6. Right-click in the Camera01 viewport to activate it. Click the Quick Render button. You'll see that the scene is severely overlit, so you need to apply the Exposure Control setting, much as you would with a film camera to compensate for the bright sunlight (see Figure 4.14).

Figure 4.14   *As you can see, the scene looks overlit.*

7. In the Advanced Lighting dialog box, Radiosity Processing Parameters rollout, Interactive Tools section, click the Setup button (see Figure 4.15) to set up exposure control. In the Environment dialog box, Exposure Control rollout, click the drop-down arrow next to No Exposure Control, and select Logarithmic Exposure Control in the list (see Figure 4.16). This option adjusts exposure more in the brighter and darker areas than in the midtone areas. Render the scene; you'll see that it is still bright but has more color.

8. The skydome should not be lit by the sun; it already has its own Omni light. Select Daylight01, and in the Modify panel, Sun Parameters rollout, click the Exclude button (see Figure 4.17) and send Skydome from the left column to the right column to exclude it.

tip   Shadow calculations can be a major part of render times, especially when using raytraced shadows. Always try setting Max Quadtree Depth to 10, and then reduce it if your shadows show artifacts or other problems.

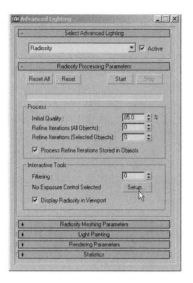

FIGURE 4.15
Click the Setup button to access the Exposure Control settings.

FIGURE 4.16
Select the Logarithmic Exposure Control option.

9. Also the skydome should not be included in the Radiosity processing because in the real world, a sky object does not bounce light back to earth. The skylight component of Daylight01 simulates the bounced light, and the skydome is necessary to show the sky image. In the Front viewport, select Skydome. Right-click on Skydome and choose Properties in the Quad menu. In the Adv. Lighting tab of the Object Properties dialog box, ensure the By Object option is displayed on the button (click By Layer if it's not, to toggle the setting), and select the Exclude from Adv. Lighting Calculations check box. Click OK to close the dialog box (see Figure 4.18).

10. Because this is a daylight exterior scene, you need to select the Exterior Daylight check box in the Logarithmic Exposure Control Parameters rollout of the Environment dialog box. Render the scene, and you'll see that the sky is very dark and the building's lighting is blotchy. The sky is dark because it is excluded from radiosity and has only a very weak standard light that radiosity attenuates

FIGURE 4.17
In the Modify panel, Sun Parameters rollout, click Exclude and exclude the Skydome object from the sun.

(diminishes over distance) to nothing very quickly. You need to boost the Physical Scale setting in the Environment dialog box to match the sun's strength. In the Logarithmic Exposure Control Parameters rollout, enter 95000 in the Physical Scale field to match strength of the sun as seen in the Modify panel, Sun Parameters rollout for Daylight01 (see Figure 4.19). This multiplies the effect of standard lights to match the sun's strength. Render the Camera01 viewport, and you'll see that the sky is brighter.

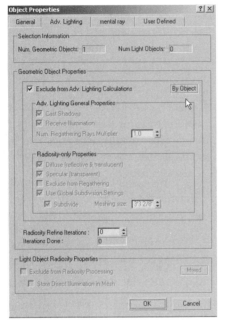

FIGURE 4.18
Use the Adv. Lighting tab in the Properties dialog box to set radiosity properties for individual objects.

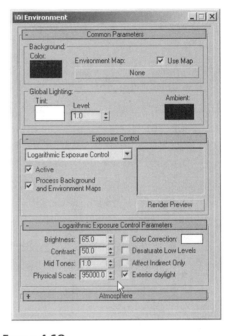

FIGURE 4.19
Entering the Daylight01 intensity value in the Physical Scale field multiplies the strength of the standard Omni light in the scene to match the intensity of the photometric sun.

11. Close all dialog boxes and windows and save the file. It should already be called Daylight02.max.

In this exercise, you have taken an outdoor scene with a skydome and applied a Daylight system. Daylight is made of a direct Sun light and a Skylight component. You learned to assign the Radiosity renderer and set up the Logarithmic Exposure Control option.

tip

The Physical Scale setting also can help adjust raytrace reflections in a radiosity scene. The 95000 value you entered is just a starting point; you might have to adjust from there for better reflection results.

Excluding the skydome from the sunlight was necessary because it must be lit by an Omni light from below to ensure even illumination. You had to use the Exterior Daylight option and increase the Physical Scale setting to 95000 to match the strength of the sun with standard lights.

You still don't have a good rendering, but these steps are vital preparation for adjusting the mesh later for more accuracy.

Adjusting the Mesh for Radiosity Lighting

Remember that all radiosity calculations are stored in vertices and faces of the mesh. With efficient modeling methods, you seldom have vertices of one object corresponding with vertices on an adjacent object to transfer and store the radiosity effects correctly.

For example, if you have two boxes—one a small column object sitting in the middle of a large floor object—there are no vertices in the floor that match up with the column's vertices, and the calculations are interpolated over a large area. If you add meshing to the floor to create a vertex every three feet, there will be new vertices close to the column, making the calculations more localized.

You must generate new meshes that have a more regular layout of vertices and faces to better store the radiosity solution. This can be done in four ways:

- Model so that you specifically place vertices at key points.
- Apply Global Meshing parameters to all objects in the scene.
- Change the properties of each individual object in the Properties dialog box for a specific meshing subdivision.
- Apply Subdivide modifiers to mesh objects.

tip After some testing, it appears that the easiest and most efficient method of meshing is to select objects and change their meshing properties. Global meshing is the fastest but least efficient method, and the others fall somewhere in between.

warning Global meshing applied to this scene would take a very long time because of the landscape's size and offer little benefit.

In this exercise, you use the Properties meshing option to adjust the meshing of some objects in the scene for more accurate radiosity calculations.

Exercise 4.4: Meshing Parameters for Radiosity

1. Open the Daylight02.max file, and save it as `Daylight03.max`. Choose Rendering, Advanced Lighting from the menu or press **9**. In the Advanced Lighting dialog box, Radiosity Processing Parameters rollout, click Reset All, and then click Start to ensure the processing is up to date. Render the Camera01 viewport. Open the RAM Player and click the Open Last Rendered Image in Channel A button. After viewing the rendering, minimize the RAM Player.

On the CD

exercises\CH04\
Daylight02.max

2. On the main toolbar, click on the Named Selection field and choose BREWERY in the list. This selects all objects associated with that building. In the Camera01 viewport, right-click on any of the selected buildings, and choose Properties in the Quad menu. In the Adv. Lighting tab, make sure By Object mode is active. In the Radiosity-only Properties section, clear the Use Global Subdivision Settings check box, and make sure the Subdivision check box is selected.

note

The By Object option is a toggle button that might read By Layer or Mixed, depending on the object selected. Clicking the button toggles through all three choices.

3. The Global Subdivision Enabled option is disabled by default in the Radiosity Meshing Parameters rollout of Advanced Lighting, so having Use Global Subdivision Settings selected was doing nothing. Now, however, you are using a meshing size of 3'3–2'8" for all the building objects. Enter 2' in the Meshing Size field, and press Enter (see Figure 4.20). This sets a minimum of 2 feet between vertices in the building, making it more likely that there are vertices in one object in close proximity to the vertices in another to store the radiosity solution for that area of the mesh. Click OK to close the dialog box.

tip

The Named Selection feature has been expanded and improved on in 3ds max 5. Take the time to investigate its new functionality in the online help file.

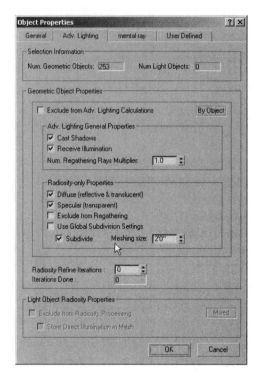

FIGURE 4.20   *In the Object Properties dialog box, set Meshing Size to 2' for the building objects contained in the named selection set.*

4. In the Advanced Lighting dialog box, click Reset All, and then click Start to generate a new radiosity solution. Render the Camera01 viewport, and maximize the RAM Player. Click the Open Last Rendered Image in Channel B button. Comparing the two renderings shows more blotchiness in the newer rendering, but the variations are smaller and more consistent over the surface (see Figure 4.21). The upper half of the building has no meshing, and the lower half shows the results of the 2' mesh setting.

note

The objects with 2' meshing have more accurate lighting data because of the smaller mesh and look more varied and blotchy. You will use this accurate data in the next exercise to smooth the results.

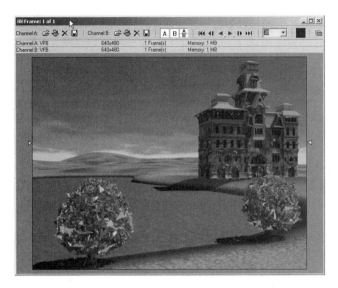

FIGURE 4.21   *The RAM Player with a horizontal split screen to compare the effects of different mesh settings.*

5. Close all dialog boxes and windows and save the file. It should already be named Daylight03.max.

The radiosity solutions are stored in the MAX files, so the file sizes are becoming very large, in the neighborhood of 18MB for this file.

You can reduce the file sizes by going to the Advanced Lighting dialog box, clicking the Reset All button, and saving again to discard the radiosity solution. Next time you open the file, recalculating the solution before rendering would be a good idea.

You also can enable the Compress on Save feature in the File tab of the Customize/Preferences dialog box, which retains the data and results in smaller files.

Refining the Solution for Better Results

The rendering is still unacceptable at this point, so you will learn to adjust parameters in the Advanced Lighting dialog box that refine and smooth the results of the random calculations so far. For example, the Refine Iterations setting is something that can be done globally or locally. The landscape and water in the scene look okay and the skydome is excluded from radiosity, so it would make sense to confine Refine Iterations locally to those objects that need it.

Exercise 4.5: Fine-Tuning the Radiosity Solution

1. Open Daylight03.max, and save it as
   Daylight04.max. On the main toolbar, Named
   Selections field, choose BREWERY to make sure the
   entire building is selected. Right-click on any part
   of the building, and choose Properties in the Quad
   menu. In the Adv. Lighting tab, set the Radiosity
   Refine Iterations field to 3 (see Figure 4.22).
   Click OK.

On the CD

exercises\CH04\
Daylight03.max

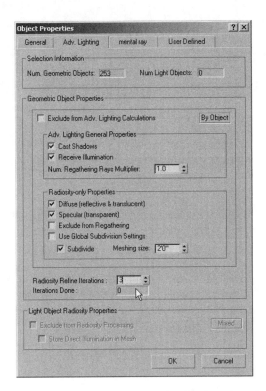

FIGURE 4.22 *Changing the Radiosity Refine Iterations setting for the selected building object.*

2. Choose Rendering, Advanced Lighting from the
   menu or press **9**. In the Advanced Lighting dialog
   box, Radiosity Processing Parameters rollout, click
   Reset All, and then click Start. Notice that the
   Process Refine Iterations Stored in Objects check
   box is selected.

tip

The Reset All option resets
the entire solution's mesh. If
only lighting parameters have
changed, you can use the
Reset button for faster results.

3. Render the Camera01 viewport with the new radiosity solution, and you will see a greatly improved image, with only a small amount of variation in the building surface (see Figure 4.23).

FIGURE 4.23 *Setting refinement to 3 in Object Properties for only the selected objects improves the building radiosity solution significantly.*

4. In the Advanced Lighting dialog box, enter 5 in the Filtering field in the Interactive Tools section. Click the Reset button (filtering does not change the mesh), and click Start. This blurs the edges of random bright and dark areas in the calculation with minimum impact on calculation times.

5. The scene is looking much better than in the first exercise, but you will adjust a few Exposure Control settings and turn on the reflections for the final rendering. The skydome is a bit bright, so in the Advanced Lighting dialog box, Radiosity Processing Parameters rollout, click the Setup button to open the Environment dialog box. In the Logarithmic Exposure Control Parameters rollout, reduce Physical Scale to 85000 to dull the standard Omni lighting the sky. Enter 62 in the Brightness field to reduce overall brightness slightly, and enter 100 in the Contrast field to increase contrast (see Figure 4.24).

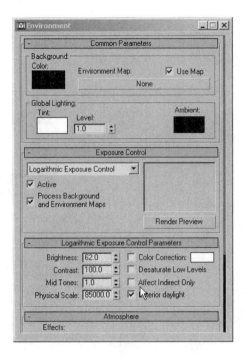

FIGURE 4.24 *Adjust Exposure Control settings to improve your rendering.*

6. Open the Material Editor and click on the WATER
    Sample Window to activate it (third from left, top
    row). In the Raytrace Basic Parameters rollout, click
    the Reflect check box twice to enable the color
    swatch.

7. In the Material Editor, right-click on any sample
    window and choose 5 × 3 Sample Windows from the
    shortcut menu. Click on the WINDOORwGLAZING
    sample window (third from left, third row). In the Multi/Sub-Object
    Basic Parameters rollout, click on GLAZING (Raytrace) and toggle the
    color swatch option for Reflect as you did for the WATER material. Close
    all windows and dialog boxes.

note

You must click the Reflect check
box twice to toggle through
a Fresnel setting so that you
can activate the color swatch
option.

8. Click the Render Scene button on the main toolbar, and in the Max Default
    Scanline A-Buffer rollout, select the Auto Reflect/Refract and Mirrors check box.

9. In the Advanced Lighting dialog box, click Reset All, and then click Start to calcu-
    late the reflections in the radiosity solution. Click the Render button. Reflections
    in the windows and on the water add a lot of visual interest to the scene (see
    Figure 4.25).

FIGURE 4.25 *Rendering the scene with reflections enabled produces a much more interesting view.*

10. Close all windows and dialog boxes and save the file. It should already be called Daylight04.max.

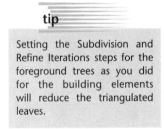

tip

Setting the Subdivision and Refine Iterations steps for the foreground trees as you did for the building elements will reduce the triangulated leaves.

You have learned to set local Refine Iterations options to recalculate, which reduces the randomness of the radiosity solution, and to change the Filtering setting to blend the remaining variations in the bounced light.

Other Exposure Control adjustments, such as Brightness and Contrast, were changed to fine-tune the look of your rendering, and the Physical Scale setting was reduced to lower the amount of light from the standard Omni light illuminating the skydome.

Summary

In this chapter, you have learned to set up two lighting schemes: Sunlight and Daylight. The Sunlight system uses standard lights and usually renders much faster than the Daylight system. However, setup times are longer because you must add fill lights to simulate bounce light in the scene. The Daylight system is quick to set up, but the time required to tweak modeling and light parameters, and the long render times could make it less efficient in a production environment.

You have focused on the following lighting concepts and skills in this chapter:

- **Standard Sunlight system**   You learned to place and adjust a Sunlight system for a specific time and location. Sunlight is a standard light type.

- **Faking bounced light**   You learned to add lights that simulate the effect of bounced light from surface to surface to fill the dark areas that the direct illumination from Sunlight does not penetrate.

- **Daylight system**   You learned the fundamentals of setting up an outdoor scene with the new Daylight system, composed of a direct Sun light and a fill Sky light. You also learned to set up and adjust Advanced Lighting parameters to calculate the light bouncing from surface to surface in the scene. This adds a depth that's difficult to achieve with standard lights and rendering.

- **Modeling concerns**   The bounced light, or radiosity solution, is stored in mesh objects in the scene. You learned to adjust the size of that mesh to balance quality and speed.

- **Fine-tuning the process**   After the basic radiosity solution was processed, you learned some refinement adjustments and exposure control settings that helped you fine-tune the basic radiosity calculations.

- **Optimization**   With either lighting scenario, you learned the importance of optimization. In the Sunlight scene, you reduced rendering times by increasing the Max Quadtree Depth setting of raytraced shadows. You did the same in the Daylight scene and learned to set meshing and refinement locally instead of globally for more efficiency.

Practice the two lighting schemes on simple models to get a feel for the effects of adjustments and the controls you have in each method. Then you will be able to make an intelligent choice in your production workflow.

CHAPTER 5

New Animation Concepts

In This Chapter

The medieval street scene is a little boring without some action to liven things up, so you'll animate a catapult rolling into firing position and tossing barrels up the street.

These exercises walk you through the process of animating both individual objects and several objects as a group. You also learn about using the new Character feature to copy animation from one object to another, which increases your productivity. After you have the basic animation set, you learn to adjust it with Graph Editors that display a graphical representation of your animation.

In this chapter on animation, you will learn about important animation concepts in 3ds max 5:

- **Dummy objects** Helper objects that are never rendered in a scene, but can be used as a secondary pivot point location or a new level of animation control. Dummy objects function in a hierarchical parent-child relationship.

- **Set Key Animation mode** A method of animating by setting keys and refining between the poses.

- **Graph Editors** You'll learn about the new Dope Sheet and Curve Editor and another great improvement to animation called Auto Tangents.

- **Characters** Assemblies of predefined animation that can be inserted as a unit in time.

The exercises focus on the fundamental application of each concept and the workflow you might apply to production. As with everything you learn in this book, try to apply the methods and concepts to scenes of your own as soon as you can. Tutorials should not be a "paint by the numbers" exercise, but a learning tool to use as a guideline. When practicing these techniques and methods on your own, start with simple scenes and objects to get a feel for how the process functions, and then work your way up to more complex examples.

Key Terms

Bézier   A French mathematician; much of computer curve description is based on his work.

Character   A container to hold an animated event.

Dummy object   A Helper object to add extra control and pivot points to other objects.

Keyframe   A point in time where an action has been recorded.

Transform   To move, rotate, or scale an object.

Hotkeys and Keyboard Shortcuts

h   Open the Select Objects or Pick Object dialog box

A Primer on Dummy Objects

Dummy objects and hierarchical linking are central to understanding animation in 3ds max 5. *Dummy objects* act as helpers in a parent-child relationship to aid in setting up complex animations. They can provide secondary pivot points or act as handles to control child objects that are linked to them.

A *hierarchy* can consist of a whole ancestry nested as deeply as you need and can keep track of. Think of your arm, from shoulder to fingertips, as an example of a hierarchy. The upper arm is the great-grandparent, the lower arm the grandparent, the hand the parent, and the fingers the children. Where the upper arm goes, the rest will follow, but the fingers can be playing the piano.

You will use a parent Dummy object to control the movement of multiple objects as though they were a single entity, but you also will animate the child catapult arm so that it rotates to throw a barrel. Using the Dummy relieves you of keeping track of many moving objects at once.

A single Dummy object can have any number of children, but a child can have only one parent. For hierarchical linking to work, it is not absolutely necessary to use Dummy objects. In the example of the human arm mentioned earlier, the fingers would be linked directly to the hand, the hand to the lower arm, and the lower arm to the upper arm, without the need for any Dummy objects in between.

note

There also are Point helpers in 3ds max 5. The functionality is the same as Dummy helpers, but the form is different.

Creating and Linking Dummy Objects

In this exercise, you create a Dummy object in a street scene that includes a catapult and a table with three barrels sitting on it. The various parts of the catapult are then hierarchically linked to the Dummy—that is, the Dummy will be the parent of the catapult parts. You use the Align tool to align the Dummy with the catapult frame and to orient the Dummy's axis to correspond to the axis of the catapult frame. You then select and link all catapult parts to the Dummy in one operation.

Exercise 5.1: Linking a Dummy Object as a Parent of the Catapult Parts

1. Open SetKey01.max from the CD-ROM. Choose File, Save As from the menu, select a new subdirectory, and save the file as SetKey02.max. It is the street scene from Chapter 4, "Exterior Lighting: Standard and Advanced Methods," with a catapult made of multiple small parts, a table in the street, and three barrels on the table.

On the CD

exercises\CH05\
SetKey01.max

2. Right-click in the Top viewport to activate it. In the Create panel, Helpers category, Object Type rollout, click the Dummy button (see Figure 5.1). In the Top viewport, click near the center of the viewport and drag to create a Dummy object slightly larger than the catapult.

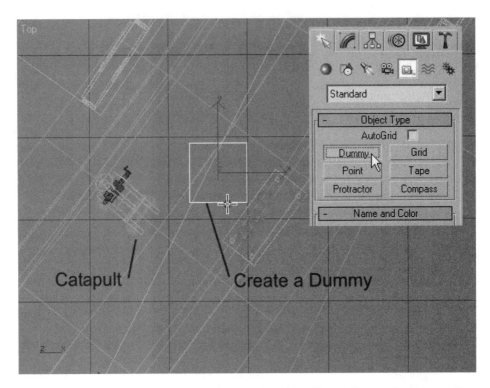

FIGURE 5.1   *Selecting the Dummy helper object in the Object Type rollout and creating a Dummy in the center of the Top viewport, slightly larger than the catapult to the left.*

3. On the main toolbar, click the Align button. Press **h** to open the Pick Object dialog box, and double-click Frame01 in the list to use it as the Align command's target object.

4. In the Align Selection (Frame01) dialog box, select the X, Y, and Z Position check boxes. Make sure Center is selected in both columns and select the three Align Orientation (Local) check boxes (see Figure 5.2). These settings align Dummy's geometric center with Frame01's geo-metric center in all three axes, and then rotates Dummy's local axis to match Frame01's. Click OK.

tip

A Dummy object has no para-meters that can be modified. It is simply a wireframe box used as a helper. For an editable Helper object, use the Point helper.

note   Although the Pick Object dialog box looks much like the Select Objects dialog box, the end result has different consequences. You pressed **h** in the middle of the Align command to pick an object to process as part of the Align function. The Select Objects dialog box enables you to select objects for any editing process that follows.

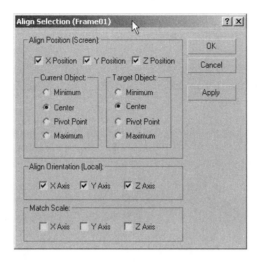

FIGURE 5.2   *Use these settings to align Dummy's geometric center with Frame01's geometric center.*

5. On the main toolbar, click the Named Selection Sets button. Three named selection sets are already created. Expand Catapult by clicking the + sign to the left of the name to see what is in the set (see Figure 5.3). Double-click Catapult in the list to select all objects in that set.

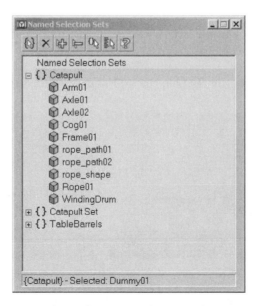

FIGURE 5.3   *Catapult contains three selection sets: the catapult parts in Catapult; the catapult, tables, and barrels in CatapultSet; and the table and barrels in TableBarrels.*

6. On the main toolbar, click the Select and Link button. In the Top viewport, move the cursor over selected objects until you see a double box cursor. Click and drag to any edge of the Dummy object. You will see black dotted lines from the selected objects' pivot points to the cursor (see Figure 5.4). Release the left mouse button over the edge of the Dummy, and you will see the Dummy briefly flash white to indicate the link was made.

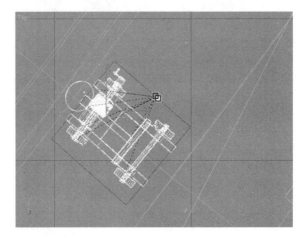

FIGURE 5.4   *Linking Catapult's pivot points to the Dummy helper object.*

7. On the main toolbar, click the Select button and press **h**. At the bottom left of the Select Objects dialog box, select the Display Subtree check box. If the link was successful, the parts of the catapult will be indented in the list of objects (see Figure 5.5). Double-click Dummy01 in the list to select it.

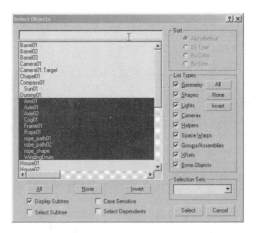

FIGURE 5.5   *In a successful hierarchical link, child objects are indented below the parent object.*

8. Close any open windows and dialog boxes, and save the file. It should already be named SetKey02.max.

To animate all the catapult parts as a single entity, all you have to do is animate their parent object, Dummy01. For rotation purposes, the Dummy01 object forms a single pivot point for all children. Linking is a simple concept, but one that can be used in complex scenarios to ease the management of animated groupings and to give objects multiple pivot points.

New Keyframe Animation Techniques

In previous versions of 3ds max, the general method for animating objects was to toggle the Animate button on, go to any frame other than frame 0, and make a change that would generate a key. This method, known as *keyframe animation*, automatically created the keys as you went along. It was a linear process from start to finish.

As with anything done automatically, this method had problems that new users often found confusing. As keys were added to fine-tune the animation, objects developed secondary or curving motion that the user had not specified and found difficult to avoid or correct. This problem was a combination of automatic keying and a process called *overshoot*, which has been compensated for in 3ds max 5. For example, if a lunar lander were keyed to land on the moon surface and take off again, you would have a key for the start position in space, another for the position on the surface, and yet another back in space. The problem would manifest itself by the lander sinking into the ground on landing and again on take-off.

note

The automatic key creation mode is still an option and is now known as AutoKey mode. The two methods can be mixed in the same scene.

Another new animation feature in 3ds max 5 is called Auto Tangents. The default animation controllers on most objects in max are Bezier Controllers, and as you know by now, *Bezier* refers to curves. As keys were added or copied, the incoming and outgoing tangencies would interact with each other, and you would get the unwanted motion.

note

The lunar lander example mentioned previously would create curves with overshoot. Figure 5.6 compares a function curve for curves with overshoot (top graph) and without.

3ds max 5 adds a slightly different method of generating keys for animation. The process is still keyframe animation, but with a new approach. It's called Set Key mode, a method of animating and setting specific keys only when the user specifies and only for certain aspects of animation—position, rotation, or color, for example.

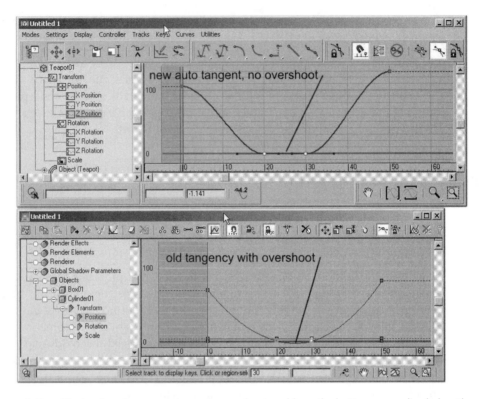

FIGURE 5.6   *The top function curve shows no overshoot problem; the bottom curve dips below the area between keys, indicating overshoot.*

This Set Key workflow makes it easier to fine-tune parameters without automatically generating new keys that interfere with what you have already animated. The approach with Set Key animation is to block out the main poses and set the keys for each pose; then you start working between the main keys to set intermediate poses. Finally, you use tools such as Function Curves and Ease Curves to fine-tune so that you can achieve the subtlety that makes a good animation.

Animating Position in Set Key Mode

In this exercise, you animate the Dummy01 object in the scene to move the catapult into firing position from across the street to beside the table. To do this, you need to animate Dummy01's position and rotation in Set Key mode.

After the catapult is in position, you animate the arm through one firing cycle, and then adjust it to repeat over the entire length of the animation.

Exercise 5.2: Set Key Animation for Position

1. Open SetKey02.max from Exercise 5.1 or from the CD-ROM, and save it as SetKey03.max. It contains the catapult parts linked to Dummy01. You need to get the catapult across the street in front of the table to assume firing position up the street, so the catapult needs to move and rotate into position.

On the CD

exercises\CH05\
SetKey02.max

2. In the Top viewport, zoom so that you can clearly see the catapult and the table. Place the cursor at the intersection of the four viewports, and when you see the four-way cursor, click and drag to enlarge the Top viewport (see Figure 5.7). Select Dummy01.

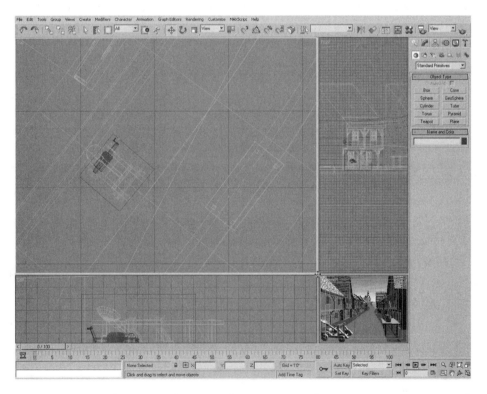

FIGURE 5.7   *Dragging the viewport frame enables you to resize the viewports to resize your work area.*

tip   You can reset the viewports by moving the cursor to the intersection of the four viewports, right-clicking, and clicking the Reset Layout button.

3. Click the Set Key button at the bottom of the display (see Figure 5.8). It will turn pink, as will the Time slider bar and the outline around the active Top viewport. The color change indicates you are in Set Key mode. You will notice that you are setting keys for selected objects. Click the Key Filters button and select only the Position check box in the Set Key Filters dialog box (see Figure 5.9). Setting keys only for the attributes you need is often helpful. Close the Set Key Filters dialog box.

FIGURE 5.8   *The Set Key button at the lower right of the display turns red when it's toggled on.*

4. Make sure the Time slider is set to frame 0 and click the key icon button to the left of Set Key. This sets a position key at frame 0 for Dummy01 to record its current position in time.

5. On the main toolbar, click the Select and Move button. Click the View Reference Coordinate field to the right of the button and choose Local in the list (see Figure 5.10). The Move Transform Gizmo will align itself with Dummy01's axis.

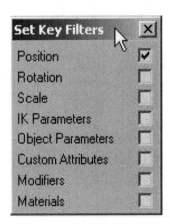

FIGURE 5.9
Select only the Position attribute for setting keys.

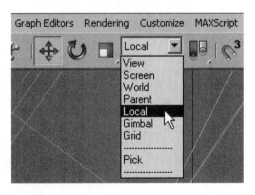

FIGURE 5.10
Setting the current Reference Coordinate System to Local enables you to transform the object on its own axis rather than just the world axis.

6. Drag the Time slider to frame 10. In the Status Bar, toggle the Absolute Mode button in the Transform Type-In field to Offset Mode. Enter -7' in the X field, and press Enter. This moves Dummy01 (and the catapult) 7 feet in the local negative-X axis, closer to the table. Click the key icon button to set a new key. Scrub the Time slider from frame 0 to frame 10 and back, and you will see the catapult move toward the table.

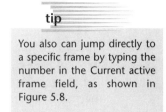

tip

You also can jump directly to a specific frame by typing the number in the Current active frame field, as shown in Figure 5.8.

7. Drag the Time slider to frame 15. Enter 9' in the Z field (you're still in Offset Mode in the Transform Type-In area), and press Enter. Click the key icon button to set a key. The catapult is now in front of the table. Scrubbing the Time slider shows it moving across the street and into place. Toggle the Set Key button off.

8. In the Display panel, Display Properties rollout, select the Trajectory check box (see Figure 5.11). In the Top viewport, you will see a red trajectory of the Dummy01 pivot point. The white boxes are the keys, and the white dots are the other frames in between. Notice that the default Bezier Controller type that is on most objects you create has introduced curvature to the trajectory that you did not specify.

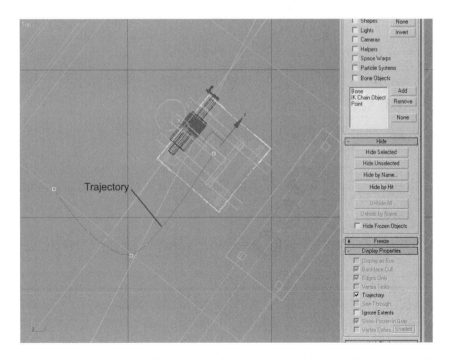

FIGURE 5.11 *The Trajectory option lets you see the pivot point trajectory of the selected object in the viewport.*

9. Save the file; it should already be called SetKey03.max.

You have animated Dummy01, which is the hierarchical parent of all the catapult parts, and used Set Key to create position keys only where you needed them.

Try using Set Key mode to get the hang of it. You can experiment with Auto Key mode as well, and when you get comfortable with the differences, you can mix and match to suit your needs.

note

A big advantage of Set Key mode is that you create keys only when you click the key icon button in Set Key mode. This avoids accidentally creating new keys when you adjust a control, as is apt to happen in Auto Key mode. The downside is that if you forget to click the Set Key button, no animation is recorded.

Animating Rotation in Set Key Mode

Setting rotation keys so that Dummy01 turns as it rounds in front of the table is essentially the same process. You activate Set Key mode, select only Rotation in the Set Key Filters dialog box, and set keys at various points in time.

With the position attribute for Dummy01, you set a key at frame 0 because that is when you wanted the object to start moving to the next keyframe. With the rotation attribute for Dummy01, you want to hold Dummy01's orientation until it nears the turn and then finish the rotation shortly after it completes the turn. You also will animate the catapult arm to swing up in a firing action.

Exercise 5.3: Set Key Animation for Rotation

1. Open SetKey03.max, and save it as `SetKey04.max`. The Dummy01 position has been animated, but it should turn the corner rather than slide around the corner. Click the Set Key button to turn it red. Click the Key Filters button and select only the Rotation check box in the Set Key Filters dialog box. Close the dialog box.

On the CD

exercises\CH05\
SetKey03.max

2. Make sure Dummy01 is selected. Drag the Time slider to frame 5 and click the key icon button. This records the current rotation of the Dummy01—that is, 0 rotation.

3. Drag the Time slider to frame 12. Click the Select and Rotate button. In the Transform Type-In area, make sure you're in Offset Mode, enter 90 in the Z field (you are in View Reference Coordinate System and the Top viewport), and press Enter. Dummy01 will rotate to face down the street. Scrub the Time slider, and you will see the catapult turn the corner smartly as it moves in front of the table.

4. Move the Time slider to frame 20. Next, you will animate the catapult arm in a throwing motion from frame 20 to frame 30. Select Arm01, the shaft with the dish at the end, in the Top viewport. Make sure Select and Rotate is toggled on and set the Reference Coordinate System to Local, as the default View Reference Coordinate System has no relevance to the orientation of the Arm01, but uses the screen axis (see Figure 5.12). Click the key icon button to set a rotation key for Arm01.

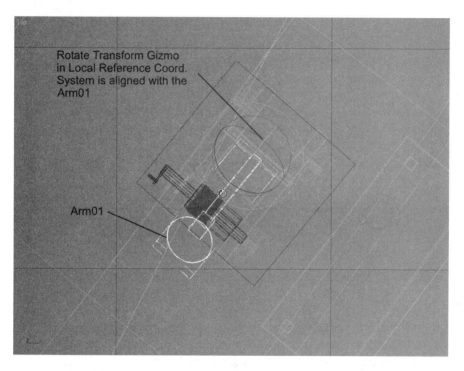

Figure 5.12   *The Rotate Transform Gizmo aligns with the axis of Arm01, making easier to rotate correctly.*

5. Drag the Time slider to frame 25. In the Transform Type-In area, enter –55 in the Y field and press Enter. Arm01 will rotate almost vertically toward the front of the catapult. Click the key icon button to create a key. Move the Time slider to frame 30, enter 55 in the Y field in the Transform Type-In area, and click the key icon button. Arm01 now has three rotation keys. Scrub the Time slider, and you'll see the catapult move, turn in front of the table, and pause slightly. The catapult arm will fire once and return to the rest position.

6. In the Track bar, below the Time slider, select and drag the key at frame 25 to frame 22 (see Figure 5.13). Scrub the Time slider again, and you will see that the arm fires more quickly and returns to rest more slowly. The distance between keys determines speed. More distance is more time—in other words, slower.

FIGURE 5.13 *In the Track bar, drag the key at frame 25 to frame 22 to shorten the upswing and slow the return.*

7. Right-click at the intersection of the four viewports, and click Reset Layout to return to four equal viewports. Click the Maximize Track Bar button to the left of frame 0 on the Track bar. This opens a new Track bar with expanded capabilities, including function curve editing. In the left column's tree view, highlight Z Rotation for Arm01. Zoom and pan by clicking the appropriate icons or using the mouse wheel, if you have one, in the Track bar to clearly see the blue function curve (see Figure 5.14).

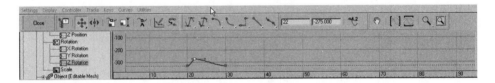

FIGURE 5.14 *Zoom and pan in this view of the Track bar to clearly see the function curve.*

8. You would like Arm01 to fire continuously through the rest of the animation. To do this, choose Controller, Out-of-Range Types from the Track bar menu. In the Param Curve Out-of-Range Types dialog box, click the right-pointing arrow below the Cycle window (see Figure 5.15), and click OK. This repeats the three key animation

tip

When Track bar is maximized, you can scrub the two vertical bars in the graph field to play the animation.

over the rest of the animation, as shown by a dotted function curve. Activate the Camera01 viewport and click the Play Animation button. After the catapult stops, it should fire continuously for the remainder of the animation. Stop the animation.

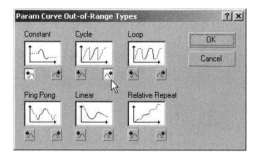

FIGURE 5.15   *Select Cycle in the Param Curve Out-of-Range Types dialog box to make Arm01 continue firing throughout the rest of the animation.*

9. Minimize the Track bar with the Close button. Save the file; it should already be called SetKey04.max.

   You have set animation keys for Dummy01's rotation as it pulls the catapult around the turn and for the arm as it swings into firing mode. You then adjusted the timing by moving the key that determines the peak of rotation back in time. You learned to maximize the Track bar to access the Out-of-Range Controller to cycle the firing keys through the rest of the animation.

   Set Key mode promises to be a productive method of keyframing an animation without generating unwanted keys or movement. You have more specific control than you do with Auto Key mode.

The New Dope Sheet Editor and Function Curve Editor

You have worked with the Track bar and maximized the Track bar with a "mini" function curve editor to repeat the arm animation over time. However, two new features, the Dope Sheet Editor and the Curve Editor, expand the possibilities of editing and controlling the animation.

The Dope Sheet Editor enables you to manipulate a variety of keys in a timesheet form (see Figure 5.16). It provides a view analogous to a traditional animator's exposure sheet, more commonly known as a *dope sheet*. Typically, this sheet is arranged as a simple graph, showing marks in time so that the animator can get a sense of timing and relationship between objects. The keys are color-coded for the axis based on RGB=Move/Rotate/Scale. You can move keys, select and right-click keys to change tangency, assign new animation controllers, and perform a myriad of other functions. Visually, however, getting a feel for exactly what is happening in the animation is difficult.

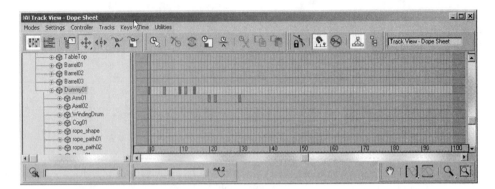

FIGURE 5.16   *The Dope Sheet Editor for your current scene.*

The Curve Editor offers much more visual feedback by displaying the animation as function curves (see Figure 5.17 for the same animation in the Curve Editor). With a little practice, you can judge at a glance exactly what your animation is doing and see the relationships of the curves for highlighted tracks in the left column.

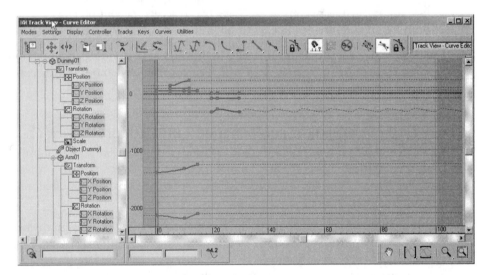

FIGURE 5.17   *The Curve Editor for the current scene with all animated tracks highlighted in the left column.*

> **tip**   A dual monitor setup is very helpful when animating, as the Curve Editor and Dope Sheet can be on one monitor while you work on the other.

In the next exercise, you use the Curve Editor to adjust the trajectory of a barrel flying through the air. You also use Set Key mode to create 3 keys over 15 frames to move a barrel from the table through the air and up the street. This flying barrel will then be coordinated in another exercise with the catapult arm.

Exercise 5.4: Flying Barrels and Function Curves

1. Open SetKey04.max from the previous exercise or from the CD-ROM. Save it as `SetKey05.max`. Click the Select button, and in the Camera01 viewport, select the barrel closest to you on the table (Barrel03).

On the CD

exercises\CH05\
SetKey04.max

2. In the Status Bar, toggle the Set Key button on; it will turn pink. Open the Key Filters dialog box and select the Position and Rotation check boxes. Drag the Time slider to frame 30, and click the key icon button to set initial position and rotation keys for Barrel03.

3. Drag the Time slider to frame 37. Click the Select and Move button on the main toolbar. Toggle the button in the Transform Type-In field to Offset Mode. Enter `10'` in the X axis field and press Enter. Enter `20'` in the Y axis field and press Enter. Enter `10'` in the Z axis field to move Barrel03 up. Click the key icon button to set the keys. Barrel03 will move straight down the street and be at roof level.

4. Drag the Time slider to frame 40. Enter `5'` in the X axis field, `10'` in the Y axis field, and `-14'` in the Z axis field, and press Enter. Click the key icon button to set the keys. Toggle Set Key off. Barrel03 moves farther up the street and down to the road surface (see Figure 5.18).

5. Choose Track View - Curve Editor from the Graph Editor menu. Highlight the Y Rotation curve for Barrel03 in the left column. You will see a flat green curve with three control points. Select the middle control point on the green curve. At the bottom of the Curve Editor, you will see a numeric field with 37 for the current frame and 0 for the current rotation in the Y axis. Enter `180` in the current rotation field, and press Enter. Use the Zoom Horizontal and Zoom Value Extents buttons to see the new curve (see Figure 5.19).

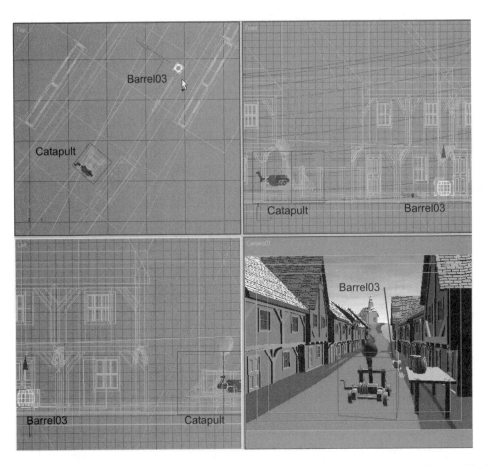

Figure 5.18 *Move Barrel03 through the air and to the street by using three keys at frames 30, 37, and 40.*

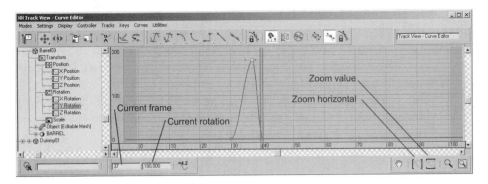

Figure 5.19 *Changing the value of the Y rotation key at frame 37 rotates the barrel as it flies through the air.*

6. Play the animation, and you will see Barrel03 roll 180 degrees from the table to the trajectory's high point, and then return to 0 rotation by the time it is on the ground again.

7. Close all windows and dialog boxes and save the file. It should already be called SetKey05.max.

You have used Set Key mode to animate Barrel03 along its Local axis system. You then used the Curve Editor to change Barrel03's rotation at its peak height and then back to its original rotation as it hits the ground. After you have your base animation keyed, editing the motion in the Curve Editor is often easier than adding more keys because you get more visual feedback in the Curve Editor.

note

The Z Position graph for the Barrel03 object shows the parabolic path typical of projectile motion. The X and Y Position graphs show the almost linear horizontal velocity of the projectile.

Characters Feature

Another entirely new tool in the arsenal of 3ds max 5 animators is Characters. You might think of them as containers for animations that can be reused on other sets of objects that will have the same animation.

The Character becomes another object in the scene that is non-renderable, much like the Dummy helpers. It is assigned to animated objects, and the animation is saved in the Character. Another object has a Character assigned to it, and then you can merge the animation from the first Character to the second, in absolute time (exactly the same as the original) or relative time (from a new position in relation to the original).

Characters are primarily designed to help with actual character animation; for example, a walk cycle for one leg can be pasted to the other leg with the proper offset in relative time. You will learn to use Characters in a more basic manner to fire the remaining two barrels in the scene. You create a Character for the animated barrel and save its animation to a file, and then create Characters for the remaining barrels and insert the animation in relative time mode to have the barrels fire at the right frame. You have to map the animation from Barrel03 to another specific barrel for it to merge correctly. As a final step, you have to animate each Character to be at the catapult arm at the correct frame.

Exercise 5.5: Character Assemblies as Animation "Containers"

1. Open SetKey05.max, and save it as `SetKey06.max`. It is the street scene with one animated barrel and an animated catapult with a firing arm. Make sure the Time Slider is set to frame 0.

On the CD

exercises\CH05\
SetKey05.max

2. In the Top viewport, select Barrel03. Choose Character, Create Character from the menu. You will see a small "Da Vinci man" icon at Barrel03. Repeat this step for Barrel02 and Barrel01 (see Figure 5.20).

3. Select Character01, which is on Barrel03, and, in the Modify panel, Character Assembly rollout, click the Save Animation button (see Figure 5.21). Name the file `Barrel.anm` in the subdirectory of your choice. This file stores the animation of the barrel flying through the air from frame 30 to frame 40.

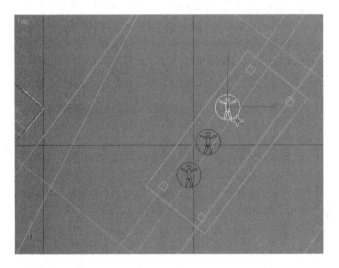

FIGURE 5.20 Create a Character for each of the three barrels in the scene.

FIGURE 5.21
You can save or insert animations to or from ANM files from the Modify panel, Character Assembly rollout.

4. In the Top viewport, select Character02 (on Barrel02). In the Modify panel, Character Assembly rollout, click the Insert Animation button. You will now insert the animation from Barrel03 onto Barrel02, but apply that 10-frame animation at frame 40, a relative offset of 10 frames from the original frame 30. In the Source File dialog box, double-click Barrel.anm, which you saved in the previous step. In the Merge Animation dialog box, expand the Object Mapping rollout (see Figure 5.22). In the Source Time Range section at the top, select the Paste to Existing Animation radio button, select the Match Source File Time check box,

and enter **40** in the Insert Animation to Frame field. These settings copy the flying animation to the barrel at Character02 and specify it should start at frame 40, when the catapult arm will fire again.

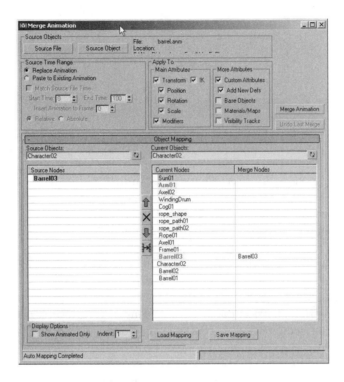

FIGURE 5.22   *The Merge Animation dialog box enables you to paste animation files from one Character to another.*

5. In the Object Mapping rollout, you will see that the source object Character02 is using Barrel03 as the source node for the animation in the left column. However, in the right column there is direct mapping, so the merge node for Barrel03 is on Barrel03's current node. This setting would just repeat the existing animation. In the Merge Nodes column, choose Barrel03 and click the X button between the Source Objects and Current Objects columns to remove the animation mapping from Barrel03 to Barrel03.

6. In the Source Nodes column on the left, click and drag Barrel03 to the Merge Nodes column for Barrel02 (see Figure 5.23). Click the Merge Animation button to complete the transfer, and close the Merge Animation dialog box. If you scrub the Time slider, you will see that Barrel02 flies off the table 10 frames later than Barrel03.

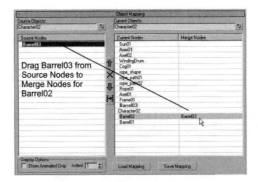

FIGURE 5.23   *The animation from Barrel03 needs to be mapped onto Barrel02.*

7. In the Top viewport, select Character03. In the Modify panel, Character Assembly rollout, click the Insert Animation button. Double-click Barrel.anm in the dialog box to insert it. You will now insert the animation from Barrel03 onto Barrel01. Double-click the Barrel.anm file you saved in the previous step. In the Merge Animation dialog box, expand the Object Mapping rollout. Select the Paste to Existing Animation radio button, select the Match Source File Time check box, and enter **50** in the Insert Animation to Frame field. These settings copy the flying animation to the barrel at Character03 and specify it should start at frame 50.

tip

Direct mapping from one object to the next is a useful technique for animating something like a leg bone configuration for a human character. You would want the left thigh bone to be mapped directly to the right thigh bone, for example.

8. In the Object Mapping rollout, notice that the source object Character03 is using Barrel03 as the source node for the animation in the left column. Again, there is direct mapping in the right column, so the merge node for Barrel03 is on Barrel03's current node. To map it to the correct barrel, choose Barrel03 and click the X button between the columns. This removes the animation mapping from Barrel03 to Barrel03.

9. This time, in the Source Nodes column on the left, click and drag Barrel03 to the Merge Nodes column for Barrel01. Click the Merge Animation button to complete the transfer, and close the Merge Animation dialog box. If you scrub the Time slider, you will see that all three barrels fly off the table with a 10-frame offset between barrels.

10. You will now position the barrels in Set Key mode to the catapult arm. In the Top viewport, select Character01. Drag the Time slider to frame 28. In the Status Bar, toggle the Set Key button to turn it red. Click the key icon button to set a position and rotation key for the character. Drag the Time slider to frame 29 and move Character01 left and up into place over the dish at the end of the catapult arm. Click the key icon button to create a key.

11. In the Top viewport, select Character02. Drag the Time slider to frame 38. Click the key icon button to set the keys. Drag the Time slider to frame 39. On the main toolbar, click the Align button and pick Character01 in the dish. In the Align Selection (Character01) dialog box, select the X, Y, and Z Position options and make sure the Center option is selected in both columns. Click OK to align the Characters in exactly the same location. Click the key icon button to set the keys.

12. Select Character03 and repeat step 12 at frames 48 and 49. Play the animation, and the barrels should be fired smartly, one after the other, down the street.

13. Save the file. It should already be called SetKey06.max.

    You have learned to use Characters in a basic way, as containers of animation that can be passed along to other objects. Characters can also be used to switch between high-density models and low-density models for scene optimization. You would have the high-density version when the camera is close and the low-density model at a distance where the detail is not visible.

tip

You will have to move Character01 in at least two viewports to place it in the dish. Do not worry about being too accurate because it happens over two frames, too quick for the eye to see.

warning

Do not rotate the Character, as it will change the direction of the animation. Rotating the Character could be useful for aiming the barrel, but not for this scene.

tip

Any of the align tools—Align, Normal Align, Array, and so forth—can be used to create animations, as long as the rules for setting keys are observed. They are just transform tools, as Select and Move is.

Summary

You have learned new animation features in 3ds max 5 that give you the ability to set keyframes only where you need them and only for specific purposes without creating confusing and unnecessary keys.

- **Dummy objects**   Can be used as Helper objects to give you more animation control and flexibility. These objects act as a parent to one or more objects in the scene and offer a common pivot point for child objects.

- **Set Key animation mode**   Sets animation keys only at specific points in time and for only specific purposes, such as position or rotation.

- **Graph Editors**   The Dope Sheet Editor displays animation keys as points in time to offer a view of the relative timing of animated objects. The Curve Editor displays the animation as plotted function curves so that you can visually compare parameters.

- **Characters**   Animation files that can be reapplied to objects offset in time, or be applied to different objects in the scene.

PART III

An Interior Scene

CHAPTER 6

Modeling for Radiosity and Efficiency

In This Chapter

Modeling efficiency should always be of utmost importance as you plan your workflow in 3ds max 5. Whether you are modeling for games or film, you should avoid creating unnecessary faces and vertices. Also, as you will learn in this chapter, modeling with radiosity rendering in mind requires additional planning. It's not that modeling for radiosity or efficiency need be difficult; it is just that you should develop work habits that produce models that can be easily edited, which gives you the flexibility of quick fixes to adapt to any radiosity lighting problems. Some of the topics covered in this chapter are as follows:

- **Modeling for radiosity**   You will learn about lighting adjustments that work along with modeling techniques for improving radiosity rendering.

- **Layer management**   You will learn about a new concept in 3ds max 5 called Layers, which are another level of managing objects as a group with similar attributes. In this chapter, you define a layer to manage radiosity meshing.

- **Daylight and interior radiosity**   You will learn how good modeling for exterior day lighting does not always translate to good results for interior lighting.

■ **More on efficient modeling**   You have learned about creating 3D objects from a 2D mesh; in this chapter, you learn more about "borrowing" 2D splines from shapes to create multiple 3D objects from a minimum of 2D information. You will loft an object with efficiency in mind and plan ahead for material application.

As always, it is important that you use these step-by-step exercises as a guideline for learning concepts and approaches, instead of as the definitive way to do anything specific in 3ds max 5.

Key Terms

Attach option   Separate objects, whether 2D or 3D, can be attached to a single object for better management or material application.

Detach option   When editing 2D or 3D objects, this option can be used to turn sub-object selection sets into new geometry.

Grid objects   Grids define new work planes in space that can be aligned with other geometry or positioned freely in space; these objects are found in the Helpers category.

Isolate Selection   With this tool, you can clear everything from the viewports except the selected objects for a less cluttered workspace.

Layers   A new object-management tool in 3ds max 5 that enables you to group objects by layers and then set parameters for all objects in a layer.

Hotkeys and Keyboard Shortcuts

8   Open the Environment dialog box

9   Open the Advanced Lighting dialog box

c   Toggle to Camera viewport

h   Open the Select Objects or Pick Object dialog box

Comparing Exterior and Interior Radiosity Lighting

Why open with a lighting exercise in a modeling chapter? Because radiosity lighting and modeling are tied closely together, and you have to prepare the lighting in the scene to learn the effects of making changes in the model.

In 3ds max 5, there is often more than one solution to a problem, but this chapter takes an approach that parallels movie set design. Set designers do not build a complete building for a movie. Usually, they build a facade for the outdoor shots and, in a separate sound stage, build several rooms for the interior scenes. This approach is good with a 3ds max 5 workflow because it keeps models small and offers you more flexibility overall. As with movie sets, the audience never knows the difference.

First, the Comparison

In the following exercise, you open a model of a bungalow similar to a Sears Vallonia home kit, sold between 1910 and 1940. The scene has been set up with a Daylight system like the one you used in Chapter 4, "Exterior Lighting: Standard and Advanced Methods." The model's radiosity meshing has been set for efficiency yet retains acceptable results. The sky background is a simple Gradient Ramp map used as an environmental background image.

You will render the Camera01 viewport of this scene and open the image in the RAM Player. You will then switch to Camera02, an interior view, and compare the lighting.

The model for the exterior scene is similar to the one for the interior scene, but the interior has some changes introduced to the model to illustrate new workflow and techniques unrelated to the exterior scene. This is not a continuation of the exterior scene, which showed only how direct daylight radiosity is not as dependent on modeling to achieve good results.

Work through the modeling exercises and focus on the lessons; the radiosity improvements will be revealed toward the end of the chapter. This chapter is hard work! There is no simple solution to good radiosity rendering, and you must learn to recognize potential problem areas and some methods to fix those problems.

Have patience.

Exercise 6.1: Daylight Systems with Interior and Exterior Scenes

1. Open Bungalow_Exterior01.max from the CD-ROM. You do not need to save it as you will not be making changes in this file. This exercise is for comparison only.

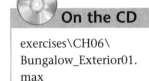

exercises\CH06\
Bungalow_Exterior01.
max

2. Make sure the Camera01 viewport is active. Choose Rendering, Advanced Lighting from the menu (keyboard shortcut: **9**) to open the Advanced Lighting dialog box. Click the Start button in the Radiosity Processing Parameters rollout to process the radiosity solution. When the solution is finished, click the Quick Render button on the main toolbar. The image should look

like Figure 6.1. Choose Rendering, Environment from the menu (keyboard shortcut: **8**) to open the Environment dialog box and view the Logarithmic Exposure Control Parameters for the scene.

note   On a single PIII 1.13GHz processor, the solution takes about 1 minute, 30 seconds. The rendering, at the default 640×480 resolution, takes 58 seconds.

FIGURE 6.1   *A simple bungalow rendering with Daylight system lighting. Meshing is moderate on major objects and Exposure Control has been adjusted.*

3. In the Camera01 viewport, press **c** to open the Select Camera dialog box, and double-click Camera02. The viewport becomes a dark interior view looking out toward the Daylight, onto the porch. Click the Quick Render button, and you'll see that the radiosity solution from step 2 is still valid. The rendered image will be very dark, similar to Figure 6.2. You can see strange greenish light leaks at the top of the walls and some sunlight on the floor as it streams through the windows— not at all what you would expect on a bright sunny day.

FIGURE 6.2   *An image of the same bungalow and Daylight from an interior perspective. The lighting is not convincing as a sun-flooded interior.*

4. Close all windows and dialog boxes. Choose File, Reset from the menu, and click Yes in the reset prompt dialog box. You have not intentionally made any changes, so you do not want to save this file.

> **note**
>
> The odd floor tiles have nothing to do with modeling or lighting. You will correct the tiles in Chapter 7, "Materials and Mapping: Deeper into the Details."

You have compared the result of the Daylight system on exterior and interior renderings of the same model. Obviously, some serious problems in the interior need to be corrected to achieve an acceptable rendering. It might be possible to make some changes to the model to make it acceptable for both interior and exterior views, but it would involve a dense, inefficient mesh and many compromises.

Often, you'll be faced with a similar workflow dilemma. Do you work with large complex models that can be used for a wide variety of scenes, or do you create and modify smaller models for specific uses? Only you can make the decision based on previous experience, but in this case, you will opt for smaller efficient models.

Lighting Adjustments for Interior Daylight

Before you can see the effects of modeling changes on the lighting, you have to set the lighting up for an interior scene. The light was created for an exterior scene, with the primary light sources being direct illumination from the sunlight and skylight. Indirect, or bounced, light is secondary for filling under the porch roof and eaves. The light bouncing off the floor as it streams through the windows, on the other hand, lights the interior almost entirely.

You will adjust the Daylight system for new shadow methods; however, most of the changes will be in the Exposure Control settings.

Exercise 6.2: Switching Daylight to Interior Use

1. Open Bungalow_Interior01.max from the CD-ROM. Save it as Bungalow_Interior02.max on your hard drive. This file contains modeling changes that will be discussed later. On the main toolbar, click the Select by Name button and double-click the [Daylight01] group in the Select Objects dialog box.

On the CD

exercises\CH06\
Bungalow_Interior01.
max

tip

The object name Daylight01 is in brackets because it is a group of objects containing Sunlight and Skylight. You can create your own groups in 3ds max 5 from the Groups menu.

caution

Groups occasionally cause odd behavior, with no clear-cut explanations. Named selection sets and the new Layers tool offer similar functionality with no ill effects.

2. In the Modify panel, Sun Parameters rollout, click the drop-down list in the Shadows section and choose Adv. Ray Traced in the list (see Figure 6.3). Advanced Ray Traced shadows offer more control for radiosity scenes. Explaining the adjustments in depth is beyond the scope of this book, but the setting for transparent shadows is important for this exercise.

3. In the Modify panel, Optimizations rollout, select the On check box in the Transparent Shadows section (see Figure 6.4). This step can prevent frustration for new users. Without this setting on, sunlight cannot pass through the transparent window glass and the room would be black. Standard Ray Traced shadows automatically respect transparency.

4. Choose Rendering, Advanced Lighting from the menu or press **9**. In the Advanced Lighting dialog box, Radiosity Processing Parameters rollout, select the Display Radiosity in Viewport check box to show a representation of the lighting in the Camera02 viewport and the wireframe meshing in the other viewports. This display will help you judge the effects of Exposure Control changes without actually rendering each time. In the Radiosity Processing Parameters rollout, click the Start button. After processing, the viewport will display the radiosity. Click the Setup button in the Interactive Tools section (see Figure 6.5) to open the Exposure Control dialog box.

5. In the Exposure Control dialog box, Logarithmic Exposure Control Parameters rollout, the Exterior Daylight check box is currently selected for the exterior camera view. However, you are no longer in an exterior scene, so clear that check box. The Camera02 viewport will become very washed out with the current exposure settings. To bring the exposure down, enter **30** in the Brightness field, **50** in Contrast, and **1** in Mid Tones. Make sure the Camera02 viewport is active, and click the Quick Render button. The rendered scene shows a soft light bounced from the floor and from the exterior Skylight entering the windows. However, there are light leaks and random coloration (see Figure 6.6). Close the Virtual Frame Buffer window.

FIGURE 6.3
Select [Day-light01] group and, in the Modify panel, Sun Parameters rollout, switch to Adv. Ray Traced shadows.

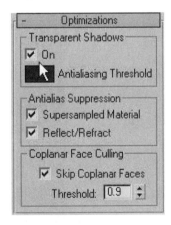

FIGURE 6.4
Enable the Transparent Shadows setting in the Optimizations rollout so that the window panes don't block the light.

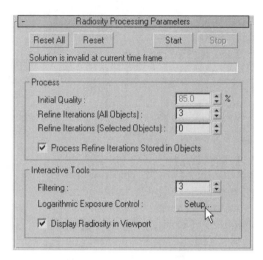

FIGURE 6.5 *The Display Radiosity in Viewport option helps you see the effects of changes to Exposure Control settings.*

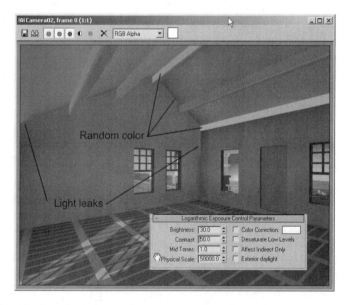

FIGURE 6.6 *The Exposure Control setting and a quick render of the Camera02 viewport shows light leakage at the walls and roof and random green coloration on some of the roof beams.*

6. Close all windows and dialog boxes. Save the file. It should already be called Bungalow_Interior02.max.

Exterior lighting is primarily direct light, but an interior scene being lit from the exterior is primarily bounced light that comes through the windows. The first step in changing from an exterior scene to an interior scene with the same light sources is to switch modes by clearing the Exterior Daylight option and then adjust the Exposure Control settings so that you can see the scene well enough to make corrections. The adjustment to exposure control would be somewhat analogous to your pupils dilating or having to adjust the f-stop on a camera lens.

You also have been introduced to Advanced Ray Traced shadows in the Daylight system. These shadows must have the Transparent Shadows setting turned on manually to take the window panes into account and let light through into the room.

Modeling and Radiosity

Again, you may have been able to force a very tight meshing and work with a concept called "light painting" to correct the problems in the interior scene, but more often than not, reworking the model is more sensible. In any case, adjusting this model will make you aware of why the lighting behaves this way, and you can make the choice for which solution is best for your workflow.

Remember that the radiosity calculations are stored in the model's vertices and faces. If a vertex on one wall has no corresponding vertex on another wall to share radiosity information, 3ds max 5 has to interpolate to the next available vertex.

The model has already been changed from the exterior example. The side roof overhangs have been aligned with inside and outside edges of the gable walls, and the dormer has been removed and the roof "patched" to make it a continuous surface. The roof beams have been made flush with the inside surface of the walls. There are still several areas at the roof eaves and wall intersections where vertices do not match closely enough for good results, however.

Adjusting the Model for Radiosity

In the next exercise, you edit the roof and learn about Grid objects to help keep things aligned. To help you produce fast and accurate alignments, you also learn about using the Align tool to align sub-object selections of one object with other objects, and using the Isolate tool to reduce clutter when working with specific objects.

You don't know at what angle the roof is pitched, but it would be handy to be able to move the vertices without changing that angle. There is no Reference Coordinate System in alignment with the roof pitch, however. You will learn about creating Grid objects aligned to the roof surface, and then move the vertices in the correct plane. You will be concerned only with the walls that are visible from the camera viewpoint in this exercise.

Exercise 6.3: New Productivity Tools for Editing

1. Open Bungalow_Interior02.max, and save it as Bungalow_Interior03.max. Choose Rendering, Advanced Lighting from the menu, and clear the Display Radiosity in Viewport check box. On the main toolbar, click the Select by Name button and highlight ROOF, WALL_BACK, WALL_FRONT, and WALL_RIGHT in the Select Objects list (see Figure 6.7). Click the Select button.

On the CD

exercises\CH06\
Bungalow_Interior02.
max

caution   If you are not continuing from Exercise 6.2, you will have to perform steps 4 and 5 from that exercise for the proper radiosity solution.

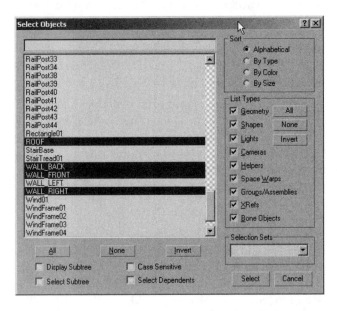

FIGURE 6.7   *Select ROOF, WALL_BACK, WALL_FRONT, and WALL_RIGHT so that you can isolate these objects in your scene.*

2. Choose Tools, Isolate Selection from the menu. This option temporarily hides all objects in the scene except the ones you have selected, which reduces clutter and makes editing easier by giving you much better visibility and control.

3. Right-click in the Top viewport to activate it. You will use a shortcut to create and align a Grid object on the front roof plane. In the Create panel, Geometry category, click the Box button in the Object Type rollout. Select the AutoGrid check box in the Object Type rollout (see Figure 6.8). AutoGrid will read the plane of the face under the cursor and allow you to create geometry directly on that plane. You will use the Alt key to make the grid a permanent object.

4. Move the mouse around the objects in the Top viewport, and you will notice that the tripod under the cursor changes angle, depending on the face normals of the face directly below it. Hold the Alt key down and click somewhere in the middle of the front roof plane and drag a Box primitive. A box will be created on the roof plane as well as a new permanent Grid object that is made active and automatically named Grid02 (see Figure 6.9). Delete the Box01 object; it was only a shortcut for creating the new Grid.

5. Click and drag the intersection of the four viewports to enlarge the left viewport, and zoom in to see the top of the front wall and the roof overhang. The light is leaking through where the top of the front wall touches the underside of the roof and where the overhang of WALL_RIGHT extends past WALL_FRONT (see Figure 6.10).

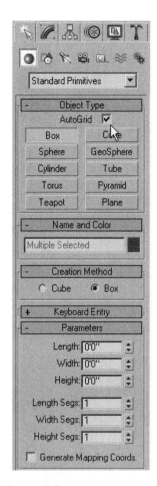

FIGURE 6.8
Select the Auto-Grid option to automatically create a Grid object when you create a primitive object.

tip

AutoGrid is an override operation that reverts back to the World Grid as soon as the creation process is complete. Holding down the Alt key during creation creates a permanent active Grid, or active work plane object, for use until you change it.

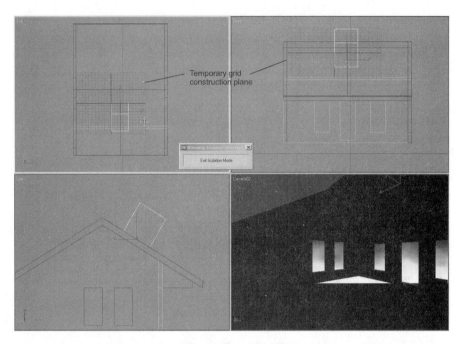

FIGURE 6.9   *Use AutoGrid to create a Box primitive and a Grid object on the front roof plane.*

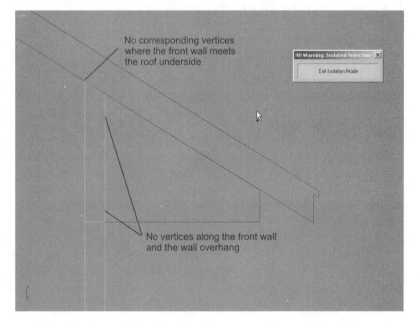

FIGURE 6.10   *Light leaks occur in areas with no vertices in close proximity where two object intersect. The roof has no vertices near the top of the wall, for example.*

tip   When used with the Alt key, AutoGrid is turned off at creation. 3ds max 5 presumes that if you are creating a permanent Grid object, you intend to use it for editing.

6. You will adjust the roof first. Click the Select button on the main toolbar, and pick ROOF in the Left viewport. In the Modify panel, Stack display, choose Vertex sub-object level. Drag a selection window around the vertices at the end of the roof overhang, including the vertex about halfway to the wall (see Figure 6.11).

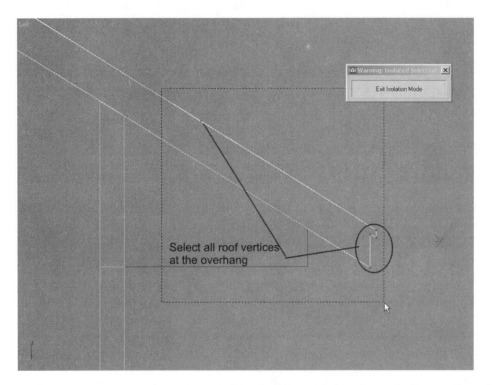

FIGURE 6.11   *Select all the vertices at the end of the overhang, including the one halfway to the wall.*

7. On the main toolbar, click the Select and Move button and switch the Reference Coordinate System from View to Grid (also on the main toolbar), so the Transform Gizmo aligns itself with the current Grid object, allowing you to move in the roof's plane. Move the roof vertices, using the Transform Gizmo to restrict movement to the Y and Z axes, until it is at the top inside of WALL_FRONT (see Figure 6.12). This minimizes radiosity light leaks in that area. In the Modify panel, Stack display, exit Vertex sub-object mode and return to the top of the stack (UVW Mapping level).

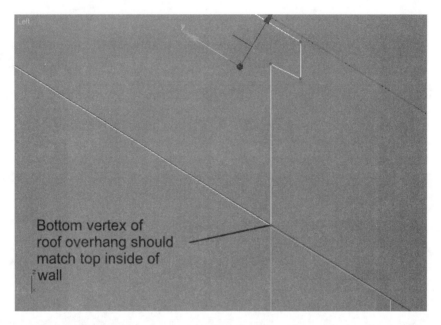

FIGURE 6.12 *Move the selected vertices in the Grid object's Y and Z axes, and align them as closely as you can with the inside of WALL_FRONT to minimize radiosity light leaks.*

8. Right-click at the intersection of the four viewports, and click Reset Layout to return to four equal viewports. Right-click in the Top viewport to activate it, click the Select button, and pick the Grid02 object. Right-click with the cursor over Grid02, and choose Activate Home Grid in the Quad menu (see Figure 6.13). The default World Grid planes appear and are active, but the Grid02 object is still in the scene. Press the Delete key to delete it because you are finished with it.

9. Repeat steps 3–8 to adjust the vertices of the back overhang, so that you align them with the outside edge of the back wall (see Figure 6.13). This time you can just select and delete the Grid object to return to the World Grid as the active grid. You do not have to deactivate the grid first.

note

Remember that you are optimizing this model for interior radiosity rendering only. Changing the roof line at the exterior is of no consequence to the interior's appearance.

tip

When you are finished editing at the sub-object level, always remember to return to the top of the Stack display. Otherwise, you won't be able to select other objects, or the top operations might not function.

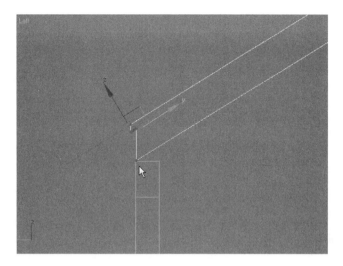

FIGURE 6.13   *Adjust the rear overhang to be aligned with the outside edge of the back wall.*

10. Click the big yellow Exit Isolation Mode button to show all objects in the scene again. Save the file; it should already be called Bungalow_Interior03.max.

You have learned some important productivity tools in this exercise. AutoGrid, Grid objects, and Grid Reference Coordinate Systems can give you much more control than you would have with only the standard Home Grid system. The Isolate tool enables you to reduce clutter in the viewports to work on only the important objects in that stage of editing.

Using the Align Tool at Sub-Object Level

In this exercise, you learn to use the Align tool to clean up the overhanging gable end to align it with the inside of the front wall. Again, this results in vertex-to-vertex matching to better calculate the radiosity solution when the time comes. Remember that the Align tool is based on an object's bounding box (the extents of the object in World Coordinate axes) or the bounding box of a sub-object selection to determine the minimum and maximum alignment limits.

As a reminder, the procedure in this exercise is not necessarily the only way to get a better interior radiosity solution. This exercise highlights a cause-and-effect process so that you will know what to look for in your scenes and will learn how to use some new tools in 3ds max 5.

Exercise 6.4: Using the Align Tool to Prepare for Radiosity

1. Open the Bungalow_Interior03.max file, and save it as Bungalow_Interior04.max. In this exercise, you clean up the overhanging section of the gable wall to better match the inside edge of the front wall, in an effort to prevent light leaks. On the main toolbar, click the Select by Name button and select WALL_FRONT and WALL_RIGHT. Choose Tools, Isolate Selection from the menu. In the Left viewport, zoom in on the overhang area at the right where you adjusted the overhang in the previous exercise. Click and drag on the intersection of the four viewports, and enlarge the Left viewport.

On the CD

exercises\CH06\
Bungalow_Interior03.
max

2. You will work at Vertex sub-object level to move the overhang and the right edge of the gable wall to match the left edge of the front wall. There are horizontal faces under the overhang that will cause problems when the edges are aligned, so you will use the Weld option on vertices to clean up the extra faces (see Figure 6.14). Select WALL_RIGHT. In the Modify panel, choose Vertex sub-object in the Stack display. In the Left viewport, drag a selection window around the top vertices at the end of the overhang (see Figure 6.15).

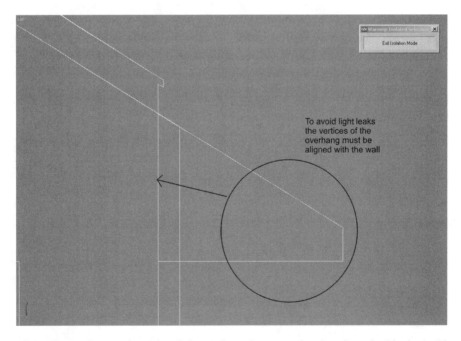

To avoid light leaks the vertices of the overhang must be aligned with the wall

FIGURE 6.14 *The vertices at the right of the wall overhang need to be aligned with the inside of the front wall to prevent light leaks.*

tip When selecting vertices in an orthographic viewport, you must use a selection window. Simply picking the vertices would fail to select the vertices stacked behind the ones you can see in the viewport.

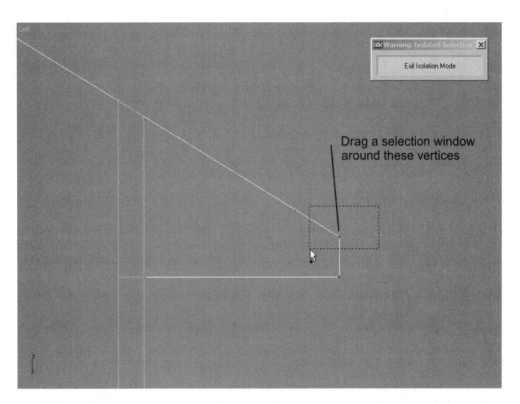

FIGURE 6.15 *In Vertex sub-object mode, drag a selection window around the top overhang vertices.*

3. On the main toolbar, click the Align button. In the Left viewport, pick a vertical edge of the front wall. In the Align Sub-Object Selection dialog box, select the X Position check box, and in the Target Object section, select the Minimum radio button. This moves the wall overhang vertices directly left, to the inside of the front wall. You are not done with the Align tool yet, however. Click the Apply button to set the alignment and clear the dialog box options. Select the Y Position check box and the Maximum radio button under Target Object. This aligns the wall overhang vertices with the top inside edge of the wall (see Figure 6.16). Click OK to finish that alignment.

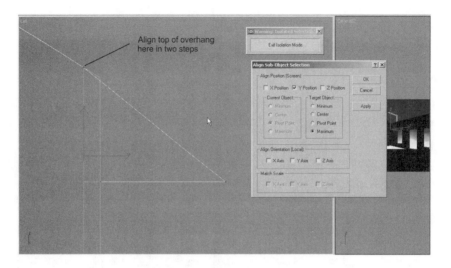

FIGURE 6.16   *Align the top vertices of the overhang with the top inside edge of the front wall.*

4. Select the bottom vertices of the overhang and align them to the inside front wall with X Position set to Minimum. Perform the same alignment procedure for the vertices at the inside of the overhang (see Figure 6.17).

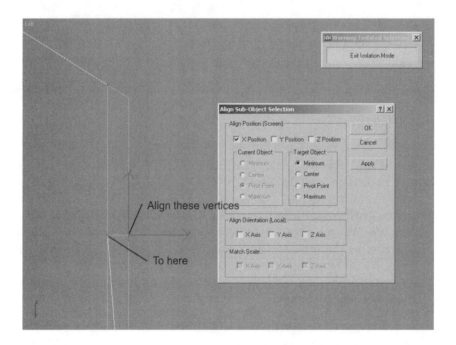

FIGURE 6.17   *Align the inside corner vertices of the overhang to the inside of the front wall.*

5. You have now compressed the bottom horizontal faces of the overhang into a infinitely small space by stacking vertices on top of vertices. You will now select and weld those vertices to collapse the faces and clean up the vertices. Drag a selection window around the new alignment area to get all the vertices. In the Modify panel, Edit Geometry rollout, enter 1" in the field next to the Selected button in the Weld section (see Figure 6.18). Click the Selected button to weld the vertices and collapse the extra faces.

caution

It is very important that you enter 1" (inch), not 1' (foot). The number describes a sphere around each vertex. If two or more spheres overlap, the vertices are welded into a single vertex. In your line of sight in the Left viewport, the vertices are separated by 6 inches. A 1-foot weld threshold would collapse the vertices in two directions, ruining the gable wall.

6. One more alignment at the bottom of the wall is necessary. Pan up in the Left viewport to see the base of the walls (see Figure 6.19). Align the vertices to the inside bottom of the front wall by setting X Position to Minimum and clicking OK. In the Stack display, exit sub-object mode, and then return to the top of the stack to UVW Mapping level.

7. Click the Exit Isolation button and move the cursor over the intersection of the four viewports. Right-click and choose Reset Layout. Save the file. It should already be called Bungalow_Interior04.max.

Whew, that was a tough exercise! You might be wondering if it was worth all that trouble just to clean up the model for radiosity, but it's a very typical scenario that you will encounter over and over in production, and being aware of the potential problems is important. The process seems difficult because it's so new, but try repeating it until you understand the workflow. This type of editing and alignment can be helpful in all your modeling, so do not pass this exercise off as too much trouble to work through. The Align tool is underused in 3ds max because it requires an understanding of the Reference Coordinate Systems to determine which way X, Y, and Z refer and to realize that alignments use the bounding box of objects or the midpoint of sub-objects.

FIGURE 6.18

Use a 1" (inch) setting to weld the vertices in what was the bottom horizontal faces of the overhang.

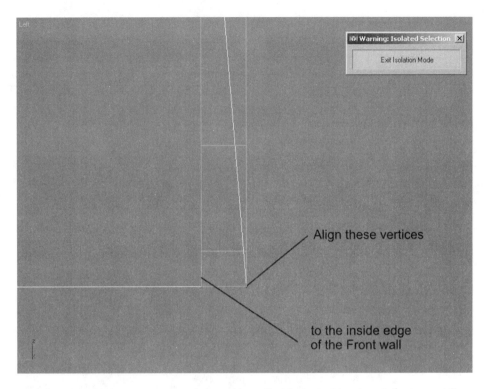

Figure 6.19   *Align the bottom vertices of the gable wall with the inside edge of the front wall.*

Efficient and effective radiosity solutions require that the model have vertices that are aligned to pass lighting information from object to object. Although there are methods available in the Advanced Lighting controls to generate a very fine radiosity mesh that might overcome these modeling problems, it would not be at all efficient.

The interior scene follows the analogy of movie sets; you need to be concerned only with what the audience will see. Having two models, an exterior and an interior, is usually more productive than trying to build one model that fills both radiosity requirements.

Layer Concepts in 3ds max 5

Layers, a new feature in 3ds max 5, is an object-management tool. It enables you to define sets of objects as layers with particular attributes, such as viewport visibility, object color, advanced lighting parameters, and so forth. The Layers feature gives you another level of control separate from groups or named selection sets.

You access layers from their own toolbar. To open the Layers toolbar, position the cursor between buttons on the main toolbar, right-click, and choose Layers from the shortcut menu (see Figure 6.20). You can create as many layers as you need, set the attributes for each layer, and then add or delete objects from that layer.

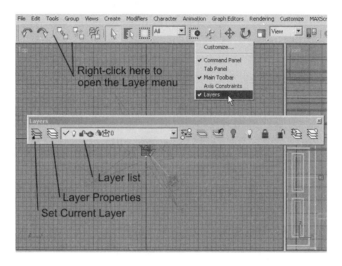

FIGURE 6.20   *Use the Layers toolbar to create new layers, set layer properties, and choose from a list of layers.*

This next exercise shows you the basic steps for creating a new layer expressly for objects that have a radiosity meshing of 3 feet. In previous exercises, you have set radiosity meshing parameters on individual objects by right-clicking on a selected object and going to the Properties dialog box, Adv. Lighting tab. The layers just make it easier to keep common objects grouped. Don't forget to explore the 3ds max 5 online help files to learn more about layers.

Exercise 6.5: Fundamental Layer Concepts

1. Open Bungalow_Interior04.max, and save it as `Bungalow_Interior05.max`. It contains the interior model of the bungalow that has been edited for radiosity solutions. You will set the major objects in the scene on a newly created layer for the purpose of setting the radiosity meshing size for all objects on the layer. Move the cursor to

On the CD

exercises\CH06\
Bungalow_Interior04.
max

the gray vertical line between some of the buttons, or on the space below the buttons on the main toolbar, right-click, and choose Layers from the shortcut menu.

2. You must first create a new layer. On the Layers toolbar, click the Layer Properties button to open that dialog box (see Figure 6.21). Click the + symbol to the left of 0 (the default Layer 0) in the Name column to expand the list and see that all objects are currently on Layer 0. Collapse the list after you have looked at it. In the Layer Properties dialog box, click the New button, and in the Name column, enter 3FootMesh. Click the Current button to make 3FootMesh the current layer. Now all objects you create will be on 3FootMesh layer (see Figure 6.22). The check mark to the right of the name indicates the current layer. Click OK to close the Layer Properties dialog box.

tip

One default Layer 0 already exists in 3ds max 5. All objects you create or import are placed on this special layer, which has attributes for random colors, visibility in viewports, and so on.

caution

You must click OK to save your changes. Simply closing the dialog box discards changes without saving.

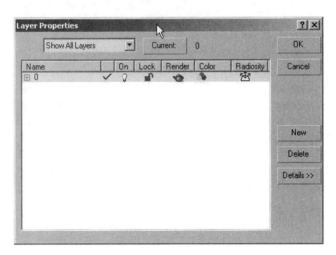

FIGURE 6.21   *The Layer Properties dialog box showing the default Layer 0.*

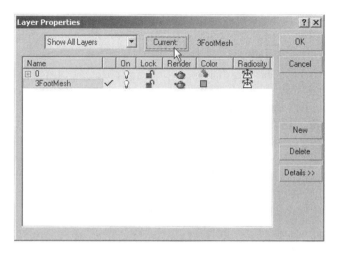

FIGURE 6.22   *The new 3FootMesh layer is now the current layer.*

3. All the objects in the scene were created on Layer 0, and you want to switch some objects to the 3FootMesh layer. On the main toolbar, click the Named Selection Sets drop-down arrow and choose Roofs (see Figure 6.23) to select the roof objects in the scene. On the Layers toolbar, Layer 0 will appear in the layer list because Roofs is on that layer. Choose 3FootMesh layer in the layer list to make it the current layer and click the Set Properties By Layer button. In the Set Object Properties to By Layer prompt window, click Yes, which moves the roof objects from Layer 0 to the 3FootMesh layer and turns on the By Layer properties for those objects. Now, instead of right-click-

FIGURE 6.23
Choose Roofs in the Named Selection Sets field to select those objects in the scene.

ing on Roofs, choosing Properties from the menu, and setting properties by object, you can change the properties of all objects on the 3FootMesh layer at once by changing the layer properties. Repeat the process, including Set Properties By Layer, for these named selection sets: Walls, PorchStuff, RoofBeams, and Floors.

If you click the Layer Properties button and expand 3FootMesh in the Layer Properties dialog box, you will see that the objects from the named selection sets are now listed as belonging to that layer.

4. In the Layer Properties dialog box, click the Details button. Under the Layer Information section, click the Adv. Lighting tab. In the Radiosity Properties section, clear the Use Global Subdivision Settings check box, select the Subdivide check box, and enter 3' in the Meshing Size field (see Figure 6.24). Click OK to close the Layer Properties dialog box and save the new settings.

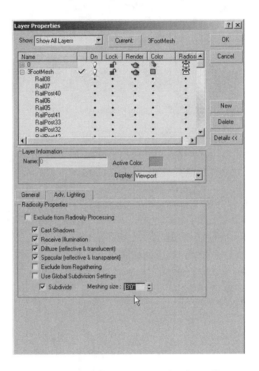

FIGURE 6.24   *The Details display in the Layer Properties dialog box allows you to set common properties for objects sharing a layer. Here the Advanced Lighting settings are set to subdivide the radiosity mesh to a 3' size for all objects on the 3FootMesh layer.*

5. In the Top viewport, select Ground01, right-click on the object, and choose Properties from the Quad menu. Go to the Adv. Lighting tab and make sure that the button in the Geometric Object Properties section is toggled to By Object mode. In the Radiosity-only Properties section, clear the Subdivide check box.

Click OK to close the dialog box. The Ground01 object is large but has little effect on the interior scene, so leaving it to mesh at 1 meter is a waste of processor time. You now have most of the major bungalow objects meshed at 3' by layer. There is not much sense in making a layer with just one object (Ground01, in this case), so you adjusted its meshing at the Object Properties level.

6. Right-click in the Camera02 viewport to activate it. Choose Rendering, Advanced Lighting from the menu to open the Advanced Lighting dialog box (keyboard shortcut: **9**). In the Radiosity Processing Parameters rollout, click the Reset button if it is not grayed out, and then click the Start button. When the radiosity solution is calculated, click the Quick Render button. The interior should have no light leakage along the intersections of walls and roofs (see Figure 6.25). If you see light leakage, you might have to manually fine-tune the vertices of the roof intersection with the front wall again to align them as closely as possible (see Figure 6.26).

7. Close all windows and dialog boxes. Save the file; it should already be called Bungalow_Interior05.max.

In this exercise, you learned to edit at sub-object level using the Align tool to match edges of objects to edges of other objects. Occasionally, hand-tweaking the model is necessary to close any open areas. Remember, radiosity solutions work much better if objects have shared vertices.

FIGURE 6.25 *This quick render shows no light leaks at the wall-to-roof intersections.*

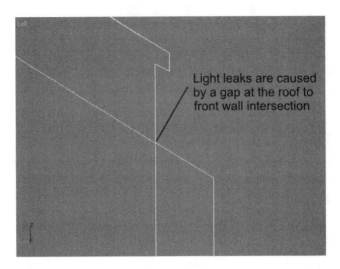

Light leaks are caused by a gap at the roof to front wall intersection

Figure 6.26   *If you still have light leaks, use Exercise 6.4 to close the gap in the wall to roof intersection.*

note   Often hand-tweaking is necessary for good radiosity solutions. Learn to recognize the problem areas and become comfortable with sub-object editing, and you will be able to fix problem areas quickly.

Another solution to the problem of light leaks is increased mesh sizing, but it can slow calculations and rendering times. Recognizing the problem areas and being comfortable with sub-object editing will quickly cure most problems.

note   You might have noticed that the rendered interior is currently too bright and has blotchy coloration, but you'll address this materials issue in Chapter 7.

Modeling Custom Windows

Most of the windows are already placed in the window openings, but there is a hole next to the door with no window. In the next exercise, you learn a process of borrowing 2D splines from a compound shape to create an efficient, yet presentable, window. This process was used to create the door; although the 2D shape was created in 3ds max 5, it could have been imported from a CAD program or another vector drawing program that exports Adobe Illustrator (AI) files.

You can use this same borrowing process to create fancy 3D company logos from 2D shapes or produce latticework similar to that on the bungalow porch. The basic concept is that you have simple 2D geometry that represents a view of more complex 3D objects. You detach 2D splines from the shape to create 3D objects with the Bevel modifier. However, if you simply detach the shapes for the window frame, for example, the spline is no longer available to define the outside edge of the sash. What you must do is detach copies of the splines from the shape so that the original is still available for other uses.

Exercise 6.6: 3D Windows from 2D Shapes

1. Open Bungalow_Interior05.max, and save it as Bungalow_Interior06.max. On the main toolbar, click the Select By Name button and double-click Wind01 in the list. Choose Tools, Isolate Selection from the menu. Click the Zoom Extents All navigation button to fill all orthographic viewports with the 2D shape of a window with frame. Right-click in the Front viewport to activate it (see Figure 6.27). The 2D shape includes the frame, the sash, and the glass panes.

On the CD

exercises\CH06\
Bungalow_Interior05.
max

FIGURE 6.27   *Wind01 is isolated in the Front viewport.*

2. In the Modify panel, choose Spline sub-object level in the Stack display. Select the two outermost splines that create the window frame (see Figure 6.28). In the Modify panel, Geometry category, select the Copy option for Detach (see Figure 6.29), and then click the Detach button. In the Detach dialog box, name the new shape WinFrame01 (see Figure 6.30). Click OK.

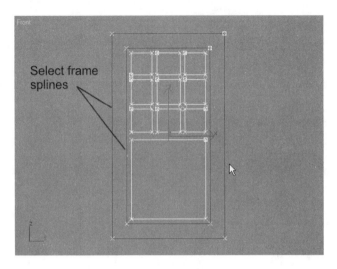

Select frame
splines

FIGURE 6.28   *The two outer frame splines turn red when they are selected.*

3. Select the inside frame rectangle and all the window pane rectangles. Make sure the Copy option is still selected, click Detach, and name the new compound shape WinSash01. Click OK. Click only the 10 inner pane rectangles, click Detach, and name the new shape WinPane01. Exit sub-object mode. You now have three new compound shapes that can be turned into 3D objects with the Bevel modifier.

FIGURE 6.29
Select the Copy option for detaching the 2D splines so that the original still exists in the scene.

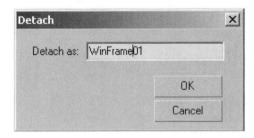

FIGURE 6.30   *Name the new detached shape WinFrame01 and click OK.*

4. On the main toolbar, click the Select By Name button and double-click WinFrame01 to select it. In the Modify panel, Modifier List, click the Bevel modifier. It remembers the settings from the last use, but make sure the entries are Level 1: Height to 1", Outline to 0", Level 2: Height to 4/8", and Outline to -4/8". These settings generate a 3D frame 1-1/2" thick with a 45-degree chamfer on the outer edges.

5. Press **h** and double-click WinSash01 in the Select Objects dialog box list. Apply the Bevel modifier to it; the same settings are fine. Select WinPane01, but this time put the cursor over the edge of the shape in the Front viewport and right-click. Choose Convert to Editable Mesh in the Quad menu. You will not see any change to WinPane01 in the Front viewport because it is in wireframe mode, and you will not see any change in the Camera01 viewport because the face normals of WinPane01 point away from you. The shape did, however, convert to a flat mesh with no thickness.

6. Click the Exit Isolate Mode button to show all objects. Right-click in the Top viewport to activate it. Next you will move the window parts into place within the wall's window opening, next to the door. WinFrame01 is in the proper location, so select WinSash01. On the main toolbar, click the Select and Move button. In the Status Bar, toggle the Absolute Mode button in the Transform Type-In area to Offset Mode. In the Y axis field, enter 4", and press Enter. WinSash01 will move back to near the center of the wall (see Figure 6.31).

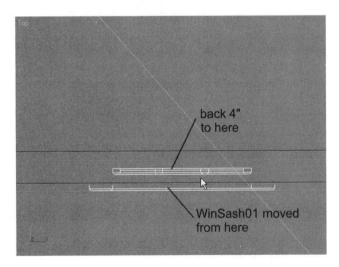

FIGURE 6.31   *The window sash has been moved back, near the center of the wall.*

7. Select WinPane01 in the Top viewport and move it 3.5" in the Y axis to center it in the sash. In the Modify panel, Edit Geometry rollout, click the Attach button, and in the Top viewport, pick WinSash01 and WinFrame01. Click the Attach button again to disable this tool. The three objects are attached into a single object named WinPane01. This makes it easier to keep track of the window as a unit.

8. Open the Material Editor (keyboard shortcut: **m**), and select the Window sample window (see Figure 6.32). Click the Assign Material to Selection button below the sample windows. The WinPane01 object now has the material applied, but the Material ID assignments will be corrected in upcoming steps. Close the Material Editor.

FIGURE 6.32 *In the Material Editor, select the Window sample window and click Assign Material to Selection.*

9. Click the Zoom Extents Selected navigation button. In the Front viewport, right-click on the viewport label and choose Smooth + Highlights in the menu to shade the Front viewport (see Figure 6.33).

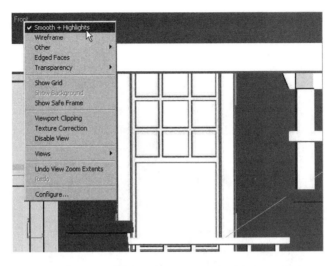

FIGURE 6.33   *Choose the Smooth + Highlights option to shade the Front viewport.*

10. In the Modify panel, click Element sub-object in the Stack display. Pick the window frame in the Front viewport to turn it red. In the Modify panel, Surface Properties rollout, enter 1 in the Material ID field. In the Front viewport, select the sash element, and change the Material ID to 2. Select a window pane, hold down the Ctrl key and add the other panes to the selection, and change their Material ID to 3. The elements of the WinPane01 object now have the correct material assignments for the Multi/Sub-Object material called Window. Exit sub-object mode in the Stack display.

11. In the Advanced Lighting dialog box, Radiosity Processing Parameters rollout, click the Reset All button and then the Start button to recalculate the radiosity solution. Activate the Camera02 viewport and click the Quick Render button. The scene will have a window in the front wall opening, and less light will be coming through the new glass panes (see Figure 6.34).

12. Close all windows and dialog boxes and save the file. It should already be called Bungalow_Interior06.max.

In this exercise, you have learned to detach 2D splines from an existing shape to create new 3D objects. The underlying 2D shape is still available for other uses because you used the Copy option for the Detach tool. You then applied a Bevel modifier to turn the 2D frame and sash into 3D objects and converted the WinPane01 shapes into a flat mesh with no thickness. You attached the new 3D objects into a single window unit, and at Element sub-object level, changed the Material ID numbers to match the Multi/Sub-Object window material. The whole process is fast and efficient and easy to edit at any time.

FIGURE 6.34   *The front wall now has a window with glass.*

More Lofting: Advantages with Materials

In this exercise, you use two 2D shapes to loft a dining counter for the interior. This will give you a little more practice with lofting and highlight some methods of optimizing face count in preparation for applying materials in the next chapter.

3ds max 5 has several methods you can use to create a counter, as shown in Figure 6.35. All three counters are visually similar, but the lofted object offers more flexibility and efficiency in editing material application, as you will see in Chapter 7.

tip   You can open the Counter_Options.max file noted next to the CD icon to investigate the three creation methods for the counter.

You will learn to optimize the lofted counter by adjusting the path and adding new 3D parts to the counter by attaching to the 2D shape.

On the CD

exercises\CH06\
Counter_Options.max

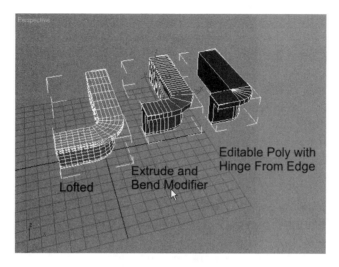

FIGURE 6.35 *Of the three creation methods shown here, lofting is the most flexible in editing and material application.*

Exercise 6.7: More Lofting Techniques

1. Open the file called Bungalow_Interior06.max, and save it as Bungalow_Interior07.max. On the floor in the Camera02 viewport, you should see two 2D shapes for a counter. You will loft counter_shape along counter_path to create a 3D counter. Select counter_path in the Camera02 viewport. In the Create panel, Geometry category, choose Compound Objects from the subcategory list (see Figure 6.36).

On the CD

exercises\CH06\ Bungalow_Interior06. max

2. In the Create panel, Object Type rollout, click the Loft button. In the Creation Method rollout, click the Get Shape button, and pick the counter_shape object in the Camera02 viewport. Click the Zoom Extents All Selected button to zoom in on the counter in all viewports. Right-click on the Front viewport label, and switch to Wireframe mode. The counter is not at all what you might expect (see

Figure 6.37); it sinks into the floor, the geometry overlaps itself at the inside corner, and it is backward. You will learn where the problems lie and how to correct them in the following steps.

3. First, you will keep the counter from sinking into the floor. The shape's pivot point determines where the shape attaches to the path, so you must move the pivot point and loft again. Click the Select button, and press **h** to open the Select Objects dialog box. Choose Loft01, counter_shape, and counter_path in the list and click Select. Choose Tools, Isolate Selection from the menu. Click Zoom Extents All Selected to fill the viewports with the objects. In the Top viewport, select counter_shape. In the Hierarchy panel (right of the Modify panel tab), click the Affect Pivot Only button (see Figure 6.38).

FIGURE 6.36
Choose Compound Objects for the type of objects you'll be working with in this exercise.

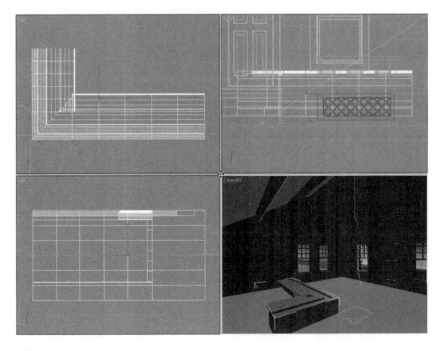

FIGURE 6.37   *The lofted counter is a mess.*

> **caution** You are still in Get Shape mode. If you do not click the Select button or right-click in the viewport, you will pick only another loft shape. You must exit Get Shape mode to actually select a new object.

4. The pivot tripod appears in the shape. Click the Align button, and pick the edge of counter_shape in the Top viewport. In the Align Selection (counter_shape) dialog box, select X Position and Y Position, select the Pivot Point radio button under Current Object, and select the Minimum radio button under Target Object (see Figure 6.39). Click OK. In the Hierarchy panel, click the Affect Pivot Only button again to toggle it off.

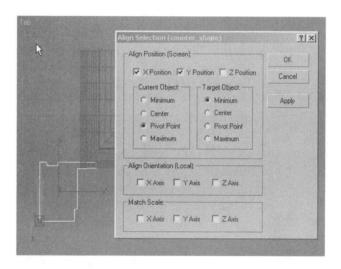

FIGURE 6.39
These alignment settings move the pivot point to the lower-left corner of the shape, as seen in the Top viewport.

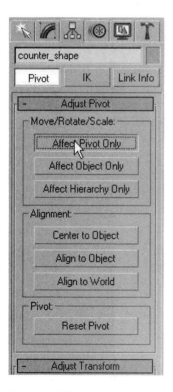

FIGURE 6.38
In Affect Pivot Only mode, any transformations reposition just the pivot point, not the whole object.

5. In the Camera02 viewport, select the Loft01 object. In the Modify panel, Creation Method rollout, click the Get Shape button and pick counter_shape in the viewport. The modified loft object sits on the floor, but is still backward. With Get Shape still active, hold down the Ctrl key and pick counter_shape again. This causes the shape to flip 180 degrees on the path, which is the right configuration (see Figure 6.40). Right-click in a viewport to exit Get Shape mode.

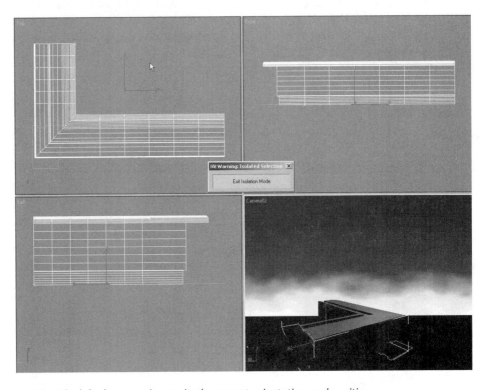

FIGURE 6.40   *The lofted counter is now in the correct orientation and position.*

caution   When performing step 5, you must be in the Modify panel. If you were in the Create panel, you would be creating a new loft object over the existing one.

6. You will now round the corner of the counter by editing counter_path and optimizing the mesh. Select counter_path in the Top viewport. It will be difficult to see under the counter, but you will still be able to edit it. In the Modify panel, choose Vertex in the Stack display. In the Top viewport, drag a selection window around the inside corner of the counter area (see Figure 6.41).

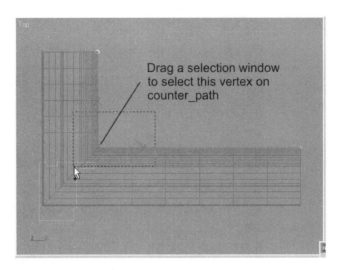

Drag a selection window to select this vertex on counter_path

FIGURE 6.41 *Select the corner vertex on counter_path.*

7. In the Modify panel, Geometry category, enter 1' in the Fillet field and press Enter to create a 1' radius fillet (a narrow strip of molding) at the inside corner of the counter. Exit sub-object mode. In the Top viewport, select Loft01. In the Modify panel, Skin Parameters rollout, set Path Steps and Shape Steps to 0 (see Figure 6.42). This reduces the density of the mesh, but destroys the rounded corner.

8. If you do not have Path Steps to define curvature between vertices, it stands to reason that you might add vertices to replace them. In the Top viewport, select counter_path again. In the Modify panel, Stack display, choose Segment. Pick the rounded segment at the inside corner of the counter. You will not see it turn red, but you will see the pivot move to its center to indicate it is selected. In the Modify panel, Geometry category, enter 4 in the Divide field, and then click the Divide button. This adds four new vertices on the curved segment and rounds the counter, but does not add geometry to the rest of the object. Exit sub-object mode (see Figure 6.43).

FIGURE 6.42

Reducing Path and Shape Steps optimizes the object by reducing the mesh's density, but sacrifices detail in curved areas.

note   Remember that Path Steps are intermediate steps that define curvature in the path.

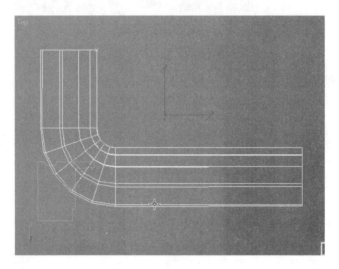

FIGURE 6.43   *Adding vertices to curved segments with Divide is a good compromise between detail and efficiency.*

9. Click the Exit Isolation Mode button to view all objects in the scene. Save the file. It should already be called Bungalow_Interior07.max.

This exercise has refreshed your memory of lofting and you have learned that the pivot point's position on the shape determines where the shape will attach to the loft path. You also learned that by holding the Ctrl key down while performing Get Shape, the shape will flip 180 degrees on the path.

You can optimize a lofted object by setting Path and Shape Steps to 0, and then add vertices to the curved segments to regain the necessary detail. This method works equally well whether you are adjusting the path or the shape or both. Always be aware of the density of your lofted objects, as it can get out of hand quickly.

Summary

Modeling is an important factor in the quality and efficiency you can achieve with radiosity rendering. Because radiosity information is calculated between corresponding vertices in adjacent objects, it's important to model carefully to match vertices as closely as possible. Creating the initial model with this in mind allows you to use a larger radiosity meshing parameter when 3ds max 5 calculates the radiosity solution, thus improving productivity.

You've learned the following lessons in this chapter:

- **Daylight and interior radiosity** You learned to adapt the Advanced Lighting Daylight system for interior usage—that is, light streaming through windows. The Exterior option in the Exposure Control dialog box needs to be cleared and the Exposure Brightness setting needs to be adjusted for the scene.

- **Modeling for radiosity** You learned to adjust the positions of object vertices by transforming and aligning them to eliminate radiosity light leaks.

- **Layer management** Layers are an important new object-management tool in your complex scenes. You learned to create a new layer and move objects onto that layer expressly to control the radiosity meshing size of everything on that layer. New objects added to the layer automatically assume the new parameters.

- **Using existing geometry** Rather than start from scratch each time, you learned to "borrow" 2D geometry from a compound shape by detaching splines that could be used for multiple purposes.

- **More on efficient modeling** During a refresher exercise on lofting, you learned that lofting offers more control over the density of the mesh than other modeling methods as well as better editing capabilities. You learned how to adjust the shape's pivot point and use the Ctrl key when lofting to better position the shape on the path.

- **Grid objects** In adjusting the mesh geometry for better radiosity solutions, you learned to make Grid objects with the AutoGrid option and the Ctrl key. You then learned to use the Grid Reference Coordinate System to control editing at sub-object levels.

- **Align tool** While adjusting the model at sub-object level, you learned that you could use the Align tool to align sub-object selections of one mesh with other meshes or the object itself.

CHAPTER 7

Materials and Mapping: Deeper into the Details

In This Chapter

Would you like your 3D scenes to stand out from all the others? The fundamental topics learned in this chapter will start you toward that goal.

Although the models you create are certainly important, it is the materials and lighting that capture the imagination of the audience. You can make mediocre models look great with materials and lighting, and you can make perfect models look absolutely terrible.

You will learn to create materials that fit the scene you are working on. That is, you'll learn to apply mapping coordinates so that you can size the patterns that make up the material; more accurate sizing improves the sense of scale and space, making the material more convincing to viewers. In Chapter 3, "Applying Materials and Maps for a Convincing Outdoor Scene," you used mapping coordinates generated in Object XYZ space and adjusted the map sizes accordingly. In this chapter, you apply specific mapping coordinates by using the UVW Map modifier and adjusting special coordinates in lofted object. The exercises in this chapter will cover the following:

- **UVW Map modifier** Materials with patterns that closely resemble real-world sizes are important to the credibility of your scene. You will learn to adjust pattern sizes with this modifier.

- **Nested maps** Using maps within maps add to the realism of your materials.

- **Lofted mapping coordinates** Learn to take advantage of the built-in mapping coordinates in lofted objects.

- **Flat Mirror reflections**   Learn about creating and adjusting efficient reflections for flat surfaces.

- **Reflect/Refract maps**   Curved surfaces can be made reflective with the Reflect/Refract map type.

- **Raytrace maps**   Learn about applying the most accurate of the reflection maps, which function on both flat and curved surfaces.

- **Advanced Lighting Override material**   See how a special material can offer adjustments to color bleeding and light reflectance values for radiosity rendering.

Take the information from this chapter and begin to build your own "signature" materials from what you learn here. Using your own custom materials will give your scenes a style that others will come to recognize and respect.

Key Terms

Bitmap   A photograph, scanned image, or computer-generated image used as a pattern within a material.

Color Bleed   A control to adjust the amount of color that is picked up and transferred by bounced light.

Mapping coordinates   Settings that describe how a pattern fits and repeats on a surface.

Reflectance   Light bounced from a surface in a radiosity solution; also a setting in Advanced Lighting Override for controlling the amount of bounced light.

Hotkeys and Keyboard Shortcuts

9   Open the Advanced Lighting dialog box

Alt+q   Isolate selection

h   Open the Select Objects or Pick Object dialog box

m   Open the Material Editor

Accurate Real-World Mapping

As you learned in Chapter 3, materials are the surface attributes of objects in the scene, and maps are the patterns within the material. You have learned to adjust the size of procedural maps, such as Noise, Smoke, and Gradient Ramp, so that they look appropriately sized on an object. With other types of maps, such as Bricks, Checker, and Bitmaps, adjusting them to match real-world units, instead of making them visually pleasing on the objects they're applied to, will make them more convincing to the viewer.

In the next exercises, you learn to use the UVW Map modifier to adjust the scale of maps being used in the material. Think of the UVW Map modifier as a type of projector that projects the map pattern on the surface. There are several options for the type of mapping applied: Planar, Cylindrical, and Spherical, to name the more commonly used. The rule of thumb is to use the mapping type that most closely fits the object's actual shape, but be willing to experiment with variations to get the fit you need.

You also learn how to take advantage of the special attributes of lofted objects, which can generate mapping coordinates that flow with the curvature of the loft path. For example, the mapping for a brick arch would be impossible to achieve with UVW Map, but if the arch is lofted, the bricks follow the shape of the arch.

tip

Bitmap is a term you will encounter often in 3ds max. It is an image file that might have been scanned, photographed, painted in other software, rendered in a 3D program, or downloaded from the Web. Bitmaps can be used to generate patterns in material attributes, such as color, bumps, opacity, or shininess, to name a few.

warning

Unless you create a bitmap yourself, it is wise to assume that federal and state copyright laws protect it from illegal use.

All images on the 3ds max 5 CD can be used freely.

The UVW Map Modifier for Adjusting Maps

In this exercise, you open a file similar to the interior scene you saved in Chapter 6, "Modeling for Radiosity and Efficiency." This scene has a Brick Floor material applied to Foundation01, which serves as the floor. The material has been assigned to the object, and the Show Map in Viewport option has been enabled to make the Bricks map in the Diffuse Color slot visible in the viewport.

It is immediately obvious, even to the untrained eye, that the bricks are much too large, which makes the interior seem like a dollhouse rather than a room. This look is caused by the Brick pattern fitting the entire Foundation01 object when it's assigned. To fix this problem, you learn to apply and adjust the pattern's mapping coordinates so that the bricks are a real-world scale. You also learn to adjust the Bricks map so that it looks more like terra-cotta tiles in size and layout.

Exercise 7.1: Adjusting Maps and Mapping Coordinates to Real-World Sizes

1. Open the Bungalow_Materials01.max file noted next to the CD icon, and save it as `Bungalow_Materials02.max`. The shaded Camera02 viewport shows that the Bricks map pattern in the Brick Floor material's Diffuse Color slot fits over the entire floor surface. To make the map look more convincing, you must first analyze the pattern to determine how much area it would cover in real-world units.

On the CD

exercises\CH07\
Bungalow_Materials01.
max

2. On the main toolbar, click the Material Editor button (keyboard shortcut: **m**). In the sample windows, scroll to the right, or right-click on any sample window and choose 5 × 3 Sample Windows from the shortcut menu. Click the Brick Floor sample window to make sure it is the active sample window. At the lower right of the sample windows, click the Material/Map Navigator button to see a hierarchical list of components in this material (see Figure 7.1).

FIGURE 7.1   *View a hierarchical list of the Brick Floor's attributes in the Material/Map Navigator.*

3. In the Material/Map Navigator, click Diffuse
   Color: Map #11 (Bricks) to go to that level in the
   Material Editor. In the Standard Controls rollout,
   click the Preset Type drop-down arrow, and select
   Stack Bond in the list (see Figure 7.2). This option
   adjusts the brick pattern to stack on top of each
   other, the way floor tiles are generally laid, rather
   than be offset by half a brick every other course.

caution

The map numbers in the
Material Editor (Diffuse Color:
Map #12) are assigned automatically, so they might be different in your file from in the
figures you see in this book.

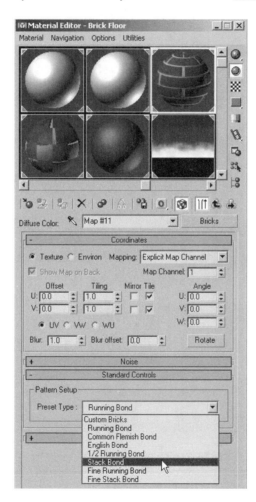

FIGURE 7.2   *The Stack Bond option for the floor tile pattern mimics the way floor tiles are usually laid.*

4. In the Material Editor, Advanced Controls rollout, you will see options that define the pattern layout. Currently the Horiz. Count is 3 bricks and the Vert. Count is 8 bricks, but this pattern is not the square one you need for your tiles. Change the Horiz. Count field to 8 to create a square pattern. Below the sample windows, toggle the Show End Result button off (see Figure 7.3) so that you can see just the pattern in the sample window instead of the end result of all maps applied to the sphere.

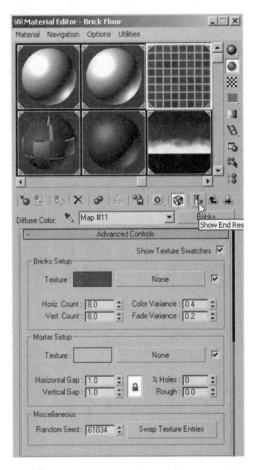

FIGURE 7.3   *Set the Horiz. Count to match Vert. Count for a square pattern, and toggle Show End Result off.*

5. The current pattern now shows a square brick, but you must determine the area covered by one repetition of the Bricks map. First, decide how large each tile is.

Tiles can range from smaller than 1" × 1" to over 2' × 2', but you will use 1' × 1' tiles, a common size in the United States. Also, the math is easy: 8 bricks times 1 foot on each side means one repetition of your map covers 8' × 8' feet of area in the real world. Remember that size.

6. In the Mortar Setup section, enter 0.6 in the Horizontal Gap field (see Figure 7.4). You are subjectively reducing the width of the mortar or grout for a better appearance. The Vertical Gap field also changes when you press Enter because the lock button to the right of the fields keeps them equal.

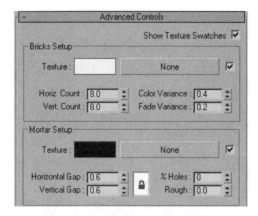

FIGURE 7.4   *Change the Horizontal Gap field to narrow the grout lines.*

7. On the main toolbar, click the Select button and select Foundation01 in the Camera02 viewport, or press **h** to select it from the Select by Name dialog box. In the Modify panel, Modifier List, choose UVW Map. This automatically creates a Planar map gizmo that fits the extents of the Foundation01 object. This gizmo "projects" one repetition of the map perpendicular to its plane, in both directions.

Box mapping instead of Planar mapping would be appropriate for this map as well. Box mapping would enable you to adjust the pattern on the sides of Foundation01, and Planar causes the pattern to streak on the sides. However, because you are viewing only the top surface, Planar will do nicely in this case.

8. In the Modify panel, Parameters rollout, enter 8'0" in both the Length and Width fields to resize the gizmo (see Figure 7.5). These settings resize one repetition of the map to an area of 8' × 8', and the pattern repeats to the edge of Foundation01.

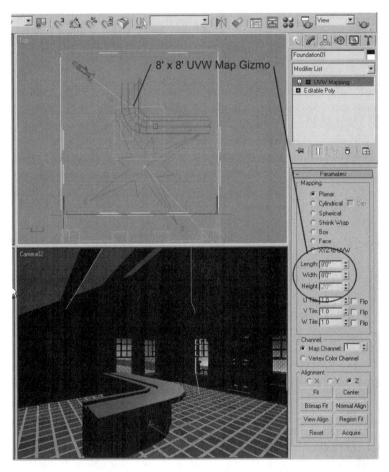

8' x 8' UVW Map Gizmo

FIGURE 7.5   *One repetition of the Bricks map fits an area 8' × 8', resulting in tiles that are 1 foot square, as you determined in step 5.*

9. You have adjusted the Diffuse Color map for the Brick Floor material, but there is also a Bump map that gives the illusion that the tiles are raised above the grout in the rendered scene. The Bump: Map #12 (Bricks) is the original pattern and must be changed. In the Material Editor, use the Material/Map Navigator to return to the top level of the Brick Floor material. In

tip

When you drop the map onto a new slot, the cursor looks like a rectangle with a white arrow. You must place the white arrow on the slot, not the box.

the Maps rollout, click and drag the map from the Diffuse Color slot and drop it over the map in the Bump slot (see Figure 7.6). Select the Copy radio button in the Copy (Instance) Map dialog box, and click OK.

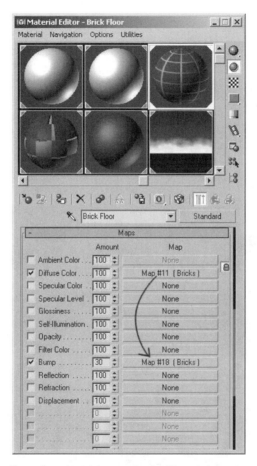

FIGURE 7.6   *In the Maps rollout, drag the Bricks map from Diffuse Color to Bump to replace the old pattern.*

10. In the Material/Map Navigator, choose Bump: Map (Bricks) in the list to go to that level. In the Advanced Controls rollout, click the Texture color swatch in the Bricks Setup section, and change it to pure white. Click the Texture color swatch in the Mortar Setup section, and set it to pure black.

Remember from Chapter 3 that Bump maps use the Luminance value, or whiteness, of the color to determine the amount of the bump effect. White creates bumps; black does nothing. Changing the colors in the Bump map will create the illusion that the bricks are higher than the grout in the rendered image.

11. Right-click in the Camera02 viewport to activate it, and click the Quick Render button on the main toolbar to render the scene. The tile pattern is now more convincing, and in areas of sunlight, you'll see the tile raised slightly above the grout (see Figure 7.7).

You have not recalculated the radiosity solution, so the counter is not included and appears very dark. The lighting comes from the previous solution that was calculated in Chapter 6 and is stored in the radiosity mesh.

FIGURE 7.7   *Activate Camera02 viewport and click the Quick Render button to render the scene. The tile floor is adjusted for 1' × 1' tiles.*

12. Close all windows and dialog boxes. Save the file; it should already be called Bungalow_Materials02.max.

You have learned to analyze and adjust the Bricks map to replicate floor tiles you'd find in the real world. You then assigned and adjusted the UVW Mapping modifier to cover an area the size of a single repetition of the map you created. Adjusting the size of your maps in this way makes your materials much more convincing to the viewer.

tip

The process would be the same for a bitmap that was photographed or scanned from a brick sample. In that case, you would not be able to adjust the pattern as you did with the procedural Bricks map.

Wood Plank Material and Lofted Object Mapping

In this exercise, you learn another material creation method and another mapping coordinate technique. You create a material that represents wood planks with caulking between the planks, such as what you'd find in industrial or boat flooring. The material is based on the Bricks map again to create the planks and the caulking, but instead of a solid color in the Bricks texture slot, you apply another map that generates a procedural wood-grain pattern. This pattern appears only in the area of the planks, not in the grout.

This material is then assigned to the counter in the scene. The counter is lofted along a path to create a 90-degree bend. You want the planks to bend, too, which is easily accomplished with the built-in mapping coordinates of the lofted object.

Exercise 7.2: Maps Within Maps and Lofted Mapping Coordinates

1. Open Bungalow_Materials02.max, and save it as `Bungalow_Materials03.max`. In the Camera02 viewport, select the counter, called Loft01. Choose Tools, Isolate Selection from the menu (keyboard shortcut: **Alt+q**) to hide all other objects.

2. Open the Material Editor (keyboard shortcut: **m**) and scroll the sample windows to find an unused one. Click the sample window to make it active, and name the material `Planking`. Drag the sample window to the counter in the Camera02 viewport. The counter turns gray when the material is assigned.

On the CD

exercises\CH07\
Bungalow_Materials02.
max

3. In the Material Editor, Blinn Basic Parameters rollout, click the gray map shortcut button to the right of the Diffuse color swatch. (The tooltip "None" appears if you hold the cursor over it for a few seconds.) This shortcut button opens the Material/Map Browser, where you can double-click Bricks in the list to open it. Click the Show Map in Viewport toggle to see the Bricks map on the counter in the Camera02 viewport. The Running Bond pattern closely resembles the way planks would be applied, so that is okay, but if you want your planks to be a certain size, you can adjust it, as you did the floor tiles Exercise 7.1. Assuming each plank will be 6 inches wide by 4 feet long, enter a Horiz. Count of 2 and a Vert. Count of 8 to maintain the map's aspect ratio so that it does not distort when you apply the appropriate UVW Map modifier settings. In the Coordinates rollout, enter 90 in the W field under Angle to rotate the map 90 degrees (see Figure 7.8). This makes the plank's long axis match the counter's long axis.

4. Given that each plank is 6 inches wide and 4 feet long, this map would cover an area of 8 feet horizontally (2 planks at 4' each) by 4 feet vertically (8 planks at 6" each). Applying a UVW Map modifier to this object would cause the planks to be linear and not bend around the corner, so you will use the lofting coordinates instead of a modifier. You need to find the counter's length and the distance around a cross-section cut to determine how many planks will cover those dimensions. Exit Isolate Mode. On the main toolbar, click the Select by Name button and double-click counter_path in the list to select it. In the Utilities panel, Utilities rollout, click the Measure button and see that the path length is 15'4 6/8" long. You will call it 16 feet. Select counter_shape. You will see it is 12'3 1/8", but 12' even will be close enough (see Figure 7.9).

tip

You are not limited to only 24 materials, even though you can see only 24 sample windows at a time in the Material Editor. When you use up all the sample windows and have assigned the materials to objects in your scene, you can clear the sample window with the Reset Map/Mtl to Default Settings button. You can then reuse the sample window without removing the current material from objects in your scene.

You also can save materials in sample windows to a material library for safekeeping and to be accessible from any 3ds max file. See the online user reference by choosing Help from the main menu for more information.

tip

In step 3, you're setting the aspect ratio, not the size of the planks. If you had, for example, 8 bricks by 8 bricks, and then adjusted mapping coordinates for a long thin plank, the caulking gap would be distorted and look very thin at the sides and very wide at the ends of the planks. Setting up a count with an aspect ratio close to the real thing reduces or eliminates the distortion.

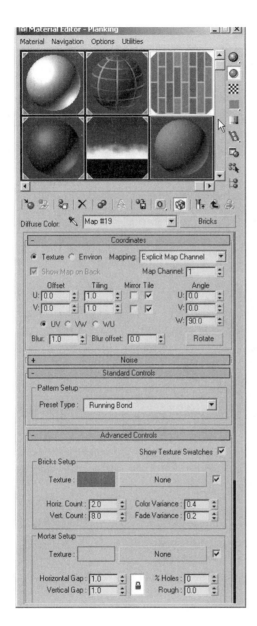

FIGURE 7.8
Set the aspect ratio to match a 6-inch-wide by 4-foot-long plank.

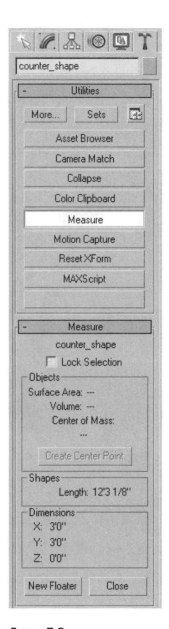

FIGURE 7.9
Use the Measure utility to determine the length of splines and overall dimensions of objects.

5. Select Loft01, the counter, in the Camera02 viewport. In the Modify panel, Surface Parameters rollout, the Apply Mapping check box had already been selected in the Mapping section. You will use the Length Repeat and Width Repeat fields to adjust the mapping coordinates. The counter_path is 16 feet long and one repetition of the map covers 8 feet, so you need to enter a Length Repeat of 2. The total length of counter_shape is 12 feet, and one repetition of the map covers 4 feet. Enter 3 in the Width Repeat field. The planks are now sized appropriately and bend around the counter, as though a fine craftsman had built it (see Figure 7.10).

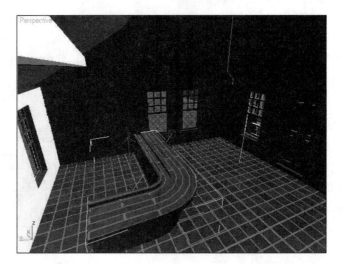

FIGURE 7.10   *The number for the Length Repeat field is the path length divided by the map coverage in that direction (16 ÷ 8). The Width Repeat field is the total counter_shape length divided by the map coverage in that direction (12 ÷ 4).*

6. In the Material Editor, Bricks map level, Advanced Controls rollout, make the Texture color swatch in the Mortar Setup section pure black to set the caulking color. In the Bricks Setup section, click the None button to the right of the color swatch and double-click Wood in the list. In the Wood Parameters rollout, select Explicit Map Channel in the Source drop-down list to use the loft object coordinates. In the Coordinates rollout, enter 90 in the W field under Angle to rotate the map, and in the Wood Parameters rollout, enter 0.05 in the Grain Thickness field to resize the map (see Figure 7.11).

tip

Even if you were applying only the material to the counter top, you still need to consider the total length of counter_shape to determine the number of repeats.

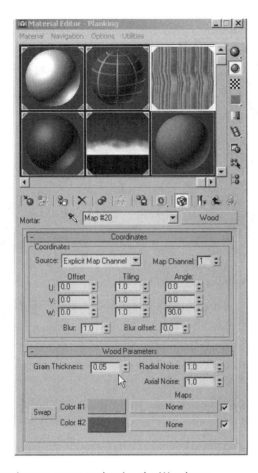

FIGURE 7.11   *Use these settings to rotate and resize the Wood map.*

7. Press **9** to open the Advanced Lighting dialog box and click the Reset All button. Click the Start button to calculate a new radiosity solution that includes the counter and the new materials. Quick render the Camera02 viewport, and you will see the planking on the counter (see Figure 7.12).

tip

You could go back to the Bricks map level and set the Horizontal and Vertical Gap values lower for thinner caulking lines, and you could change the horrible default colors of the Wood map, as you did in Chapter 3.

FIGURE 7.12   *Rendering the Camera02 viewport with new materials and radiosity solution.*

8. Close all windows and dialog boxes and save the file. It should already be called Bungalow_Materials03.max. The materials have a pattern scaling more closely related to real-world units.

You have learned to create a material that uses a map within another map to determine Diffuse Color patterns. The Wood map is a pattern only within the area of the bricks, and the caulking is still a solid color.

You also learned to size maps based on geometry and repetitions of the patterns and to use the special mapping coordinates generated by lofted objects that enable maps to conform to the flow of the path. This is very difficult with non-lofted objects.

Creating Reflections in Materials

Reflections are an important addition because they contribute to the sparkle of the scene and they give the illusion of depth in surfaces. 3ds max 5 offers several methods of creating reflective materials, but each method requires a compromise in quality, speed, or control. You will learn the basic components and applications of reflection methods in this section. You should then apply them to simple scenes to compare the advantages and disadvantages so that you can quickly decide during production which method is most effective in terms of time and cost.

The four reflection methods are summarized in Table 7.1.

Table 7.1   Comparison of Commonly Used Reflection Methods in 3ds max 5

Map	Surface	Disadvantages	Advantages
Bitmap	Curved surfaces	Does not reflect surrounding scene	Renders very quickly
Flat Mirror	Coplanar, contiguous faces	Moderate accuracy	Renders quickly
Reflect/Refract	Curved surfaces	Moderate accuracy	Renders quickly
Raytrace	Flat and curved surfaces	Difficult to blur, renders slower	High accuracy
Raytrace Material	Flat and curved surfaces	Difficult to blur, renders slower	High accuracy, blends well with other material components

In the next set of exercises, you apply these reflection maps to objects in the scene for a quick comparison of the results. The reflections will be somewhat exaggerated so that you can more clearly judge how they function.

The objects that will become reflective are the tile floor and the wood counter. The floor is a flat surface, so you apply the Flat Mirror reflection first and then make some adjustments. You then substitute Raytrace map reflections for comparison.

The counter, on the other hand, is composed of partly flat and partly curved surfaces. You will try Reflect/Refract maps first, and then create a new plank Raytrace material.

tip

I have found when adjusting materials and maps that exaggerating the effect I'm trying to achieve is often helpful. When you see how the patterns develop, you can then back the settings down to a more convincing value.

Flat Mirror Reflections

Flat Mirror reflections can be applied only to sets of faces that are coplanar and contiguous—that is, they share edges. The reflections can be easily distorted and blurred to make them more convincing. The Flat Mirror reflection map "looks" in six directions from the center of the object and reads the scene. It then composites what it sees on the object's surface in the rendering.

Exercise 7.3: Adding Flat Mirror Reflections to Materials

1. Open Bungalow_Materials03.max, and save the
   file as Bungalow_Materials04.max. You have
   applied and mapped tile material to the floor and
   plank material to the counter, but the scene is flat
   and lifeless when rendered. Open the Material
   Editor and activate the Brick Floor sample window. In the Maps rollout, click the None button to
   the right of Reflection, and double-click Flat
   Mirror in the list (see Figure 7.13).

On the CD

exercises\CH07\
Bungalow_Materials03.
max

warning   Do not apply the Flat Mirror map to the Refraction slot by mistake. Refraction, the
effect of light bending through clear materials, would make the floor transparent.

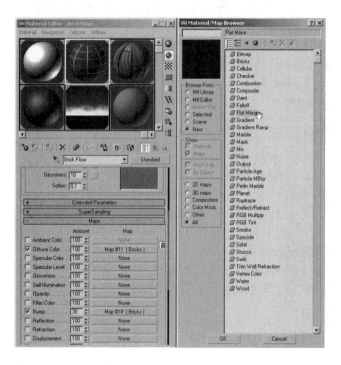

FIGURE 7.13   *Select Flat Mirror for the Reflection slot.*

2. If you rendered the Camera02 viewport, you would see that the floor is not reflective yet. Remember that Foundation01 is a Box primitive; therefore, all the faces
   are not coplanar. The Foundation01 object in the Bungalow_Materials files has

been edited to change all the top faces to Material ID #1, and make them coplanar. In the Material Editor, Flat Mirror Parameters rollout, select the Apply to Faces with ID 1 check box (see Figure 7.14). Also, notice the note at the bottom of the Flat Mirror Parameters rollout.

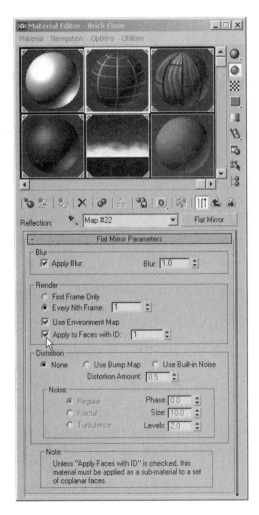

FIGURE 7.14 *Foundation01 has been edited to make the top faces coplanar; Material ID #1 is being applied to those faces.*

3. Render the Camera02 viewport, and you will see that the floor is highly reflective (see Figure 7.15). You will tone down the reflections shortly, but first you'll add a bit of distortion. In the Material Editor, Flat Mirror Parameters rollout, Distortion

section, select the Use Built-in Noise radio button and set the Distortion Amount to `0.1`. Render the scene again, and you'll see that these settings randomly distort the reflection to make it more convincing.

FIGURE 7.15   *The Flat Mirror reflection map with default settings is highly reflective.*

4. At the top of the Flat Mirror Parameters rollout, enter `5.0` in the Blur field to soften the reflections. Render the scene again to see the results.

5. To reduce the amount of the reflection, use the Material/Map Navigator to return to the top of the material hierarchy and enter `50` in the Amount field next to the Reflection slot (see Figure 7.16). Render the Camera02 viewport again to see that the reflection's level and softness are more convincing.

tip

Between the Render Scene and Quick Render buttons on the main toolbar is a drop-down list of render options. If you choose Region Render in the list, you can select a small area in the Camera02 viewport to speed the test renders.

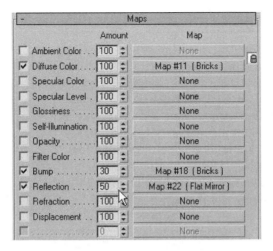

FIGURE 7.16   *Use the Maps rollout to reduce the amount of reflection.*

6. Close all windows and dialog boxes and save the file. It should already be called Bungalow_Materials04.max.

You have learned to apply a Flat Mirror reflection map and apply it to coplanar faces that have Material ID #1 assigned. You blurred and distorted the reflections by adjusting those settings in the map's parameters. Adding the soft reflections to the floor has given the scene much more depth than it would have with no reflections.

tip

There is a check box to the left of the map name in the Maps rollout. After you have assigned a map, you can use the check box to disable the map. This is handy when you are experimenting or when the reflections mask the effect of the bumps while you are trying to adjust them, for example.

Reflect/Refract Map Reflections

As the name of this map implies, it can be used to calculate reflections and/or refractions. You will learn to apply it as a reflection map. It functions similarly to Flat Mirror map in that it renders six views and composites what it "sees" onto the surface at render time.

Exercise 7.4: Using the Reflect/Refract Map

1. Open Bungalow_Materials04.max, and save it as `Bungalow_Materials05.max`. Open the Material Editor and click the Planking sample window. In the Maps rollout, click the None button next to the Reflection slot and double-click Reflect/Refract in the list. Notice that Reflect/Refract map has blur settings, but no noise or distortion settings in the Reflect/Refract Parameters rollout (see Figure 7.17). The map gets distortion information from any Bump maps in the material.

On the CD

exercises\CH07\
Bungalow_Materials04.
max

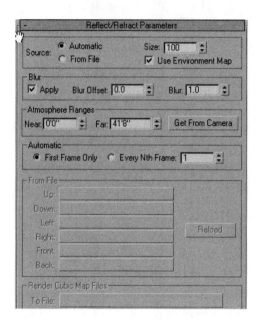

FIGURE 7.17   *The Reflect/Refract map has blur settings but no distortion settings.*

2. In the Material Editor, toggle the Background button to the right of the sample windows. It turns on a checkered background that reflects on the sample sphere (see Figure 7.18).

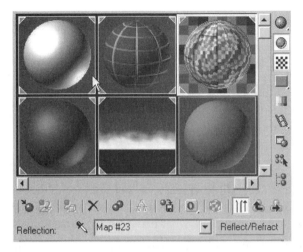

FIGURE 7.18 *Toggling the Background button on reflects the checkered background in the sample window, which enables you to preview the Reflect/Refract map.*

3. Render the Camera02 viewport. Notice that the preparation time for the reflections has increased noticeably with the new map; however, the rendered scene is a mess. Bright colors and washed-out areas abound, with only a few areas showing acceptable reflections (see Figure 7.19). Remember that the Reflect/Refract map was described as functioning only on curved surfaces. The counter is a mix of curved and flat surfaces, so the map acts unpredictably.

FIGURE 7.19 *The Reflect/Refract map functions predictably only on curved surfaces.*

4. Close all windows and dialog boxes and save the file. It should be called Bungalow_Materials05.max.

This short exercise illustrates a common frustration for users new to 3ds max 5. You work hard to get a good-looking reflective material in the sample window and apply it to the scene, only to have it become totally dysfunctional. The sample sphere is curved and returns good results, but the reflections fail on the flat surfaces in the scene.

Raytrace Maps, a New Level of Reflections

Flat Mirror and Reflect/Refract maps use snapshots of the scene that are distorted like reflections on a surface, but the Raytrace reflection map actually shoots sample rays around the scene to calculate what pixels on the surface can see.

The resulting reflections are much more accurate and can simulate mirrors many levels deep; Flat Mirror and Reflect/Refract can reflect only one level deep. The price, of course, can be longer render times, but with new hardware capabilities and shorter setup times, the use of Raytrace reflections might still be efficient in terms of time.

In this next exercise, you change the Reflect/Refract map in the Planking material to a Raytrace map that works equally well on curved or flat surfaces of an object.

Exercise 7.5: Changing to Raytrace Mapped Reflections

1. Open Bungalow_Materials05.max, and save it as Bungalow_Materials06.max. Open the Material Editor, click the Planking sample window, and make sure you are at the Reflection map level (use the Material/Map Navigator, if necessary).

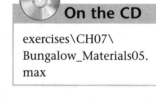

On the CD

exercises\CH07\
Bungalow_Materials05.
max

2. This material already has a Reflect/Refract map in the Reflection slot that you want to replace with the Raytrace map. At the map level, click the Reflect/Refract map button below the sample windows (see Figure 7.20) to open the Material/Map Browser, where you double-click Raytrace in the list. Select the Discard Old Map radio button in the Replace Map dialog box, and click OK.

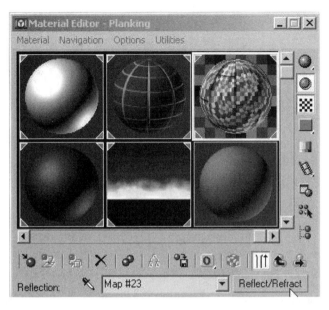

FIGURE 7.20   *To replace an existing map, click the map button below the sample windows while you are at that map level.*

3. To reduce the amount of the Raytrace reflection, go the top level in the Material/Map Navigator. In the Material Editor, Maps rollout, and enter 25 in the Amount field next to Reflection.

4. Choose Rendering, Advanced Lighting from the menu, and in the Radiosity Processing Parameters rollout, click the Reset All button. Click the Start button to process the radiosity solution with the new materials, and then render the Camera02 viewport. The reflections have changed the dynamics of the radiosity solution. There is much more green bleed from the door reflection on the far side of the counter. The reflections, however, are good on curved or flat surfaces (see Figure 7.21).

tip

The Keep Old Map as Sub-map option in the Replace dialog box is valid when you want to use the existing map in a slot of a new map. Maps can be used inside other maps to infinite depths.

FIGURE 7.21   *The Raytrace map has changed the dynamics of the radiosity solution; notice the increased color bleed, particularly from the door.*

5. Close all windows and dialog boxes. Save the file; it should already be called Bungalow_Materials06.max.

Raytrace reflections are accurate, but can take longer to calculate than Flat Mirror or Reflect/Refract. However, they have more predictable results because they function equally well on curved and flat surfaces of the same object.

The reflections of Raytrace Material are calculated similarly to the Raytrace map, with many of the same attributes. The major difference is how the reflections interact with the other material components. With the Raytrace map, the reflections are applied on top of color, shininess, or transparency. With Raytrace Material, the reflections and other components are blended together and influence each other. This offers more subtle control for materials in which reflections are critical. In the Raytrace map, the Reflection color swatch controls the strength of the reflection: White is pure reflection; black is none.

tip

Raytrace Material can be used with reflections off—that is, a black color swatch. Blending maps within Raytrace Material can give you subtle effects.

Advanced Lighting Override Material

With the advent of radiosity rendering and photometric lighting, you'll also find a new set of issues with reflectance values and color bleeding. When light bounces off a surface, you must describe how much light leaves the surface and how much color it takes with it from that surface.

The overall Reflectance values of materials can be adjusted by changing the value of the Diffuse color in the Color Selector; the darker the color is, the less light it bounces to its neighboring faces. You can adjust Reflectance values of materials that get their Diffuse color from bitmaps by changing the map's Output Amount setting in the Output rollout (see Figure 7.22).

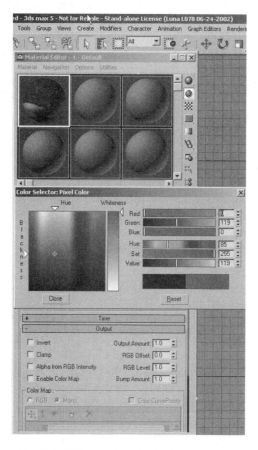

FIGURE 7.22 *In materials with plain Diffuse color, the Value setting in the Color Selector will adjust reflectance. Materials with bitmaps in the Diffuse slot can be adjusted with the Output Amount field in the Output rollout.*

Lowering either the Diffuse color value or the Diffuse bitmap's Output Amount setting reduces the material's overall reflectance, but because the Material Editor does not use radiosity in the sample windows, the materials there can get exceedingly dark and difficult to adjust.

To solve this problem, 3ds max 5 has a new material type called Advanced Lighting Override. When applied to existing materials, it overrides the basic material settings. This way, the material is still visible in the sample window, but both reflectance and color bleed can be reduced to improve radiosity solutions.

Advanced Lighting Override also can be used with self-illuminated materials to cause the material to actually cast light, as though the object with the material were a photometric light source. You will learn more about that in Chapter 11, "Materials and Lighting: The Magic Combination." In this section, you learn to apply Advanced Lighting Override to materials in your scene to control reflectance and color bleed.

Material Override and Reflectance

The amount of light bouncing from the floor and lighting the walls and ceiling of your scene is a bit much, but the colors of the floor are just the way the client wants them. If you start to play with the Value settings of the brick color swatch to reduce the amount of bounced light, you will change the color too much. As an alternative, you add an Advanced Lighting Override material to the floor material and reduce the Reflectance value.

Exercise 7.6: Using Advanced Lighting Override Material to Control Reflectance

1. Open Bungalow_Materials06.max, and save it as `Bungalow_Materials07.max`. Render the Camera02 viewport. The radiosity solution was stored in the mesh from the previous exercise.

2. Choose Rendering, RAM Player from the menu. In the RAM Player, click the Open Last Rendered Image in Channel A button. Click OK in the RAM

On the CD

exercises\CH07\ Bungalow_Materials06. max

Player Configuration dialog box. Notice that the room is quite bright from the light bouncing off the floor to the ceiling and walls. Minimize the RAM Player.

3. Open the Material Editor and click the Brick Floor sample window. Click the Standard button to the right of the material name field, and double-click Advanced Lighting Override in the Material/Map Browser list. This time, make sure the Keep Old Material as Sub-material radio button is selected in the Replace dialog box, and click OK.

4. In the Advanced Lighting Override Material rollout, enter 0.5 in the Reflectance Scale field (see Figure 7.23).

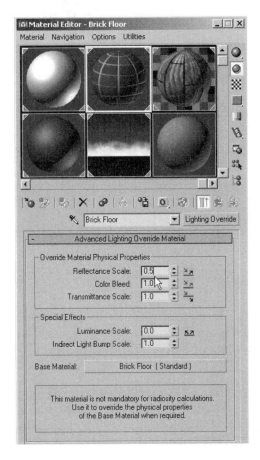

Figure 7.23 *Enter 0.5 in the Reflectance Scale field to reduce the amount of reflectance.*

5. Open the Advanced Lighting dialog box and click the Reset All button. Click Start for a new radiosity solution. Render the Camera02 viewport. Maximize the RAM Player, and click Open Last Rendered Image in Channel B. The light levels in Channel B are noticeably lower, but the floor color is just a little darker (see Figure 7.24).

FIGURE 7.24   *The light reflectance from the floor to the walls and ceiling has been reduced without affecting the color of the floor.*

6. Close all windows and dialog boxes and save the file. It should be called Bungalow_Materials07.max.

You have reduced the reflectance of the floor material without changing the map's color or output level.

Using Advanced Lighting Override to Control Color Bleed

The room has a decidedly green tint to the lighting, primarily from the grass areas outside the window. The Daylight bounces off the grass and into the room, bringing the green of the grass with it.

The amount of light bouncing from the grass is acceptable; it is just the amount of green color that is overwhelming. To fix this problem, you use the Advanced Lighting Override material to lower the color bleed while retaining the reflectance.

Exercise 7.7: Using Advanced Lighting Override Material to Control Color Bleed

1. Open Bungalow_Materials07.max, and save it as Bungalow_Materials08.max. Open the Material Editor and activate the Ground sample window, a Multi/Sub-Object material with three materials.

2. Click on the first sub-object material, also called Ground. Click the Standard button, and choose Advanced Lighting Override in the Material/Map Browser. Select the Keep the Old Material as a Sub-material radio button, and click OK.

3. In the Advanced Lighting Override Material rollout, enter 0.1 in the Color Bleed field (see Figure 7.25).

FIGURE 7.25   *In the Advanced Lighting Material Override Material rollout, enter 0.1 in the Color Bleed field.*

4. In the Advanced Lighting dialog box (keyboard shortcut: **9**), click Reset All, and then click Start to calculate the new radiosity solution.

5. Render the Camera02 viewport and notice the reduction in the green tint on the walls and ceiling; the grass outside the window is still a very bright green color, however.

6. Close all windows and dialog boxes and save the file. It should be called Bungalow_Materials08.max.

You have adjusted the material's color bleed while leaving the Reflectance value as is. Again, the Advanced Lighting Override material should be used only when there is no good alternative to reducing the a material's reflectance or color bleed without affecting the color adversely.

Summary

- **UVW Map modifier**   You have learned to apply the UVW Map modifier to objects to adjust the scale of projected maps or patterns in your materials, thus creating a more convincing look. You learned to determine how much area one repetition of the map pattern would cover, and then adjusted the UVW Map Gizmo to reflect that size in the scene. The map then repeats over the surface to fill it with the pattern.

- **Nested maps**   You learned to use maps within maps to create a planking material that has black caulking between wood planks.

- **Lofted mapping coordinates**   You assigned a material to a lofted object and used its built-in mapping coordinates to adjust the number of repeats and have the material flow around the curvature of the loft path.

- **Flat Mirror reflections**   You learned how to create and adjust efficient reflections for flat surfaces.

- **Reflection maps**   You learned to create reflections in your materials to give them more depth and presence. You learned that Flat Mirror reflections are fast to calculate and can be blurred, but are restricted to coplanar faces only. You learned the Reflect/Refract maps work only on curved surfaces, not on objects with both flat and curved surfaces. Raytrace map reflections are very accurate and function on any surface form, but can take longer to render.

- **Advanced Lighting Override material**   You learned to use the new Advanced Lighting Override material to control material attributes such as reflectance and color bleed without adjusting the actual colors. You also learned that it should be used judiciously, as it can slow production.

CHAPTER 8

Interior Lighting with New Photometric Lights

In This Chapter

This chapter focuses on the new 3ds max 5 lighting enhancements. You will apply photometric lights to a simple interior scene and adjust those lights and their shadows to strike a balance between quality and efficiency. Among the topics you will cover are the following:

- **Photometric lights** Learn the fundamentals of photometric light placement and the effects of light intensity, color, and distribution patterns.

- **New lighting types** Learn about the new 3ds max 5 photometric lighting types, such as Linear and Area, and some of their applications.

- **Shadows** Learn the importance of shadows in a scene, the shadow types that can be used with the new photometric lighting, and shadow features that aren't available with standard lighting. You'll also learn that shadows can be a drain on system resources.

Developing a good understanding of the fundamentals of photometric lighting will help make you more productive and give you an artistic advantage over your competition.

note Photometric lighting makes sense only when used with radiosity rendering.

Key Terms

Advanced Ray Traced shadows
Accurate shadows with controls available
to soften the edges.

Area lights   New 3ds max 5 lights that
radiate from an area as opposed to a
point. Creates soft lighting effects.

Area shadows   Shadows that are
sharper at the base of objects and grow
diffuse as the distance from the object
increases.

Linear lights   New lights that simulate fluorescent tube lights.

Hot Keys

h   Open the Select Objects or Pick Object
dialog box

m   Open the Material Editor

9   Open the Advanced Lighting dialog box

Some Principles of Photometric Lighting and Radiosity

The behavior of light in the real world is based on good old-fashioned physics.
Electricity heats an element and then converts the electrical energy into light energy
and heat. The light energy speeds willy-nilly through space, crashing into surfaces
that it reflects from or passes through, or is absorbed by the surface to become more
heat. Even if light energy does not strike a surface on its trip, it is still converted to
other forms of energy by decay and interaction with the atmosphere.

Photometric lights in 3ds max 5 try to mathematically
simulate as much of these real light physics as practical to achieve a visual quality that is important to
you, the artist.

Photometric lights do, however, bounce from surfaces and decay in strength as they pass through
space. You set a light intensity at the source, and the
software calculates the decay based on a formula
called the *Inverse Square law*. Light diminishes at a
rate inversely to the square of the distance from the
source. If the light has a certain strength at the
source, at 4 feet it has $1 \div distance^2$, or $1 \div 16$, the
strength. At 16 feet, it has $1 \div 256$ as much strength.
This accurate falloff of light adds to the illusion that
convinces the viewer the scene is real.

note

The conversion of light energy
to heat energy is usually not
visible in the real world. The
software engineers have seen
fit to leave that aspect out of
3ds max 5 lighting. You will
not burn down the house with
3ds max lights yet, although
there are probably those who
complain about the omission.

The preceding note is in jest.

In previous versions of 3ds max, lighting scenes could be difficult because bounced light was not calculated in a scene. In the real world, light hitting an object is partly absorbed and partly reflected to continue on to nearby objects. Certain wavelengths of light, depending on surface conditions, bounce more than other wavelengths, effectively tinting the reflected light. For example, white sunlight streaming through a window and hitting a red carpet reflects much more of the wavelength's red and absorbs more of the blue, thus tinting the wall red.

This effect is not so much something we see in our day-to-day surroundings as something we perceive unconsciously. When it is missing, as in previous versions of 3ds max, viewers knew something was wrong with the scene, even if they could not put a finger on what it was. The solution in previous 3ds max versions was to use extra lights judiciously placed and colored to simulate the bounced light. This method of "painting with light" is not necessarily a bad lighting method. After you learn the technique, it's efficient and convincing to the viewer.

With photometric lights in 3ds max 5, you are faced with the choice of extra time for radiosity calculations or extra time setting and adjusting lights in the painting-by-light method. Learn both methods, and choose the one that makes the most sense for your application.

The New Photometric Lighting with Radiosity

This chapter's exercises walk you through the fundamental steps of creating and adjusting photometric lights in an interior scene. In Chapter 4, "Exterior Lighting: Standard and Advanced Methods," you applied a Daylight system to an exterior scene. Although radiosity rendering did enhance the scene somewhat with bounced light under the eaves and the porch roof, it was a minor contributor to the scene's look. In Chapter 6, "Modeling for Radiosity and Efficiency," you adjusted your interior model for better radiosity rendering results, but you did not get into the finer points of lighting.

In this chapter, you learn to use some of the controls in photometric lights to see how lights and surfaces interact to fill the volume with light and color. You will switch between light types, such as Point, Linear, and Area, to see how the type of light affects the quality of the lighting. You'll also learn the effects of some distribution patterns available in 3ds max 5, and see how light color can be affected by changing the bulb type.

Photometric Light Placement and Fundamental Adjustments

The photometric lights you will learn about in these exercises come in three forms:

- **Point**   Point lights are just that—a single point in space with light that radiates in all directions. A Point light can be used to simulate a typical bare incandescent light bulb.

- **Linear**   Linear lights are similar to fluorescent light tubes in a light fixture. The light radiates downward and outward from the source, as though directed by the fixture.

- **Area**   Area lights can be used to simulate an array of fluorescent bulbs in a fixture or the skylight through a north-facing window. This simulates a softer flood of light with little direction.

The placement of photometric lights in a scene usually corresponds to typical lighting fixtures in the real world. You then rely on the Radiosity renderer to bounce light from surfaces to fill in the dark areas not directly illuminated by the light. Lighting a scene with Standard lights is more analogous to painting the scene with light brushes—that is, getting light to fall on surfaces with no regard for the light's positioning in the scene.

These exercises use the interior scene from Chapter 7, "Materials and Mapping: Deeper into the Details," with major objects placed on a layer that has radiosity meshing parameters set to 2 feet. This setting produces a reasonable quality radiosity solution with an acceptable render time.

The scene includes a glass vase on the counter and two hanging light fixtures created from a 2D closed spline and the Lathe modifier. The inside segments of the spline were assigned Material ID #2, corresponding to a pure white Multi/Sub-Object material, to bounce the light from the fixture. The fixture's outside material is a green enamel. The floor material's reflections have been disabled so that you can better see the shadows from the counter.

Point Lights and Distribution Patterns

In this exercise, you create a Target Point light in the scene and clone it as an Instance. Remember that with Instance clones, you can edit either light to affect all instances. You calculate a radiosity solution for the default Target Point light and render the camera viewport to see the effect of the lights on the scene. You then learn to change the light distribution with some typical fixture types and by using a manufacturer's file for specific distribution patterns.

Exercise 8.1: Placing Point Lights in Fixtures

1. Open Bungalow_Lighting01.max from the CD-ROM.
   Choose File, Save As from the menu, select a subdirectory, and click the + button to increment the new
   filename to Bungalow_Lighting02.max. Right-click
   in the Left viewport to activate it. In the Create
   panel, Lights category, click the drop-down arrow
   next to Standard, and choose Photometric from the
   list (see Figure 8.1). There are three types of lights
   you'll use in these exercises: Point, Linear, and Area.

2. In the Create panel, Lights category, Object Type
   rollout, click the Target Point button. In the Left
   viewport, click in the middle of the hanging lightshade (to set the lightshade as the source) and drag
   straight down to the floor (to set the floor as the
   target), as shown in Figure 8.2. The target is automatically named for the light it's associated with.

3. With the new light selected, click the Align button
   on the main toolbar, and pick the light fixture in
   the Left viewport. In the Align Selection dialog
   box, select the Y Position check box and select the
   Center radio button under Current Object and the
   Minimum radio button under Target Object. Click
   the OK button to exit the dialog box. This sets the
   light's height in relation to the fixture.

On the CD

exercises\CH08\
Bungalow_Lighting01.
max

FIGURE 8.1
*Select Photometric for the light-
ing system.*

---

tip

Target and Free lights behave the same. Target lights are intended for fixed lights that
are aimed at a special Dummy object called the "target." Free lights are generally animated through the scene, such as a flashlight or car headlights, and are aimed with
the Select and Rotate tool.

---

note

The IES Sun and Sky lights are the two components of the Daylight system you used
in Chapter 4 for the street scene. They can be accessed independently of the
Daylight system in this menu.

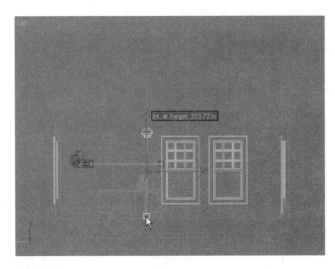

FIGURE 8.2   *Setting the source and target for the Target Point light.*

caution   Step 2 does not position the light correctly, even though it might look correct in the Left viewport. Remember that objects are created on the active grid plane that passes through the 0,0,0 coordinate point. You must move the light into its final position after setting the source and target.

tip   The distance from the light source to the light target has no affect on the light; it's simply a visual aid for placement.

4. On the main toolbar, click the Select By Name button and chose Point01 and Point01.Target in the list (see Figure 8.3). You will align the light and target under the fixture.

5. On the main toolbar, click the Align button. In the Top viewport, click the lamp_shape01 object on the right. In the Align Selection dialog box, select the X Position and Y Position check boxes and the Center radio button in both columns (see Figure 8.4). Click OK. This centers the light and target under the fixture.

note   Aligning Point01 alone would cause it to point off in the original target direction rather than straight down from the fixture.

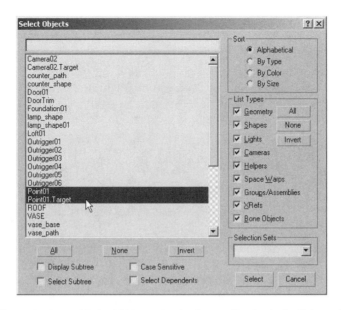

FIGURE 8.3   *Select Point01 and Point01.Target in the list to align both the light and the target.*

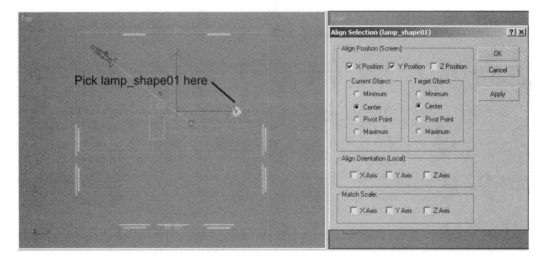

FIGURE 8.4   *Align the light and its target below the fixture. The Z-axis position was set properly when you created the light.*

6. Click the Select and Move button on the main toolbar. Hold the Shift key down, and in the Top viewport, click the X restrict arrow shaft of Transform Gizmo, and clone the light and target to the center of the other fixture. Select the Instance radio button in the Clone Objects dialog box (see Figure 8.5), and click OK. This makes an Instance clone, so if you edit one light, the other changes, too. Repeat the align operation in step 5 for this light and fixture.

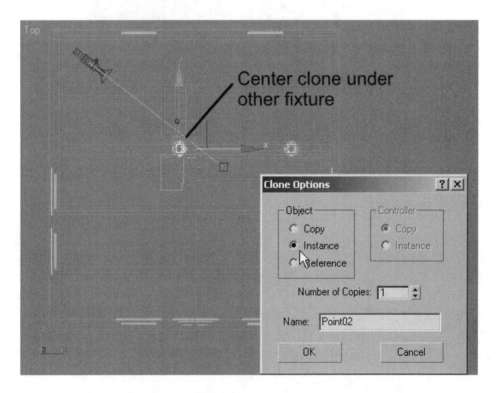

FIGURE 8.5   *To clone the light and target to the center of the other fixture, select the Instance radio button in the Clone Objects dialog box, and click OK.*

7. Click the Select By Name button on the main toolbar, and double-click Point01 to select the light only. In the Modify panel, Intensity/Color/Distribution rollout, enter 10000 (ten thousand) in the Intensity section (see Figure 8.6). This raises the strength of both lights (because you're using an Instance clone) to 10,000 candelas, which will be bright enough for reasonable lights and good shadows in this scene.

8. Choose Rendering, Advanced Lighting from the menu (keyboard shortcut: **9**). In the Advanced Lighting dialog box, Select Advanced Lighting rollout, make sure the Active check box has been selected for the Radiosity option. In the Radiosity Processing Parameters rollout, make sure Initial Quality is set to 85%, Refine Iterations (All Objects) to 3, and Filtering (under Interactive Tools) to 3. Click the Start button. (see Figure 8.7).

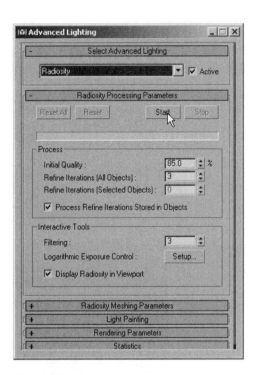

FIGURE 8.7
Enter these settings for the radiosity solution.

FIGURE 8.6
Set the intensity of both lights to 10,000.

note

Photometric lighting in 3ds max 5 is based on real-world engineering principles and uses terms such as *candelas*, *lumens*, and *lux* to describe the power of the light source.

Candelas measure the source's intensity, lumens measure the rate at which light leaves the source, and lux measures the actual illumination on an object. Each measurement represents a way to determine a light source's relationship to the objects around it.

Artists don't usually have light engineering backgrounds, however, so adjusting the strength of lights for the best appearance is still a "best guess" process.

9. When the radiosity solution is finished, right-click in the Camera02 viewport to activate it. On the main toolbar, click the Quick Render button. The scene should have moderate light on the floor and counter, with some light bouncing and lighting the ceiling. The vase and the counter are casting fairly hard-edged shadows (see Figure 8.8).

note

The quality of the light, especially on the walls and ceiling, is much better than in Chapter 7. This is not because of the lighting itself, but because the objects in this scene are being meshed at 2 feet, resulting in more vertices and faces to calculate a radiosity solution. Also note that the sunlight has been deleted from the scene.

FIGURE 8.8   *Quick render the Camera02 viewport to see moderate light levels with fairly hard-edged shadows.*

10. The default distribution pattern of a Point light type is called Isotropic, which casts light in all directions equally. This works fine for the fixture type in your scene, where the light bouncing from inside the fixture is important. At times, however, you need to direct the light in a more controlled fashion. In the Intensity/Color/Distribution rollout, click the Distribution drop-down arrow and choose Spotlight from the list (see Figure 8.9).

11. The viewports now display two cones: a light blue Hotspot and a dark blue Falloff from the light source (see Figure 8.10). The light now shines only in the area defined by the cones. Choose Rendering, Advanced Lighting from the menu (keyboard shortcut: **9**). In the Radiosity Processing Parameters rollout, click the Reset All button, and then click the Start button. When the radiosity solution is complete, quick render the Camera02 viewport. The cones concentrate the light in such a small area that no light is bounced from inside the fixtures, and minimal light is bounced from the dark counter and floor. The light pools are soft-edged, going from full light in the Hotspot cone and falling off to no light outside the Falloff cone (see Figure 8.11).

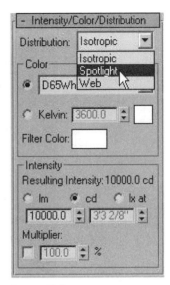

FIGURE 8.9
Switch to the Spotlight distribution pattern to see how a different distribution pattern affects the scene.

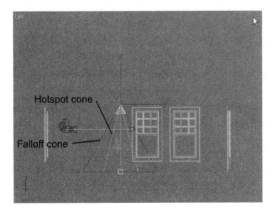

FIGURE 8.10 *The Spotlight distribution pattern focuses the light from the light source within two cones, Hotspot and Falloff.*

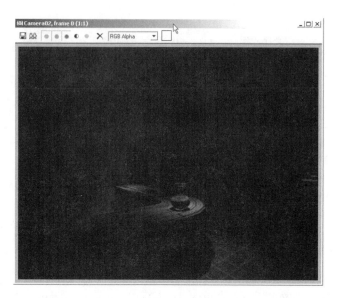

FIGURE 8.11   *The Point lights with Spotlight distribution concentrate the light in two small circles on the counter and floor. This contributes almost no bounced light to the scene.*

tip

You can adjust the softness of the light pool's edge by setting the size of the Hotspot and Falloff cones in the Spotlight Parameters rollout. The closer the numbers are to each other, the harder the light edge.

12. In the Intensity/Color/Distribution rollout, click the Distribution drop-down arrow and choose Web from the list. In the Web Parameters rollout, click the None button under Web File, and load point_ street.ies from the CD-ROM. This is a distribution pattern for a generic type of street light. In the Advanced Lighting dialog box, click Reset All and then click Start. When the solution is done, quick render the Camera02 viewport. This yields a result similar to Isotropic, but without as much bounced light. The light is mostly distributed downward and sideways, giving less light from the fixture and, therefore, less bounced light, even though the light strength is much higher (17840 candelas versus 10000 candelas for the Isotropic light).

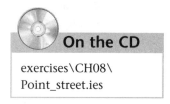

On the CD

exercises\CH08\ Point_street.ies

tip

You might use Web distribution if you are working for an architect who needs accurate lighting effects, or if you are doing forensic work for the courts, where accuracy is a must.

13. Set the Distribution setting back to Isotropic and the Intensity setting back to 10000 candelas for a brighter scene, which will be easier to work with in upcoming exercises. Close all windows and dialog boxes. Save the file. It should already be called Bungalow_Lighting02.max.

With two photometric lights, you have accomplished what would have taken at least four to eight Standard lights to approximate. By adjusting meshing and light parameters judiciously, you can achieve a balance of quality and render speed and still maintain productivity.

You may have noticed that, especially with Point lights, the fixture type and material can greatly affect the lighting. Much of the light in the scene rendered with Point lights and Isotropic distribution came from the light bounced from the highly reflective inside of the fixtures. The Spotlight distribution directed all the light downward, for example, and the lack of light bounced from the fixture left the room very dark. The Web distribution bounced only a little light at the edge of the fixture.

You have seen that different distribution patterns can also affect the lighting. Spotlight distribution focuses the light within the two cones and reduces the light that can be bounced in the scene. Web distribution can be used when lighting accuracy is paramount, from an engineer's point of view. For proper application, you need information from specific lighting manufacturers in the form of .ies files and a background in light engineering.

tip

You can use Spotlight distribution much as you would use barn door spotlights, with the four adjustable wings, on a movie set—not so much to add light to the scene, but to draw the viewer's attention to objects or characters important to your story.

Treat lighting as part of the storytelling process, not just to illuminate the scene.

Application of New Linear Lights

Although Point lights with Isotropic distribution can simulate standard Omni lights, and Spotlight distribution can simulate standard Spotlights, there is a new light type in 3ds max 5 with no equivalent in previous versions: the Linear light type.

Linear lights are similar to fluorescent tube lighting in the real world—not the tube itself, which is long and radiates in all directions, but like a fluorescent fixture with one or two bulbs. The default Linear lights distribute light in a long pattern diffused downward and to the sides. The length of the light can be adjusted from its 1-meter default length.

In the next exercise, you convert the Point lights in the scene to Linear lights to see the difference in lighting patterns in the room. You then adjust the length of the light to see how much a longer fixture affects the scene.

Exercise 8.2: Using the New Linear Light Type

1. Open Bungalow_Lighting02.max, and save it as
   `Bungalow_Lighting03.max`. The scene contains
   two Target Point lights in round hanging fixtures.
   Select the Point01 light in the scene. In the
   Modify panel, General Parameters rollout, click
   the drop-down arrow next to On in the Light
   Type section and choose Linear in the list (see
   Figure 8.12). It is not necessary to delete the Point
   light and add the Linear light to the scene, as the
   light type can be changed at any time. Notice that
   the light icon in the scene has a line running
   through the top to indicate the length of the
   Linear light. The light shines in the direction of
   the sphere below the line.

2. Choose Rendering, Advanced Lighting from the
   menu (keyboard shortcut: **9**). In the Advanced
   Lighting dialog box, Radiosity Processing
   Parameters rollout, click the Reset All button and
   then the Start button to recalculate the solution
   for the new lights. When the calculation is done,
   quick render the Camera02 viewport. The scene is
   again much darker overall because the light is diffused downward and sideways, and the lighting
   fixtures contribute no light (see Figure 8.13).

3. Choose Rendering, RAM Player from the menu. In
   the RAM Player dialog box, click the Open Last
   Rendered Image in Channel A button. Accept the
   default settings and minimize the RAM Player. In
   the Modify panel, expand the Linear Light
   Parameters rollout and enter **10** in the Length
   field. This makes the Linear lights 10 feet long in
   the scene.

On the CD

exercises\CH08\
Bungalow_Lighting02.
max

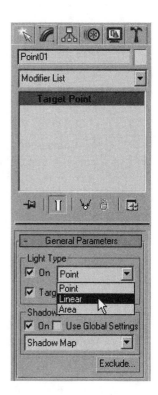

Figure 8.12
*Select Linear from the list to
change the light type.*

caution   The name of the light does not change to reflect the new light type. The Linear lights are still called Point01 and Point02. This can lead to confusion if you do not rename your lights as you create them in a production environment.

tip   You can change the new lights from Target to Free by clearing the Targeted check box in the General Parameters rollout, Light Type section.

Figure 8.13   *The Linear light casts light down and out to the sides but not into the fixture.*

4. In the Advanced Lighting dialog box, click Reset All, and then click Start to recalculate the radiosity. When the solution is finished, quick render the Camera02 viewport. Maximize the RAM Player, and click Open Last Rendered Image in Channel B. You might have expected a longer light to add more illumination, but the actual amount of light added to the scene is minimal and overall a bit more diffuse. The render also took noticeably longer. In the Modify panel, Linear Light Parameters rollout, set the light back to a 1-meter length.

tip

When entering numeric values, you can convert units simply by adding the appropriate suffix. For example, to get the equivalent of a 1-meter light, enter 1m, and it will be converted to 3'3 2/8" automatically.

To simulate a string of fluorescent lights, you would need to use three 1-meter lights instead of a single 10-foot light.

5. Notice in the Modify panel, Intensity/Color/ Distribution rollout, that the color of the light is set to D65White. Click the drop-down arrow and select Fluorescent in the list (see Figure 8.14). Reset and recalculate the radiosity solution, and render the scene. You'll see a slight change in the wall colors. Set the light back to D65White.

6. Close all windows and dialog boxes, including the RAM Player. Save the file; it should already be called Bungalow_Lighting03.max.

Switching to a Linear light type changes the distribution to an elongated pattern that casts light downward and sideways. To simulate a string of fluorescent bulbs, you need to create multiple Linear lights, not just lengthen one light.

You can adjust the color of any light by choosing a specific light type or, more accurately, by looking up values and entering a Kelvin temperature amount. You can find some common values in the online User Reference by searching on `kelvin`.

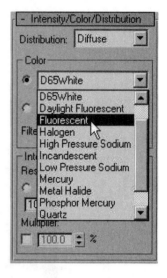

FIGURE 8.14
Use the color list to select the color temperature of common light sources. For example, switching from D65White to Fluorescent gives the scene a greenish cast.

The effects of changing lights' colors in a scene vary widely depending on whether materials are absorbing or bleeding the light color.

You can also enter specific Kelvin temperatures in the Intensity/Color/Distribution rollout to adjust color: Incandescent is around 3200K, and daylight is around 10,000K. Select the Kelvin radio button to access the numeric field.

Investigating the New Area Lights

Area lights, a new light type in 3ds max 5, offer a soft diffuse light that emanates from a wide area to simulate, for example, lighting from a fixture that usually contains four or more fluorescent bulbs with a diffusing lens that spreads the light downward and outward. You also could use Area lights to simulate the soft, diffuse north light coming through an artist's loft window or skylight.

Exercise 8.3: Using the New Area Lights

1. Open Bungalow_Lighting03.max, and save it as Bungalow_Lighting04.max. Select the Point01 light in the Top viewport. In the Modify panel, General Parameters rollout, click the drop-down arrow in the Light Type section, and select Area in the list. The icons in the scene become square with a sphere indicating the direction of the light (see Figure 8.15).

On the CD

exercises\CH08\ Bungalow_Lighting03. max

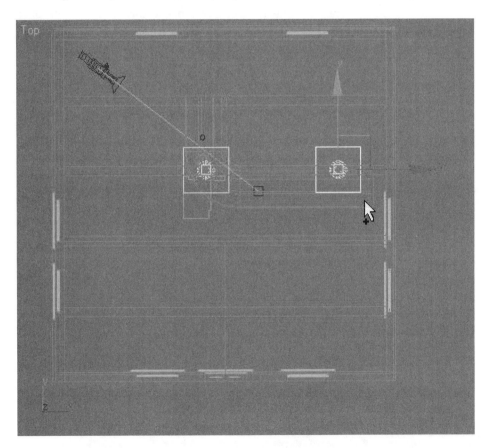

FIGURE 8.15 *Area light icons as seen in the Top viewport. The light emanates from a 1-meter square area diffused downward and outward.*

2. In the Advanced Lighting dialog box, click Reset All and Start to calculate a new radiosity solution. When it's finished, quick render the Camera02 viewport. Notice that there's not much difference from the two Linear lights used in the previous exercise.

note

You'll see a thin bright area at the bottom of each light fixture. The Area lights extend beyond these fixtures and light the bottom edge.

3. Right-click in the Top viewport to activate it. On the main toolbar, click the Select By Name button and choose Point01, Point02, and the two corresponding targets. Click the Select and Move button, and holding down the Shift key, move and clone the lights (selecting Instance in the Clone Options dialog box) to about halfway between the original lights and the wall with the door at the bottom of the viewport (see Figure 8.16).

tip

In the Select By Name dialog box, you can filter the object names by selecting only the categories you want to see in the List Types section, making it much easier to select only lights, for example.

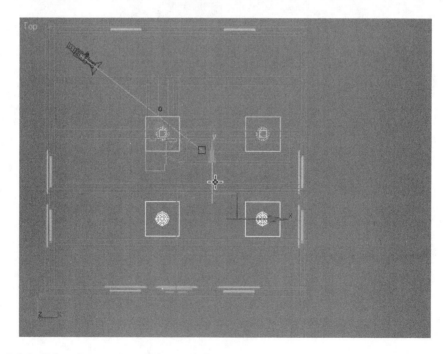

Figure 8.16   *Select the two Area lights and their targets and clone them as Instances between the original lights and the wall with the door.*

4. In the Advanced Lighting dialog box, click Reset All and then Start to recalculate the radiosity solution. Quick render the Camera02 viewport. There is noticeably more soft light, and the scene is developing more complex shadow patterns.

5. Close all windows and dialog boxes. Save the file. It should already be named Bungalow_Lighting04.max.

You learned that Area lights are similar to Linear lights, but have a broader coverage sideways. They tend to be used in arrays in a large interior space, but could also be used to simulate the soft, diffuse light from a north-facing window or skylight.

note

When using the old method of Standard lights, avoiding hotspots where two lights overlapped on surfaces was difficult. In a radiosity solution, the new lights do not exhibit that same problem.

New Shadow-Casting Options in 3ds max 5

Shadows give objects weight in the scene by anchoring them to the surfaces they sit on. There are a wide variety of shadow types and shadow effects in 3ds max 5, some of which are new to this release.

So far, you have been using Shadow Map shadows in the bungalow interior scene. The shadows have a fairly hard edge and constant density over the entire shadow. Shadow Map shadows have been around for a long time and are popular for their fast rendering times, even though they are not particularly convincing. Many viewers don't focus on the detail of the shadows, and you can get away with a lot before the viewer becomes suspicious.

You can adjust the softness/hardness of Shadow Map shadow edges with the Size and Sample Range settings and shift the shadows away from or toward the light source by using the Bias setting. Shadow color and density can also be adjusted. Keep in mind that increasing the Size setting can quickly deplete your computer resources when you have many lights, thus slowing production.

In Chapter 4, you created lighting for an outdoor scene and used Ray Traced Shadows (available in previous 3ds max versions) to cast the shadows. They are more intensive, mathematically speaking, and can render quite slowly in scenes with dense mesh objects. The shadow edges are always crisp and harsh, well suited to bright outdoor scenes.

New to 3ds max 5 are Advanced Ray Traced shadows and Area shadows. Advanced Ray Traced shadows are similar to the Ray Traced Shadows option you've used previously, but you have more control over the quality of the shadow, especially at the edges.

When light shines obliquely onto objects, Area shadows add another dimension to your shadows entirely. These long shadows are denser, with sharper edges near the base of objects, and become lighter with softer edges as the shadow becomes more distant from the top of the object.

As each shadow type is required to do more math, you will, of course, have to compromise productivity. Learn how shadows function at their fundamental levels, and then apply them to very simple scenes to learn the effects of adjustments. After you are comfortable with the fundamentals, you can rapidly build on that knowledge to work with more complex scenes.

> **warning**
>
> Even in this simple scene, the render times are going to increase significantly with the new shadow types. Make sure you allow enough time and have patience. It is worth it.

Advanced Ray Traced Shadows

In this exercise, you delete the two newly created lights and switch back to Point lights for the original lights. Next, you render the scene with Shadow Map shadows and view the results in the RAM Player. You then switch to Advanced Ray Traced Shadows, render again for comparison, and make adjustments to vary the shadows in the scene.

Exercise 8.4: Using Advanced Ray Traced Shadows

1. Open Bungalow_Lighting04.max, and save it as Bungalow_Lighting05.max. On the main toolbar, click the Select By Name button and choose Point03 and Point04 in the list. Click the Select button to select them and close the dialog box. Press the Delete key on the keyboard. The lights and their targets will be deleted, as the targets cannot exist separately. Select Point01 in the Top viewport and, in the Modify panel, General Parameters rollout, switch the light type back to Point. In the Shadows section, switch to Shadow Map.

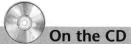

On the CD

exercises\CH08\ Bungalow_Lighting04. max

2. Choose Rendering, Advanced Lighting from the menu (keyboard shortcut: **9**). Click Reset All and then Start. When the radiosity solution is finished, quick render the Camera02 viewport. Choose Rendering, RAM Player from the menu, and click Open Last Rendered Image in Channel A. Note that the edges of the Shadow Map shadows are slightly soft.

3. In the Select By Name dialog box, double-click Point01 to select it. In the Modify panel, General Parameters rollout, click the drop-down arrow in the Shadows section and choose Adv. Ray Traced in the list (see Figure 8.17).

4. Quick render the Camera02 viewport, and in the RAM Player, click the Open Last Rendered Image in Channel B button. Click in the RAM Player window, and scrub back and forth while holding down the left mouse button to compare the Shadow Map and Advanced Ray Traced shadows. The Advanced Ray Traced shadows have become crisper, but the scene took longer to render.

5. You might not have noticed, but the shadow of the glass vase on the counter has been solid with both types of shadows. Shadow Map shadows do not respect the transparency of materials and always have solid shadows. Standard Ray Traced shadows take transparency into account, as you saw in Chapter 4 with the sun coming through the windows. In the Modify panel, Optimizations rollout, select the On check box in the Transparent Shadows section (see Figure 8.18). Quick render the Camera02 viewport and notice that the shadow from the vase is much lighter. The scene also takes longer to render.

6. To create softer shadow edges with Advanced Ray Traced shadows, you must adjust the Shadow Spread setting. In the Modify panel, Adv. Ray Traced Params rollout, enter 5 in the Shadow Spread field. Quick render the Camera02 viewport, and click Open Last Rendered Image in Channel A in the RAM Player. The shadow edges are much softer, but the render times are a bit longer.

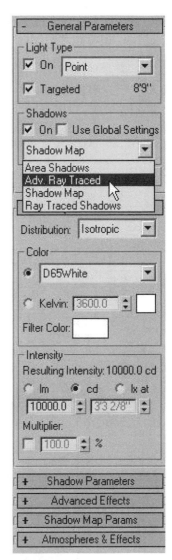

FIGURE 8.17
Select Adv. Ray Traced as the shadow type.

tip

As long as lights and objects have not been moved in the scene, you can test shadow changes without recalculating the radiosity solution. However, it would be a good idea to click Reset All and Start to calculate the solution before the final render.

7. You might notice that the shadow on the far wall from the fixture is somewhat striped (see Figure 8.19). In the Modify panel, Adv. Ray Traced Params rollout, enter 0.18 in the Jitter Amount field. Quick render the Camera02 viewport, and you will see that the jittering has blended the stripes to make them less noticeable.

8. Close all windows and dialog boxes and save the file. It should already be called Bungalow_Lighting05.max.

You have learned to switch from the default Shadow Map shadows for the Point light to Advanced Ray Traced shadows. With this shadow type, you need to enable the Transparent Shadows option for the shadows to respect transparent materials and adjust the Shadow Spread and Jitter Amount settings to produce soft-edged shadows and reduce artifacts at the edge of shadows. You also learned that there is a price to pay in rendering time for higher quality shadows.

FIGURE 8.18
Enable the option for Transparent Shadows to allow Advanced Ray Traced shadows to respect transparent materials.

FIGURE 8.19   *Striped artifacts show at the fixture's shadow edge on the far wall.*

Area Shadows in 3ds max 5

Area shadows are the most accurate shadows in 3ds max 5 and have the most options. You should use them when you need a shadow that changes density and edge sharpness, but be forewarned that they can take a long time to render compared to the other shadow types.

Area shadows, like Area lights, emanate from an area you describe and can have various shapes, such as rectangular, disk, or box. The shape can affect the look of the shadow. Like Advanced Ray Traced shadows, you can soften the edges and apply a jitter to clean up any artifacts that might be created.

Exercise 8.5: Using Area Shadows

1. Open Bungalow_Lighting05.max, and save it as `Bungalow_Lighting06.max`. Select Point01 light with the Select By Name button on the main toolbar.

2. In the Modify panel, General Parameters rollout, click the drop-down arrow in the Shadows section and choose Area Shadows in the list.

3. The Area shadow should usually be set to match the shape of the light or fixture; in this case, the Disc Light option best matches the shape of the lighting fixture. In the Area Shadows rollout, click the drop-down arrow in the Basic Options section and choose Disc Light in the list (see Figure 8.20). In the Antialiasing Options section, enter `0.05` in the Jitter Amount field, as 1.0 will cause artifacts in this scene, and set the Sample Spread to 3 for softer edges.

4. In the Optimizations rollout, select the On check box in the Transparent Shadows section. Quick render the Camera02 viewport. The render time is considerably longer than with other shadow types, but the shadows are very soft and have a quality you cannot achieve with the other shadow types. As the counter shadow curves away from the light toward you, you can see that it is softer as it gets farther from the light (see Figure 8.21).

On the CD

exercises\CH08\
Bungalow_Lighting05.
max

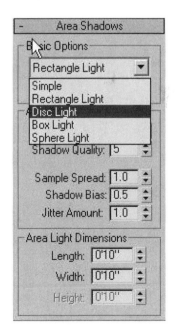

FIGURE 8.20
Switch to Disc Light to match the shape of the lighting fixture.

Figure 8.21   *Area shadows are soft and increase in softness as the distance from the light increases. Notice the change in the counter shadow on the floor as it curves from below the light toward you.*

5. Close all dialog boxes and windows and save the file. It is already called Bungalow_Lighting06.max.

In this exercise, you have learned how to switch to the Area Shadow type and adjust the settings to match the shape of the light or fixture. Area shadows can add considerable render time, but are worth it when quality is important.

Summary

In this chapter, you have learned the fundamental process of applying and adjusting the new photometric lights and shadow types in 3ds max 5:

- **Point lights**   You learned about the new Point light type and saw how to change the distribution pattern from Isotropic to Spotlight to Web, which uses manufacturers' IES files to describe the pattern of light from the source.

- **Linear lights**   The new Linear light type can be used to simulate fluorescent tube lighting fixtures. You learned that you can lengthen the source of the light, but that it has little effect on the amount of light. Use a series of short Linear lights instead of a single long one. Linear lights can also be used as accent lights in wall valances or under counters, too.

- **Area lights**   Area lights emanate from a rectangular source that you can resize as you please.

- **Advanced Ray Traced shadows**   These shadows have more options for adjusting the edge conditions than the standard Ray Traced shadows in previous versions.

- **Area shadows**   These new shadows offer much more realism because the shadows sharpen as they get closer to objects and grow increasingly diffuse as they get farther from objects.

CHAPTER 9

Taking Control with Animation Controllers

In This Chapter

A speeding car careens down narrow streets, leaning precariously as it races around corners. The car bounces roughly over areas of cobblestones while the passenger holds a steely gaze on the pursuing police cruiser.

Although you will not create as complex a scene as this, you will learn the basic tools that enable you to animate and control such action. In Chapter 5, "New Animation Concepts," you learned to animate objects moving and rotating through space by setting animation keys with the new Set Key mode. This is a common method of creating basic animation, but sometimes you need more control than the Set Key method offers.

Animation controllers handle all animation in 3ds max 5. So far, the default controllers in 3ds max 5 have been enough to perform the Set Key animation exercises. Objects created with 2D or 3D primitives tend to have a default controller for the position keys: the Position XYZ controller. Each position axis of the object, in turn, has a Bezier Position controller assigned that causes curved motion. In addition to the default controllers, you'll learn about the following controllers and constraints:

- **Path Constraint** This constraint allows you to assign one or more 2D shapes to define the position of an object, such as a car speeding around corners.

- **Noise Controller**   This controller causes an object to move randomly in the scene to simulate vibration or undulation—a car on cobblestones, for example.

- **List Controller**   This controller acts as a container for multiple controllers and constraints enables you to "stack" animation effects for compound results.

- **LookAt Constraint**   This constraint is used to make an object track another object animated through the scene; it could be used to make a character's head watch another animated object in the scene, for example.

There are too many controllers and constraints in 3ds max 5 to cover in this book, but the exercises walk you through the process of assigning controllers to objects and show you how to combine controllers. Use these exercises as a guide to the fundamental process of assigning controllers, and then experiment on your own with simple scenes so that you can focus on how the controllers function.

Key Terms

Animation constraint   A special class of controller that uses relationships with other objects to provide control over the animation.

Animation controller   An interchangeable option assigned to an object that defines the animated behavior of a specific attribute, such as position, size, shape, or color.

Range bars   Graphic elements that encompass a range of time and enable you to adjust the overall timing of animation keys within the range as a group.

UpNode   An option for defining "up" for purposes of orientation on some controllers and constraints. It might be the World Z axis or the position of some other object in the scene, for example.

Hotkeys and Keyboard Shortcuts

h   Open the Select Objects or Pick Object dialog box

Fundamental Assignment of Animation Controllers and Constraints

Many aspects of 3ds max 5 scenes can be animated with controllers. Figure 9.1 shows the Dope Sheet Editor for a scene with a box object. The column on the left, called the *Controller view*, shows a hierarchical listing of the scene. The icons to the left of the name represent the current controller type. The small gray bar to the left of the highlighted Length item for the Box object means that there's no current controller but one can be assigned.

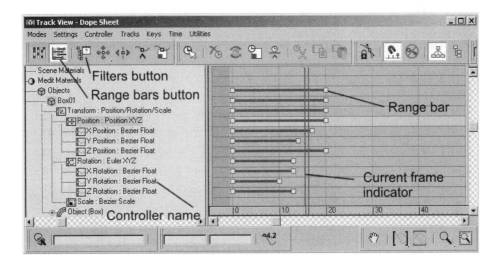

FIGURE 9.1   *Icons in the Controller view indicate the controllers assigned to various aspects of the scene.*

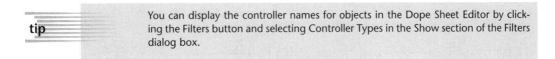

> **tip**
>
> You can display the controller names for objects in the Dope Sheet Editor by clicking the Filters button and selecting Controller Types in the Show section of the Filters dialog box.

Figure 9.2 shows several sets of controllers that can be assigned to the object's rotation, position, or Diffuse color of the material, for example. Not all objects can have the same controller types assigned to them; for example, it would make no sense to assign a Path Constraint to the color of an object.

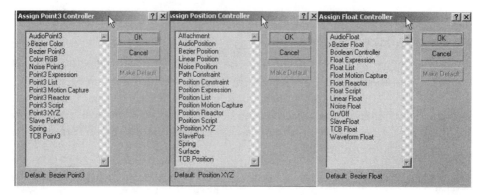

FIGURE 9.2   *Different aspects of the scene can have different controllers assigned, as shown in this sampling of controller types.*

All objects created or imported into 3ds max 5 have animation controllers pre-assigned to objects' positions, rotations, or orientation in the scene, to name a few. Primitive objects you create are automatically assigned Position XYZ controllers and EulerXYZ Rotation controllers, for example. These two controllers have other controllers assigned to the XYZ axes.

You can assign animation controllers and constraints in several places in 3ds max 5 with the same results. In the Motion panel for the selected object in the scene, for example, you can assign controllers for transformations as a whole or to an individual transform—move, rotate, or scale. You can also use the Curve Editor, which displays animation as function curves, or the Dope Sheet Editor, which displays animation as keys, to assign controllers to transforms. To assign controllers to other aspects of the scene—such as ambient light, object color, or materials, for example—you need to use either the Curve Editor or the Dope Sheet Editor.

Changing Controllers in the Motion Panel

In the first exercise, you learn the basic process for changing the Position Controller on an animated box to affect the overall type of animation. The box has been animated to move in a *W* shape through the scene. Five animation keys defining the points of the *W*-shaped path have been set with the Set Key mode.

In the Object Properties dialog box for Box01 (see Figure 9.3), the option for showing the trajectory of the object's pivot point has been switched on (see Figure 9.4).

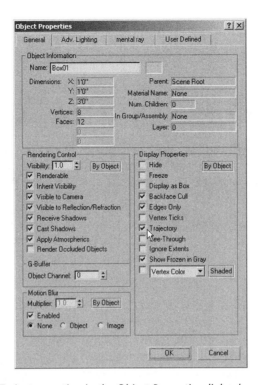

FIGURE 9.3   *Select the Trajectory option in the Object Properties dialog box.*

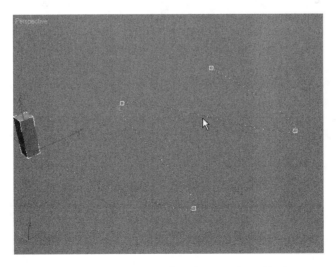

FIGURE 9.4   *The red line indicates the pivot point's trajectory; the white boxes represent key positions in the animation.*

Along the trajectory are white boxes that represent the five key positions set to create the animation. Between the white boxes are yellow dots that represent the pivot point's position in all 100 frames of the animation.

If you look at the trajectory, you'll notice that the object did not travel in a straight line from keyframe to keyframe, but curved into and out of the points. If you look closely, you can see that the yellow frame dots on the trajectory's red line are closer together in the tight curve areas than on the straight sections. This indicates that the object slows down in the curves (more frames to cover in that distance) and speeds up in the straight sections (fewer frames for the same distance). The animator did not intend for this to happen; rather, it is the result of Bezier Position controllers on the X, Y, and Z transform axes.

In the Motion panel, you'll substitute a Linear Controller for the Position XYZ controller that is the parent of the three axes. A Linear Controller causes the box to go directly, or linearly, from key to key at a constant speed.

Exercise 9.1: Using the Motion Panel to Change Transform Controllers

1. From the CD-ROM, open the Position_Cont01.max file. Choose File, Save As from the menu, select a subdirectory, and click the + button to increment the filename to Position_Cont02.max. In the Perspective viewport, pick the Box01 object to select it and display the trajectory. Click the Play Animation button in the Track bar to see the animation play in the active viewport, and notice the object slow down at the curves. Stop the animation playback.

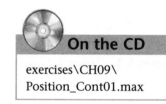

On the CD

exercises\CH09\
Position_Cont01.max

2. In the Motion panel, Assign Controller rollout, expand the Position: PositionXYZ item by clicking the + sign left of the name. Highlight Position: PositionXYZ in the list (see Figure 9.5). Remember that transform controllers can be changed in the Motion panel, the Dope Sheet Editor, or the Curve Editor with the same end results.

3. Just above and to the left of the Controller view, click the Assign Controller button. In the Assign Position Controller dialog box, select Linear Position, and click OK. The trajectory in the viewports is now a straight line with evenly spaced yellow dots along the trajectory indicating constant speed (see Figure 9.6). Play the animation to verify that, and then stop the animation.

4. Close all windows and dialog boxes and save the file. It should already be called Position_Cont02.max.

You have successfully changed Box01's Position Controller in the scene to convert the motion from a Bezier curve trajectory with variable speeds to a linear trajectory with constant speed. You can access only the transforms of an object in the Motion panel.

FIGURE 9.5
Expand Position: PositionXYZ in the list.

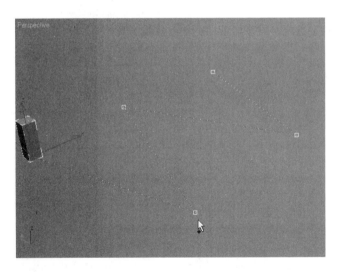

FIGURE 9.6
Assigning a Linear Position controller to Box01 eliminates the curves from the trajectory; the evenly spaced yellow dots represent constant speed.

note

When placing keyframes, you are setting specific positions (or orientation, scale, and so forth) at a specific time. 3ds max 5 determines the in-between frames based on the algorithm within the controller. The Bezier Position controller provides smooth movement into and out of the key. A Linear Position controller is designed specifically to provide a straight path from key to key.

Assigning Animation Constraints for Control by Other Objects in the Scene

Often you want more visual feedback and control in determining the trajectory that an object's pivot point follows through space. To do this, you can use one or more 2D shapes to define animation trajectories.

You can then assign a Path Constraint to the object and add the path or paths to constrain the pivot point's motion. If you have more than one path constraining the position of an object, you can weight the influence of either path on the object. This weighting can be animated as well.

tip

By default, the first vertex on the shape determines the start point of the animation, but you can change that at any time in the Modify panel, Vertex sub-object mode.

This next exercise shows you how to assign a Path Constraint to an object and make adjustments that affect the object's velocity and attitude as it travels along the path. The scene is an undulating elevated track in a hilly landscape. Atop the track sits the catapult from Chapter 5, "New Animation Concept." The timber tower in the middle has a strange device mounted at the top that will come into play in a later exercise. The scene is lit with a standard Sunlight system (no radiosity) and one Omni light as a fill light (see Figure 9.7). The material applied to the track is very bumpy where the catapult sits and is smooth everywhere else.

tip

Take some time to select each object in the scene to see how it was constructed. This scene was built very quickly, in about 15 minutes, using primarily 2D shapes, a Quad Patch, and several modifiers. The catapult was merged as one object from another file.

Analyzing the Modifier Stack of objects built by others is a great way to learn different approaches to modeling. Viewing the Material Editor can also give you some insights on creating materials.

You never want to use other people's work directly unless given express permission, but you do want to study others' work to learn from them.

By default, the first vertex on the shape determines the start point of the animation, but you can change that at any time in the Modify panel, Vertex sub-object mode.

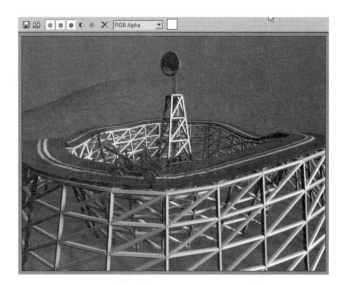

FIGURE 9.7   *The camera view of the catapult from Chapter 5 running along an undulating elevated track.*

In this exercise, you create a Dummy object and assign it a Path Constraint in the Dope Sheet Editor. This animates the dummy along a 2D shape in the center of the track. You then align the catapult with the Dummy and link it as a child to the parent Dummy, and the Dummy pulls the catapult around the track. You learn to adjust the Dummy's velocity on the path and its angle in relation to the track as it travels around the track.

Exercise 9.2: Using the Path Constraint and a 2D Shape

1. From the CD-ROM, open the Cat_Animate01.max file, and save it as `Cat_Animate02.max`. Right-click in the Top viewport to activate it. In the Create panel, Helpers category, click the Dummy button. Click anywhere outside the track in the Top viewport and drag to create a Dummy object roughly the width of the track.

On the CD

exercises\CH09\
Cat_Animate01.max

2. Choose Graph Editor, Track View – Dope Sheet from the menu. You used the Dope Sheet Editor in Chapter 5 to see the animation's keys displayed in a graph. You can also assign animation controllers by using this graphical interface.

3. In the Dope Sheet Editor, highlight Position for the Dummy01 object. It will turn yellow when selected. The current animation controller is PositionXYZ. From the Dope Sheet Editor menu, choose Controller, Assign (see Figure 9.8).

| tip | Even though there are several objects in the scene, the Dope Sheet Editor displays the tracks for the Dummy01 object because it was the selected object when you opened the Dope Sheet Editor. This saves searching through long lists of objects in your scene's hierarchy. |

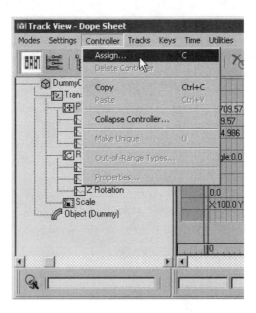

FIGURE 9.8   *In the Dope Sheet Editor, choose Controllers, Assign to open the Assign Position Controller dialog box.*

4. In the Assign Position Controller dialog box, double-click Path Constraint (see Figure 9.9). If you tried to move the Dummy01 object in the scene now, you could not do it because it no longer has an animation controller. Instead, it has an animation constraint without a path to constrain itself to.

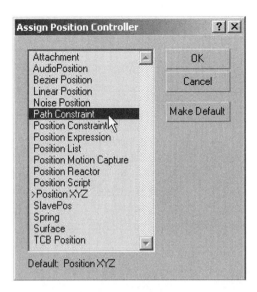

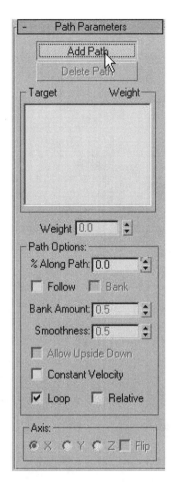

FIGURE 9.9   *Double-click Path Constraint to assign the controller to Dummy01's Position transform.*

5. In the Motion panel, Controller view, you will see that the Path Constraint has been added next to the Position transform. You also will see a new Path Parameters rollout that has expanded. In the Path Parameters rollout, click the Add Path button (see Figure 9.10). Press **h** and double-click loft_path in the Pick Object dialog box. Click the Add Path button again to toggle it off.

6. Several things have occurred from the actions in step 5. In the Path Parameters rollout, loft_path is displayed with a weight of 50. In the Track bar, below the viewports, two keys have been created at frame 0 and frame 100. The keys also have been created in the Dope Sheet Editor to the right of Dummy01, Transform, Position, and Percent. The Dummy01 object has jumped to the First Vertex of the loft_path shape. Scrub the Time slider, and notice that Dummy01 is animated

FIGURE 9.10
Use the Path Parameters rollout to assign a path for the Dummy01 object.

from 0% along the path at frame 0 to 100% along the path at frame 100. Right-click in the Camera01 viewport and click the Play Animation button. Dummy01 will move around the track in the active viewport. In the Path Parameters rollout, the value in the % Along Path field will continually be updated (notice that the spinners have red brackets to indicate an animated feature). Stop the animation.

7. Close the Dope Sheet Editor. Click the Select By Name button and double-click Cat in the list to select it. On the main toolbar, click the Align button, and in the Camera01 viewport, pick the Dummy01 object. In the Align Selection (Dummy01) dialog box, click the X, Y, and Z Position check boxes. Select the Pivot Point radio button under both Current Object and Target Object, and select the three check boxes for the X, Y, and Z axes under Align Orientation (local). See Figure 9.11. Click OK to align the objects. This ensures that the objects share a common pivot point and that their local axes run in the same direction.

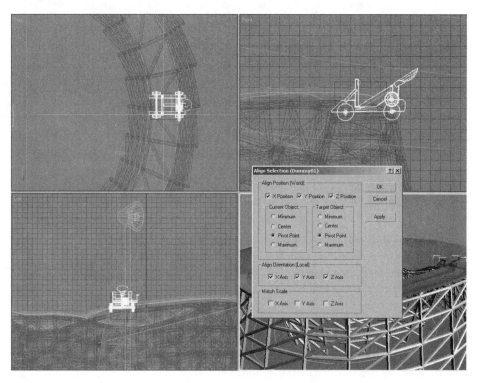

FIGURE 9.11   *Aligning the catapult with the Dummy01 object.*

8. On the main toolbar, click the Select and Link button. Press **h** and double-click Dummy01 in the list. The Cat object is now a child of the parent Dummy01. Play the animation; Cat is dragged around the track, always holding its original rotation from the start.

9. Drag the Time slider to move Dummy01 to the track closest to you in the Camera01 viewport. Select Cat, and on the main toolbar, click the Select and Move button. On the main toolbar, switch the Reference Coordinate System to the Local option. In the Camera01 viewport, move Cat in its local Z-axis until the front wheels seem to be sitting on the track (see Figure 9.12). The shaded Camera01 viewport enables you to see when the wheels are roughly on the track.

FIGURE 9.12   *Move Cat up in the local Z axis until the front wheels seem to be sitting on the track.*

10. Select Dummy01 in the Camera01 viewport. In the Motion panel, Path Parameters rollout, select the Follow check box in the Path Options section. Scrub the Time slider, and you will see that Dummy01 and Cat stay oriented to the path while traveling along the track, but are traveling backward. Select the Flip check box and the X radio button at the bottom of Path Parameters rollout to flip the Dummy01 and Cat objects 180 degrees on the path (see Figure 9.13). Select the Bank check box under Path Options, and you'll see that Dummy01 reads the curves and banks into the turns. This is not appropriate for a flat track, however, so clear that check box after you see how it functions.

note The Follow option reads the path curvature in all directions, so the objects tilt up and down the hills as well.

11. Close all windows and dialog boxes and save the file. It should already be called Cat_Animate02.max. Play the animation in the Camera01 viewport to see the results. The Dummy01 object pulls the Cat object along the path and keeps the orientation perpendicular to the path, making the catapult wheels appear to follow the track's surface.

You have learned to apply a Path Constraint to a Dummy helper object to animate it along a single 2D shape, which much easier than setting individual keys at positions along the track. You linked the Cat to the parent Dummy01, which pulls the child (Cat) along with it. However, you were able to adjust the child Cat object to place its wheels on the track surface. You also learned to make adjustments to the Path Constraint in the Motion panel that cause the dummy to stay perpendicular to the path's curvature.

Noise Controllers for Random Motion

In the next exercise, you learn how to apply a new controller type to Dummy01's Position aspect to produce randomly generated position changes in all three axes. This short exercise will not seem to make much sense at this point, but will lead you into another exercise that illustrates an important concept in animation controllers.

FIGURE 9.13
The Follow option causes Dummy01 to stay perpendicular to the path as it moves along. Selecting the Flip option for the X axis makes the catapult go forward.

Exercise 9.3: Assigning a Noise Controller to Position

1. Open Cat_Animate02.max, but do not save this file under another name. In the Camera01 viewport, select the Dummy01 object. In the Motion panel, expand the Assign Controller rollout. The Position Controller is the Path Constraint you assigned in Exercise 9.2.

On the CD

exercises\CH09\
Cat_Animate02.max

2. In the Assign Controller rollout, Controller view, highlight Position: Path Constraint. Click the Assign Controller button, and double-click Noise Position in the Assign Position Controller dialog box. Dummy01 and its child jump inside the timber structure, and the Noise Controller dialog box opens (see Figure 9.14). Drag the Time slider, and you will see that the objects jump randomly in a narrow area. You have replaced the Path Constraint with a Noise Controller that has control of Dummy01's position—not exactly what you wanted.

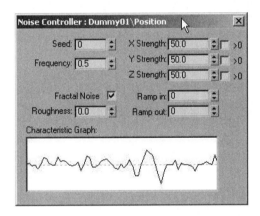

FIGURE 9.14 *Use the Noise Controller dialog box to set range of motion and frequency of movement in the three axes and view the motion in a graph.*

3. Do not save this file. Choose File, Reset from the menu, and click No when asked if you want to save the current file and Yes when asked if you really want to reset.

    The exercise has taught you that you can have one controller per animation track—in this case, Position. When you assign a different controller, the information from the previous controller is lost.

Using List Controllers to Allow Controller Stacking

With animation controllers, there is a way to eat your cake and have it, too. The List Controller feature creates a stack of controllers somewhat similar to a stack of modifiers when modeling. The controllers act independently and can go as deep as you can manage.

In this exercise, you learn to apply a List Controller to the Position aspect of Dummy01. This maintains the Path Constraint as the top controller in the list, not just replace it as assigning a Noise Controller did. It also creates an Available slot, where you can assign another controller below the Path Constraint. You will place the Noise Controller in the Available slot and learn to adjust the range of its effect, so that Dummy01 and Cat bump along only over the rough track area.

Exercise 9.4: Assigning List Controllers

1. Open Cat_Animate02.max, and save it as Cat_Animate03.max. In the Camera01 viewport, select Dummy01. In the Motion panel, Assign Controller rollout, highlight Position: Path Constraint in the Controller view. Click the Assign Controller button, and double-click Position List in the list. The Controller view shows that Position List is current, but the Dummy01 object is still in place.

2. In the Controller view, click the + sign next to Position: Position List to expand it (see Figure 9.15). Highlight the Available slot in the Controller view. Click the Assign Controller button and double-click Noise Position. The Noise Controller dialog box opens, and the Dummy01 is still in place. Scrub the Time slider. The objects travel along the path and randomly jump up and down. You have combined the effects of two Position Controllers. Close the Noise Controller dialog box.

On the CD

exercises\CH09\
Cat_Animate02.max

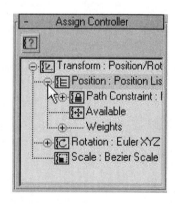

FIGURE 9.15
Expand Position: Position List in the Controller view to reveal the Path Constraint and a new Available slot.

3. You want the objects to jump only between frames 62–72, when the Cat object is over the rough area of track, and you want it to bump upward, not down into the track surface. Choose Graph Editor, Track View - Dope Sheet from the menu. In the Dope Sheet Editor, highlight Noise Position in the Controller view. There are currently no keys created for the Noise Controller; it just animates over the full frames (see Figure 9.16).

Notice that when you assign a controller to an Available slot, another Available slot is created, ready for another controller.

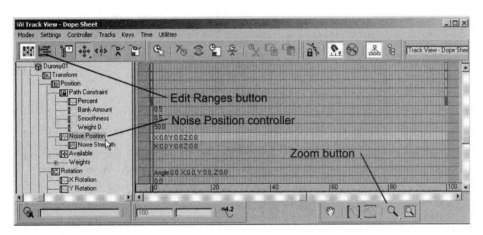

Figure 9.16 *Highlight Noise Position in the Dope Sheet Editor in preparation for viewing and editing range bars.*

4. On the Dope Sheet toolbar, click the Edit Ranges button to display range bars in the tracks, indicating that the entire animation covers frame 0 to frame 100. Move the cursor over the white box for frame 0 in the Noise Position range bar. You will see a cursor with a left-pointing white arrow. Drag the end of the range bar to near frame 60. Drag the right end of the range bar to near frame 70. Zoom in on the range bar with the mouse wheel or click the Zoom button at the bottom of the Dope Sheet Editor. Set the left end at frame 62 and the right end at frame 72, using the yellow lines as guides (see Figure 9.17). These settings restrict the Noise Controller to the time indicated by the range bar. Close the Dope Sheet Editor.

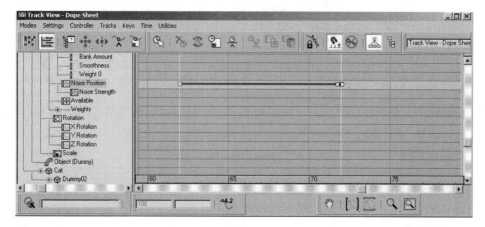

FIGURE 9.17   *Restricting the Noise Controller to a specific time range.*

5. In the Noise Controller dialog box, you will see a Strength setting of 50 in all three axes, which means the random numbers that determine Dummy01 noise range from –25 units to +25 units. You need Dummy01 to bump only in the Z axis and only above the track. Right-click on the spinners for X Strength and Y Strength to zero them out, and select the >0 check box next to the Z Strength field to generate random numbers between 0 and +50 units (see Figure 9.18).

tip

If you have closed the Noise Controller dialog box, you can highlight Noise Position in the Controller view, right-click on it, and choose Properties from the Quad menu. You must be in Edit Keys mode to access Properties.

6. Drag the Time slider, and you'll see that the jumping produced by the Noise Controller happens only between frames 62 and 72, but that the objects are above the track the rest of the time. This is because the controller uses the Noise amount set at frames 62 and 72 on either side of the range. In the Noise Controller dialog box, enter 1 in the Ramp In and Ramp Out fields. This tells the Noise Controller to start one frame before the range and end one frame after.

7. In the Noise Controller dialog box, enter 2.0 in the Frequency field and 25 in the Z Strength field to adjust the amount of bumping. The amounts are exaggerated somewhat so that you can see the effect.

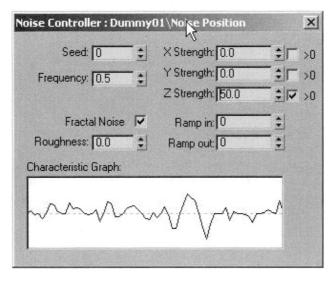

FIGURE 9.18   *Select the >0 option next to Z Strength to constrain movement in the Z axis to the upward direction.*

8. Close all windows and dialog boxes and save the file. It should already be called Cat_Animate03.max.

You have learned to assign multiple animation controllers and constraints to a single aspect of an object. You used the Dope Sheet Editor to adjust the Noise Controller's range bar to limit the frames affected by the noise. You also adjusted the Noise Controller's parameters to limit the motion in the Z axis and create a one-frame ramping effect before and after the time set in the range bar.

Assigning a LookAt Constraint Rotation

Your imagination is going to get a workout in the next exercise. The strange device mounted on the tower in the middle of the track structure is a medieval laser device that powers the catapult as it moves along the track. How did you think it moved?

However, to power the Cat object, everyone knows the device has to be pointing at the catapult; otherwise, the power would be interrupted. Again, you could use Set Key mode to rotate the laser at a particular frame and set a key, move to another frame, set another key, and so forth. However, in this exercise you learn a more automatic method that enables you to essentially set and forget the laser device. This method uses a LookAt Constraint assigned to the Laser head's Rotation track that uses Dummy01 as the LookAt target. No matter where Dummy01 moves in the scene, the LookAt Constraint attempts to point an axis of the Laser head object at Dummy01.

Exercise 9.5: Using the LookAt Constraint

1. Open Cat_Animate03.max, and save it as Cat_Animate04.max. In the Camera01 viewport, select the Laser head object at the top of the tower mast. It has a Standard Free Direct light linked to it that you will use in Chapter 11, "Materials and Lighting: The Magic Combination." In the Motion panel, Assign Controller rollout, highlight Rotation: EulerXYZ in the Controller view.

On the CD

exercises\CH09\
Cat_Animate03.max

2. Click the Assign Controller button and double-click LookAt Constraint in the list (see Figure 9.19). If you tried to rotate the Laser head now, you could not do it because it's waiting for you to assign a LookAt target.

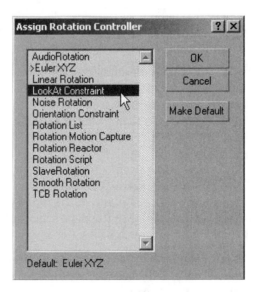

FIGURE 9.19   *The LookAt Constraint determines the rotation of the Laser head based on a target you assign.*

3. In the Motion panel, LookAt Constraint rollout, click the Add LookAt Target button. Press **h** and double-click Dummy01 in the list. The Laser head flips around, and you'll notice a short blue line pointing toward Dummy01 (see Figure 9.20). Click the Add LookAt Target button again to toggle it off.

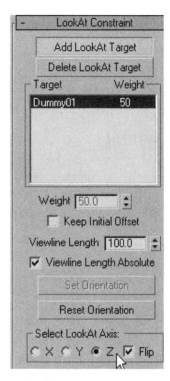

FIGURE 9.20   *After the LookAt Constraint target is assigned, the Laser head flips and a blue line points toward Dummy01.*

FIGURE 9.21
The object's positive local X axis points to the Dummy01 pivot point. Choosing the Z and Flip options points the Laser head's local –Z axis at Dummy01 for the correct orientation.

4. In the LookAt Constraint rollout, select the Z radio button under Select LookAt Axis, and select the Flip check box (see Figure 9.21). This forces the Laser head's local –Z axis to point at Dummy01.

5. Scrub the Time slider, and watch the Laser head hold the correct orientation as it tracks Dummy01 moving around the path. Save the file. It should be called Cat_Animate04.max.

You have learned to place a LookAt Constraint on an object's Rotation track and adjust the orientation. The LookAt Constraint enables you to point any axis of an object at a target object and determine which way is up as an alignment tool. This frees you from hand-animating such alignments. The LookAt Constraint also could be used to, for example, align the wheels of a train to track correctly around corners or to control a character's eye movement.

The blue line represents the Laser head's axis, and it points at the LookAt target's pivot point.

A third method of assigning controllers to objects is through the Animation menu. In the Motion panel, Dope Sheet Editor, or Curve Editor, you can assign a new controller to replace an existing controller.

When you add a controller from the Animation menu, it automatically creates a List Controller with the existing and new controllers. This can speed the process of creating List Controllers.

Summary

Assigning and adjusting different animation controllers on objects offers more variation in your approach to animation than the Set Key process you learned in Chapter 5. Some of the topics covered in this chapter include:

- **Assigning controllers** You have learned that controllers and constraints can be assigned in the Motion panel, Dope Sheet Editor, Curve Editor, or Animation menu.

- **Changing controllers** You learned the fundamentals of how the controller type affects animation by viewing a standard Position XYZ controller with a Bezier Controller on each axis that caused unexpected curvature and changes in velocity in the animation. You learned to substitute one controller type for another to make a linear animation.

- **Path Constraint** You learned to use a Path Constraint to determine one or more 2D shapes that describe an object's position and rotation. You made adjustments to change the object's orientation on the path.

- **List Controllers** You saw that replacing one controller with another can cause a loss of animation data, and learned to control it by using the Position List controller. This enables you to add controllers to an object while keeping any existing animation—a way of "layering" the animation effects.

- **LookAt Constraint** You learned to apply and adjust a Rotation constraint called LookAt that points a specific axis of an object at the pivot point of a target object.

PART IV

A Personal Transporter

CHAPTER 10

Introduction to Freeform Modeling

In This Chapter

In this chapter, you learn the fundamentals of a modeling method quite different from what you have learned so far. The technique, called Surface modeling, is a more free-form approach to creating soft or curved surfaces.

You will build a two-wheeled Segway-style personal transport device with handlebars. As with the loft modeling techniques you have already learned, you start with 2D shapes. However, you do not extrude those shapes along a path; rather, you use them to define a cage to which the surface is applied. Some of the topics covered in this chapter include

- **Surface modeling** You'll learn about two new modifiers to generate the new surface: the CrossSection modifier and the Surface modifier. CrossSection effectively "connects the dots" of the 2D shapes—that is, it uses vertices to define the cage. The Surface modifier then generates a skin over the cage to further define the surface.

- **Symmetrical halves** Often, it's more efficient to create only one of a pair of objects or only half of one object and then mirror that object for an opposing pair or a symmetrical object. You will learn two methods of mirroring your models.

- **More complex 3D from simple 2D**   You also will learn about the Bevel Profile modifier, which creates a surface from two 2D shapes. The simple Bevel modifier you've used previously has three levels of control, but you can define as many levels as you want with Bevel Profile to make much more complex objects.

- **Complex primitive objects**   You'll be introduced to another class of 3D primitive objects called Extended Primitives.

Key Terms

Bevel Profile modifier   Extrudes a base 2D shape according to a 2D profile shape.

CrossSection modifier   Prepares a wireframe cage by connecting vertices to accept Patch surfaces.

Extended Primitives   Primitive 3D objects, such as a box or cylinder, with extra parameters to add chamfered or rounded edges.

Patch surface   A mathematical surface, defined by four spline edges or as a Patch Grid, that has weighting between vertices, thus producing smoother flowing surfaces.

Surface modeling   Covering a wireframe cage with Patch surfaces.

Surface modifier   Uses a wireframe cage to define a Patch surface.

Symmetry modifier   Mirrors, trims, and welds half an object into a symmetrical whole object.

Hotkeys and Keyboard Shortcuts

h   Open the Select Objects or Pick Object dialog box

m   Open the Material Editor

F3   Toggle the Wireframe/Smooth+ Highlights option

Surface Modeling Technique: More Than One Way to Skin a Shape

In Chapters 2, "Modeling: A Medieval Street Scene," and 6, "Modeling for Radiosity and Efficiency," you created and used 2D shapes in a variety of ways to generate 3D objects. These methods involved extruding the object along some form of path, defined by the shape's Z axis or by another shape entirely. This affords you an efficient and flexible workflow.

At times, however, you need a more fluid way of working that enables you to push and pull the surface, much as an artist working with clay might approach a 3D task. The exercises in this chapter introduce you to *Surface modeling*—a method of creating and editing 3D objects that have smooth-flowing surfaces and are still easy to edit in a production environment. You'll use this method to create your own platform with curved fenders for a personal transporter.

The type of surface defined in this process is not a mesh object, like the ones you have created in previous chapters; rather, it is called a *Patch surface*. When you move a vertex of a Patch, for example, the surface bulges rather than spikes because the vertices are weighted to their surrounding neighbors. Notice in Figure 10.1 that each 4×4 segment surface has the middle vertex moved the same distance.

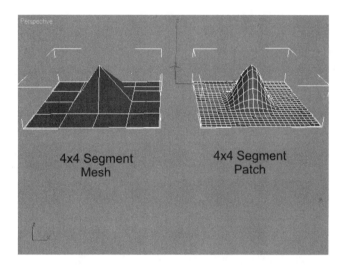

FIGURE 10.1   *Notice the bulging effect when vertices are moved in the Z axis on the Patch object.*

You will use a Patch surface to create just one half of the transporter platform. To finish the other half, you'll learn about a new 3ds max 5 modifier called Symmetry that mirrors an object and then welds the seam to make a single seamless surface.

Creating Half a Platform as a Patch Surface

In this first exercise, you open a file containing a number of 2D shapes; several of them are cross-sections of a surface that have been attached into a single compound shape. You use two modifiers to convert the shape: the CrossSection modifier to convert the shape into a wireframe cage, and the Surface modifier to convert it into a Patch. This modeling method enables you to efficiently rough out your complex object with 2D information that's easy to see and manipulate, and then create and tweak the surface later.

Exercise 10.1: Generating a Patch Surface over a Wireframe Cage

1. From the CD-ROM, open the Transporter01.max file. Choose File, Save As from the menu, select a subdirectory, and click the + button to increment the filename to Transporter02.max. The file contains several 2D shapes and one 3D object called Grip01. You will convert the 2D compound shape called platform_shape01 into an editable 3D Patch surface.

On the CD

exercises\CH10\
Transporter01.max

2. Right-click in the Perspective viewport to make sure it is active, click the Select button on the main toolbar, and select the platform_shape01 compound shape. When in Select mode, if you hold your cursor for a second over an object, you'll see a tooltip with the name of the object (see Figure 10.2).

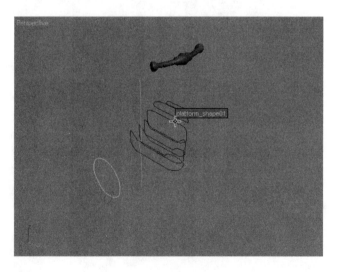

Figure 10.2 *A tooltip showing the object name when you're in Select mode is a helpful selection aid.*

3. The 2D wireframe cage shape is made of multiple splines that were separate from each other. For you to create a valid Patch surface from the shapes, they must form a wireframe cage composed of areas that have four edges each. The original shapes were all cloned as copies from a single shape, edited, and then attached into a single new shape, so they have the same number of vertices in each spline. You will take advantage of that fact and use a CrossSection modifier to connect vertex to vertex so that you can define the required four-edged areas. In the Modify panel, Modifier List, select CrossSection under Object-Space Modifiers (see Figure 10.3). In the Parameters rollout, select the Bezier radio button to ensure the connections have smooth curves that you can adjust later. You can see in Figure 10.4 that the vertices have all been connected to form the four-edged areas that will define the patch surfaces.

FIGURE 10.3
Select the Cross-Section modifier to create a wireframe cage.

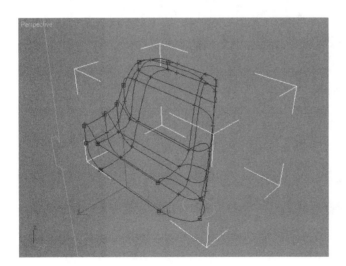

FIGURE 10.4   *To see the vertices better, you can enable Vertex Ticks in the Display panel, Display Properties rollout, which has been done in this figure.*

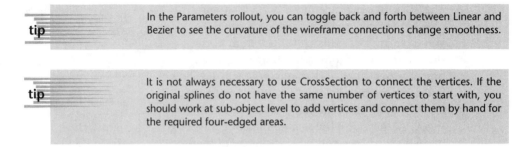

tip In the Parameters rollout, you can toggle back and forth between Linear and Bezier to see the curvature of the wireframe connections change smoothness.

tip It is not always necessary to use CrossSection to connect the vertices. If the original splines do not have the same number of vertices to start with, you should work at sub-object level to add vertices and connect them by hand for the required four-edged areas.

4. In the Modify panel, Modifier List, choose Surface. This modifier skins over the cage with a smooth patch surface (see Figure 10.5). No end caps are created, so the faces with face normals pointing away from you are invisible. In the Parameters rollout, Patch Topology section, enter in the Steps field to reduce the complexity of the surface (see Figure 10.6). As with other types of objects in 3ds max 5, you should always strive to get the visual results you want with the minimum amount of surface information.

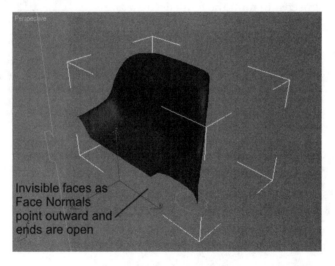

Invisible faces as Face Normals point outward and ends are open

Figure 10.5 *A Surface modifier skins the wire cage with a Patch surface. The inside surface is invisible because there are no end caps and the face normals point outward from the center.*

5. The open end of the patch that you can see in Figure 10.5 would not be a problem because you are creating only half the platform and that end will be hidden. However, the other smaller end must be capped, so you'll add a modifier that caps both open ends of the platform. In the Modify panel, Modifier List, choose Cap Holes. In the Parameters rollout, select the Smooth With Old Faces check box to smooth the edge between the cap and the original surface for a better appearance (see Figure 10.7).

FIGURE 10.6
Lower the Steps value in Patch Topology to reduce the surface's complexity yet maintain adequate detail.

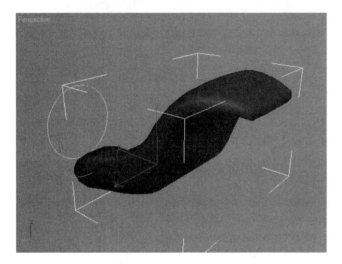

FIGURE 10.7
The Cap Holes modifier closes both ends of the open patch object, and the Smooth With Old Faces option smoothes the edges of the caps.

6. In the Modifier Stack, scroll down to the Editable Spline level and choose the Vertex sub-object level. This makes the Patch object disappear in the viewports and enables you to edit the splines at vertex level. In the Modifier panel, click the Show End Result On/Off Toggle button below the Stack display (see Figure 10.8). Toggling it on enables you to see the end result of the whole Modifier Stack while

you edit, not just the result to the current modifier. You won't actually do any editing at this level
in this exercise—just be aware that it's possible
and is simplified by seeing the end result as you
edit. Click the Editable Spline level to exit Vertex
mode and click the top Patch Select to return to
the top of the stack.

7. Save the file; it should already be called
Transporter02.max. You have created one half of a
flowing platform patch object.

You have learned to use attached 2D shapes with
the CrossSection modifier, apply the Surface modifier to create a smooth-flowing patch surface, and
apply the Cap Holes modifier to close the open
ends of the patch with mesh surfaces.

Complex Modifier Stacks are often normal in a
production environment. They enable you to
build complex models that are easy to edit at
almost any point in the model's history.

Figure 10.8
*Setting the Show End Result
On/Off Toggle to on allows you
to edit in the stack yet still see
the object with all modifications.*

The New Symmetry Modifier

You have created only half the platform, so now you
need to create a mirror image and attach it to the
existing half to form a seamless platform. In previ-
ous versions of 3ds max, this process could be time consuming: You had to convert
to an Editable Patch or Editable Mesh, create the mirror image, attach the two into
a single editable object, delete all the faces between the two halves, weld the vertices
at the adjoining edges, and adjust the smoothing to make the object look seamless.

The new Symmetry modifier makes the process infinitely easier and more productive. Because it is a modifier, it rides on the stack and enables you full editing at any
sub level, and it can be disabled or removed at any time. When you do edit the patch
lower in the stack, both halves update and remain symmetrical. The modifier also
handles the face removal, the welding, and the smoothing processes automatically.
Although you are applying the Symmetry modifier on a mechanical type of object,
it is very useful for creating characters and other creatures or beings.

Exercise 10.2: Applying the New Symmetry Modifier

1. Open Transporter02.max, and save the file as Transporter03.max. In the Perspective viewport, select the half-platform object called platform_shape01.

2. In the Modify panel, Modifier List, choose the Symmetry modifier. You will not see much happen, but an exact clone of the half-platform has been created directly over the existing object. You also will see an orange Gizmo with an orange arrow that represents the clone's mirror axis (see Figure 10.9).

note   The name of the 3D platform half is platform_shape01. If you are using lowercase naming conventions to identify 2D shapes, you might want to rename the object "Platform," for example, to fit a naming scheme for 3D objects. You do not need to do that for this exercise, however.

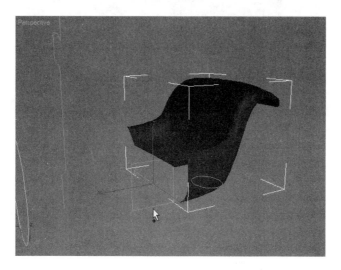

FIGURE 10.9   *The Symmetry modifier creates a clone of the half-platform. The orange Gizmo indicates the clone's mirror axis.*

3. In the Modify panel, Parameters rollout, select the Y option in the Mirror Axis section. The clone mirrors itself below the original. Select the Z option, and you'll see the half flip into place with a smooth seam automatically created by slicing the overlapping caps between the two halves and welding the vertices (see Figure 10.10).

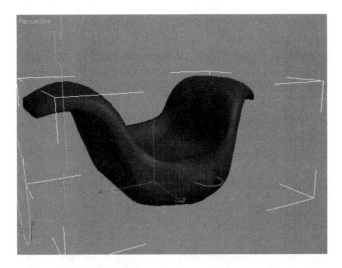

FIGURE 10.10   *The Symmetry modifier creates a clone, orients it, slices overlapping faces, and welds the seam smoothly.*

4. In the Modify panel, Parameters rollout, toggle the Slice Along Mirror check box to see that this function slices away the end caps where the two halves meet to allow clean welding at the seam. When the check box is cleared, there's a visible seam in the surface. Make sure it is selected.

5. In the Modify panel, Parameters rollout, toggle the Weld Seam check box. When the check box is cleared, the vertices at the seam are not welded and the seam is visible. Make sure you leave it selected.

6. Save the file; it should already be called Transporter03.max. It is now one continuous object that can be edited by changing the original shapes, which you can access at the bottom of the Modifier Stack.

note

The Threshold setting enables you to weld vertices that are not coincident, but within the Threshold distance.

You have learned some of the wonders of the new Symmetry modifier in 3ds max 5. You have applied it to half an object, and it performed the necessary trimming and welding to produce a continuous smooth surface that can easily be edited.

Bevel Profile Modifier: Beveling and Then Some

In Chapters 2 and 6, you learned to use the Bevel modifier, which gave you three levels of height and outline adjustments so that you could create chamfered edges on two sides of an object. In this section, you learn about the Bevel Profile modifier, which can do all the things that Bevel does, but with a lot more flexibility and control. With Bevel Profile, you need two pieces of 2D information: a base shape and a profile shape. The *base shape* can be simple or compound and open or closed. The *profile shape* should be a simple shape that can be open or closed. As with so many of the tools in 3ds max 5, Bevel Profile enables you to create complex 3D objects with simple 2D shapes. You then have full control of editing the 3D mesh by adjusting only the sub-object levels of the 2D shapes.

In this exercise, you use the Bevel Profile modifier in two examples. First, you create a support shaft for the handgrips that are already in the scene and adjust the position of the shaft coupling. Then you create a star hub for the transporter wheels from two 2D shapes and adjust the shapes to make the hub a little fancier.

Exercise 10.3: Creating a Support Shaft with the Bevel Profile Modifier

1. Open the Transporter03.max file from the previous exercise or from the CD-ROM, and save it as `Transporter04.max`. On the main toolbar, click the Select By Name button and double-click Handlebar_shaft_shape in the list (see Figure 10.11). This elliptical shape inside the front of the platform is the base of the shaft.

On the CD

exercises\CH10\
Transporter03.max

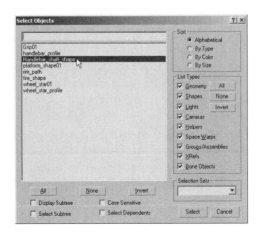

Figure 10.11   *Double-click Handlebar_shaft_shape in the Select Objects dialog box.*

caution

The Bevel Profile modifier is always applied to the base shape. A common mistake for new users is to apply Bevel Profile to the profile shape, realize they wanted the modifier on the base shape, but forget to remove Bevel Profile from the profile shape.

If you make the same mistake and try to pick the correct profile shape, you won't be able to because the added Bevel Profile modifier means it is technically no longer a 2D shape, even though it appears to be in the viewports.

2. In the Modify panel, Modifier List, choose Bevel Profile. Nothing will happen that you can see, but the elliptical shape has changed from a 2D shape to a flat 3D surface that is waiting for a profile to be defined. In the Modify panel, Parameters rollout, click the Pick Profile button (see Figure 10.12).

3. Press **h** and double-click handlebar_profile in the list (see Figure 10.13). Be aware that this is the Pick Object dialog box, not the Select Objects dialog box. The Pick Object dialog box enables you to pick the profile by name instead of finding it in a viewport. After you pick the profile, the 3D shaft appears at the front of the platform.

4. In the Modify panel, Parameters rollout, clear the Start and End check boxes in the Capping section. Both ends of the shaft are hidden inside other geometry, so the end caps are just extra faces that serve no purpose in this file. Deleting them saves 72 faces.

5. The coupling in the middle of the shaft should be moved down 2 3/4". You could apply an EditMesh modifier or convert the shaft to an Editable Mesh to get access to vertices, edges, or faces and make the change, but it's easier to edit the original 2D profile. To do that, first click the Zoom Extents All button at the lower right to fill all viewports with all objects in the scene.

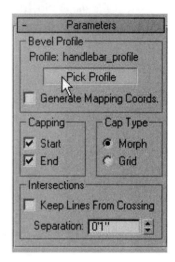

Figure 10.12
Click the Pick Profile button to add a profile shape to your new 3D surface.

note

The elliptical shape is hidden in the transporter body in the shaded viewport. You can switch to a Wireframe view (hotkey: **F3**) if you want to see it.

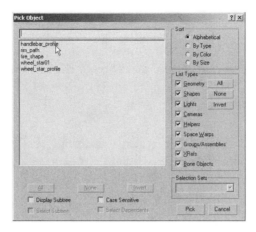

FIGURE 10.13   *Selecting the profile shape in the Pick Object dialog box.*

6. In the Front viewport, pick the handlebar_profile line just to the right of the platform. It looks like the shaft. In the Modify panel, Stack display, make sure Line is expanded and select Vertex sub-object mode (it will be highlighted yellow). Drag a selection window around the coupling vertices on handlebar_profile (see Figure 10.14).

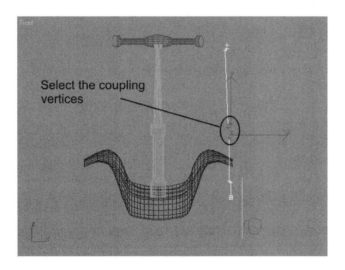

FIGURE 10.14   *In the Front viewport, select the coupling vertices of handlebar_profile.*

7. On the main toolbar, click the Select and Move button. At the center of the Status Bar, toggle the Absolute Mode button in the Transform Type-In area to Offset Mode. In the Y field, enter -2.75, and press Enter to move the vertices down an exact amount. The vertices and the 3D mesh change accordingly.

8. In the Modify panel, Stack display, exit Vertex sub-object mode by selecting Line in the list.

9. Save the file; it should already be called Transporter04.max. You have created a relatively complex 3D mesh with simple 2D shapes. The base shape can be edited in the Modify panel as well if you select the Handlebar_shaft_shape object and drop to Ellipse in the Stack display.

> **caution**
>
> Simply clicking the + sign next to Line and closing the list is not the same as exiting sub-object mode. You must click on the text Line in the list to make the vertex symbol to the right of the name disappear.

You have learned to use and adjust the Bevel Profile modifier to convert two 2D shapes into a 3D mesh, to optimize the 3D mesh's face count by eliminating the hidden end caps, and to select and make changes to the original profile shape that are automatically reflected in the 3D mesh object.

> **note**
>
> Bevel Profile is similar to other shape-based 3D tools. In some ways, it is like Lathe, except the result isn't the result of revolution. It is like Extrude, except the result isn't straight. It is like a deform-fit loft, but with the ability to make concave, overlapping faces.

Bevel Profile can be used to make mechanical objects, lampposts, even complex roofs. The building on the cover of this book has three roofs that were created in minutes with Bevel Profile. You have seen the tool's basic functioning; now use your imagination to put it to work in your own artistic ways.

The Bevel Profile Modifier for a Wheel Hub

This next exercise leads you through using the Bevel Profile modifier again to create a five-spoke hub for the transporter wheel. The 2D shape you'll load from the scene file was created from a Star and a Circle primitive that were attached into a single compound shape. At the Spline sub-object level, the Trim command was used to trim off unnecessary portions, and all vertices were welded to form a continuous closed shape. Another small circle was centered with the Align tool and then attached to the hub shape.

You will use the Bevel Profile modifier to turn the 2D shape into a 3D mesh with filleted edges on the front surface. You then adjust it to raise it slightly above the front surface for a 3D relief effect.

Exercise 10.4: Creating a Hub with Bevel Profile

1. Open the Transporter04.max file, and save it as Transporter05.max. In the Perspective viewport, select wheel_star01 shape. You can use the viewport tooltip to find the shape or use the Select By Name button. Zoom in and use Arc Rotate until your view looks similar to Figure 10.15.

On the CD

exercises\CH10\
Transporter04.max

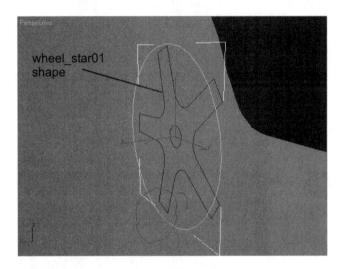

FIGURE 10.15   *The wheel_star01 shape in the Perspective viewport will be turned into a complex hub.*

2. In the Modify panel, Modifier List, choose Bevel Profile. In the Parameters rollout, click the Pick Profile button, and in the Perspective viewport, pick the small hook shape called wheel_star_profile (see Figure 10.16).

3. You might notice that some faces appear to be missing, as shown in Figure 10.17. This is because you cleared the Capping check boxes in the previous exercise, and modifier settings are remembered in the current session until you change them. In the Parameters rollout, select Start and End in the Capping section to turn them back on. If you had shut down 3ds max 5 and then restarted it, the modifiers would be back to their default settings, so the Capping option would be enabled.

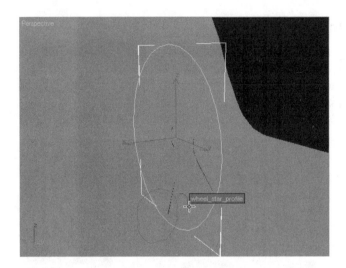

FIGURE 10.16   *The small hook-shaped wheel_star_profile will define the profile of the 3D wheel.*

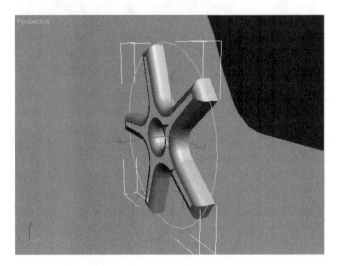

FIGURE 10.17   *Faces are missing on the Bevel Profile object because the Capping option was disabled in the previous exercise.*

4. Right-click in the Front viewport to activate it. On the main toolbar, click the Select By Name button and double-click wheel_star_profile in the list. Click the Zoom Extents Selected button to fill the Front viewport with the profile.

5. In the Modify panel, Stack display, choose Vertex sub-object mode. In the Front viewport, pick the upper-right end vertex of wheel_star_profile. Pick the green Bezier handle to the left and move it upward so that the tangency is at about a 45-degree angle and the yellow tangent lines do not change length (see Figure 10.18). Exit Vertex sub-object mode.

tip

The Zoom Extents Selected button is a flyout under Zoom Extents. Click Zoom Extents, hold the mouse button down, and choose the white box button instead of the gray box button.

tip

When trying to adjust vertex tangency handles, the Transform Gizmo might be frozen in a previously picked axis. To free it to move in two axes, pick the edge of the yellow shaded square in the Transform Gizmo.

You can also change a setting in the 3dsmax.ini file called TransformGizmoRestoreAxis=0 by changing the 0 to 1. This setting prevents the Gizmo from locking.

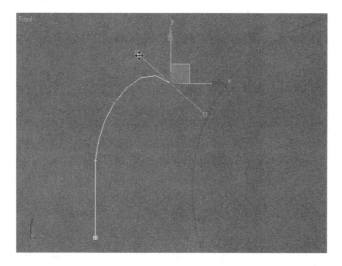

FIGURE 10.18 *Move the green Bezier handle upward to about a 45-degree angle.*

6. After adjusting the profile shape's curve, you have a raised relief area on the front surface of the hub (see Figure 10.19). Save the file. It is already called Transporter05.max. The wheel hub is a complex object, again created with simple 2D shapes.

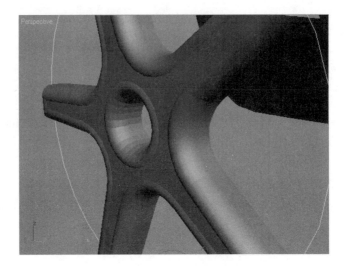

FIGURE 10.19   *Adjusting the curve of the profile shape adds a raised relief effect to the hub's front surface.*

You learned that making small adjustments to your shapes can greatly affect the 3D mesh. You also learned that modifiers retain any setting changes until you restart 3ds max 5, which can result in some surprises. When you exit 3ds max 5 and come back to a new session, the modifiers are reset to their defaults.

Lofting Revisited

The hub you created for the transporter needs a rim and tire, so in this next exercise, you use lofting to create a single object that can serve as both the rim and the tire. You also assign Material ID numbers to segments or splines of the loft shape to determine material assignments. Also, to refresh what you learned in previous chapters about the orientation of the loft shape on the loft path, you edit the lofted mesh to get the correct results.

Exercise 10.5: Lofting a Tire and Rim Object

1. Open the Transporter05.max file, and save it as Transporter06.max. Right-click in the Perspective viewport to activate it. On the main toolbar, click the Select By Name button, and double-click rim_path in the list. Click the Zoom Extents All Selected button (in the flyout below Zoom Extents All) to fill all viewports with rim_path.

On the CD

exercises\CH10\
Transporter05.max

2. In the Create panel, Geometry category, click the drop-down arrow next to Standard Primitives, and choose Compound Objects from the list (see Figure 10.20). In the Object Type rollout, click the Loft button.

3. In the Loft panel, Creation Method rollout, click the Get Shape button. In the Perspective viewport, pick the tire_shape object (see Figure 10.21). The resulting loft looks quite strange because the shape's Local axis aligns with the path's Local axis by default. You can correct it better after lofting.

4. In the Modify panel, Stack display, click the + sign next to Loft to expand it and choose the Shape sub-object level. In the Perspective viewport, pick the shape at the First Vertex of the loft path. The shape on the loft path is displayed as a bright green line in the shaded mesh when deselected, shows as white before you enter Shape sub-object mode, and turns red when selected (see Figure 10.22).

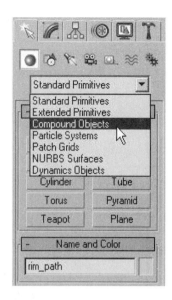

Figure 10.20
Choose Compound Objects from the list.

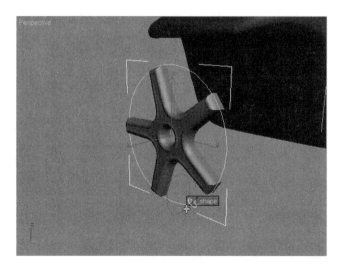

Figure 10.21   *Pick tire_shape in the Perspective viewport.*

It can be difficult to see the shapes on the loft object. You can use the F3 hotkey to toggle to Wireframe mode or pass the cursor over the loft object until it changes from an arrow to a small crosshair to locate the shape on the loft object.

The First Vertex of a circle is always at the right cardinal point as viewed down its Z axis.

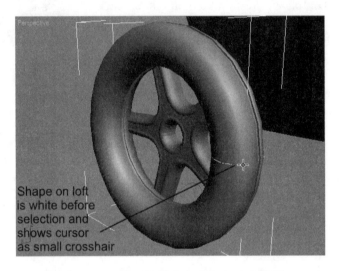

FIGURE 10.22   *In Shape sub-object mode, pick the shape on the loft mesh.*

5. On the main toolbar, click the Select and Rotate button. In the Status Bar, make sure the Offset Mode button in the Transform Type-In area is toggled on. In the Z field, enter 90, and press Enter to finalize the rotation. In the Modify panel, Stack display, click Loft at the top of the stack to exit sub-object mode. The shape on the path rotates 90 degrees counterclockwise on the path, orienting the rim and tire correctly in relation to the hub (see Figure 10.23).

6. Next, you'll prepare the loft object to accept two materials in Chapter 11, "Materials and Lighting: The Magic Combination." In the Modify panel, Surface Parameters rollout, select the Use Shape IDs check box in the Materials section (see Figure 10.24). This tells the loft object to use Material IDs along the loft, matching Material IDs of the loft shape. When you assign a Multi/Sub-Object material in the next step, the sub-materials will correspond to the correct faces.

FIGURE 10.23   *Rotating the tire_shape on the path 90 degrees in the Z axis orients the rim and tire correctly on the hub.*

7. Click the Select button, and in the Front viewport, select tire_shape. In the Modify panel, Stack display, choose Segment sub-object level. Make sure the top three segments that make up the tire portion of the shape are selected and red. In the Modify panel, Surface Properties rollout, set the Material ID to 2 (see Figure 10.25). Exit sub-object mode in the Stack display.

8. In the Material Editor, create a Multi/Sub-Object material with two materials and set the Diffuse colors to a dark and light color. Drag and drop the sample window onto the tire and rim loft object. It will look similar to Figure 10.26.

FIGURE 10.24
The Use Shape IDs option enables the loft object to make use of Multi/Sub-Object materials.

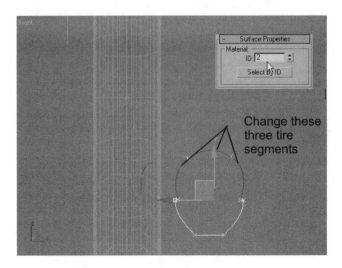

FIGURE 10.25   *In the Surface Properties rollout, enter 2 in the Material ID field.*

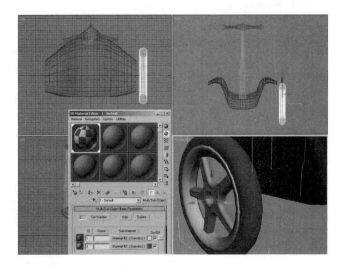

FIGURE 10.26   *Applying a Multi/Sub-Object material to the tire/rim object assigns two materials to a single object based on the shape's Material ID numbers.*

tip

It is important that you perform steps 6 and 7 to make material assignments on loft objects work correctly. You must set the loft object to use shape IDs and then set the shape IDs to correspond to the material components of a Multi/Sub-Object material.

9. In the Front viewport, use Zoom Extents to see the transporter platform. Select Loft01 and wheel_star01 and move them in the negative axis until they are in position under the fender of the platform (see Figure 10.27).

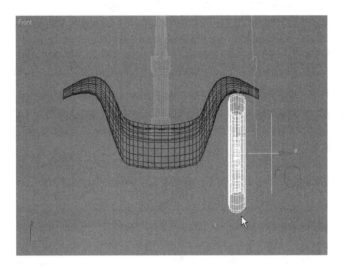

Figure 10.27   *In the Front viewport, move Loft01 and wheel_star01 in position under the fender of the platform.*

10. Save the file. It should already be called Transporter06.max. You now have a platform, a shaft and handlebars, and a tire and hub.

You are getting ready to finish the transporter and have yet to create any 3D objects directly. Instead, you have converted 2D shapes into 3D objects to make editing the objects more efficient.

In this exercise, you refreshed what you knew about lofting and making adjustments to the shape on the path for proper orientation of the loft object. You also made changes to the loft to use shape IDs to determine material assignments and to set the shape's segments to the correct ID numbers.

Mirroring Objects in 3ds max 5

You used the Symmetry modifier to mirror half the platform and weld the two halves into a seamless object. You need another wheel that is the mirror image of the one you created, but Symmetry is not appropriate for that task because the new wheel will be a separate object, not the second half of a single object, like the transporter body.

You have a couple of options in this case. You could rotate the hub and wheel 180 degrees with the Shift key to clone another wheel. That method would work fine here because the object is symmetrical from front to back and would look okay, but it wouldn't work at all for asymmetrical objects. You can also use the Mirror command on the main toolbar, but the Mirror command is really just a form of scaling an object with a –1 Scale factor. As mentioned in previous chapters, you should avoid scaling objects in 3ds max 5 because, as a transform, scaling gets evaluated after all modifiers. This can lead to problems later that are difficult to troubleshoot and fix.

So to get the best results for this exercise, you'll use the Mirror modifier to create and position a mirrored clone. Because Mirror is a modifier, it is always evaluated at the appropriate time in the Modifier Stack, so it causes no problems later in the editing process.

Exercise 10.6: Using the Mirror Modifier

1. Open the Transporter06.max file, and save it as Transporter07.max. Select the Loft01 and wheel_star01 objects (the hub and tire) in the Front viewport.

2. In the Modify panel, Modifier List, choose Mirror. A mirrored clone of the wheel is created, and you can see an orange mirror Gizmo showing the mirror axis in the World X axis.

On the CD

exercises\CH10\
Transporter06.max

> **note** The Stack display is blank when you first open the Modify panel because you have multiple objects selected with different histories, and the stack can display only one at a time. You will be able to apply a new modifier to the multiple objects you have selected. The name appears in italics in the stack to show that it's applied as an instanced modifier to multiple objects—change parameters for either instance, and the other will change, too.

3. In the Parameters rollout, Options section, enter -2.5 in the Offset field and press Enter (see Figure 10.28). The mirrored object moves to the other side of the platform, but the orange Gizmo remains in place.

4. Select the Copy check box in the Parameters roll-out, and the original wheel reappears (see Figure 10.29). To center the two wheels on the platform, click the Align button on the main toolbar, and pick the platform in the Front viewport. In the Align Selection (platform_shape01) dialog box, select the X Position check box and select Center under both Current Object and Target Object. Click OK. The wheels are now centered on the platform.

5. Save the file; it should be called Transporter07.max. You now have a pair of identical but mirrored wheels centered on the platform.

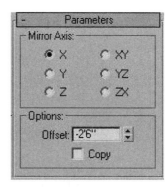

FIGURE 10.28
The value in the Offset field mirrors the wheel 2.5 feet to the other side of the platform.

Despite the fact that you could have cloned and rotated the original wheel or used the Mirror command from the main toolbar, you used the Mirror modifier instead. It is perhaps the best way to get a mirrored object without the editing problems caused by –1 scaling. The wheels also are treated as a single entity when the Mirror modifier is applied to one set of the tire-and-hub combo with the Copy option selected.

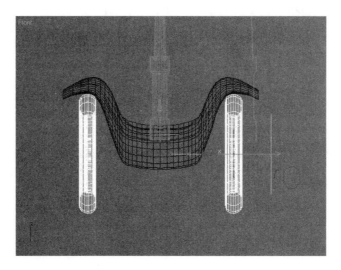

FIGURE 10.29   *The Copy option was used to make the original wheel objects reappear.*

Introduction to Extended Primitives

You have been using 2D shapes and modifiers or lofting to build 3D mesh objects. Sometimes a standard primitive object, such as Box, Cylinder, or Cone, is sufficient for an object or as a starting point for objects.

Sometimes you need a simple 3D object that is a bit more complex than standard primitives. In this short exercise, you create an axle for the transporter that is just a cylinder with chamfered ends. You could do this with a circle and the Bevel or Bevel Profile modifiers, but you want to keep it simple. To create this object, you'll use an extended primitive object called ChamferCyl, which is simply a parametric cylinder with chamfered ends, just the ticket for the axle.

Exercise 10.7: Creating an Axle with Extended Primitives

1. Open Transporter07.max, and save it as Transporter08.max. Right-click in the Left viewport to activate it and zoom in on the wheel.

On the CD

exercises\CH10\
Transporter07.max

2. In the Create panel, Geometry category, click the drop-down arrow next to Compound Objects, and choose Extended Primitives in the list.

3. In the Create panel, Object Type rollout, click the ChamferCyl button. This is similar to creating a Cylinder standard primitive with one extra step for the chamfer. In the Left viewport, click and drag anywhere to set the radius of the cylinder; any setting will do for now. Release the mouse button, and move the mouse up to define a height. Click to set the height. Move the mouse around to define a chamfer amount at the top and bottom edges of the cylinder, and click to set it. Name the object Axle.

4. In the Modify panel, set Radius to 1.5", Height to 2.5, and Fillet to 0.25" to make the axle the size you need.

tip

Do not worry about sizes for now. Defining an exact size by dragging the mouse can be frustrating, especially for the chamfer amount. You will edit it in the next step.

5. In the Left viewport, click Align on the main toolbar, and pick the tire. In the Align Selection dialog box, select X Position and Y Position, and make sure Center is selected for both Current Object and Target Object. Click OK. The axle is centered in the tire.

tip If you were aligning to the hub object, you could not use the Center option for both the current and target objects. Because the hub has five spokes, the bounding box is not square, so the axle would not center correctly. You would have to use the Pivot Point option for both the current and target objects.

6. Click the Align button again, and pick the platform in the Left viewport. In the Align Selection dialog box, select Z Position, and select Center under both Current Object and Target Object to center the axle between the wheels.

7. Save the file. It is already called Transporter08.max. You have a complete transporter that is simple and can be easily edited both to make changes to the form and to optimize the mesh (see Figure 10.30).

tip

If you edit the height of the axle, you need to align in this axis again. The ChamferCyl object grows from its base, not from its center.

Figure 10.30 *You have a finished transporter that can be easily edited for both form and optimization of the mesh density.*

Summary

Creating and editing free-form surfaces from a wireframe cage is an intuitive way to build flowing surfaces in 3ds max 5. The resulting Patch surfaces are molded into shape by pushing and pulling them into the form you need. The following topics were covered:

- **Patch surfaces**   Surfaces weighted from vertex to vertex cause the patch to bulge rather than spike when a vertex is moved.

- **Surface modeling**   Create cages of 2D shapes and add a combination of a CrossSection modifier and a Surface modifier to generate a smooth Patch surface.

- **Symmetrical objects**   Create only half of a transporter platform and then add the new Symmetry modifier that mirrors, slices, and welds two halves into a smooth continuous surface.

- **Bevel Profile modifier**   By manipulating the 2D shapes used in Bevel Profile, you learned a new method to create objects for your transporter that are easy to edit.

- **Mirror modifier**   The Mirror modifier creates the second wheel in a mirrored configuration and treats the pair of wheels as a single object. This method of mirroring is more reliable than the Mirror command.

- **Extended Primitives**   A class of 3D primitive objects that have more parameters, such as chamfered edges or rounded end caps.

CHAPTER 11

Materials and Lighting:
The Magic Combination

In This Chapter

In this chapter, you learn more about the interaction of light and materials in your scene so that you can add depth and sparkle to your renderings. Some options available in 3ds max 5 include

- **Specular highlights** These bright spots on rendered objects simulate light scattering from the surface, which adds sparkle and depth to your scene.

- **Material masking** Masking techniques enable you to layer maps, or patterns, within materials to hide or reveal underlying colors or other maps.

- **Unwrap UVW modifier** With the new UVW Unwrap map type, you can flatten the surface of objects to make it easier to place map patterns.

- **Standard lights** This lighting method is still efficient for many scenes, so you will learn to place and adjust Spot and Omni lights to produce a crisp rendered image with plenty of sparkle that renders very quickly.

- **Light Tracer** The new Light Tracer render engine, although somewhat slower, works with the new Skylight option to give you a global illumination solution that fills the scene with bounced light.

- **Special effects** To create the illusion of a laser beam, you'll add some special light effects to enhance the catapult track scene you worked on previously.

Key Terms

Global illumination   Advanced Light methods, such as Light Tracer or Radiosity, that simulate bounced light in the scene.

Light Tracer   A rendering method that uses a Skylight to simulate bounced light.

Masking   Using the brightness value or alpha channel (transparency) of maps to mask out or reveal underlying color or maps.

Scanline renderer   The default 3ds max 5 renderer, which does not calculate bounced light.

Specular highlights   Light scattered from the surface of an object, based on the material's molecular makeup and surface conditions in the real world.

Hotkeys and Keyboard Shortcuts

m   Open the Material Editor

9   Open the Advanced Lighting dialog box

h   Open the Select Objects or Pick Object dialog box

Materials, from Realistic to Cartoons

Certainly there's a major difference between a realistic rendering and a cartoon rendering, but what elements set them apart and how do you simulate those differences in 3ds max 5? There are many methods of adjusting materials to achieve the level of realism you want, which help you control your scene's look and mood.

Often, specular highlights are one of the first aspects you can adjust to increase your rendering's realism. In this chapter's exercises, you will create materials for the transporter you modeled in Chapter 10, "Introduction to Freeform Modeling," and adjust its specular highlights to enhance the scene's depth and punch.

You also will learn to use masking to increase your control over materials. This technique uses values in maps to hide or reveal other parts of color or maps below the mask to produce layered effects in materials. You will use masking to enable flexible color assignments to racing numbers and footpads on the transporter. Masking also was used in Chapter 3, "Applying Materials and Maps for a Convincing Outdoor Scene," to reveal brick below stucco in the exterior walls.

Positioning map patterns on objects can often be challenging, to say the least. 3ds max 5 makes this procedure a lot easier with the introduction of the improved Unwrap UVW modifier, which enables you to control the surface coordinates to match patterns in the current material's bitmaps. You'll use this modifier to make positioning the footpads and racing numbers on your transporter a snap.

But what if the client would rather see a light-hearted rendition of the transporter for a marketing spot on television? The new Ink 'n Paint material type, which you'll use in Exercise 11.3, simulates a more traditional cartoon look: inked outlines with painted infill.

Specular Highlights: All That Sparkles . . .

Specular highlights are an essential material attribute that aren't usually given enough attention. We generally take specular highlights for granted in our day-to-day life, so you need to train yourself to recognize them before you can reproduce them in 3ds max. These highlights, caused by light scattering off the surface of objects, are crucial to indicating whether the material is wood, plastic, metal, and so forth, and convey much more about material composition than color or reflections.

A material's molecular makeup and surface conditions influence the specular highlights. The molecules in metal, for example, are close together and reflect a large portion of the light straight back from the surface, which causes bright, hard-edged specular highlights. Rubber molecules, on the other hand, are widely spaced, enabling the light to be absorbed and then scattered in all directions. The result is a softer, more diffuse specular highlight.

Specular highlights are often the brightest areas in your rendering, and creating a full tonal range from the darkest shadows to the specular highlight enhances the 3D quality of your scenes. Several components are available for adjusting the quality of specular highlights in most 3ds max 5 material types (see Figure 11.1), including

- **Shader Type** The shader type determines the shape of the specular highlights and helps simulate the effects caused by a material's molecular layout and surface conditions.

- **Specular Color** Specular highlights are usually very white, regardless of the material's color. Generally, the exceptions are pure metal, such as gold and copper, in which the specular highlights take on the metal's hue. In anodized aluminum, the color is "baked into" the molecules, so the specular highlights are tinted with the material's base color.

- **Specular Level** This setting controls the brightness of the specular color. Increasing the Specular Level setting simulates more light being scattered at a tighter angle back to the viewer. Generally, the harder the material, the higher the specular level should be.

- **Glossiness**   The setting in the Glossiness field determines the size of the specular highlight. A higher number results in a small, tight specular highlight; a lower number produces a softer, more diffuse highlight. The Specular Level and Glossiness settings usually work with each other and, as a rule of thumb, should be within 20 to 30 points of each other.

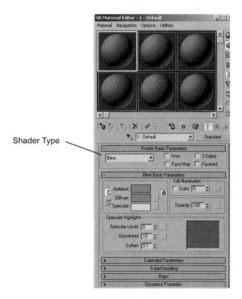

Shader Type

FIGURE 11.1   *The Material Editor has four important settings for adjusting specular highlights.*

An entire chapter, if not an entire book, could be written about specular highlights, but this overview is intended to get you thinking about specular highlights and how they can enhance your work. The following are some of the typical applications for shader types and their effect on specular highlights:

- **Blinn and Phong**   These two shaders are quite similar in their controls and uses, varying mostly in how they react in backlit situations. The Blinn shader is a newer mathematical formula, but can be used interchangeably. Blinn and Phong shaders are appropriate for manmade materials, such as plastic and paint, that tend to have very regular molecular makeups. The light falling on the material is scattered back in a round highlight with a smooth transition at the edge.

- **Anisotropic**   This shader, used for extruded plastic or rolled metal (the molecules are aligned much like the grain in wood), has two extra adjustments for highlight shape: Anisotropy and Orientation,. The Anisotropic setting determines the highlight's elongation amount; a setting of 50 makes the highlight about twice as long as it is wide, and a setting of 0 makes the highlight round.

The Orientation adjustment is set in degrees and rotates the highlight around the viewing axis. There also are Diffuse Level and Roughness settings that affect the influence of the Diffuse color. At 100, the Diffuse color has a normal influence on the surface. Lower settings reduce the Diffuse color influence and increase the effect of the Ambient color.

- **Multi-Layer**   This shader has two Anisotropic components, which enables you to create two specular highlights similar to those on stainless steel, for example. One specular highlight is light scattered by the molecular makeup, and the other is scattered by scratches in the surface.

- **Oren-Nayer-Blinn**   This shader is intended for use in soft porous materials, such as rubber, fabric, or human skin. The highlights are broad and soft. An added Roughness control reduces the effect of the specular highlight in the Diffuse zone beyond the edge of highlight, darkening the material somewhat. It also slightly brightens the object's outer curved edges, as though the light were being scattered obliquely to the material's rough surface.

- **Strauss and Metal**   Like Blinn and Phong, Strauss and Metal are two similar shaders, with Strauss being the newer version. They are unique in that the Specular Color cannot be set by changing a color swatch, but is derived from the Diffuse color swatch. Metal has an Ambient color swatch, but Strauss takes the Ambient component from the Diffuse color. Table 11.1 compares this shader to Phong to clarify these differences. These shaders mimic the specular highlights from pure metals or from materials such as anodized aluminum, in which the color is actually a physical property of ("baked into") the material's molecular level and influences the color of the highlights.

Table 11.1   Comparing Shader Type Settings

Shader	Ambient	Diffuse	Specular
Phong	User controllable color swatch	User controllable color swatch	User controllable color swatch
Metal	User controllable color swatch	User controllable color swatch	Derived from Diffuse
Strauss	Derived from Diffuse	User controllable color swatch	Derived from Diffuse

note   Although these general rules are a good guideline, feel free to experiment with uncommon variations of shader types to get the look you need for your materials.

Many rendering are much too flat and lifeless. By adjusting the specular highlights, you can create the bright spots we often take for granted to add sparkle to your scenes. Take the time to study your surroundings and examine the effect of specular highlights so that you can accurately re-create them in 3ds max.

From Bland to Grand (Almost): Adjusting Specular Highlights

In this exercise, you open the transporter created in Chapter 10 and render the Perspective viewport to see a lifeless scene with little apparent depth. By creating materials with specular highlights, you will breathe life into the scene and change its mood.

Exercise 11.1: Creating and Adjusting Specular Highlights in Materials

1. Open the TransMatl01.max file from the CD-ROM, and save it as `TransMat102.max`. This is the transporter from Chapter 10 with a couple of stand-in materials applied to the handlebars and the platform. Right-click in the Perspective viewport to activate it, and click the Quick Render button on the main toolbar to render the scene as is (see Figure 11.2). Choose Rendering, RAM Player from the menu, and click the Open Last Rendered Image in Channel A button. Click OK in the RAM Player Configuration dialog box, and minimize the RAM Player. You will use it for comparison later.

On the CD

exercises\CH11\
TransMatl01.max

2. Close the Virtual Frame Buffer. Open the Material Editor by clicking the Material Editor button (keyboard shortcut: **m**). The scene file has four materials already in the Material Editor, and three have been assigned to objects in the scene, as indicated by triangles in the corners of the sample windows. Click the first sample window in the top row to make sure it is active (with a heavy white border). This material, Chrome_wheel_shaft, has been assigned to the Handlebar_shaft_shape and Grip01 objects in the scene. You will adjust the specular highlights to make the material look hard and shiny.

3. First, in the Material Editor, Blinn Basic Parameters rollout, click the Specular Color swatch to open the Color Selector. It's set by default to a very light gray. Enter 255 in the Value field to make it pure white.

4. In the Material Editor, Blinn Basic Parameters rollout, enter 50 in the Specular Level field and press Enter to increase the specular color's brightness. You'll see a broad bright white spot on the sample sphere in the Material Editor.

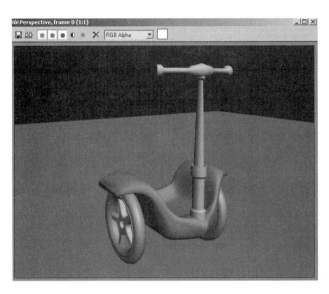

FIGURE 11.2 *The transporter rendered with flat materials and default lighting. The scene is lifeless, and the plane's back edge is somewhat distracting against the black background.*

5. Enter 35 in the Glossiness field and press Enter to reduce the size of the specular highlight. Notice in the Material Editor that the smallish, bright specular highlight makes the sample sphere look like a hard plastic.

6. Render the Perspective viewport by clicking the Quick Render button. Maximize the RAM Player and click the Open Last Rendered Image in Channel B button. Click OK in the RAM Player Configuration dialog box. Pick anywhere in the RAM Player display and drag the mouse back and forth to compare Channel A (left side) and Channel B (right side). The only real difference is in the grip and the wheel closest to you (see Figure 11.3). This is not a radical change in the material's look, but it's an important first step. Minimize the RAM Player

7. In the Material Editor, click on the second sample window in the top row to activate Metallic_platform material. Set the Specular Color to pure white, set Specular Level to 50, and set Glossiness to 30. Use Quick Render in the Perspective viewport, maximize the RAM Player, and click Open Last Rendered Image in Channel B. Drag the mouse back and forth in the RAM Player to compare Channels A and B. The specular highlights show more on the transporter platform, even though they are a bit softer. Minimize the RAM Player.

tip

The lighting in the scene can have an enormous influence on your materials. Here you are using the default lighting and are seeing only small but significant changes in the materials. The materials look harder and stand out more against the background.

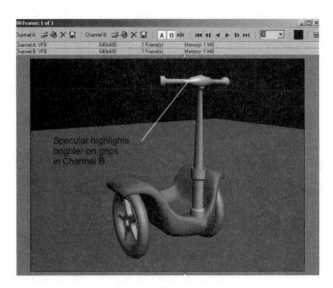

FIGURE 11.3 *Increasing the specular level makes the specular highlight brighter, and increasing the glossiness makes it smaller and tighter.*

8. Activate the third sample window in the top row called Tires. This is a Multi/Sub-Object material made of two materials: Handlebars, which is assigned to all faces with Material ID #1, and Tire tread, which is assigned to faces with Material ID #2. In the Material Editor, click the Material/Map Navigator button to see a hierarchical listing of the Tires material, and click (1): Handlebars (Standard) in the list to highlight it (see Figure 11.4). This sets the Material Editor to that level in the material hierarchy.

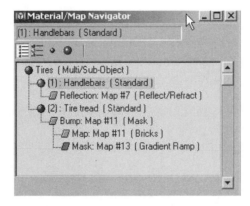

FIGURE 11.4 *By using the Material/Map Navigator in the Material Editor, you can quickly navigate complex material hierarchies.*

9. In the Material Editor, drag and drop the 1: Handlebars (Standard) level material in the Material/Map Navigator onto Grip01, wheel_star01, Handlebar_shaft_shape, and Axle objects in the Left and Front viewports (see Figure 11.5). This replaces the material on those objects with a new Handlebars material with reflections and specular highlights. Quick render the Perspective viewport, maximize the RAM Player, and click Open Last Rendered Image in Channel B. Compare the new materials with the original rendering in Channel A to see a dramatic difference. Minimize the RAM Player.

tip

You also can use the Select by Name dialog box, and choose Grip01, wheel_star01, Handlebar_shaft_shape, and Axle. Drag (1): Handlebars (Standard) from the Material/Map Navigator onto one of the selected objects. When the Assign Material dialog box pops up, choose Assign to Selection and click OK.

caution

Do not drag and drop the sample sphere, or you will assign the complete Multi/Sub-Object material called Tires, not just the Handlebars material. If you make a mistake, just drag and drop the correct materials to the correct objects to "overwrite" the incorrect assignment.

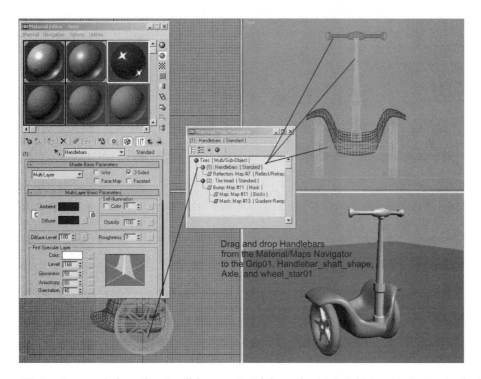

Drag and drop Handlebars from the Material/Maps Navigator to the Grip01, Handlebar_shaft_shape, Axle, and wheel_star01

Figure 11.5 *Drag and drop the Handlebars material from the Material/Map Navigator to the four objects to reassign the material.*

tip

You can check your material assignments by choosing File, File Summary Info from the menu (see Figure 11.6).

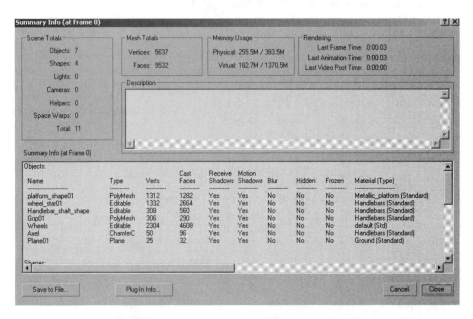

FIGURE 11.6   *In the Summary Info dialog box, you can view material assignments, mesh density, and other information about objects in your scene.*

note

The Handlebars material is more complex than any you have used so far. The specular highlight appears as a bright cross on the dark blue sample sphere because the Multi-Layer shader type allows two separate specular highlights.

The Handlebars material also has a Reflect/Refract map in the Reflection slot that reflects the surrounding scene in the objects. This type of reflection map works only on curved surfaces.

Take the time to investigate this Multi/Sub-Object material to see what adjustments have been made. Change settings one at a time, and re-render the scene to see the changes.

tip

One of the best methods of learning about materials is to dissect materials created by others.

10. In the Material Editor, drag and drop the Tires sample sphere onto the Wheels object in the Perspective or Front viewport. The tires will turn brown. This assigns the complete Multi/Sub-Object material to Wheels, so the rims get the Handlebars material, and the tires get the Tire tread material. Render the Perspective viewport, and you will see that the Tire tread material has a Bump map that gives the illusion of raised treads (see Figure 11.7). The tread does not wrap around the tire's entire width because the material includes a Mask map that reveals the tread bump only in certain areas of the tire. Again, investigate the material to see how the effect is created. You will learn more about Mask maps in the next exercise.

11. Close all windows and dialog boxes. Click OK in the Exit RAM Player dialog box when prompted. Save the file; it should already be called TransMatl02.max.

You have adjusted the specular highlight components to make materials look harder and shinier in the rendered image. You also have assigned materials that have reflection maps and bump maps to give the illusion of more depth and texture.

FIGURE 11.7 *A reflective chrome material with specular highlights and a material with Bump maps enhance the rendered image.*

Masking in Maps and Materials

You can create interesting and convincing materials in 3ds max without drilling too deeply into the Material Editor. However, for good control of materials and for materials that will separate your work from your competition, you can use a technique called *masking* in 3ds max.

The concept is simple: A *mask* is a pattern that hides something and reveals something else. Masks perform their function based on the Luminance value, or brightness, of each pixel in the pattern used as the mask. For this reason, using a grayscale image as the mask usually makes it easier to visualize the values. Color patterns will work fine, but it might be difficult to tell the difference in brightness between a yellow pixel and a bright green pixel, for example. However, you can convert these images from color to grayscale in most photo paint or image manipulation software.

Masks can be used at the material or map level in the Material Editor. At the material level, for example, you could have a Blend material made up of two materials: a red plastic and a bumpy blue material. When a black-and-white checkered mask is applied, the red plastic shows where the checks are white, and the bumpy blue material shows where the checks are black. With this form of masking, two complete materials can be hidden or revealed as needed. A simpler but equally powerful masking can be done at the Map level by using the Mask map type.

Who Was That Masked Map?

In Exercise 11.2, you learn to use a Mask map in the Diffuse Color slot to allow the map color—in this case, white—to show through the dark blue Diffuse Color. You then learn to use a RGB Tint map to adjust the color of the revealed underlying map.

A single map is used several times in this next exercise as both the color and the mask, and eventually as the bump map. Masking is a more complex technique, but this exercise walks you through the basics of using it so that you can understand the concept behind it.

tip

Reusing a single map for multiple purposes is an efficient way to work in 3ds max 5. The map has to be loaded into memory only one time. If you had separate Diffuse maps, Bump maps, and Mask maps, the memory requirements would be three times as great.

Exercise 11.2: Masking and Tinting for Flexible, Efficient Materials

1. Open the TransMatl02.max file from Exercise 11.1 or from the CD-ROM, and save it as `TransMat103.max`. Open the Material Editor and click the second sample window in the top row to activate the Metallic_platform material.

On the CD

exercises\CH11\
TransMatl02.max

2. In the Material Editor, click the Standard button to the right of the material name. In the Material/Map Browser, double-click the Raytrace material type, which will give you better control of the reflections. In the Raytrace Basic Parameters rollout, click the Diffuse Color swatch to open the Color Selector. In the RGB value fields, set Red to 6, Green to 20, and Blue to 66 for a dark blue color.

On the CD

exercises\CH11\
TransBump.png

3. Click the gray map shortcut box to the right of the Diffuse Color swatch to drop to the material's map level. Double-click Bitmap in the Material/Map Browser and open the TransBump.png file noted next to the CD icon. This simple black-and-white image includes footprints and the number 42 (see Figure 11.8). In the Material Editor, click the Show Map in Viewport button just below the sample windows. The platform will change color, but will not actually show the map until the object has mapping coordinates assigned.

Figure 11.8 *This black and white bitmap, created in the Top viewport, consists of text and two shapes converted to Editable Mesh objects. A white material with full self-illumination was applied, and the Top viewport was rendered as a PNG file.*

4. The sample sphere will turn black with white figures, as the black-and-white bitmap is controlling
100% of the Diffuse Color. You want blue with
white figures for your material, so you will substitute a Mask map for the bitmap, but keep the
bitmap as a sub-map. In the Material Editor, click
the Bitmap button to the right of the map name.
In the Material/Map Browser, double-click Mask.

In a mask, the white pixels are
opaque and the black pixels
are transparent, allowing the
base color to show through
that portion of the mask.

In the Replace Map dialog box, make sure the Keep Old Map as Sub-map radio
button is selected, and click OK. The Material Editor should look like Figure 11.9.

FIGURE 11.9   *By choosing Mask map and keeping the bitmap as a sub-map, you now have a Mask slot
below the current map.*

5. In the Material Editor, Mask Parameters rollout, drag and drop the Map button
onto the Mask button. Select the Copy radio button and click OK in the Copy
(Instance) Map dialog box. The sample sphere shows a blue sphere with white figures. Click the Material/Map Navigator button to see the material's hierarchy so far
(see Figure 11.10).

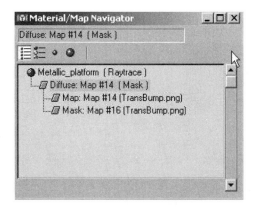

Figure 11.10 *The Material/Map Navigator shows that you have the same map used twice in the material—once for color and again to mask where the base color is shown in the material.*

6. The client for this project is not sure what colors the figures should be, so you will apply a RGB Tint map to this material's map level so that you can change the map color at any time. In the Material/Map Navigator, click the first Map level indented under the Diffuse slot to go to that level. In the Material Editor, click the Bitmap button to the right of the map name and double-click RGB Tint in the Material/Map Browser. In the Replace Map dialog box, make sure Keep the Old Map as Sub-map is selected, and click OK. The RGB Tint map has equal parts of pure red, green, and blue to make white, so it has no effect on the white map. In the RGB Tint Parameters rollout, drag and drop the red color swatch onto the green and the blue slots, selecting Copy in the Copy or Swap Colors dialog box for each action. The RGB Tint map is now tinting the figures bright red, and the Mask map is still revealing the blue base color.

7. Next, you'll add the TransBump.png map to the material's Bump slot. The white pixels in the map make the figures appear raised, and the black pixels do nothing. In the Material/Map Navigator, click the top level, and in the Material Editor, Maps rollout, resize the Material Editor and scroll, if necessary, to see the Bump slot.

8. In the Material/Map Navigator, click and drag the Mask: Map #16 (TransBump.png) level onto the None button next to the Bump slot in the Maps rollout. Select the Instance radio button in the Instance (Copy) Map dialog box and click OK (see Figure 11.11). The text looks slightly raised on the sample sphere. In the Maps rollout, enter in the Bump Amount field to heighten the illusion. Close the Material Editor and Material/Map Navigator.

note

The actual map numbers might be different in your scene.

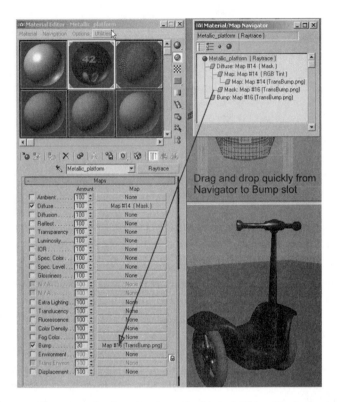

FIGURE 11.11 *You can clone maps by dragging from the Material/Map Navigator to the buttons in the Material Editor.*

9. Quick render the Perspective viewport. You'll see a Missing Map Coordinates message box indicating that the platform_shape01 object has no mapping coordinates to place the map pattern on the surface. Click Cancel to cancel the render. On the main toolbar, click the Select button and click on the platform_shape01 object in the Perspective viewport. In the Modify panel, Modifier List, double-click the UVW Map modifier. Quick render the Perspective viewport. Because of the way the object was created, the default Planar map is perpendicular to the object's Local Z axis, which stretches the footprints across the width of the platform and places the numbers backward (see Figure 11.12). In the Modify panel, click the Remove Modifier from the Stack button to remove UVW Map. It will not give you the correct orientation for the maps.

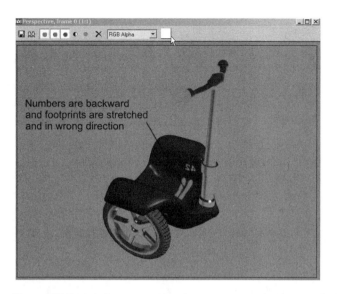

FIGURE 11.12   *The Planar UVW Map does not orient the maps correctly on your platform.*

10. You want the footprints on the platform facing forward and the number 42 on top of each fender. You have only one 42, which is in front of the footprints. You will use the improved Unwrap UVW modifier to give you the control you need. With the platform_shape01 object selected, go to the Modify panel, Modifier List, and click Unwrap UVW. In the Parameters rollout, click the Edit button. This opens the Edit UVWs dialog box and shows the mesh from the side with some selected vertices. In the Modify panel, Selection Parameters rollout, click the minus button to deselect the vertices.

On the CD

exercises\CH11\
TransBump.png

11. Click the UV drop-down list at the top right of the Edit UVWs dialog box, and select Pick Texture from the list (see Figure 11.13). Double-click Bitmap in the Material/Map Browser and open TransBump.png from the CD-ROM. This drops it into the dialog box background. The mesh in the dialog box represents the mapping coordinates on the surface, and you can see the relationship to help align the pattern.

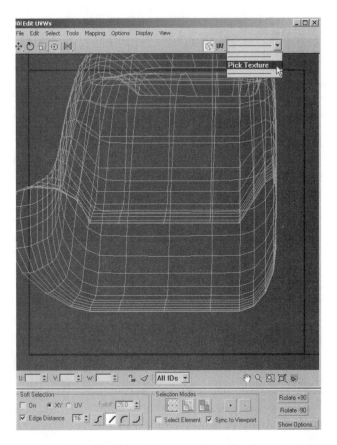

Figure 11.13 *You can view a bitmap in the Edit UVWs dialog box by selecting Pick Texture in the UV drop-down list.*

12. You do not want the default mapping because you need a more complex positioning on the object's surface. Choose Mapping, Flatten Mapping from the Edit UVWs menu. In the Flatten Mapping dialog box, enter 40 in the Face Angle Threshold field and click OK (see Figure 11.14).

13. At the bottom of Edit UVWs dialog box, in the Selection Modes section, click the Select Element check box. Click on the shapes in the display, and each element will be highlighted in red as it's picked. In the Edit UVWs display, zoom out slightly to see that the map is tiled in the background. Drag a selection window around half of the elements, and move them to the right into the black space away from the map figures. Move the other half to the left so that the figures do not appear on the object.

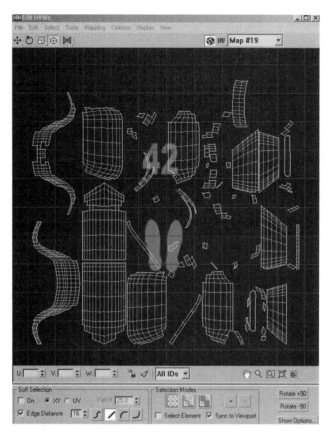

FIGURE 11.14 *The Flatten Mapping option groups faces that meet at 40 degrees or less and flattens them onto the Edit UVWs display with the bitmap visible in the background.*

14. Click the Freeform Mode button at the top left of the Edit UVWs dialog box. Also make sure the Show Map in Viewport button is toggled on in the Material Editor. In the Edit UVWs display, select the large element in the middle of the second column of elements on the left (see Figure 11.15), pick any of its vertices, and move the element over the footprints. Zoom in to see the alignment better. The footprints now show on the platform in

By default, the Edit UVWs cursor is in Freeform Mode. Clicking the corner points scales the selection, clicking the midpoints rotates the element, and clicking on a vertex moves the element. If you hold Ctrl down while dragging, you lock the Element Gizmo's aspect ratio. Holding down Shift restricts scaling to one axis.

the Perspective viewport. You are adjusting the mesh's mapping coordinates to match the map patterns. Click on one of the yellow corners of the Element Gizmo, and scale the element so that the footprints fit in the rectangular area. Move the element again to center it on the footprints (see Figure 11.16).

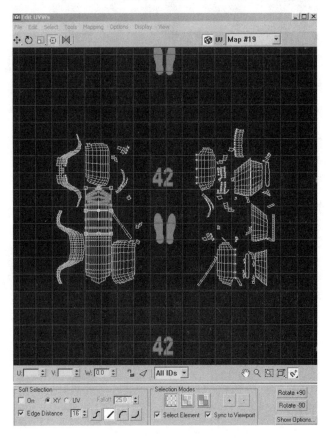

FIGURE 11.15 *By selecting elements in the Edit UVWs display and moving them away from the bitmap figures, the map will not show anywhere on the mesh in the scene. Then select the middle element in the left grouping.*

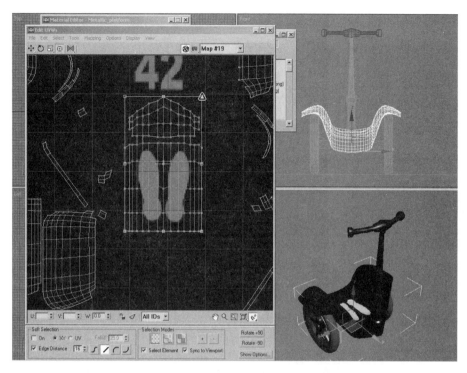

FIGURE 11.16 *Scaling the element large makes the pattern look smaller on the surface. Moving the element adjusts the position of the pattern on the surface.*

15. Next, you'll align the top coordinates of the left and right fenders (see Figure 11.17) over the 42 in the map. You need to rotate and scale the elements for the right fit. In the Edit UVWs display, rearrange the fender's top elements to make the numbers smaller so that they can be read on each side (see Figure 11.18).

If this pattern were too crowded to get the results you wanted, you could zoom out and move elements to any of the other tiled map locations in the display.

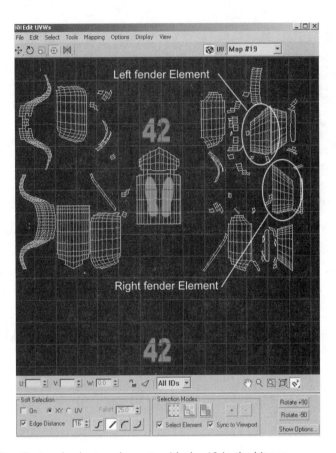

FIGURE 11.17　*Align the two fender top elements with the 42 in the bitmap.*

16. Close all windows and dialog boxes. Right-click in the Perspective viewport and click the Quick Render button. The shiny blue platform should have bright red figures raised from the surface. Open the Material Editor, and at the top level of the Metallic_platform material, click the Reflect Color swatch in the Raytrace Parameters rollout. In the Color Selector dialog box, enter 100 in the Values field, and press Enter. In the Raytrace Parameters rollout, enter 100 in the Specular Level field and press Enter. Quick render the Perspective viewport. You should have a shiny blue platform with chrome fixtures and rubber tires.

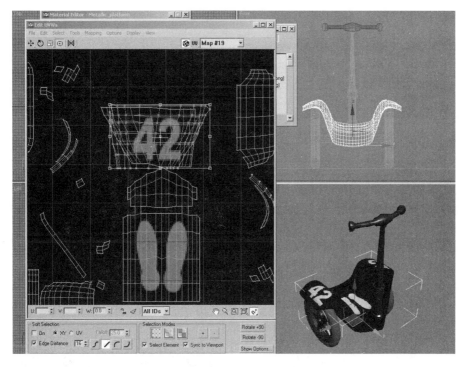

FIGURE 11.18   *You can position the numbers on each fender by moving, rotating, and scaling the elements in the Edit UVWs dialog box.*

17. Close all windows and dialog boxes, and save the file. It should already be called TransMatl03.max.

   Complex mapping is now much easier to solve in 3ds max 5 with the new Unwrap UVW modifier, which has the option of flattening the mesh coordinates into manageable elements that can be positioned on the bitmap.

Cartoons or Technical Illustrations

In this next exercise, you use the new Ink 'n Paint material in 3ds max 5. Essentially, this material puts flat color on surfaces and outlines objects in a contrasting color. It can be used to render a cartoon effect or to create technical illustrations.

Exercise 11.3: Applying Ink 'n Paint Material

1. Open the InknPaint01.max file from the CD-ROM, and save it as InknPaint02.max. It is the transporter with the basic materials assigned.

2. Click the Select By Name button. In the Select Objects dialog box, click the All button, and then click the Select button to select all objects in the scene.

3. Open the Material Editor and click the lower-left sample window to activate it. Name this material Cartoon. Just below the sample window, click the Assign Material to Selection button. This turns all objects a flat gray color. Render the Perspective viewport to see a flat, relatively uninteresting image.

4. In the Material Editor, click the Standard button for the Cartoon material, and double-click Ink 'n Paint in the Material/Map Browser. The sample sphere turns a solid blue, and all the objects in the shaded viewport turn blue. Render the Perspective viewport (see Figure 11.19).

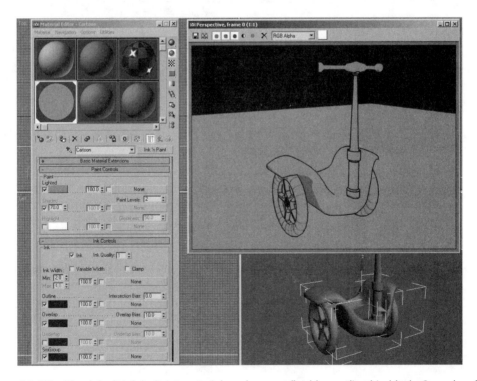

FIGURE 11.19   *The default Ink 'n Paint material renders as a flat blue outlined in black. Curved surfaces show lines that indicate the curvature, and shaded areas appear slightly darker.*

5. In the Material Editor, Paint Controls rollout, select the Highlight check box and quick render the Perspective viewport. Specular highlights are simulated with white lines on the surface.

6. In the Ink Controls rollout, click the Outline color swatch and change it to bright yellow. Quick render the Perspective viewport. You'll see that objects are outlined in yellow to make them stand from the black background and against other objects. Outlines within each object are still black, however.

7. Click the Lighted color swatch in the Paint Controls rollout and change the Lighted color in the from light blue to brick red, and quick render to see a totally different look to the scene (see Figure 11.20).

8. Close all windows and dialog boxes and save the file. It should already be called InknPaint02.max.

The Ink 'n Paint material gives your renderings a cartoon or technical illustration look and includes options that help you focus viewers' attention where you want. The look can range from very flat to one with depth and specular highlights.

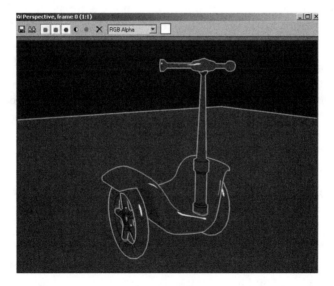

Figure 11.20 *Changing the paint and outline colors radically affects the look of objects with the Ink 'n Paint material. These settings can be used to draw the viewer's eye to important areas of the scene.*

Lighting: Bring in the New and Take Out the Old

With the new lighting features in 3ds max 5, we should probably abandon the old methods, right? Not at all! It still makes sense to take advantage of the rendering speed and efficiency of the Standard lights that have been around since the early 3D Studio DOS days. In this section, you learn your way around the fundamentals of using Standard light types, including

- **Spot**   Spot lights cast their light within a cone emanating from the light source. By default, the light does not attenuate and shines to infinity within that cone.

- **Omni**   Omni lights, as the name implies, shine their light in all directions from the source. Like Spot lights, they shine to infinity by default.

- **Direct**   Direct lights shine within a cylinder and are useful for creating parallel shadows or, as you'll see in a later exercise, simulating laser beams when combined with special effects.

Standard lights are not intended for general use with the Advanced Lighting features, even though they can be combined with photometric lights, such as Point, Linear, Area, Sky, and Sun, as you learned in Chapter 4, "Exterior Lighting: Standard and Advanced Methods," while lighting the street scene. Standard lights are used with the Scanline renderer and offer speed and control not available with photometric lights.

Because the Standard light types do not use Advanced Lighting, bounced light in the scene is not calculated. The approach to lighting a scene is more akin to painting the scene with lights rather than placing lights in real-world arrangements. You control the action with Standard lights, whereas the Radiosity or Light Tracer renderers control many aspects of bouncing photometric lighting. The following features increase your control of Standard lights:

- **Angle of Incidence**   Angle of incidence is the angle at which lights strike a surface. The closer the angle is to perpendicular to the surface, the brighter the light.

- **Attenuation**   Attenuation is the diminishing of light along its path.

- **Shadows**   Shadow calculations can be a major component of balancing rendering speed and memory use.

In addition to features of Standard lights, you'll learn about the new Light Tracer renderer, which calculates bounced light in a scene but is not physically accurate like the Radiosity renderer. Light Tracer is primarily intended for open outdoor scenes that benefit from soft shadows and uses the new 3ds max 5 Skylight as its light source.

Finally, you will add a special effect to the Direct light you placed in the catapult track scene in Chapter 9, "Taking Control with Animation Controllers." This special effect simulates a laser beam.

Standard Lighting: The Old Efficient Standby

As mentioned earlier, Standard lights can be an effective and efficient lighting method after you understand the fundamentals of placing and adjusting the light settings and learn the shadow-casting capabilities.

Because bounced light isn't calculated when you use Standard lights with the Scanline renderer, you have to add fill lights to control the areas of light and dark. Another control you will learn about is the ever-important Attenuation setting, the decay of light as it travels away from the source. It is handled automatically with the Advanced Lighting system, but must be manually controlled with Standard lights.

Spot Lights: Placement and Control

Spot lights tend to be the most commonly used Standard light type in 3ds max. The light emanates from the source within two cones: the *Hotspot cone* for full-intensity light, and the *Falloff cone*, within which the light diminishes laterally from the hotspot cone to the area of no light (see Figure 11.21).

Setting the light source's position and then dragging it to the light target's position creates the light in the scene. The distance from the light source to the light target has no effect on the brightness; it is used primarily as a visual aid for aiming the light.

In this next exercise, you place a Target Spot light to light the transporter and then adjust the light for intensity and shadow quality.

Exercise 11.4: Creating and Adjusting Target Spot Lights

1. Open the TransMatl03.max file from Exercise 11.2 or from the CD-ROM, and save it as `TransMat104.max`. It is the transporter with materials applied. Right-click in the Front viewport to activate it and click the Zoom Extents button to fill only the Front viewport with all objects in the scene.

On the CD

exercises\CH11\
TransMatl03.max

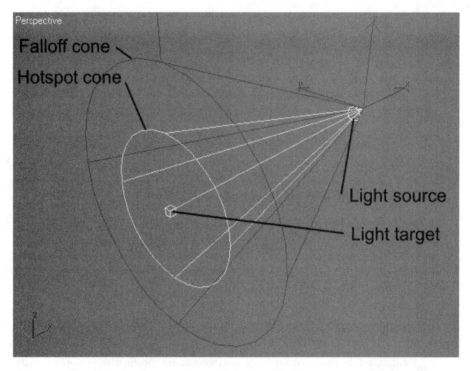

Figure 11.21 *A Standard Target Spot light has a light source, a light target, a hotspot cone, and a falloff cone.*

2. In the Create panel, Lights category, make sure you are in the Standard category, and click the Target Spot button in the Object Type rollout. In the Front viewport, click above right of the transporter to set the light source, and drag to the bottom middle of the platform at roughly a 45-degree angle to set the light target (see Figure 11.22).

3. In the Perspective viewport, zoom out so that you can see the two circles formed by the Hotspot and Falloff cones. On the main toolbar, click the Quick Render button, and you will see the pool of light created by the Target Spot light (see Figure 11.23). The pool is brighter on the left and somewhat darker on the right because of the angle of incidence of the light striking the ground object. The light strikes at a more perpendicular angle on the left. The edge of the light pool is a sharp line because the two cones are separated by the default 2 degrees, resulting in rapid falloff.

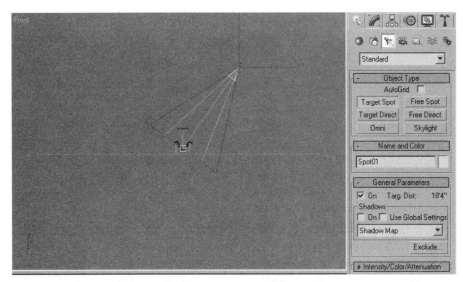

FIGURE 11.22 *Create a Target Spot light that's aimed at the platform from the upper right of the Front viewport.*

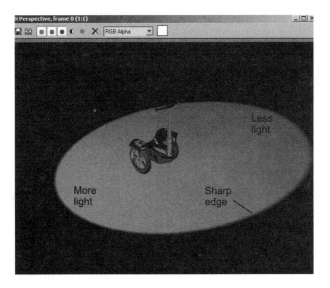

FIGURE 11.23 *The light pool from a Target Spot at about 45 degrees to the ground plane is brighter closer to the source and has a sharp edge.*

4. In the Modify panel, Spotlight Parameters rollout, enter 65 in the Falloff/Field field to increase the size of the Falloff cone. Render the Perspective viewport, and you will see that the edge of the light pool is much softer. The greater the distance between the Hotspot and Falloff cones, the softer the edge of the light pool.

5. To adjust the light intensity, you change the Multiplier value in the Intensity/Color/ Attenuation rollout. Enter 1.2 and press Enter. Render the Perspective viewport to see the brighter light effect.

6. You have probably noticed there are no shadows by default with Standard lights. In the Modify panel, General Parameters rollout, select the On check box in the Shadows section. Render the Perspective viewport to see shadows being cast on the ground plane. The shadow type is set to Shadow Map, which superimposes a bitmap representing the shadows on the rendered image. Shadow Map shadows tend to have softer edges than Ray Traced shadows, the other type of shadow in Standard lights.

7. In the General Parameters rollout, click the drop-down arrow next to Shadow Map and choose Ray Traced Shadows from the list. Render the Perspective viewport, and you will see much sharper shadow edges. Ray Traced shadows do not create bitmaps; rather, they calculate the shadows mathematically by shooting sample rays to generate the shadows at render time. You might not have noticed, but it took almost twice as long to render the Ray Traced shadows in this scene. In the Ray Traced Shadow Params rollout, enter 10 in the Max Quadtree Depth field and render the scene again. Render times will drop back closer to the Shadow Map times, yet retain the sharp shadow edge.

tip

You can also adjust a light's brightness by clicking the color swatch and changing the Value setting up to a strength of 255. You can, of course, also change the color of the light. Multiplier settings enable you to increase a light's brightness above the color setting.

tip

Ray Traced shadows generally take longer to render than Shadow Map shadows, which can use much more RAM. If you are using Ray Traced shadows, always try setting the Max Quadtree Depth to 10 to speed things up.

To adjust the quality of Shadow Map shadows, you can change settings in the Shadow Map Params rollout. The Bias setting moves the shadow toward or away from the light source, Size is the resolution of the shadow map, and Sample Range is the softness of the shadow's edge.

Shadow Map quality depends on the scene size, range of object sizes, and distance of the light from objects.

8. In the Intensity/Color/Attenuation rollout, click the Decay Type drop-down arrow, and choose Inverse Square from the list. The Perspective viewport will go dark. In the Front viewport, you will see a green lens-shaped object just below the light source. This is the start range for Inverse Square decay, and the light dies quickly from that point outward in the cone. In the Intensity/Color/ Attenuation rollout, enter 14'0" in the Decay Start field. This should move the lens-shaped object near the top of the handlebars in the Front viewport. Adjust the Decay Start setting if that is not the case (see Figure 11.24).

Attenuation not only lends an air of realism to your lighting, but also cuts down on the amount of geometry on which shadows must be calculated.

The Far Attenuation option enables you to define a start and end attenuation range, with linear falloff between the two ranges. This does not match the laws of physics, but is easy to control.

9. In the General Parameters rollout, set the shadows back to the Shadow Map type. Save the file; it should already be called TransMatl04.max.

Two important concepts in 3ds max 5 Standard lighting are shadow-casting techniques and attenuation methods. Shadows give your objects the illusion of weight by anchoring them to the objects they sit on. However, shadows can be expensive in rendering time, so use them only when necessary. Attenuation simulates the natural decaying of light as it gets farther away from the source and adds realism and efficiency to your scenes.

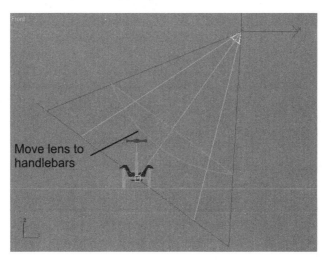

FIGURE 11.24 *Setting the lens-shaped object near the handlebars causes the light to attenuate from that point outward in the cone, using the Inverse Square law.*

Omni Lights: Filling Out the Scene

Although standard Omni lights can be used as the main lights in any scene, using them as fill and effects lights is generally more efficient. An Omni light streams from the source equally in all directions to infinity by default. Omni lights have the same shadow capabilities and intensity/color adjustments as Spot and Direct lights.

In this next exercise, you use one Omni light to fill out your scene and another to add some sparkle to the scene.

caution

Omni light shadows are actually generated by six spotlights pointing front, back, up, down, left, and right. A special algorithm blends the overlapping areas to avoid bright spots caused by two lights hitting the same surface. For this reason, Omni lights can take six times the computer resources to calculate shadows, so use shadow-casting Omni lights only in special circumstances, such as a candle flame or campfire.

Exercise 11.5: Adding Omni Lights to Augment the Main Spot Light

1. Open the TransMatl04.max file, and save it as `TrasnsMatl05.max`. The scene has one standard Spot light shining from a 45-degree angle to the ground plane. Because Standard lights and the Scanline renderer do not calculate bounced light, the side of the transporter opposite the Spot light gets no light at all.

On the CD

exercises\CH11\
TransMatl04.max

2. Activate the Front viewport, and click Zoom Extents to fill the viewport with all objects. In the Create panel, Lights category, make sure you're in the Standard category, and click the Omni button in the Object Type rollout. Click in the Front viewport at the left edge of the ground plane and about halfway up the transporter (see Figure 11.25). An Omni light is a Point light, so there is no target. In the Modify panel, Intensity/Color/Attenuation rollout, enter 0.8 in the Multiplier field to dim this light. In the Left viewport, move the Omni light to the left so that it's slightly in front of the transporter.

tip

By keeping the Omni light low to the ground plane, you are adding minimal extra light to that surface because the angle of incidence is very low.

3. In the Perspective viewport, zoom in to fill the viewport with the transporter and render the scene. The far side of the transporter has more light, and the tire is now visible where it was in shadow before.

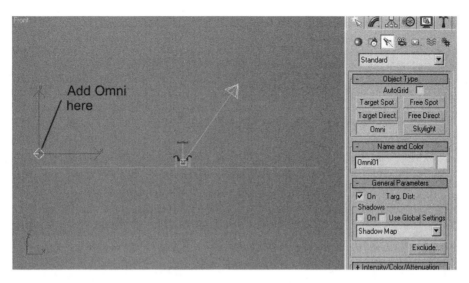

FIGURE 11.25   *Add an Omni light in the Front viewport to act as a fill light.*

4. The rendered scene has good depth cues and the materials are rich, but there is very little sparkle. You will add another Omni to the scene that contributes just sparkle, which also will add more apparent depth to the scene. In the Create panel, click the Omni button, and in the Perspective viewport, click anywhere in front of the transporter.

In a more typical scene, you might need four or more Omni lights away from and around the scene to fill where necessary. Remember you are painting the scene with light.

5. In the Modify panel, Intensity/Color/Attenuation rollout, enter 3 in the Multiplier field. This adds very bright light to the front underside of the transporter, turning the tires almost white. You do not want this light to affect the whole scene, however. In the Advanced Effects rollout, clear the Diffuse check box. The light now affects only the specular areas of the scene.

6. In the General Parameters rollout, click the Exclude button. Highlight Plane01 in the left column and click the >> button between columns to send Plane01 to the right column (see Figure 11.26). The Exclude radio button is selected, thus excluding Plane01 from any effects of the light. Click OK to close the dialog box.

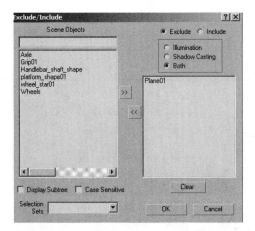

FIGURE 11.26   *In 3ds max 5, objects can be excluded from the effects of lights for more control of lighting.*

7. Next, you will use a special alignment tool intended for placing specular highlights where you want them on objects. You must be in a non-orthographic viewport (such as Camera, Perspective, User, Light) and must have a light selected. On the main toolbar, click and hold on the Align tool to open the button flyouts. Click the Place Highlights button indicated in Figure 11.27.

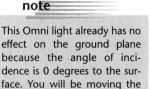

note

This Omni light already has no effect on the ground plane because the angle of incidence is 0 degrees to the surface. You will be moving the light, however.

8. In the Perspective viewport, click on the vertical handlebar shaft and, while holding the mouse button down, move the cursor across the surface. You will see a blue normals vector at the cursor position, and the light will move to be at a angle to that normals vector that causes the specular highlight to be brightest there. Release the mouse button when the highlight is on the front of the shaft (see Figure 11.28).

9. Render the Perspective viewport. The scene lighting should be fairly well balanced, with good shadows to give the transporter the illusion of weight. Bright specular highlights add a good dynamic range between the lightest and darkest portions of the scene. Close all windows and dialog boxes and save the scene. It should already be called TransMatl05.max.

You can add Omni lights, or any other lights for that matter, for fill and to simulate bounced light. You can also restrict lights to affect only the specular highlights, and exclude or include certain objects in the scene for more lighting control. The Standard light types are versatile and efficient to render.

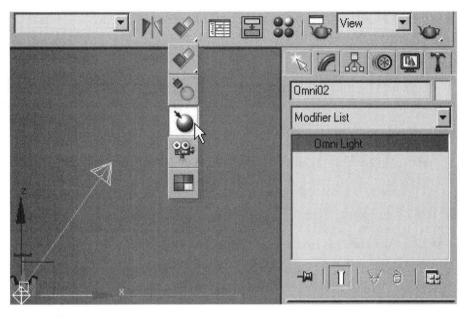

FIGURE 11.27   *Use the Place Highlights alignment tool to specify the surface locations for specular highlights.*

FIGURE 11.28   *By dragging the Place Highlights cursor over surfaces, you can move lights.*

Light Tracer Rendering Engine

Next, you'll combine the Skylight component of the Daylight system (used in Chapter 4) with the new Light Tracer renderer. Light Tracer rendering fills the scene with light that appears to come from an overhead dome.

Lighting setup with a Skylight is straightforward, and the rendering times can be faster than radiosity rendering. However, both are slower than the Scanline renderer.

tip

You can control the direction of shadows by the placement of the IES Sky photometric light. IES Sky is a Target light type.

Exercise 11.6: Using Light Tracer with a Skylight

1. Open the LightTracer01.max file from the CD-ROM, and save it as `LightTracer02.max`.

2. In the Create panel, Lights category, make sure you're in the Standard category and click the Skylight button. In the Top viewport, click to the left of the transporter near the edge of the viewport. The Skylight icon looks like a dome. Its position in the scene is not important.

On the CD

exercises\CH11\
LightTracer01.max

3. Choose Rendering, Advanced Lighting from the menu (keyboard shortcut: **9**). In the Advanced Lighting dialog box, choose Light Tracer for the lighting plug-in (see Figure 11.29).

4. Right-click in the Perspective viewport to activate it and click the Quick Render button. The rendering might progress rather slowly with the default settings, depending on your processor speed. The resulting render has soft shadows, and even though the light source is behind the transporter, all areas have some light. The bump maps on the tires hardly show with the soft shadows.

note

The handlebar grips, shaft, and wheels are currently black. The Reflect/Refract reflection maps have been disabled to speed the rendering process. You will turn them on later.

5. In the Advanced Lighting dialog box, Parameters rollout, enter **100** in the Rays/Sample field and render the Perspective viewport again. The render time will be cut almost in half, but the reduced number of rays makes the shadows somewhat blotchy.

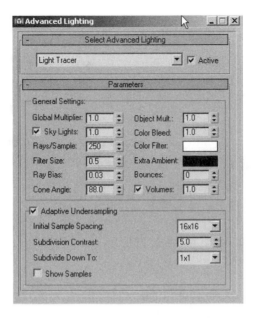

FIGURE 11.29   *The Light Tracer rendering plug-in has fewer controls than the Radiosity renderer.*

6. In the Parameters rollout, enter 1 in the Bounces field and render the Perspective viewport again. The shadows become somewhat lighter because of the light bouncing from the underside of the platform, and the render times increase again. Set Bounces back to 0.

7. In the Parameters rollout, enter 33 in the Cone Angle field and render the Perspective viewport. This concentrates the light and makes the shadows darker and their edges more pronounced.

8. In the Parameters rollout, increase the Rays/Sample setting to 150. Click the Render Scene button (not Quick Render), and in the Render Scene dialog box, MAX Default Scanline A-Buffer rollout, select the Auto-Reflect/Refract and Mirrors option to enable it again. Click the Render button in the dialog box. The scene will take a while to calculate reflections and render, but result is very good for only one light source (see Figure 11.30).

9. Close all windows and dialog boxes and save the file. It should already be called LightTracer02.max.

Light Tracer Advanced Lighting with a Skylight or photometric IES Sky is quick to set up and adjust. The quality of the soft light lends itself to quiet outdoor scenes.

FIGURE 11.30 *Light Tracer renderings with Skylight have a soft, evenly lit quality.*

Adding Special Effects to Lights

A number of special effects can be added directly to most lights. In this exercise, you revisit the catapult track scene from Chapter 9, "Taking Control with Animation Controllers." It has a Direct standard light linked to a cone with a LookAt Controller on a Rotation axis. The LookAt Controller uses the catapult on the track as its target, keeping the light pointed at it as it animates around the track.

The light has a very narrow beam and creates only a small spotlight where it hits a surface. However, you will add a special effect to the light that makes the beam visible and bright red to simulate a laser light.

Exercise 11.7: Creating Laser Effects on a Direct Standard Light

1. From the CD-ROM, open the Laser01.max file, and save it as Laser02.max. In the Camera01 viewport, click to select the yellow Direct light icon projecting from the cone on the mast. You will see the Direct light's blue cylinders for the Hotspot and Falloff cones.

On the CD

exercises\CH11\
Laser01.max

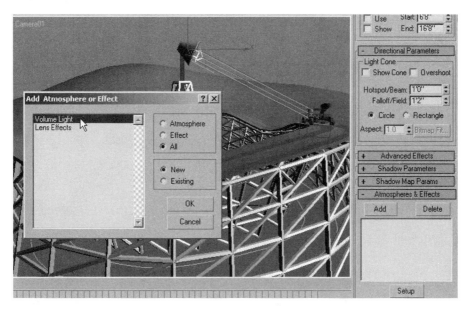

Figure 11.31 *Add a Volume Light effect to the Direct light to simulate a laser beam.*

2. In the Modify panel, Atmospheres & Effects rollout, click the Add button. Click Volume Light in the Add Atmosphere or Effect dialog box and click the OK button to enter it in the panel (see Figure 11.31).

3. Select the Volume Light entry in the Atmospheres & Effects rollout and click the Setup button at the bottom. In the Environment panel, Volume Light Parameters rollout, click on Fog Color and change it to bright red in the Color Selector. Enter 15 in the Density field (see Figure 11.32).

4. Close the Environment dialog box and render the Camera01 viewport. A thick red beam passes through the catapult. In the Modify panel, Directional Parameters rollout, enter 8" in the Falloff/Field field. The Hotspot/Beam value will automatically drop to 6". In the General Parameters rollout, select the On check box in the Shadows section.

5. Render the Camera01 viewport to see a smaller beam that now stops at any object it hits because shadow casting is on (see Figure 11.33).

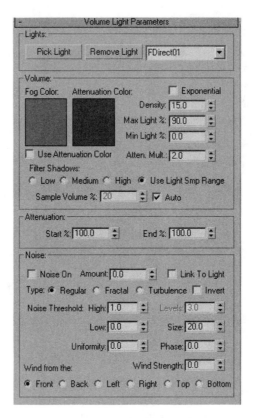

FIGURE 11.32 *Changing the color of the Volume Light effect and increasing the Density setting make the red light beam visible in the rendered image.*

6. Close all windows and dialog boxes, and save the file. It should already be called Laser02.max.

Lights can be used for much more than simply illuminating a scene. Volume Light effects can simulate a laser, as you have done here, or the soft sunlight filtering through the dusty air of an abandoned factory.

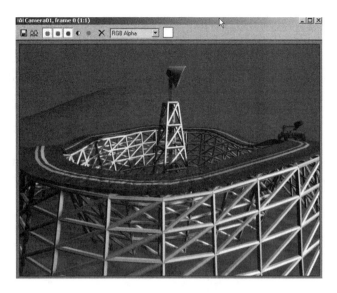

Figure 11.33 *Shadow casting causes the visible to stop at the first surface it strikes.*

Summary

You have learned to use Standard light types and the Scanline renderer for efficient fast rendering. The process of setting up Standard lights is a process of placing lights to paint the scene rather that light the scene in a more traditional sense. Because Standard lights and the Scanline renderer do not calculate bounced light, you have to add lights strategically placed to fill dark areas and to simulate bounced light. Other topics you learned about include

- **Specular highlights** Light striking the surface of any material scatters from the surface in a way that clearly clues the viewer to the material properties.

- **Masking** Using maps and images to mask a material's underlying color or other component is a powerful tool for creating convincing materials.

- **Ink 'n Paint material** Cartoon effects and technical line drawings can be simulated with this new material.

- **Standard lights** These lights, which are fast and efficient to render, are for use with the Scanline renderer and do not calculate bounced light in a scene. Placing and adjusting them is more akin to painting the scene with light than actually lighting the scene.

- **Light Tracer**   This rendering engine with a Skylight is a one-light-source setup process. The light is soft and seems to come from above. Light Tracer can be a good option for outdoor scenes and for animated sequences.
- **Special effects**   You learned to add a special effect called Volume Light to make a light beam visible in the rendered image.

Lighting and materials go hand in hand to elicit an emotional response from viewers of your rendered images. There are many approaches you can take to light scenes and to bring out the best in your materials, from Standard lights to Light Tracer renderings with Skylights. Leave yourself plenty of time in the project schedule to experiment with and tweak this art form.

CHAPTER 12

Animation: Animating in World Space

In This Chapter

In Chapter 5, "New Animation Concepts," you learned about keyframe animation, and in Chapter 9, "Taking Control with Animation Controllers," you learned to apply and adjust animation controllers. These two methods will get you through much of your day-to-day animation needs. However, at times you want to animate the space that objects exist in and have the space affect the objects. Three examples are used in this chapter: creating waves in a water surface plane, a horseshoe crab skimming the ocean bottom, and a fish wriggling around in a circle above the crab. This chapter will illustrate two basic types of animation in 3ds max 5—space warping and particle systems—and cover the following tools:

- **Wave space warp**   A Wave space warp can be used to define space in a wave form. You will bind a Plane primitive to the Wave space warp and animate the parameters to give the water surface a wave motion.

- **PathDeform World Space Modifier**   Uses a spline to deform an object as it moves though space. You'll use this world space modifier to cause a fish to "swim" around a path, distorting as it moves.

- **PatchDeform World Space Modifier**   You will apply this world space modifier to make a crab crawl across a sandy ocean floor.

- **Snapshot tool**   With this tool, you can "bake" space warp and world space modifier changes into mesh objects.

Key Terms

Native patch   A Quad Patch primitive with no topology changes applied.

Object space   The space of each object as defined by its own coordinate system. An object is deformed, but the deformations travel with it as it is moved.

Particle systems   Objects that generate particle sub-objects over time for the purpose of simulating snow, rain, dust, and so on. You use particle systems primarily in animations.

Space warps   Space warps distort space, and objects are then bound to it to become deformed as they move through space or as the space parameters deform around them.

World space   The universal coordinate system that defines space in 3ds max 5. As an object moves through world space, it is deformed by the space to which it's bound.

World space modifiers   A subcategory of space warps that act as modifiers in world space rather than object space. World space modifiers are applied directly to objects rather than having the objects bound to their space.

Hotkeys and Keyboard Shortcuts

spacebar   Lock selection set

Shift+Q   Quick Render

/   Play animation

Esc   Stop animation

Fundamentals of Space Warps

A *space warp* deforms space within the World Coordinate System. By itself, it has no effect on your scene. However, when you bind an object to a space warp, the object becomes deformed based on the space warp settings. If the object is then moved in the scene, the deformations are animated as the object moves through the space.

You'll work in an underwater scene with a rolling sand bottom and a reflective water surface above. The scene includes a fish and a horseshoe crab. The Direct light in the scene has a Projector map added to create a caustic-like effect for the light refracted from the waves on the sandy bottom. Choose Rendering, Environment from the main menu, and notice that the Fog option has been enabled in the Atmosphere rollout to make the water look murky. The finished scene is shown in Figure 12.1. Be sure you take the time to look at the materials and lighting used in the scene to learn more on your own.

FIGURE 12.1 *The underwater scene with sea life.*

These animations would be much more complex to do if you had to keyframe each position of each object, and it would not be as easy to edit the actions after the fact.

A space warp can also be moved through space, or its parameters can be animated to cause a static or moving object to be affected by the changing deformations. There are several categories of space warps in 3ds max 5, including

- **Forces** Space warps that function within a Dynamics simulation or with particle systems to cause an action to happen—wind or gravity, for example.

- **Deflectors** Space warps that deflect objects in a Dynamics simulation. A waterfall bouncing off rocks would use deflectors.

- **Geometric/Deformable** Space warps that deform 2D or 3D objects. For example, the Wave space warp can make water ripple and the Bomb space warp can blow objects up.

- **Modifier based** Space warps that mimic object space modifiers within world space, such as bending or twisting as an object moves through the space.

- **Reactor** Space warps that cause actions within a Reactor Dynamics simulation to simulate objects colliding. You will learn more about the Reactor space warp in Chapter 13, "Effects: Reacting to Reactor."

Geometric/Deformable space warps also are available in several types, including

- **FFD**   Free Form Deformation space warps use a cage structure to deform objects in world space. You could use it to simulate pushing an oyster through a key-hole, for example.

- **Wave and Ripple**   Apply wave shapes to deform objects in world space; this space warp can be used for water or cloth effects.

- **Displace**   Uses the Luminance values of bitmaps to deform objects in world space. You could simulate footprints in sand with this method.

- **Conform**   Causes one object to drape itself over another in world space. Salvador Dali would have liked this one.

- **Bomb**   Explodes objects into fragments in world space. I know you will have no trouble with what to do with this one.

You will apply a Wave space warp to the Water plane surface to deform it into the shape of undulating waves. You will then move the surface over time to cause the waves to roll.

Creating a Space Warp and Binding an Object

In this exercise, you create and adjust a Wave space warp in the underwater scene, and then bind the scene's Water object to it, causing the water to deform. You then use AutoKey animation to move the water plane through the space deformed by Wave or to move the space warp itself and leave the Water plane in place. The result of either method will be a rolling wave surface above the seabed. Although in this exercise, you'll be moving the Water plane to animate the waves, both methods work, and which one you use for your projects depends on whether the object is stationary or moving.

Exercise 12.1: Warping Space and Objects, Too

1. Open the HorseshoeCrab01.max file from the CD-ROM, and save it as `HorseshoeCrab02.max`. The Camera01 viewport has the Edged Faces option enabled so that you can see the visible mesh edges as well as the shaded view.

On the CD

exercises\CH12\
HorseshoeCrab01.max

2. In the Create panel, Space Warps category, choose Geometric/Deformable in the drop-down list. In the Object Type rollout, click the Wave button, and in the Top viewport, click and drag near the center of the small grid until the new space warp object is about

twice the size of the small grid (see Figure 12.2). Release the mouse button and move the mouse a little to define a wave Amplitude setting, and then click to set it. Do not be too concerned with sizes; you will edit them in the next step.

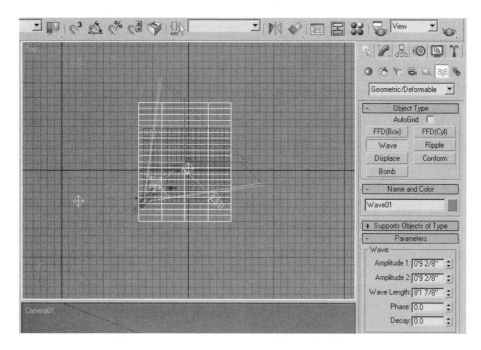

FIGURE 12.2 *A Wave space warp in the scene has no effect on objects by default.*

3. In the Modify panel, Parameters rollout, enter `0'6"` in both Amplitude fields and `8'0"` in the Wave Length field. These settings define the space deformation in the shape of a wave.

4. Right-click in the Left viewport, and click the Bind to Space Warp button left of the Select button on the main toolbar. In the Left viewport, move the cursor over the Wave space warp until you see the box-shaped cursor with wavy diagonal lines, and then click on the Wave space warp and drag the cursor to the edge of the flat plane that runs through the Direct light icon. The cursor changes to a box within a box with wavy lines. Release the mouse button on the object, which will flash white and deform in the shape of a wave (see Figure 12.3). The Water object does not have the same shape as the Wave space warp because it does not have enough geometry to bend that much.

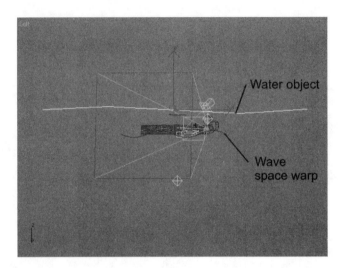

FIGURE 12.3   *Bind to Space Warp puts the Water object in the space defined by Wave space warp thus deforming it into a wavy plane.*

5. Click the Select button on the main toolbar, and select the Water object in the Camera01 viewport. In the Modify panel, you'll see the Plane and *Wave Binding items in the Stack display. The asterisk in the name indicates it is operating in world space. In the Stack display, click on Plane. In the Parameters rollout, enter 40 in the Length Segs field to add enough segments along the length to fit the Water plane to the Wave settings. Enter 1 in the Width Segs field to optimize the mesh in the direction where extra detail is not necessary—the object is not wavy in that direction (see Figure 12.4). Reducing the face count of objects is important for productivity. Return to the *Wave Binding level in the Stack display.

Using Bind to Space Warp in the Top viewport would be difficult. The Plane primitive was created in the Top viewport and rotated 180 degrees so that the face normals are pointing downward. This makes the surface visible from below. You can select objects in a scene only by picking the visible normals of the surface, so Bind to Space Warp would not see the Water object.

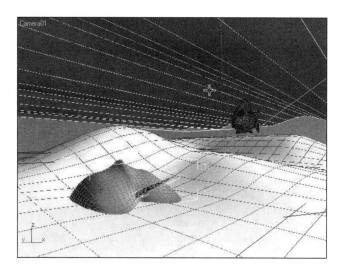

FIGURE 12.4   *Adding segments to the length of the Water plane makes it deform better to the Wave settings; reducing the Width Segs setting reduces the number of faces for more efficiency.*

6. Right-click in the Left viewport to activate it. Pick the Water object, and click the Select and Move button on the main toolbar. Move Water left in the X axis, and you'll see it slide through the space defined by the Wave space warp. Right-click while still holding down the left mouse button to cancel the move.

tip

You can cancel most operations by right-clicking while you are still in the command process and holding the left mouse button down. Otherwise, you must use the Undo button to undo the operation.

7. In the Left viewport, select the Wave space warp and move it to the left in the X axis. Right-click to cancel the move. This time the Water object remained stationary, and the wave motion passed through the object. Next, you'll animate this effect.

8. Make sure the Time slider below the viewports is set to frame 0. In the Status Bar, toggle the Auto Key button on. It will turn red. Drag the Time slider right to frame 100. In the Left viewport, move the Wave object left until the pivot point is at the left edge of the Sand object (see Figure 12.5). Toggle the Auto Key button off. Scrub the Time slider back and forth, and you will see the animated wave action over the 100 frames. Two keys were automatically created: at the beginning of the animation and at the frame where you completed the move.

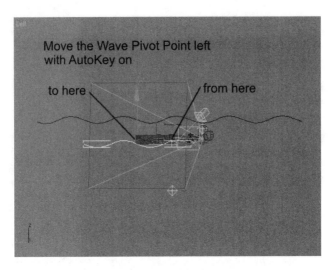

FIGURE 12.5   *At frame 100, with AutoKey toggled on, moving the Wave object until its pivot point is near the left edge of the Sand object creates an animation that causes Water to roll.*

9. Right-click in the Camera01 viewport and click the Quick Render button (hotkey: **Shift+Q**). The wavy reflective surface shows at the top of the image. Close any windows and dialog boxes. Save the file; it should already be called HorseshoeCrab02.max.

    You can create animations by moving objects that have been bound to space warps in the scene or by moving the object to make it pass through the deformations defined by the space warp. Many objects can be bound to a space warp, and many space warps can be bound to a single object.

warning

If you leave Auto Key toggled on, almost every change you make at any frame other than frame 0 will become an animation. Remember to toggle it off when you are finished animating.

World Space Modifiers

Like space warps, world space modifiers use the World Coordinate System to make changes to objects that are bound to them in the scene. For example, if you apply an Object space Bend modifier with a 90-degree angle to a cylinder you've created, you can transform the cylinder in the scene and it will remain bent in the same manner. However, if you bind a cylinder to a World Space Bend modifier, transforming the cylinder or the gizmo will have a profound effect on how the bend is applied.

tip

You will always find space warps and world space modifiers at the top of the Modifier Stack with an asterisk preceding the name. They are evaluated after all modifiers have been evaluated.

In this section, you learn about two world space modifiers that use other geometry to define how the deformations are applied to objects:

- **PathDeform World Space Modifier**   Uses a spline to deform objects in a scene. You could use it to deform text around a globe, similar to the logo for a popular movie studio.

- **PatchDeform World Space Modifier**   Uses a native patch surface to define the deformations. Drips of ice cream running down a cone modeled from a Quad Patch primitive is an example of using this world space modifier.

You will learn to create animations with the two world space modifiers to make the fish swim and the crab crawl without endless keyframe animation techniques.

Teaching a Fish to Swim: PathDeform to the Rescue

You learned in Chapter 9 to use an animation controller called Path Constraint to make the catapult race around a spline that defined the track's center line. Remember, it's actually the pivot point of any object that is animated along the path. In that chapter, a Dummy object's pivot point merely followed the path and pulled the catapult around with it.

A swimming fish is something else indeed. The fish does not remain rigid as it moves through the water, but wiggles back and forth to propel itself. You could mimic this action by animating the fish with a Path Constraint and then setting keys at appropriate frames to get the bending for the wiggle. Or you can use the PathDeform World Space Modifier to simulate both effects at once and make a fairly convincing swimming fish.

With this method, a 2D spline is used to define an object's deformations at any point on the spline. You have the option of animating a percentage of the object along the spline over time to make the object move along the spline. The fish and the spline have already been created in your underwater scene, and you will apply and animate Percent parameters to make the fish appear to be swimming.

Exercise 12.2: Using an Animated PathDeform World Space Modifier

1. Open HorseshoeCrab02.max from Exercise 12.1 or from the CD-ROM, and save the file as `HorseshoeCrab03.max`. In the Camera01 viewport, you can see the fish to the right of the viewport and a curved line above and to the left that will be the path the swimming fish takes.

On the CD

exercises\CH12\
HorseshoeCrab02.max

2. On the main toolbar, click the Select button and pick the fish in the Camera01 viewport. In the Modify panel, Modifier List, pick *PathDeform in the World Space Modifiers listing. In the Stack display, you will see *PathDeform Binding at the top of the stack. You do not have to use Bind to Space Warp for this modifier; it is applied directly to the object.

3. In the Modify panel, Parameters rollout, click the Pick Path button and pick the Ngon01 spline just above Fish01 in the Camera01 viewport. The fish will disappear from the viewport, but the pivot point will remain in place.

4. In the Parameters rollout, click the Move to Path button and the fish will jump to the path. In the lower-right corner of the display, click the Zoom Extents Selected button (a white box with a red grid—it might be a flyout), and then zoom each viewport out to see the path and fish. The orientation of the fish is not what you might expect (see Figure 12.6).

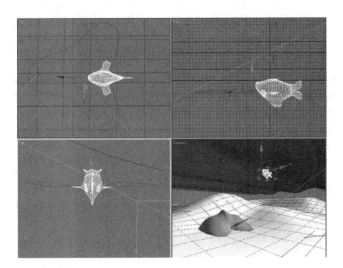

Figure 12.6 *Using the Move to Path option in PathDeform causes the fish to face inward and be upside down on the path.*

5. In the Parameters rollout, select the Path Deform Axis X radio button and the Flip check box. This causes the fish to face "down" the spline, but it is still lying on its side.

6. In the Parameters rollout, enter -90 in the Rotation field, and press Enter. The fish will right itself and be correctly oriented to swim down the spline.

7. Make sure the Time slider is at frame 0. In the Status Bar, click the Auto Key button to toggle it on. Drag the Time slider to frame 100. Enter 100 in the Parameters rollout, Percent field, and press Enter to animate the fish over 100% of the path. Toggle Auto Key off.

8. Scrub the Time slider (keyboard shortcut: /) to play the animation. Right-click in each viewport, and watch how the fish deforms based on the path's curvature as it progresses along the path (see Figure 12.7). Press **Esc** to stop the animation.

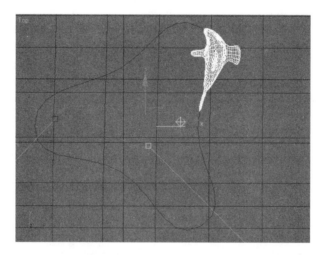

Figure 12.7   *A fish animated with PathDeform applied appears to swim along 100% of the path.*

> **caution**
>
> As the object deforms based on the path's curvature, the geometry could become self-intersecting on the inside of tight curves. For example, if the corner is too tight for the width of the fish, the inside fin could self-intersect. Making the corner less sharp would fix the problem.

9. Close all windows and dialog boxes and save the file. It should already be called HorseshoeCrab03.max.

PathDeform actually deforms the object's geometry in world space according to the spline you pick. You can use this method to form strings of text into odd shapes or to create twisting ribbons, for example. Parameters such as Twist, Stretch, and Rotation can be animated for striking effects without much effort.

> **tip**
>
> The path also could be animated to affect the deformation of the object over time. For example, you could go to the Vertex sub-object level and animate a vertex of the path moving up and down over time to get a more complex action. The whole path could be animated as moving to simulate tide drift as the fish swims.

The spline you pick can be open or closed, and it can be used for multiple purposes. For example, you could loft a roadway along the spline, and use the spline to animate a layer of asphalt being laid on the road surface or to form the yellow passing lines for the road.

The Gliding Crab: PatchDeform World Space Modifier

The crab in the underwater scene has already been animated with the Set Key process you learned in Chapter 5. However, the crab was created and animated on the World Grid in the Top viewport. Therefore, when the crab comes to a hill in the sandy seabed, it ignores the surface and travels through it, only to come out the other side when the seabed is flat again. This is all well and good, perhaps, but you want your crab to stay on top of the sand. You could create new animation keys in Set Key mode to position the crab in the World Z axis. This method would make the crab seem to stay on the sand's surface, but it would be a painstaking task, and if the seabed's profile changed, you would have to edit each Position and Rotation key.

Instead, you will take advantage of the Sand object being created from a Quad Patch primitive object. You learned about patches in Chapter 10, "Introduction to Freeform Modeling," when you built a spline cage and applied CrossSection and Surface modifiers to create a Patch surface for the transporter platform. That object was not a native patch, however, which is an important distinction. A *native patch* is a Quad Patch primitive that has no topology changes—that is, no changes in the number of sub-object vertices, edges, or patches. The native patch can be converted to an Editable Patch or have an EditPatch modifier applied to make changes to the patch's shape. All other patches will be rejected by PatchDeform modifier.

In this scene, both the crab body and the seabed are native patch objects. You will use the PatchDeform World Space Modifier to cause the crab to deform itself over the surface of the Sand object. The original animation will be retained, and the crab will appear to float over the surface of the sand. Changes you make to the Sand object will be reflected in the PatchDeform modifier.

Exercise 12.3: Applying a PatchDeform World Space Modifier

1. Open the HorseshoeCrab03.max file from Exercise 12.2 or from the CD-ROM. Save it as HorseshoeCrab04.max. Right-click in the Camera01 viewport to activate it, and play the animation or scrub the Time slider (keyboard shortcut: /). Notice how the crab moves through the Sand object.

On the CD

exercises\CH12\
HorseshoeCrab03.max

2. Click the Select button, and in the Camera01 viewport, pick the Crab01 object to select it. In the Modify panel, Modifier List, select *PatchDeform in the World Space Modifiers list.

3. In the Modify panel, Parameters rollout, click the Pick Patch button and pick the Sand object in the Camera01 viewport. The crab will deform slightly as it hugs the surface. Play the animation, and watch the crab glide over the surface instead of plunging through the sand. Press **Esc** to stop the animation.

4. In the Camera01 viewport, click the Sand object or use Select By Name to select it in the list. In the Modify panel, Stack display, expand the Editable Patch object and select Vertex sub-object. In the Camera01 viewport, pick the vertex to the right of the crab, below the fish on the Sand object and move it up in the Z axis a little (see Figure 12.8). Exit the Vertex sub-object level.

caution

Do not click the Move to Patch button, or the crab will move to the center of the patch and the animation will be offset to that position.

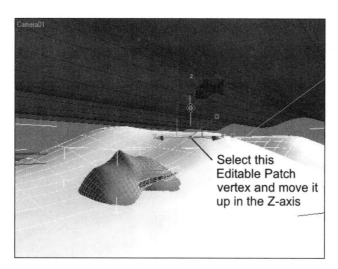

Select this Editable Patch vertex and move it up in the Z-axis

FIGURE 12.8   *Select the vertex to the right of the crab and move it up in the World Z axis to change the slope of the Sand object.*

5. Play the animation, and you will see that the path of the crab has adapted itself to the change in the Sand surface. Stop the animation.

6. In the Modify panel, Stack display, click Editable Patch at the top of the stack to exit sub-object mode.

7. Close any open windows or dialog boxes and save the file; it should already be called HorseshoeCrab04.max.

You now have a crab that crawls on the sandy seabed and will continue to do so as long as the object remains a native patch object. The fact that the crab body also is a native patch is not important in this exercise; it is the sand that must be a native patch. Any 2D or 3D object will deform to the surface as long as it has enough vertices to fit the surface.

You could use an extension of this method to animate a boat moving over the waves on the water. If you create the water as a Quad Patch and bind a Wave space warp to make the waves, you can then create a spline that represents the path of a moving boat. Just make sure it has enough vertices to deform smoothly to the waves. Bind the spline to the Wave space warp to deform it, and then use the spline for the path of a Path Constraint applied to the boat. The boat appears to stay on the surface as you animate the waves, but it's actually the boat's path that is deforming to the waves.

Space Warps and World Space Modifiers as Modeling Tools

So far you have used space warps and world space modifiers as animation tools only, but you also can use them as modeling tools to generate static objects that you can further edit. Because space warps and world space modifiers are evaluated after all object space modifiers, you cannot move bound objects in the scene without changing their form, as they are defined by deformations in world space. However, the Snapshot tool makes a clone of the deformed objects. One of Snapshot's options is Mesh, which generates a new object. The clone has the world space deformations "baked" into the object, making it an Editable Mesh that is no longer affected by the space warp or world space modifier. You will use Snapshot to create a bird wing from a lofted object, and then again to create an icicle from a particle system.

The Snapshot Tool: Using Space Warps for Modeling

In this exercise, you deform a lofted bird wing into a form that fits a Quad Patch molded into a flowing air pattern. You can then edit the native patch or reposition the wing to make changes to the wing shape. At some point, however, you want to attach the wing to a bird, but you cannot move it without affecting its shape to fit the patch. You will use Snapshot to make an Editable Mesh clone in the form you need.

Exercise 12.4: Snapshot: Winging It

1. Open the Birdwing01.max file from the CD-ROM, and save it as `Birdwing02.max`. It contains a lofted wing and an Editable Patch with vertices moved to represent the complex curves of air under a bird wing in flight (see Figure 12.9).

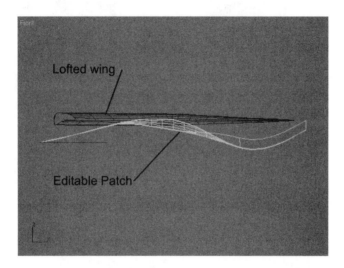

FIGURE 12.9   *A lofted wing above an Editable Patch deformed to represent flowing air.*

2. Click the Select button on the main toolbar. In the Perspective viewport, select the Wing object. In the Modify panel, Modifier List, pick *PatchDeform in the World Space Modifiers list.

3. In the Modify panel, Parameters rollout, click the Pick Patch button and select the AirFlow object in the Perspective viewport. The wing will deform to the shape of the AirFlow patch. Click the Move to Patch button in the Parameters rollout to move the wing onto the Patch surface.

4. On the main toolbar, click the Select and Move button and move the wing over the Patch surface. Right-click while continuing to hold the left mouse button to cancel the move, or click the Undo button on the main toolbar if you actually moved the wing. The wing changes as you move it through the world space defined by the Patch.

5. On the main menu, choose Tools, Snapshot from the menu. In the Snapshot dialog box, make sure the default Single radio button is enabled, select the Mesh radio button in the Clone Method section (see Figure 12.10), and click OK.

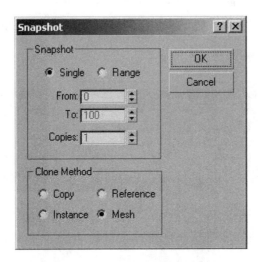

FIGURE 12.10   *Choosing the Single and Mesh options in the Snapshot dialog box creates one new mesh object in the scene.*

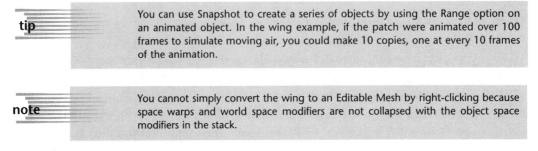

tip   You can use Snapshot to create a series of objects by using the Range option on an animated object. In the wing example, if the patch were animated over 100 frames to simulate moving air, you could make 10 copies, one at every 10 frames of the animation.

note   You cannot simply convert the wing to an Editable Mesh by right-clicking because space warps and world space modifiers are not collapsed with the object space modifiers in the stack.

6. On the main toolbar, click the Select by Name button and double-click Wing01 in the list. Move the Wing01 clone off to one side, and you will see that it remains static and is not deformed by the Patch.

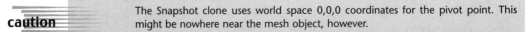

caution   The Snapshot clone uses world space 0,0,0 coordinates for the pivot point. This might be nowhere near the mesh object, however.

In the Hierarchy panel, use the Affect Pivot Only and Center to Object options to place the pivot point in the geometric center of the wing's bounding box, or position it by hand where you require the pivot point for animation.

7. Save the file. It should already be called Birdwing02.max.

The Snapshot tool is a powerful modeling option because it greatly extends the functionality of space warps and world space modifiers.

The Snapshot Tool: Using Particle Systems for Modeling

Another valuable use of the Snapshot tool is to convert particle systems into Editable Mesh objects that can be edited after creation. *Particle systems* are animated particles emitted from a source to simulate spraying, flowing, or exploding masses, to name a few examples. They are usually in motion, so they do not create a single object that can be edited. You can use the Snapshot tool, however, to capture the motion at a point in time and bake it into an Editable Mesh object.

Exercise 12.5: Snapshot: Making the Ice

1. Open the Icicle01.max file on the CD-ROM, and save it to your hard drive as `Icicle02.max`. It contains a SuperSpray particle system with an Icicle material assigned to it.

On the CD

exercises\CH12\
Icicle01.max

2. Click the Select button on the main toolbar and pick the SuperSpray emitter in the Perspective viewport. Scrub the Time slider, and you'll see the particles emitted in a straight line upward in the viewport. Set the Time slider on frame 30, the point of maximum particles for this emitter.

3. In the Modify panel, Basic Parameters rollout, Particle Formation section, enter `10` in the Off Axis Spread field and `90` in the Off Plane Spread field to make a cone-shaped spray. Leave the Off Axis and Off Plane fields set to 0. In the Viewport Display section, select the Mesh radio button and enter `100` in the Percentage of Particles field.

4. In the Particle Generation rollout, Particle Size section, enter `2'0"` in the Size field. There are now many large triangles in the scene.

5. In the Particle Type rollout, Particle Types section, select the MetaParticles radio button. MetaParticles are blobs that have an affinity to their nearest neighboring blobs; they are "attracted" to each other to form a solid objects (see Figure 12.11).

tip

The particles are now very small triangle mesh objects coming from the emitter instead of the ticks (small cross-hairs for each particle) that were displayed much faster in the viewports.

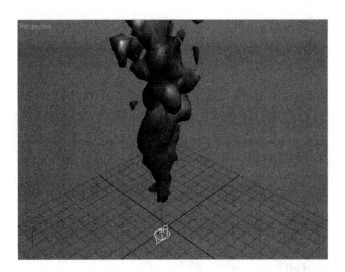

FIGURE 12.11   *MetaParticles in a SuperSpray system grow into a solid mass of blobs.*

6. Scrub the Time slider and you will see the blobs change form as they become closer or farther from their neighbors. Set the Time slider to frame 30. This is a dynamic object that could not be used as a static icicle.

7. Choose Tools, Snapshot from the menu. Make sure the Single and Mesh radio buttons are selected, and click OK in the Snapshot dialog box.

note

Depending on your computer, it might take a few seconds for Snapshot to do its job. Be patient.

8. Scrub the Time slider, and you will see you have one active SuperSpray and an Editable Mesh captured at frame 30. Delete SuperSpray01 by pressing the Delete key. It should already be the selected object.

9. Right-click in the Perspective viewport, and click the Quick Render button at the far right of the main toolbar (keyboard shortcut: **Shift+Q**). The Raytrace material, which was previously assigned to the SuperSpray emitter and remains part of the Snapshot object, makes a convincing frozen icicle (see Figure 12.12).

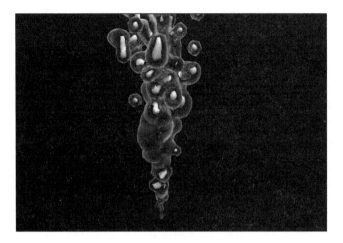

FIGURE 12.12 *Icicles are easy to create with Snapshot and SuperSpray MetaParticles.*

10. Close all windows and dialog boxes and save the file. It should already be called Icicle02.max.

Again, you have combined two tools—particle systems and Snapshot—to quickly create an object that might otherwise take hours. Experiment with 3ds max 5 constantly to try unlikely work methods that might become a standard production tool for you.

Summary

You have learned about animating and modeling in 3ds max 5, using space warps and world space modifiers that deform the space an object exists in, thus deforming the object in the same manner. You learned about the following animation features:

- **Space warps**   Objects bound to space warps deform to the space. As you change the space warp or transform the object, the deformations are reflected in the object.

- **World space modifiers**   Function similarly to space warps by deforming space. The modifiers are applied directly to the objects, however, and do not need to be bound to them.

- **Wave space warp**   Using an animated Wave space warp, you deformed a segmented plane into animated rolling waves in the water surface above the scene.

- **PathDeform World Space Modifier**   You learned to make a fish appear to swim as it deformed based on the shape of a 2D spline. You animated the object's Percent parameter along the spline for forward motion.

- **PatchDeform World Space Modifier**   A native patch object edited to look like a hilly seabed was used to change a moving crab's deformation so that it hugged the surface of the seabed. When you edited the shape of the seabed, the crab automatically adapted its motion to the changes.

- **Snapshot tool**   The Snapshot tool enabled you to capture a mesh deformed by a world space modifier and created by a particle system. This tool freezes the object in time and converts it to an Editable Mesh for more editing flexibility.

CHAPTER 13

Effects: Reacting to Reactor

In This Chapter

Special effects can grab viewers' attention and rivet them to the story you are telling better than almost any aspect of computer animation—if it is done well. Gratuitous special effects, however, can get in the way of a good story and distract from the focal point of your work. You will learn to set up short collision effects scenes that can enhance a storyline and still be cost effective in production time.

This chapter introduces you to a new feature: Reactor. Reactor is a rigid body and soft body dynamics system that calculates the collision of moving bodies in your animated scenes. You will work through two different scenes involving collisions to show you typical uses for the Dynamics system. In one scene, you try to catch a barrel fired from a catapult in a net strung across the street, as an example of rigid bodies interacting with cloth realistically. In another scene, you animate a transporter being thrown from the local palm reader's shop and reacting to the hanging beads in the doorway to learn about the interaction of rope objects, rigid bodies, and Reactor attachment modifiers.

Using the Dynamics system instead of hand-animating similar effects can save production time. Among the concepts and techniques you will learn are

- **Rigid bodies** Classifying and grouping rigid bodies that are inflexible or unyielding often set the basis for collision detection.
- **Cloth collections** These flexible, draping, open-edged objects can interact with other elements in the scene.

- **Rope collections**   This group of objects collides like strands of rope and can be attached to other objects.

- **Mass properties**   Assigning mass properties to objects gives them weight and friction so that they interact believably with other objects in collisions.

- **Keyframes and Dynamics animation**   This method enables you to animate objects to set their velocity and then pass the control to collision detection.

- **Background image**   Acts as a backdrop in your scene with very little overhead in computer resources.

- **Matte/Shadow material**   This material makes an object invisible in the rendered image, but allows a background image to show through and receives shadows from other objects. With this material, you can use a simple box object, for example, to represent a street in a collision scene.

Key Terms

background image   An image displayed as a backdrop in the rendered image or in the display viewports. This is a basic form of compositing a 3D scene against a 2D background to save rendering time.

Cloth   Animated open-edged surfaces with no thickness that simulate draping cloth in collisions with other objects in Reactor.

Reactor   A plug-in included with 3ds max 5 that calculates collisions between objects in an animated scene.

Reactor collection   A grouping of objects to be included in a Reactor collision detection simulation. Rigid Bodies, Rope, and Cloth are some of the collection types.

Rigid Bodies   A class of Reactor objects that have inflexible surfaces and can be unyielding to other objects—for example, a road or floor surface.

Rope   A fixed-end or free ropelike structure used in Reactor collisions.

Hotkeys and Keyboard Shortcuts

m   Open the Material Editor

Shift+Q   Quick render

F10   Render scene

Reactor: Planning the Attack

As with so many aspects of computer animation, preplanning the attack on a challenge can help you get the job done in a cost-effective manner. With a Reactor scene, visualizing ahead of time what you would like to see as a result and getting it down in a storyboard is paramount; then be prepared to spend time tweaking the Dynamics simulation parameters to get as close as you can to your expectations.

The process is based on physics, and you have about as much true control with Reactor as you do rolling a boulder down a hillside in real life. You can hope for a certain outcome, but must be prepared for some unexpected events along the way. Even small changes in the weight of an object, the friction of a surface, or the strength of the gravitational pull can have profound effects on the Dynamics simulation's end result.

Using small scenes with efficient mesh objects is an essential start. The more faces and vertices your scene has, the more possible collisions you must account for, and the longer the process will take. Only the objects directly involved in the collisions should be included in the Reactor collections, and when you have complex mesh objects, you should use simple proxy objects that define the boundaries for collision detection with no extraneous detail.

To increase your efficiency and free more computer resources, background images are often a good means of eliminating geometry from your scene while retaining the look of a complete scene. Background images are an entry-level step into another sophisticated special-effects science called digital compositing. Background images enable you to composite your current 3D scene atop a previously rendered image or photographic plate. Many complex productions consist of multiple layers combined with masks and image-processing tools.

Reactor: Catching Barrels in a Net

To add a little more life to your street scene from Chapter 2, "Modeling: A Medieval Street Scene," you will use the new Reactor feature to set up a collision detection simulation that catches the barrel fired from the catapult in a net and drops it to the street.

Reactor collision detection can require a lot of computer resources, so optimizing the process where you can is imperative. The buildings along the street are not involved directly with the collisions, so you will learn to use a rendered image of the street scene as a background image, with only the necessary mesh objects—the net, the catapult, and the barrel—in the foreground. The street, however, is part of the collision because the barrel drops from the net and bounces on the street cobblestones. You will take advantage of a special material called Matte/Shadow that always lets the background show through objects that have this material applied to give the illusion that the objects are in the street scene. This material eliminates the need for the street mesh object yet gives the appearance of a street surface for the collisions.

The net will be a Plane primitive that Reactor treats like a cloth object; to make it look like a net, you'll apply a material with Wire attributes enabled. The wire material renders only the visible edges of the segmented plane with a thickness you define. The net will seem to be suspended from the buildings by rigid rods; the rods are not actually part of the Reactor simulation, but the net must be anchored to the ends of the rods. To do this, you'll assign the Cloth modifier to only selected vertices. The unselected vertices are not part of the simulation, so they will remain fixed in space.

Last, the barrel must have a certain velocity and mass when it hits the net. If it is moving too fast or if it is too heavy, it will pass through the net. If it's moving too slow or if it is too light, gravity will pull it to the road before it hits the net. To achieve the correct velocity and mass, you will set the barrel's initial velocity by animating it with Set Key mode for a few frames, and then set the Reactor simulation to calculate from that point onward.

Exercise 13.1: Setting the Scene

1. From the CD-ROM, open the Reactor_net01.max file. Choose File, Save As from the menu, and save the file to a subdirectory on your hard drive with the name Reactor_net02.max. The scene contains a catapult, a barrel, a net with four supporting rods, and a box called Street. Figure 13.1 shows the rendered Camera01 viewport.

On the CD

exercises\CH13\
Reactor_net01.max

2. You will learn to apply a background image to the rendered image as an environment map, and then use the map as a viewport background. Choose Rendering, Environment from the main menu. In the Environment dialog box, Common Parameters rollout, click the None button for the Environment map. In the Material/Map Browser, double-click Bitmap, and in the Select Bitmap Image File dialog box, double-click Reactor_background.png in exercises\CH13\ on the CD-ROM. Close the Environment dialog box.

3. Right-click in the Camera01 viewport, and click the Quick Render button (keyboard shortcut: **Shift+Q**) to see the street appear behind the mesh objects in your scene. Close the Virtual Frame Buffer. Choose Views, Viewport Background from the menu. In the Viewport Background dialog box, select the Use Environment Background check box and the Display Background check box (see Figure 13.2), and click OK. The street image as well as the rendered scene now show in the Camera01 viewport.

On the CD

exercises\CH13\
Reactor_background.png

tip

You might have noticed the cyan and orange rectangles in the Camera01 viewport. They indicate safe frames, areas that prevent clipping of your image when rendering for video output. To toggle them on, right-click the viewport's label and select Show Safe Frame in the menu. Safe frames are linked to the render output resolution, which is 640×480 pixels by default in max.

In this exercise, however, the safe frames option has the effect of matching the viewport's aspect ratio to the render output and to the size of the background image, which is also 640×480 resolution. This keeps both the viewport and final rendering in registration (aligned).

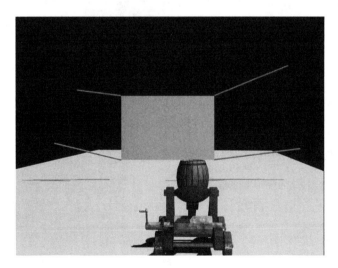

FIGURE 13.1 *The scene with a catapult, a barrel, a net, support rod, and a box rendered against a black background.*

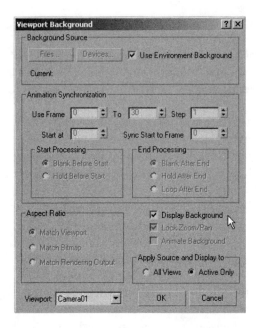

FIGURE 13.2 *Remember to select Display Background when you have selected the Use Environment Background option; otherwise, the image will be loaded but not displayed.*

4. The large Street box object hides the lower portion of the background image. You will assign a special material, called Matte/Shadow, to the box that allow the background to show through, making the box invisible yet still able to receive shadows from the mesh objects in the scene. On the main toolbar, click the Material Editor button (hotkey: **m**), and click the sample window to the far right in the second row (see Figure 13.3). Drag and drop the material onto the Street box object in the Camera01 viewport. The Matte/Shadow material already has the Receive Shadows option enabled. Quick Render the Camera01 viewport (see Figure 13.4).

On the CD

exercises\CH13\
Reactor_net.mat

note

The Reactor_net.mat material library is in the \exercises\ CH13 folder on the CD-ROM. You can open it in the Material Editor, if you do not see the materials listed as you work through this exercise.

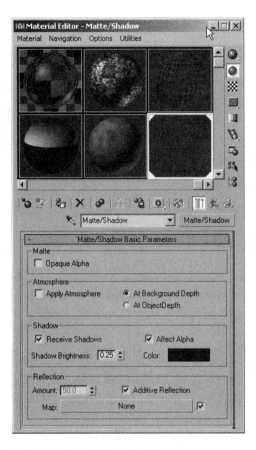

FIGURE 13.3   *Enabling the Receive Shadows option in a Matte/Shadow material allows the invisible object to receive shadows cast by other objects.*

FIGURE 13.4   *The Receive Shadows option creates the illusion that the net and catapult are casting shadows onto the background image in the rendered scene. The building shadows are part of the background image.*

5. The net in the rendered image looks like a solid object, not a net, so you'll assign a wire material that renders only the visible edges of the segmented plane. In the Material Editor, click the Net sample window (on the far right in the top row). It is a bright red color. Notice that Wire and 2-Sided are selected in the Shader Basic Parameters rollout, and the Extended Parameters rollout shows a wire size of 2 units in. Drag and drop this material onto the Net object and render the Camera01 viewport. Now you can see through the net.

> **tip**
>
> The 2-Sided option allows the Net material to be seen from both sides of the object, not just the side with the face normals. You should do this for most transparent materials.

6. Close all windows and dialog boxes. Save the file. It should already be called Reactor_net02.max. The scene is now ready for the Reactor dynamics setup.

You have a busy-looking scene with only a small amount of actual geometry. This makes rendering the scene more efficient and frees computer resources for the Reactor simulation in the following exercises.

Preparing Objects for Collision Detection

Before you are able to calculate Reactor collisions, you must assign objects to collections—Rigid Bodies or Cloth, for example—based on their physical properties in the simulation. Objects can be assigned directly to Rigid Bodies collections, but cloth objects must first have a Reactor Cloth modifier assigned before they are available to the collection.

Exercise 13.2: Using Reactor Collections and Modifiers

1. Open Reactor_net02.max from Exercise 13.1 or from the CD-ROM, and save it as `Reactor_net03.max`. Right-click in the Top viewport to activate it. This is where you will define the Reactor collections.

On the CD

exercises\CH13\
Reactor_net02.max

2. In the Create panel, Helpers category, click the drop-down arrow next to Standard, and choose Reactor in the list. This is where you find the collections that define objects to be included in the Reactor simulation. In the Object Type rollout, click the RBCollection button, and click in the lower-right corner of the Top viewport to create a Rigid Bodies collection (RBCollection) icon that looks like a box, torus, and sphere.

3. In the RB Collection Properties rollout, click the Add button. Hold down the Ctrl key and select Barrel01 and Street in the Select Rigid Bodies dialog box. Click Select in the dialog box, and the names will be added to the Rigid Bodies window in the rollout (see Figure 13.5).

4. In the Object Type rollout, click the CLCollection button to create a Cloth collection. Click near the RBCollection icon in the Top viewport to create a Cloth-Col icon (looks like a blouse or dress). Right-click in a viewport to exit CLCollection mode. If you click the Add button in the CL Collection Properties rollout, nothing appears in the list because objects in a Cloth collection must have a special modifier assigned first.

5. On the main toolbar, click the Select button and pick the Net object in the Camera01 viewport. In the Modify panel, Modifier List, select the Reactor Cloth modifier.

FIGURE 13.5 *Objects must be added to the proper collection properties list to be included in a collision detection simulation.*

6. In the Top viewport, click the Cloth-Col icon. In the Modify panel, CL Collection Properties rollout, click the Add button, and double-click Net in the Select Cloths dialog box to add it to the window in the CL Collection Properties rollout.

7. Close any windows or dialog boxes and save the file. It should already be called Reactor_net03.max.

You have added two objects to a Rigid Bodies collection and one object to a Cloth collection to make them available to a Reactor simulation. Any mesh object can be assigned to the Rigid Bodies collections, but objects assigned to a Cloth collection must have a Reactor Cloth modifier applied first.

Assigning Object Properties

Now that the objects to be included in the Reactor simulation have been assigned to collections that define their general behavior, you need to assign more specific properties to get them to interact believably. The barrel needs some weight so that it will react with gravity, for example. The net also should react to gravity, but you don't want it dropping to the street; it should appear to be held up by the rods. You do not want the street to drop from the pull of gravity or move when the barrel hits it. To define these behavioral traits, in this next exercise you assign properties to the collection objects.

Exercise 13.3: Trying to Make a Barrel Behave

1. Open the Reactor_net03.max file, and save it as `Reactor_net04.max`. Click the Select button, and in the Camera01 viewport, pick the Street object in the scene.

On the CD

exercises\CH13\
Reactor_net03.max

2. In the Utilities panel, Utilities rollout, click the Reactor button. Expand the Properties rollout, and in the Other Properties section, select the Unyielding check box. This option tells the box to be included in the simulation but not be affected by any forces it might encounter. In the Simulation Geometry section, select the Use Bounding Box radio button. This option uses the outer dimensions of the box shape to determine the extents of the simulation surface.

3. Select the Net object in the Front viewport. It is a Plane primitive with a Reactor Cloth modifier. If you were to include it in a Reactor simulation, gravity would pull the net to the street, and the force of a barrel hitting it would move it down the street. You want it to seem as though the rods are attaching the Net object to the buildings. In the Modify panel, Stack display, expand Editable Mesh and choose Vertex. Click the Hold/Yes button in the Warning dialog box.

tip

The Hold/Yes option stores the scene in a buffer file on disk. If dropping to sub-object level in the stack causes problems, you can choose Edit, Fetch from the main menu to retrieve the scene in its current state.

4. In the Front viewport, select all the vertices of the Net object, except the four corner vertices (see Figure 13.6). Remain in Vertex sub-object selection mode so that the Reactor Cloth modifier will be acting only on the selected vertices. The vertex symbol (three dots) must remain visible to the right of Reactor Cloth in the Stack display. In the Stack display, return to Reactor Cloth. Notice in the Properties rollout, Vertex Selection section, that the radio button for Non-Selected Are Fixed is selected. This means the Reactor Cloth modifier will act only on the selected vertices, so the net will appear to hang from the rods.

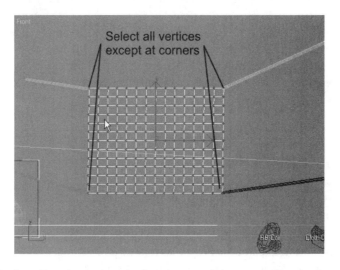

FIGURE 13.6   *Selecting all vertices except the four corners of the net enables the Reactor Cloth modifier to act on most of the object, while the four corners are stationary.*

5. To make the Net object slightly heavy, enter 5 in the Mass field in the Properties rollout. In the Force Model section, enter 0.5 in the Stiffness field to give it more body.

6. In the Camera01 viewport, select the Barrel01 object. In the Utilities panel, Properties rollout, Physical Properties section, enter 3.0 in the Mass field to make the barrel weigh less than the net (see Figure 13.7). Enter 1.0 in the Friction field to make the barrel cling slightly to the net when it strikes. In the Simulation Geometry section, leave Use Mesh Convex Hull selected. This option tells Reactor to use the barrel's actual shape in collision detection.

tip

You can also define mass and friction properties for materials in the Material Editor and then use the Get From Material and Set To Material buttons in the Properties rollout to make changes.

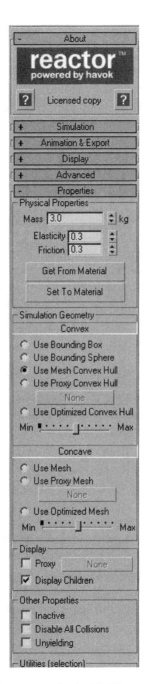

FIGURE 13.7 *Properties for Cloth objects are set in the Modify panel, but Rigid Bodies properties are set in the Utilities panel, Reactor utility.*

7. Save the file. It should already be called Reactor_net04.max.

You have assigned properties to the objects in the Reactor collections to give them behavioral parameters based on physical traits such as mass, friction, and stiffness. You also have defined the bounding box shape for the collision detection to use. The simpler the bounding box shape, the faster the calculations. However, a sphere with a box bounding shape, for example, might cause bouncing on the corner of the bounding box for an unrealistic effect in the collision detection.

For Every Action, There Is a Reaction

Without any animation in the scene, a collision detection simulation is simple. In this next exercise, you set things in motion so that Reactor has colliding objects to simulate the action. You use Set Key mode to animate the barrel moving toward the net over a period of five frames. Hand-animating ensures that the barrel's initial velocity is set in the right direction. You then tell Reactor to pick up that velocity at frame 4 and use it for the duration of the collision detection simulation. The result should be a convincing animation.

Exercise 13.4: Setting Things in Motion

1. Open the Reactor_net04.max file, and save it as Reactor_net05.max. Right-click in the Top viewport to activate it, and zoom in to fill the viewport with the catapult and the net.

On the CD

exercises\CH13\
Reactor_net04.max

2. Select Barrel01 in the Top viewport. In the Status Bar, click the Set Key button to toggle Set Key animation mode on. The Time slider and viewport border turn pink. Click the Key Filters button, and make sure only the Position check box is selected and the other check boxes are cleared. Close the Set Key Filters dialog box. With the Time slider at frame 0, click the key icon button to set an initial position key for Barrel01.

3. Drag the Time slider to frame 5. Click the Select and Move button, and in the Top viewport, move Barrel01 about one quarter of the distance from the catapult to the net (see Figure 13.8). In the Camera01 viewport, move the barrel up to align its top with the top of the catapult dish. Click the key icon button to set a position key. Toggle Set Key mode off.

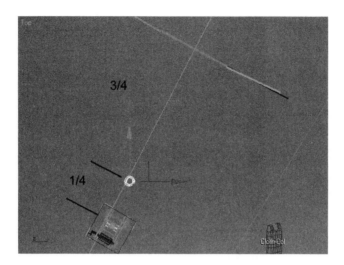

FIGURE 13.8   *Animating the barrel toward the net sets an initial velocity for the Reactor simulation.*

4. In the Reactor Utility panel, Animation & Export rollout, enter 4 in the Start Frame field to pass the barrel's velocity and trajectory at frame 4 to the Reactor simulator. From frame 4 onward, Reactor will use that initial velocity to calculate the rest of the simulation. Select the Update Viewports check box so that you can see the calculation's progress in the viewports. Click the Perform Simulation button. The first thing you will notice is the net sagging from the effects of gravity. As the barrel hits the net (see Figure 13.9), the net collapses and then rebounds, tossing the barrel back into the street. The action of the barrel and net depends on the velocity and angle that you set at frame 5. It would be different each time you tried the exercise because even slight changes in the position of the barrel at frame 5 will affect the results.

> **caution**
>
> It is important to follow all the steps in this exercise for the process to work. If it fails, start from step 1 by loading the scene and trying again. After you have it functioning and are comfortable with the process, you can experiment with variations.

5. Save the file. It should already be called Reactor_net05.max.

   Hand-animating objects to make it seem as though they are colliding with other objects and deforming under the weight of impact and gravity would be a daunting task. Reactor collision detection simulations can save you a long trial-and-error process after you have mastered the fundamentals of body dynamics. That is not to say the process doesn't have its element of trial and error when trying to set up properties for objects; it is just a different approach.

FIGURE 13.9 *The net deforms from the effects of gravitational pull and from the barrel hitting it.*

When adjusting Reactor parameters and properties, avoid the temptation to change several settings at once when fine-tuning your collisions. Set a property and perform the simulation to see the results, and then go on to the next property until you learn to predict what effect a change will probably have.

Working with Rope Collections

Another interesting option with Reactor that you will investigate is simulating the action of a rope. In this next exercise, you produce a ropelike effect for a beaded curtain in the doorway of a palm reader's shop. She has apparently seen the future in your personal transporter and has thrown it out the door, disturbing the beads and tipping over the transporter.

The scene is simple, but take the time to look at some of the materials to get ideas you can use. In the doorway is a single rope hanging from a rod across the opening to near the floor. The rope was created from a line with 17 vertices to make it flexible. It has the Renderable and Display Render Mesh options enabled in the Modify panel and a material has been assigned.

You will use a process similar to the one you used in Exercise 13.4 for the net to turn the rope into a Reactor Rope. In this next exercise, you set the floor and door trim to use the Unyielding option, and hand-animate the transporter to set an initial velocity. You then attach the rope to the rod in the doorway with a Reactor modifier to keep it from slumping to the floor under the pull of gravity. You copy the rope several times and add all the copies to a Reactor Rope collection.

Exercise 13.5: Creating Reactor Collections

1. Open the Reactor_rope01.max file, and save it as `Reactor_rope02.max` to a directory on your hard drive. Right-click in the Top viewport to activate it.

2. In the Create panel, Helpers category, click the drop-down arrow next to Standard, and choose Reactor in the list. This is where you find the collections that define objects to be included in the Reactor simulation. In the Object Type rollout, click the RBCollection button, and click in the lower-right corner of the Top viewport to create a Rigid Bodies collection icon.

3. In the Modify panel, RB Collection Properties rollout, click the Add button. Highlight transporter, Cylinder01 (the rod over the door), DoorFrame01, and Floor in the Select Rigid Bodies list and click the Select button. The four objects are then displayed in the Rigid Bodies window in the RB Collection rollout.

4. Select the DoorFrame01 object, and in the Utilities panel, Reactor utility, Properties rollout, select the Use Mesh radio button in the Concave section. Using the Bounding Box option for this object would keep the transporter from going through the door opening. Select the Unyielding check box in the Other Properties section.

5. Select Floor and then Cylinder01, and set each to Use Bounding Box and Unyielding.

6. Select the transporter, and in the Utilities panel, set the Mass field to `5.0` and the Friction field to `0.05`.

7. In the Helpers panel, Object Type rollout, click the RPCollection button and click in the Top viewport to place a Rope-Col icon (looks like a coil of rope). Click the Select button on the main toolbar, and in the Front viewport, select the Rope01 object on the left side of the doorway.

caution

In step 7 you are adding an RPCollection (for rope), not an RBCollection (for rigid body).

8. In the Modify panel, Modifier List, select the Reactor Rope modifier. In the Properties rollout, enter `0.5` in the Mass field.

9. Next, you need to select the rope's top vertex and attach it to the cylinder in the doorway. To select the vertex for the modifier to operate on, go to Modifier List, SplineSelect. Expand SplineSelect in the Stack display and choose Vertex. In the Front viewport, pick the top vertex on the rope where it meets the cylinder.

10. In the Modifier List, select Reactor AttachToRB, and in the Properties rollout, click the None button and pick the Cylinder01 object in the Front viewport. SplineSelect must be above Reactor Rope in the stack, or Reactor Rope would set the properties for just the vertex, not the entire rope. SplineSelect ensures that only the top vertex is attached to the cylinder.

11. In the Front viewport, make sure Rope01 is selected. Click Select and Move, hold down the Shift key, and move Rope01 a few inches to the right to about the center of the left tire on the transporter. In the Clone Options dialog box, select the Copy radio button, and enter 9 in the Number of Copies field. Click OK to create an array of ropes across the doorway.

12. In the Top viewport, select the Rope-Col icon. In the Modify panel, Properties rollout, click the Add button. In the Select Ropes dialog box, click the All button and click Select. The ropes are then listed in the Properties rollout window. Only objects with the Reactor Rope modifier can be added to the collection.

13. Save the file. It should already be called Reactor_rope02.max.

You have assigned objects to a Rigid Bodies collection and to a Rope collection. Then you set properties for the rope and used the SplineSelect modifier to attach just the top vertex to the cylinder across the top of the doorway. Finally, you created an array of ropes and added them to the Rope collection so that they will be included in the collision simulation.

Madame Maxine Throws a Fit and a Transporter

In this next exercise, you set objects in motion and then perform a Reactor simulation to take over the transporter's initial velocity and send it crashing into the bead ropes. The animation is a review of the process in Exercise 13.4; you will animate the transporter using Set Key mode in 10 frames and let the calculations take over at frame 9.

Exercise 13.6: Setting Initial Velocity and Performing a Reactor Simulation

1. Open the Reactor_rope02.max file, and save it as `Reactor_rope03.max`. Right-click in the Top viewport to activate it, and select the transporter.

On the CD

exercises\CH13\
Reactor_rope02.max

2. In the Status Bar, click the Set Key button. Click the Key Filters button and select only the Position check box in the Set Key Filters dialog box. Close the dialog box. Make sure the Time slider is at frame 0, and click the key icon button to set a key.

3. Set the Time slider to frame 10, and in the Top viewport, move the transporter almost to DoorFrame01 (see Figure 13.10). Click the key icon button to set a position key. Toggle Set Key off.

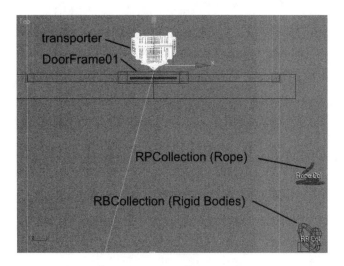

FIGURE 13.10   *Animating the transporter from its current location to the DoorFrame01 object in 10 frames will set an initial velocity for the Reactor simulation.*

4. In the Utilities panel, Reactor utility, Animation & Export rollout, enter 9 in the Start Frame field. Select the Update Viewports check box and click the Perform Simulation button.

5. Next, you'll render the completed animation to an AVI file that can be viewed from any computer. On the main toolbar, click the Render Scene button (keyboard shortcut: **F10**). In the Common Parameters rollout, Time Output section, click

> **note**
>
> Depending on your computer, the calculations could take a while because the transporter and DoorFrame01 objects are concave and the entire mesh object is used instead of a simple bounding shape.

the Active Time Segment radio button. In the Output Size section, click the 320×240 button to make the output resolution small enough to play back on almost any computer. In the Render Output section, select the Save File check box and click the Files button. In the Render Output File dialog box, choose a folder on your hard drive, name the file transporter.avi, and click OK. At the bottom center of the Render Scene dialog box, make sure Camera01 is in the Viewport field (see Figure 13.11). Click the Render button.

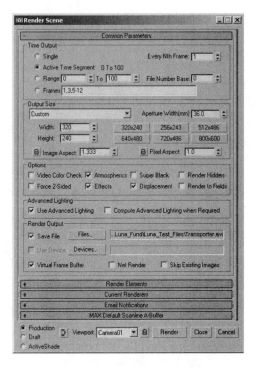

FIGURE 13.11   *Set the Render Scene dialog box to the active time segment and write to an animation file type to save the full animation to disk for others to view.*

6. Save the file. It should already be called Reactor_rope01.max. The exact behavior of your simulation could range from the transporter becoming entangled in the bead ropes and falling back into the room to shooting out and skidding across the floor. Figure 13.12 shows my final rendered frame.

Again, slight changes in the Reactor properties and the initial velocity of animated objects when the calculations begin can make large differences in the final reactions.

Go back to Exercises 13.5 and 13.6 and make changes to the transporter's mass, and then try the exercises again with different initial velocities to see what variations you can create. With a little practice, you can gain a level of comfort in how objects with certain properties might interact, but work through the process deliberately and with a little preplanning so that you have a better idea of what to adjust to fine-tune the results.

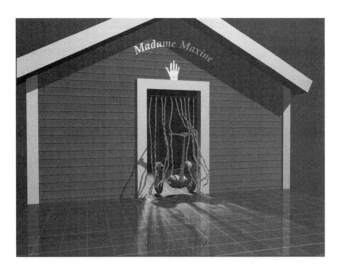

FIGURE 13.12 *The initial velocity that you set for the transporter will affect each simulation differently.*

Summary

Reactor enables you to simulate collisions between objects in a scene based on physical parameters and properties that you set for the objects. The overall shape of objects can have an effect on the calculation times, but you can optimize the process by choosing a simpler bounding shape, such as a box or sphere, to be used in the collisions instead of the complex object itself.

You learned to set up several types of object collections that define a class of behavior and define individual properties for the objects in each class. Along the way, you learned the following concepts and techniques:

- **Background image** You learned to add an image as a background in the rendering and in the viewport to reduce geometry for faster renderings.

- **Compositing** Rendering a background image behind a 3D scene is known as compositing; this skill is important for building complex scenes from layers composited over one another.

- **Matte/Shadow material** To create the illusion that a background image is a physical part of the scene, you learned to use this material to make certain objects "invisible" to the rendering and let the background image show through but still receive shadows.

- **Rigid bodies**   You learned to make these objects unyielding so that they do not move in a Reactor simulation. You can add objects directly to a Rigid Bodies collection.

- **Cloth collections**   You learned to add a Reactor Cloth modifier to the Net object so that could be added to the Cloth collection.

- **Rope collections**   You learned how to apply the Reactor Rope modifier to objects so that they could be included in the Rope collection. You learned to apply the modifier to the whole rope object, and then use the SplineSelect and Reactor AttachToRB modifiers to anchor one end of the rope to a bar called Cylinder01 in the scene.

- **Mass properties**   Setting and changing the weight of objects used in collisions can greatly influence the outcome of Reactor simulations.

- **Keyframes and Dynamics animation**   You learned to animate an object for a few frames, and then set the Reactor simulation to begin its calculation at one of the animated frames to pick up the object's initial velocity for collisions.

CHAPTER 14

Video Post: Tying It All Together

In This Chapter

Each scene you create and render in 3ds max 5 is usually just one part of a more comprehensive presentation. The presentation, based on your storyboard, is often a series of short renderings edited together to make a complete story. A typical movie that you see in the theater is literally made up of hundreds or even thousands of individual elements stitched together to produce a continuous story; if the editing is done well, the audience is not aware of the individual pieces.

With Video Post, a built-in tool in 3ds max 5, you can be your own editor and assemble pieces into a continuous story, even adding special effects to each layer. When layers are applied on top of each other in the video post phase, the last layer in the list is the one you see in the final output. You will learn to add compositing to use transparency so that lower layers show through upper layers.

In this chapter, you will edit a presentation consisting of a background, a scene, and several prerendered animations. You will apply special effects to the scene and use transitions between sequences to blend from one to the next. Some of the features you will learn about are

- **Video Post queue** A list of scene events that gets evaluated from the top down.
- **Alpha composite** A layering process that takes advantage of transparency information in a file or scene's alpha channel.
- **Composite transitions** This technique layers two scene elements with a transparent cross-fade from one to the next.

- **Lens Effects**   A class of special effects added to your scene, such as Glow, Highlight, or Flare.

- **Output event**   The final composited animation file with all layers in sequence.

Key Terms

Alpha channel   Transparency information stored in certain file types or max scenes. Up to 256 levels of transparency (ranging from fully transparent to fully opaque) information are used in compositing.

AVI   A popular file type used to save, and often compress, rendered frames for playback as an animation.

composite   To layer images or scenes with transparent elements.

transition   A blending from one scene to another using techniques such as cuts, fades, and dissolves.

Hotkeys and Keyboard Shortcuts

Shift+Q   Quick Render

Starting a Video Post Session

The exercises in this chapter use a simple file with animated text against a solid black background. This scene, part of your overall presentation, will be composited with several layers of prerendered files and special effects. The text has a material assigned to it, and two lights and a camera complete the scene. The text flies in from left to right in the upper third of the camera view, stops in the center of the view, and sits for the remainder of the sequence. This introduction portion of your presentation will take place over 30 frames of animation.

The default black background in 3ds max is rather boring, so the text will fly in over a rendered still image of the transporter. You could use the transporter image as a background as you did with the street scene in Chapter 13, "Effects: Reacting to Reactor," but you want more flexibility so that you can use different scenes over the same background. You will use Video Post to layer the 3ds max scene over the rendered image.

Exercise 14.1: Setting Up a Video Post Sequence

1. Open the Title01.max file from the CD-ROM, and save it to your hard drive as `Title02.max`. This scene contains flying text over a black background, and the animation takes place over 30 frames. Scrub the Time slider, and you will see the text animated over 15 frames and sitting still for the remaining 15 frames.

On the CD

exercises\CH14\
Title01.max

2. Choose Rendering, Video Post from the main menu. The Video Post dialog box shows an empty event queue in the left panel and a time line with a blue range bar, indicating that this scene is 30 frames long. At the bottom of the dialog box, you can read that the S: start frame is 0, the E: end frame is 29, and the total F: frame count is 30. The resolution is 640 pixels wide by 480 pixels high. The navigation buttons are at the lower right (see Figure 14.1).

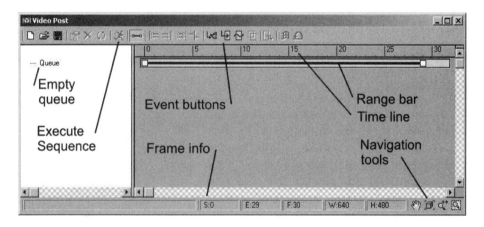

FIGURE 14.1   *The Video Post dialog box for a 30-frame scene.*

3. Events are evaluated in the order they appear in the queue, with the last event in the queue being applied last. To add a background image of the transporter, click the Add Image Input Event button on the Video Post toolbar. In the Add Image Input Event dialog box, click the Files button and open Segway01.png from the CD-ROM. Click OK to close the dialog box. Another blue range bar shows in the time line, representing the image being shown for 30 frames.

On the CD

exercises\CH14\
Segway01.png

4. To see if the image is actually there, you cannot render the scene; you must click the Execute Sequence button on the Video Post toolbar. In the Execute Video Post dialog box, select the Single radio button and enter 0 in the Single field (see Figure 14.2) to render frame 0. Click the Render button, and you should see a rendered image of the transporter in the Video Post Queue render window.

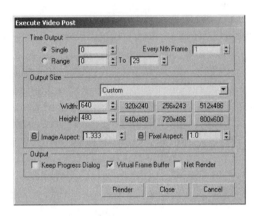

Figure 14.2 *Video Post sequences must be executed from the dialog box, not rendered with the conventional render buttons.*

5. You want the flying text animation to float in front of the image at the top. On the Video Post toolbar, click the Add Scene Event button. Make sure the Camera01 viewport is listed as the event, and click OK. It appears in the queue after Segway01.png to show that it will now be the top layer or the last event processed. Click the Execute Sequence button, enter 15 in the Single field of the Execute Video Post dialog box, and click the Render button. The Fundamentals text is rendered over a black background. This effect is not what you want, so you must composite the two events together to use the black background as alpha channel transparency.

Remember to include frame 0 in any animation lengths. Your animation is 31 frames (0–30, inclusive) and the Video Post queue is 30 frames (0–29). The last 15 frames of the title animation do not move, so cutting one off is not a problem in this case.

6. Select both events in the queue to highlight them yellow. On the toolbar, click the Add Image Layer Event button that has become active. Choose Alpha Compositor in the Layer plug-in list. The two events will be indented below the Alpha Compositor entry in the queue. Click the Execute Sequence button at frame 15, and you will see the text composited over the transporter image (see Figure 14.3).

FIGURE 14.3 *Executing an Alpha Compositor sequence uses black in the scene event as transparent information.*

7. Click in the empty space below the queue in the Video Post dialog box to deselect the events. Close the render window and save the file. It should already be called Title02.max.

   You have composited an animated scene over a still image in a 30-frame sequence. To allow the image to show through the black scene background, you used the Alpha Compositor plug-in with the two events set up as subsets to the composite. On test renders, remember to use the Execute Sequence button to see the effect of all events.

> **caution**
>
> Leaving events selected in the queue causes the next event entered to be a subset of the selected event, acting only on the event above it in the queue, not the whole queue. This is a common problem that new users encounter when setting up Video Post.

Special Effects in Video Post

You can add some special effects to a scene by choosing Rendering, Effects from the main menu. You can apply others in the Modify panel, Atmospheres & Effects rollout. Some special effects, however, can be applied only through the Video Post dialog box. In this next exercise, you apply sparkling highlights to the brightest areas of your composite with the Video Post tool.

Exercise 14.2: Adding Sparkling Highlights

1. Open the Title02.max file from Exercise 14.1 or from the CD-ROM, and save it as `Title03.max`. Choose Rendering, Video Post from the main menu. Nothing should be highlighted yellow in the queue.

2. Click the Add Image Filter Event button on the Video Post toolbar. Select Lens Effects Highlight in the drop-down list, and click OK to add the event to the queue.

3. In the Video Post queue, double-click Lens Effects Highlight, and click the Setup button in the Lens Effects Highlight dialog box. Right-click in the Camera01 viewport to activate it, and click the VP Queue button and then the Preview button just below the preview window. Drag the Time slider to frame 15. Nothing will happen in the preview window until you click the Update button. Only then will frame 15 of the composite show.

4. Select the Whole check box in the Source section to apply highlights to the whole scene. Select the Bright check box in the Filter section and wait for the effect to be processed. You'll be able to see a white progress line at the bottom of the preview area.

5. Enter 253 in the Bright numeric field and press Enter. The highlights are applied only to the brightest pixels in the composite (see Figure 14.4).

On the CD

exercises\CH14\
Title02.max

tip

Always add the filter events to the queue, and then go back to edit the parameters. Clicking the Setup button before the event is in the queue is not the correct workflow.

caution

Many special effects can be incredibly overdone, as you see in this exercise. Learn to use them and experiment with applications, but use them sparingly in your work.

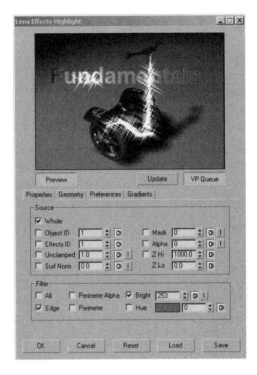

FIGURE 14.4   *You can use Video Post to apply highlights to only the brightest pixels in a composite.*

6. Click the Preferences tab in the Lens Effects Highlight dialog box, and in the Effect section, enter 6.0 in the Size field. This setting makes the highlights smaller. Click OK to close the Lens Effects Highlight dialog box.

7. Click in an empty area of the Video Post queue to deselect Lens Effect Highlight. Close the Video Post dialog box and save the scene. It should be called Title03.max.

You have learned to apply the Lens Effects Highlight filter to the brightest pixels in the composition. The filter is acting on both the image and the scene elements because it is at the same indentation level as the Alpha Compositor event in the queue. You did not need to execute the Video Post sequence to see the result of the new event because Lens Effects has a preview window for testing the setting changes.

Adding New Events and Transitions

There are two more events to add to your presentation. You have two prerendered AVI files of 100 frames in each animation. They will follow the 30 frames of animation you currently have in Video Post. You will use a *cut transition*—a sudden jump from one event to the next—from the current 30 frames into the first new animation. It is the most commonly used transition in traditional film and television, and viewers have become used to seeing it during the past 75 or so years of TV and movies.

The first animation will be a transporter crash file and the second will be the barrel toss in the street scene. Each animation is 100 frames; added to the 30 frames in your scene, you will have a total of 230 frames when the sequence is executed and saved to a new AVI animation file. However, between the transporter crash scene and the street scene, you will overlap the animation by 20 frames and blend from one to the other in a span of 20 frames, for a total of 210 frames.

Exercise 14.3: Using New Compositor Transitions

1. Open the Title03.max file, and save it as `Title04.max`. Choose Rendering, Video Post from the main menu. Again, make certain that nothing is highlighted in the Video Post queue.

exercises\CH14\
Title03.max

2. On the Video Post toolbar, click the Add Image Input Event button. In the Add Image Input Event dialog box, click the Files button, and open Transporter_crash.avi from the CD-ROM. Click OK to add it to the end of the queue.

3. Click the Add Image Input Event button again, and add Barrel_toss.avi from the CD-ROM to the end of the queue. If you executed the Video Post sequence now, you would see the Barrel_toss.avi file rendered but not saved. It is the last event in the queue and has no alpha compositing, so it would block everything below it in the queue.

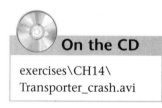

exercises\CH14\
Transporter_crash.avi

4. Select both AVI files in the queue to highlight them yellow. Click the Add Image Layer Event button on the Video Post toolbar, and select Cross Fade Transition in the drop-down list. Click OK in the Add Image Layer Event dialog box. The two AVI files are now indented below the Cross Fade Transition event in the queue. Click in the empty queue space to deselect all events.

exercises\CH14\
Barrel_toss.avi

5. At the lower right of the Video Post dialog box, click the Zoom Extents button to see all the range bars. Because the longest event is 101 frames, that is the queue's total length. Click the Zoom Time button at the lower right of the Video Post dialog box (see Figure 14.5), and click and drag to the left anywhere in the range bar area until you see the number 240 displayed at the right of the time line.

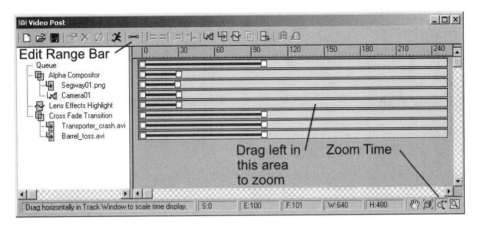

FIGURE 14.5   *Using Zoom Time in the range bar area enables you to see space to the right for editing.*

6. On the Video Post toolbar, click the Edit Range Bar button to exit zoom mode. Click and drag in the middle of the range bar for Transporter_crash.avi. You will see a double-arrow cursor, and the range bar will change from blue to red. Move it to the right until the frame numbers read S:30 and E:130, the start and end frames for 100 frames of animation. This starts the transporter segment at the end of the 30-frame intro.

7. Click and drag the range bar for Barrel_toss.avi until the start frame is S:110. This starts the barrel animation segment 20 frames before the end of the transporter segment.

8. Click the box at the left end of the Cross Fade Transition range bar and move it to frame 110. Then move the box at the right end to frame 130 (see Figure 14.6). The transition will start fading Transporter_crash out and Barrel_toss in, from frame 110 to frame 130. Click in the queue window to deselect any events.

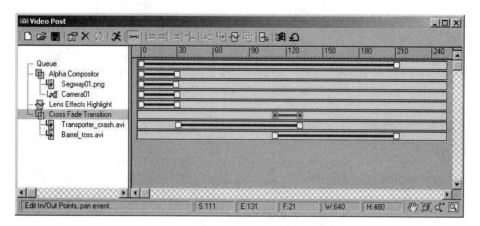

FIGURE 14.6   *Overlapping events can be composited so that one fades in while the other fades out.*

9. Executing the sequence now would create a presentation with the expected results, but it would not be saved to a file for others to view. You must set a Image Output Event at the end of the queue to tell 3ds max where to save the new animation. Click in an empty space in the queue window to deselect all events. Click the Add Image Output

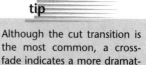

> **tip**
>
> Although the cut transition is the most common, a cross-fade indicates a more dramatic change in time or place.

   Event button on the Video Post toolbar. Click the Files button in the Add Image Output Event dialog box. Open a subdirectory on your hard drive and name the new file `Presentation.avi`. Click the Save button. In the Video Compression dialog box, select Cinepak Codec by Radius in the Compressor drop-down list, and set the Compression Quality slider to 100 (see Figure 14.7). Click OK to close this dialog box, and click OK again to close the Add Image Output Event dialog box.

10. In the Video Post dialog box, your sequence queue is complete (see Figure 14.8). Click the Execute Sequence button. Select the Range radio button in the Execute Video Post dialog box, and set the range field to a start of 0 and an end of 210. The default output size of 640×480 is fine and will match Image Input Event resolutions. Click the Render button in the Execute Video Post dialog box and let the process continue. You will notice each event being applied in sequence as it is evaluated.

> **caution**
>
> If you do not deselect all events in the queue before adding the Image Output Event, the file you save will include only the event directly preceding the Image Output Event.

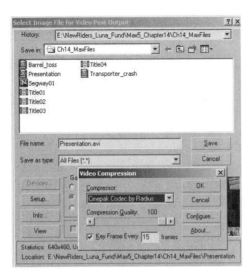

FIGURE 14.7 *The Video Post sequence must be saved as an Image Output Event, and you must choose a video compressor to write the file.*

note   Many video compressors, or *codecs*, are available for saving animations to files. Your choice depends on quality, file size, playback speed, resolution, and availability. Cinepak Codec is an older compressor of medium quality, but almost everyone has access to it on their computers so that they can play the file.

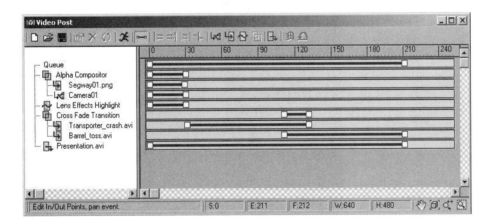

FIGURE 14.8 *The event queue is executed from the top down and the range bars indicate the start and end time of each event.*

11. Close all windows and dialog boxes. Save the file; it should already be called Title04.max.

Compositing queue events with a cross-fade transition can add information to your presentation by indicating a change in time or place. Good editing is a talent you must master to get the most from your individual animation segments and enhance the impact on your audience. Video Post is a simple but effective tool at your disposal.

Summary

If you spend some time watching feature movies and counting the number of seconds a scene is onscreen, you'll quickly realize the importance of being able to piece together short animation and still sequences into a flowing and entertaining presentation. Video Post is the 3ds max 5 tool that can help you reach those goals in your work. Some of the features of Video Post you learned about in this chapter include

- **Video Post queue**   You learned to add events in a queue that will be executed from the top down, applying each layer before moving on to the next.

- **Alpha composite**   Combining events by using alpha channel transparency allows background information to show through layers above it in the queue.

- **Composite transitions**   Progressive blending from the end of one event into the beginning of the next event can enhance the story you are telling by indicating a change in time or place.

- **Lens Effects**   You learned to add and adjust a special effect in the queue that focuses viewers' attention where you want it.

- **Output event**   You learned that Video Post sequences are not rendered with the usual methods, but must be executed and saved to a file in an Image Output Event at the end of the queue.

APPENDIX A

What's on the CD-ROM

The accompanying CD-ROM is packed with all sorts of exercise files and products to help you work with this book and with 3ds max 5. The following sections contain detailed descriptions of the CD's contents.

For more information about the use of this CD, please review the ReadMe.txt file in the root directory. This file includes important disclaimer information as well as information about installation, system requirements, troubleshooting, and technical support.

System Requirements

This CD-ROM was configured for use on systems running Windows NT Workstation, Windows 95/98/ME, Windows 2000, and Windows XP. Your machine needs to meet the following system requirements for this CD to operate properly:

- Processor: 486DX or higher
- OS: Microsoft Windows NT Workstation, 95/98/ME, 2000, or XP
- Memory: 24MB
- Monitor: VGA, 800×600 or higher with 256 color or higher
- Free space: 10MB minimum (varies depending on installation)
- Other: Mouse/pointing device, sound card, and speakers
- Browser: IE 5.5 or higher or Netscape 6 or higher
- Optional: Internet connection

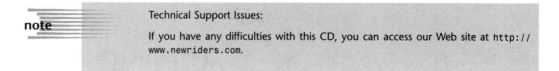

note Technical Support Issues:

If you have any difficulties with this CD, you can access our Web site at http://www.newriders.com.

Loading the CD Files

To load the files from the CD, insert the disc into your CD-ROM drive. If AutoPlay is enabled on your machine, the CD-ROM setup program starts automatically the first time you insert the disc. You can copy the files to your hard drive or use them right off the disc.

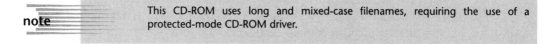

note This CD-ROM uses long and mixed-case filenames, requiring the use of a protected-mode CD-ROM driver.

Exercise Files: Scene and Image Files

This CD contains all the files you'll need to complete the exercises in *3ds max 5 Fundamentals*. These files can be found in the root directory's \exercises folder. This folder is further organized by chapter, so you'll find scene files for Chapter 8's exercises, for example, in the \exercises\CH08 folder.

All the book's grayscale figures—for example, those in Chapter 8—can be viewed in full color from the \images\CH08 folder.

Software

This CD-ROM contains the full suite of HABWare's plug-ins. You can find more information about these programs by visiting http://www.habware.at/duck4.htm.

Read This Before Opening the Software

By opening the CD package, you agree to be bound by the following agreement:

You may not copy or redistribute the entire CD-ROM as a whole. Copying and redistribution of individual software programs on the CD-ROM is governed by terms set by individual copyright holders.

The installer, code, images, actions, and brushes from the author(s) are copyrighted by the publisher and the authors.

Index

SYMBOLS

F

H

M

PHOTOSHOP® 7

Photoshop 7 Killer Tips
Scott Kelby
0735713006
$39.99

**Photoshop 7
Down & Dirty Tricks**
Scott Kelby
0735712379
$39.99

Photoshop 7 Magic
Sherry London,
Rhoda Grossman
0735712646
$45.00

Photoshop 7 Artistry
Barry Haynes,
Wendy Crumpler
0735712409
$55.00

Inside Photoshop 7
Gary Bouton, Robert Stanley,
J. Scott Hamlin, Daniel Will-Harris,
Mara Nathanson
0735712417
$49.99

**Photoshop Studio with
Bert Monroy**
Bert Monroy
0735712468
$45.00

**Photoshop Restoration
and Retouching**
Katrin Eisemann
0789723182
$49.99

**Photoshop Type Effects
Visual Encyclopedia**
Roger Pring
0735711909
$45.00

**Creative Thinking in
Photoshop**
Sharon Steuer
0735711224
$45.00

New Riders

VOICES
THAT MATTER

HOW TO CONTACT US

VISIT OUR WEB SITE

WWW.NEWRIDERS.COM

On our web site, you'll find information about our other books, authors, tables of contents, and book errata. You will also find information about book registration and how to purchase our books, both domestically and internationally.

EMAIL US

Contact us at: **nrfeedback@newriders.com**

- If you have comments or questions about this book
- To report errors that you have found in this book
- If you have a book proposal to submit or are interested in writing for New Riders
- If you are an expert in a computer topic or technology and are interested in being a technical editor who reviews manuscripts for technical accuracy

Contact us at: **nreducation@newriders.com**

- If you are an instructor from an educational institution who wants to preview New Riders books for classroom use. Email should include your name, title, school, department, address, phone number, office days/hours, text in use, and enrollment, along with your request for desk/examination copies and/or additional information.

Contact us at: **nrmedia@newriders.com**

- If you are a member of the media who is interested in reviewing copies of New Riders books. Send your name, mailing address, and email address, along with the name of the publication or web site you work for.

BULK PURCHASES/CORPORATE SALES

The publisher offers discounts on this book when ordered in quantity for bulk purchases and special sales. For sales within the U.S., please contact: Corporate and Government Sales (800) 382-3419 or **corpsales@pearsontechgroup.com**. Outside of the U.S., please contact: International Sales (317) 581-3793 or **international@pearsontechgroup.com**.

WRITE TO US

New Riders Publishing
201 W. 103rd St.
Indianapolis, IN 46290-1097

CALL/FAX US

Toll-free (800) 571-5840
If outside U.S. (317) 581-3500
Ask for New Riders
FAX: (317) 581-4663

New Riders

WWW.NEWRIDERS.COM

VOICES THAT MATTER

www.informit.com

YOUR GUIDE TO IT REFERENCE

New Riders has partnered with **InformIT.com** to bring technical information to your desktop. Drawing from New Riders authors and reviewers to provide additional information on topics of interest to you, **InformIT.com** provides free, in-depth information you won't find anywhere else.

Articles

Keep your edge with thousands of free articles, in-depth features, interviews, and IT reference recommendations— all written by experts you know and trust.

Online Books

Answers in an instant from **InformIT Online Books'** 600+ fully searchable online books.

POWERED BY

Catalog

Review online sample chapters, author biographies and customer rankings and choose exactly the right book from a selection of over 5,000 titles.

www.newriders.com

Publishing
the Voices
that Matter

OUR AUTHORS

PRESS ROOM

| web development | design | photoshop | new media | 3-D | server technologies |

EDUCATORS

ABOUT US

CONTACT US

You already know that New Riders brings you the **Voices That Matter**.

But what does that mean? It means that New Riders brings you the

Voices that challenge your assumptions, take your talents to the next

level, or simply help you better understand the complex technical world

we're all navigating.

Visit **www.newriders.com** to find:

▶ **10% discount** and **free shipping** on all book purchases

▶ Never before published chapters

▶ Sample chapters and excerpts

▶ Author bios and interviews

▶ Contests and enter-to-wins

▶ Up-to-date industry event information

▶ Book reviews

▶ Special offers from our friends and partners

▶ Info on how to join our User Group program

▶ Ways to have your Voice heard

New
Riders

W W W . N E W R I D E R S . C O M

Colophon

This book was written and edited in Microsoft Word, and laid out in QuarkXPress. The font used for the body text is Stone Serif and Mono. It was printed on 50# Husky Offset Smooth paper at R.R. Donnelley & Sons in Crawfordsville, Indiana. Prepress consisted of PostScript computer-to-plate technology (filmless process). The cover was printed at Moore Langen Printing in Terre Haute, Indiana, on 12 pt., coated on one side.